Old and New Perspectives on South Asian Languages

Grammar and Semantics

MLBD SERIES IN LINGUISTICS

General Editor
DHANESH JAIN

Volume XVI

Old and New Perspectives on South Asian Languages

Grammar and Semantics

Papers growing out of

THE FIFTH INTERNATIONAL CONFERENCE ON SOUTH ASIAN LINGUISTICS

(ICOSAL-5), held at Moscow, Russia in July 2003

Edited by

COLIN P. MASICA

MOTILAL BANARSIDASS PUBLISHERS
PRIVATE LIMITED • DELHI

First Edition : Delhi, 2007

ISBN: 978-81-208-3208-4

MOTILAL BANARSIDASS
41 U.A. Bungalow Road, Jawahar Nagar, Delhi 110 007
8 Mahalaxmi Chamber, 22 Bhulabhai Desai Road, Mumbai 400 026
203 Royapettah High Road, Mylapore, Chennai 600 004
236, 9th Main III Block, Jayanagar, Bangalore 560 011
Sanas Plaza, 1302 Baji Rao Road, Pune 411 002
8 Camac Street, Kolkata 700 017
Ashok Rajpath, Patna 800 004
Chowk, Varanasi 221 001

PRINTED IN INDIA
BY JAINENDRA PRAKASH JAIN AT SHRI JAINENDRA PRESS,
A-45 NARAINA, PHASE-I, NEW DELHI 110 028
AND PUBLISHED BY NARENDRA PRAKASH JAIN FOR
MOTILAL BANARSIDASS PUBLISHERS PRIVATE LIMITED,
BUNGALOW ROAD, DELHI 110 007

CONTENTS

PART III: OLD AND NEW DESCRIPTIVE PERSPECTIVES ON PARTICULAR LANGUAGES

EDITOR'S PREFACE

The papers in this collection represent a unique bringing together of scholarship on South Asian languages from different countries and different perspectives, not often mutually easily accessible. Scholars from six different countries have contributed – India, Russia, the USA, Canada, France, and Germany. In terms of theoretical perspective there is everything from the venerable Panini (albeit applied to modern material) and traditional historical linguistics and philology to the latest Chomskyan ideas and much else – Old perspectives and new perspectives. All four major linguistic stocks found in South Asia (Indo-Aryan, Dravidian, Austroasiatic, and Tibeto-Burman) are represented (Tibeto-Burman not explicitly in the title but abundantly in the data in Subbarao's paper). Typological and historical comparison with key languages outside of South Asia add a special dimension to a number of the papers, and make them relevant to a wider readership.

While the impetus for this collection was the Fifth International Conference on South Asian Linguistics (ICOSAL-5) held in Moscow in July 2003, the volume does not just represent the proceedings of a conference. Not all papers presented at the conference (including one whole category, those on literature) were included, and two were added (Peterson's and Oranskaia's) which were not presented at the conference. The papers included have all been extensively revised, rewritten, and expanded.

While the variety of formats, fonts, and styles entailed by the multinational character of this book, not to mention the extensive revisions, have added considerably to an editor's burden, I think the effort has been worthwhile. Fortunately, my lack of professional skill in this area has been ably compensated for by those at Motilal Publishers.

March 2005 COLIN P. MASICA

EDITOR'S PREFACE

A NOTE ON TRANSLITERATION

Due to typographical (= "font") limitations[1] faced by some of the authors, their mutual incompatibility, and to keep down the cost of the book, a Simplified Transcription, avoiding diacritical marks or keeping them to a minimum, has been employed in most of the papers in this collection. This transcription has long been widely used in linguistic papers as well as in teaching materials on South Asian languages. This well-known basic symbolism is as follows:

/T, D, N, L, R, S/ = retroflex consonants

/aa, ii, uu, oo, ee/ = (contrastively) long vowels

/a˜, aa˜, ii˜, uu˜, o˜, e˜, ai˜, au˜/ = (contrastively) nasalized vowels or diphthongs

For particular languages the following additional simplified symbols are also used:

/R/ = vocalic "r" in Sanskrit
/L/ = velarized "l" in Armenian
/M/ = *anusvâra* in Sanskrit
/A, AA, I/ = mid- and high-centralized vowels
(in Kashmiri, Munda languages, Turkish, and Tibeto-Burman languages)
/O/ = lower mid-back vowel (in Tibeto-Burman languages and Bengali)
C' = a palatal consonant (in Kashmiri)

In addition, traditional transliterations (requiring special diacritic fonts) are used by some writers, e.g., for Tamil by Chevillard, for various stages of Middle and Early New Indo-Aryan by Bubenik, and for Sanskrit by Hock and Davison. A mixed traditional/simplified transcription approaching the established roman orthography is used for Santali (with

---

[1] Although *Unicode*, commonly available in Europe, might have solved this problem, it is just beginning to become available in the U.S.A., and not for all types of computers or operating systems. Meanwhile, ad hoc interim solutions differ from user to user.

o̲, e̲ for more open mid-vowels, but with capital letters for retroflex consonants). Chinese is cited in Pinyin.

Finally, we have the problem of transliterating Russian, primarily in the reference sections, but also in some examples cited for comparison. Although the elegant "European" system of transliteration (e.g. *Južnaja Azija*) might be preferable, it involves a number of diacritical marks and special characters, which again we were trying to avoid. After first recommending the U.S. Library of Congress system (e.g. *I͡Uzhnaia Azii͡a*), to avoid the frequent occurrence of double capitals at the beginning of word – properly, with a ligature mark on top of them, itself not readily available to all contributors), the editor decided to change to the even simpler system of the U.S. Board of Geographic Names (e.g., *Yuzhnaya Aziya*), and tried to implement this throughout – possibly not with perfect consistency.

LIST OF CONTRIBUTORS

BUBENIK, VIT
Memorial University of Newfoundland, St. John's, Canada
vbubenik@mun.ca

CHEVILLARD, JEAN-LUC
CNRS, Université Paris 7
jlc@ccr.jussieu.fr

DAVISON, ALICE
University of Iowa
alice-davison@uiowa.edu

HOCK, HANS HENRICH
University of Illinois at Urbana-Champaign
hhhock@uiuc.edu

HOOK, PETER E.
Universities of Virginia and Michigan
peter.e.hook@gmail.com

KHOKHLOVA, LIUDMILA V.
Moscow University
lvik@orc.ru

KOUL, OMKAR N.
Syracuse and Cornell Universities, Indian Institute of Language Studies
onkoul@yahoo.com

LIANG, HSIN-HSIN
Universities of Virginia and Michigan
Hl9s@cms.mail.virginia.edu, h19s@virginia.edu

LIPEROVSKY, V. P.
Russian Academy of Sciences, Institute of Oriental Studies
Language Department
Rozhdestvenka 12
107996 MOSCOW
Russian Federation

MASICA, COLIN P.
University of Chicago – Emeritus
dacotah@mwt.net

ORANSKAIA, TATIANA
University of Hamburg, Department of Culture and History of India and Tibet
tatiana.oranskaia@uni-hamburg.de

PETERSON, JOHN
Univerisät Osnabrück, Germany
jpeterso@uni-osnabrueck.de

SIGORSKIY, ALEXANDER A.
MGIMO University, Moscow
asigorskiy@mail.ru

SINGH, CHARANJIT
JNU, Delhi
charanjit@mail.jnu.ac.in

SITCHINAVA, DMITRY V.
Moscow State University
dmsichinava@yandex.ru

SUBBARAO, KARUMURI V.
University of Delhi
Kvs2811@gmail.com, Kvs2811@yahoo.com

WALI, KASHI
Syracuse and Cornell Universities, Indian Institute of Language Studies
Kwali1@twcny.rr.com

ZAKHARYIN, BORIS A.
Moscow State University
lvik@orc.ru

PART I

HISTORICAL AND ETYMOLOGICAL PERSPECTIVES

ON THE EVOLUTIONARY CHANGES IN THE MIDDLE AND NEW INDO-ARYAN SYSTEMS OF CASE AND ADPOSITIONS

(WITH SPECIAL REFERENCE TO EUROPEAN ROMANI)

VIT BUBENIK

1. Restructuring of the nominal system during the Middle Indo–Aryan period

The nominal system of late MIA underwent a considerable erosion of case contrasts and Apabhraṃśa ended up with only one form for earlier Nom vs. Acc, Instr vs. Loc, and Gen vs. Abl. Table 1 (adapted from Bubenik 1998: 66) puts these matters into the diachronic perspective of Old and Middle IA (Old and Middle Prākrits represented by Pāli and Ardha-Māgadhī). Globally speaking, Old and Middle Prākrits created a new type of opposition of the direct (Nom, Acc) to the oblique cases (Instr, Gen, Abl, Loc) in both numbers: a monosyllabic ending in the direct case vs. a disyllabic ending in the oblique case (trisyllabic in the Abl in AMg). In Apabhraṃśa, in addition, a new opposition of the singular to the plural in oblique cases based on the presence of the nasalized vowel started emerging: plain vs. nasalized ultima of the ending signalized the opposition between the singular vs. plural oblique case (here we are reaching a NIA state of affairs). In morphological terminology, the cumulative exponence of grammatical significates of OIA and earlier stages of MIA gave way gradually to new types of semi-agglutinative exponence in MIA. At the end, the nasalization of the ultima became more or less consistent in the plural cases in Apabhraṃśa, whereas it was only sporadic during the previous stages (as shown by AMg).

Table 1: The nominal system (a-stems) of Old and Middle Indo-Aryan

	OIA Sanskrit	Old Pāli	Middle Amg	Late Prākrits Apabhraṃśa
Sg Nom	-aḥ	-o	-o	-u
Acc	-am	-ã	-ã	-u
Instr	-eṇa	-eṇa/ã	-eṇa	-ẽ
Dat	-āya	-assa/āya	-assa	-aho
Gen	-asya	-assa	-assa	-aho, -ahu
Abl	-āt	-asmā	-ā (o)	-ahe, -ahu
Loc	-e	-asmĩ	-ãsi	-i, -e
Pl Nom	-āḥ	-ā	-ā	-a
Acc	-ān	-e	-a,-e	-a
Instr	-ebhiḥ	-ehi	-ehĩ	-a/ehĩ
Dat	-ebhyaḥ		-aṇã	-ahã
Gen	-āṇām	-āṇã	-aṇa	-ahã
Abl	-ebhyaḥ	-ehi	-ehinto	-ahũ
Loc	-eṣu	-esu	-esũ	-ahĩ

i- and *u*-stems underwent thematization, i.e. they started being declined more and more as *a*-stems. The following global observations can be made:

(i) In the Instr Sg the *a*-stem suffix *-ẽ* (< *en* < *ena*) replaces the original *i-/u*-stem suffixes *-inā*/*-unā*.

(ii) The Abl/Gen Sg suffix *-he* (used originally with *i-/u*-stems) is also used with *a*-stems.

(iii) In the plural subparadigm several suffixes are transferred from *a*-stems: Instr *-hĩ*, Abl *-hũ* and Gen *-hã*.

For more details see Tagare (1948).

2. Evolution of the phrasal case during the Middle Indo-Aryan period

Given the drastic reduction from the seven fusional cases of OIA to four by the end of the MIA period, the adpositions (both pre- and postpositions in SVO ~ SOV syntax) grew steadily in importance in denoting relational aspects of their head nouns.

Examples in (1) and (2) are provided to contrast the grammaticalization of the notion of 'source' in Sanskrit and Apabhraṃśa:

(1)

hṛdayād	yadi	niḥsarasi	
heart+ABL	if	out-go+2/SG	(case)

'if you go out of [my] heart'

hiaya-ṭṭhiu	jai	nīsarahi	[Hc 8.4.439]
heart=ABL	if	out-go+2/SG	(postposition)

'if you go out of [my] heart'

(2)

kukavitvāt		
bad-poetry+ABL		(case)

'because of being poetaster'

kukavitvena	hetunā	(case and postposition)
bad-poetry+INSTR	cause+INSTR	

'because of being poetaster'

kukavitta-resi	[SR 21a]
bad-poetry=REF	(postposition)

'because of being poetaster'

In (1) the ablative suffix in its concrete spatial sense was replaced by the postposition *ṭhiu* whose source is the past participle *sthita* 'stood'; in (2) the causal relation 'due to/because of/on account of' is grammaticalized in several ways: in Sanskrit by the ablative suffix or by the postposition *hetunā* which actually is the instrumental form of *hetu* 'cause' (also its head-noun is in the instrumental); in Apabhraṃśa there is one of the referential postpositions, such as *resi*.

In what follows we shall study the sources of Middle Indo-Aryan adpositions and ultimately New Indo-Aryan postpositions on the basis of Apabhraṃśa data. (Their whole system organized into 12 binary pairs is presented in Table 2.) Broadly speaking, we will examine the nature of the causal nexus between the increased use of adverbial/adjectival (= participial) elements as adpositions, on the one hand, and the decreased use of the synthetic cases inherited from Old and Early MIA, on the other hand. The following semantic functions which were previously expressed by synthetic cases but came to be expressed analytically by adpositions in Apabhraṃśa will be examined in some detail: *source* (expressed in Sanskrit by the ablative), *location* (expressed by the locative) and *accompaniment/instrumentality* (expressed by the instrumental which already in OIA was reinforced with the postposition *saha* 'with').

2.1 Source

As a consequence of phonological changes the synthetic morphology of the ablative became insufficient. This happened already in Early MIA, where the old ablative *devāt* lost the final *-t* and became thus homophonous with the Nom Pl. Pāli remedied the situation by adopting the pronominal ablative suffix *-asmā* (cf. OIA *tasmāt*) ~ *amhā*, or the adverbial suffix *-to* (<*tas*). The latter suffix is continued in Middle Prākrits in the form *-āo*. In Māhārāṣṭrī, in addition to the ablative suffixes *-ā* (<*āt*) and *-āo* (< *-āt* + *tas*), there was a peculiar suffix *-ahi* (well documented in Hāla's *Sattasaī)* deriving from the postposition *adhi*, which (as far back as Vedic Sanskrit) could be attached to the ablative form of the noun in the meaning 'down from, out of'. In later developments the ablative and genitive gradually merged in both nominal and pronominal declensions.

In Apabhraṃśa the ablative suffix *-he* is probably adopted from the feminine paradigm where it may express both the ablative and genitive (vice versa, the masculine genitive suffix *-ho* has been adopted from the masculine into the feminine paradigm).

The etymology of *-he* is uncertain; it could be traced back to the feminine pronominal suffix of the Dat Sg *-asyai* (cf. *tasyai* 'to her' > Ap *tahe* 'from her').

Thus in Late MIA there arose a need to differentiate between the function of source (ablative) and appurtenance (genitive) by analytic means. In Apabhraṃśa there were two postpositions, *honta(u)* and *ṭhiu*, used for this purpose. Both are participial forms: *honta(u)* is the present participle of the verb *ho* 'be' (< OIA *bhū*) and *ṭhiu* is the past participle of the verb *ṭhā* 'remain, stay' (< OIA *sthā*). They are not recognized explicitly as ablative postpositions by the contemporary grammarian Hemacandra (1088/1089–1172/1173) but they appear in his illustrations to the sūtras in which he specifies the pronominal forms of the ablative and genitive (*hontau* in *jahāṃ hontau āgado* "Whence he has come" [Hc 8.4.355] and *ṭhiu* in [Hc 8.4.439] quoted in (1)).

2.2 Location

With regards to location there were adpositions expressing the notions of inessive 'in' (cf. Hindi *ghar=mẽ* 'in the house'), locative 'on' (cf. H. *ghar=par* 'on the house'), and adessive 'at' (cf. H. *ghar=ke=pās*).

In OIA it was enough to say *gṛh+e* 'in the house' with the locative suffix *-e*; in MIA it became necessary to use the adverb *majjhe/i* 'inside' as an adposition (< OIA *madhy+e* 'in the middle') with the noun in the genitive: *majjhe gharaho* ~ *gharaho majjhe* 'in the house'. In Apabhraṃśa both constructions (with the head *majjhe* before or after its modifier) are available:

(3) majjhi hiyayaha [Sc 707.5]
middle+LOC heart+GEN

'in the heart'
lit. in the middle of the heart

In NIA the case of the noun has been lost and the adverb *majjhe* was reduced to the postposition *mẽ* which is cliticized to the noun: H. *ghar=mẽ*. At this point the fusional case of OIA has been replaced by the phrasal (postpositional) case.

The locative postposition *par* 'on' in Hindi goes back to the OIA adverb/adposition *upari* 'over' which could be used with the noun in various cases: N+Acc 'above, over'; N+Loc 'upon, at the head of'; N+Abl 'with regard to, after', and, of course, also with the genitive. In Apabhraṃśa literature all sorts of examples are available ranging from (a) *upari/uvari* detached from its (pro)nominal modifier to (b) the immediately following one to (c) the 'compound' N=*upari*.

(4) a. iyarassu kassu vi uvari [Sc 693.2]
another+GEN what+GEN PRT on

'on whoever else'

b. kailāsho upari [Pc 13.2.6]
Kailasa+GEN on

'on the Kailasa'

c. iyar'uvari [Sc 694.8]
another on

'on another one'

The last example approximates the NIA usage of *par* as a postposition.

The notion of proximity is expressed by one of the adessive postpositions, most commonly *pās-i* 'in the proximity/nearness of'. Its concrete meaning used to be 'side, region of the ribs' (OIA *pārśva*). This concrete meaning still lurks in the following Apabhraṃśa example, where *pās-i* (with the locative suffix *-i*) is the head of the compound *pai-pāsi* (<*pati-pārśve*) 'at husband's side' → 'close to/by the husband':

(5)	kahi	vi	paipāsi	pariṭṭhiyau [Riṭṭha 1.7.7]
	who+GEN	PRT	husband-side+LOC	seat+PP

'Someone seated at the side of the husband'

It should be observed that already in OIA, with its rich system of morphological cases, there were a number of adverbial elements expressing various nuances of the notion of proximity (e.g. *antikam* 'vicinity, presence' → 'near, up to', *antike* (Loc) 'near, close to'; *samīpam* 'vicinity, proximity' → 'to', *samīpe* (Loc) 'close at hand, near, beside'). In Apabhraṃśa the two adpositions may be mentioned: *saviha* (< OIA *savidha* 'vicinity, proximity') used in the locative *savihi*; and *sammuhu* (< OIA *saṃmukha* 'confronting, facing', *saṃmukham* 'face to face' → 'towards').

As far as the OIA proximative postposition *prati* 'against, towards, to' is concerned by the late MIA period the meaning of *pai* (< *prati*) was reduced to that of an adverb (degree word) 'only' and emphatic particle (corresponding to Hindi *bhī*); in addition, the form *pai* was homophonous with *pai* 'husband' (< *pati*) and close to homophonous with *paĩ* 'you' (< OIA *tvayā*). It is therefore no surprise that this postposition had to be recreated from OIA *pratīpam* 'towards' (lit. *prati-ap-* 'against the water/stream') > Apabhraṃśa *paḍīva*:

(6) suraha	paḍīvau	[Riṭṭha 7.2]
god+GEN/PL	towards	

'towards gods'

2.3 Accompaniment/Instrumentality

In Vedic the notion of accompaniment was expressed by the preverb *sa(m)-* 'with' (from the PIE adverb **som* 'together'). *sa-* is found in the adposition *sahá* 'with' (cf. Avestan *hadā*, *haδa*) formed by adding the productive adverbial suffix *-dhā* (as in *bahu-dhā́* 'in many ways', etc.); its shortened form is found in several Vedic compounds (e.g. *sadhá-stha* 'gathering place'), and its simplified form *dh* → *h*, has several parallels elsewhere (e.g. *i-há* 'here' vs. Pāli *i-dha*). It should be emphasized that its synonym *sácā* does not contain *sa* (*sác-ā* < **sok^w-eh$_1$*). These adpositions were recreated several times: *sam-ám* (Acc) 'together with' and *sam-áyā* (Instr) 'altogether' are case forms of the adjectival derivative *sam-á* 'similar, like, equal'; *sa-rátham* 'on the same car with' → 'together with' (by the process of grammaticalization); *sākám* 'together' is probably from **sa-añc* 'going together'; *sārdhám* is the accusative form of the compounded adjective *sa-ardha-* 'together with a half'; *samānam* 'jointly' is the accusative form of the adjectival derivative in *-na* which itself is the derivative based on **sam*, i.e. *sam-ā-ná* 'identical, same, similar'.

The most common adpositions expressing these two notions are *samau* (also *samāṇu*) and *sahū* (also *sahu/sau/saī/sai*, cf. Old Hindi *se*). They may precede or follow the noun in the instrumental:

(7)	samaraṅgaṇu	samau	dasāṇaṇeṇa		Pc 12.2.6]
	war	with	ten-faced+INSTR		

'the war with Rāvaṇa'

sahu	kaṇṇae	kiu	pāṇiggahaṇu	[Pc 9.2.8]
with	girl+INSTR	make+PP	marriage	

'He married the girl.'
lit. he made the marriage with the girl

In later documents, such as *Saṃdeśa Rāsaka*, the postposition *sau* may be attached as a clitic to the noun in the absolute form (i.e. here we reach the early NIA state of affairs):

(8)	pahiya	ṇa	sijjhai	kiri	balu	maha
	traveller	not	succeed+3/SG	PRT	strength	I+GEN

kaṃdappasau [SR 99]
Cupid=with

'O traveller, my strength cannot compete with Cupid/proves of no avail against Cupid.'

The ancestor of the Hindi postposition *=ke sāth* 'with' is Apabhraṃśa *satthihi* from OIA *sa artha* (→*sārtha-*) lit. having [its] object attained → 'successful, wealthy; (travelling) company (of merchants)'. In Prākrit texts it appears in the phrase *tassa satthe* lit. he+GEN company+LOC, in his company → 'with him'.

The privative adposition *viṇu* 'without' (< OIA *vinā*) is used with the noun in the instrumental (in OIA it could be used with the accusative and also ablative and instrumental): *paĩ viṇu* 'without you', *viṇu hiae* 'without a heart', etc. An interesting way of saying 'without you' consists of combining *viṇu* with *saṃgẽ*) (Instr) 'contact with':

(9) ettiu kālu gamiu viṇu saṃgẽ [Bk 201.71]
so-much time go+CAUS+PP without contact+INSTR

'I spent so much time without you.'

The whole system of Prākrits and Apabhraṃśa local adverbs and adpositions (both pre- and postpositions) is portrayed in Table 2. It is organized in binary pairs expressing the basic topological (coincidence, interiority and exteriority, juxtaposition) and projective notions (laterality, anteriority and posteriority, inferiority and superiority, and mediality); cf. Bubenik & Hewson (forthcoming). Synthetic cases, harking back to Early MIA and OIA, are in round brackets:

Table 2. Prākrit and Apabhraṃśa local adverbs and postpositions

1.	pāsi 'at' (N+LOC)	kerau/ī (Ap) 'of' (N+GEN) (juxtaposition)
2.	pāsi, kahũ (Ap) 'to' (N+DAT)	honta(u)/ṭhiu (Ap) 'from' (N+ABL) ('to' vs. 'from')
3.	ahī (Ap) '(up)on' (N+LOC)	(preverb *ava-* > o- 'off') (location)
4.	(preverb *ud-* 'up')	(preverb *ni-* 'down') ('up' vs. 'down')
5.	majjhe 'in(to)" (N+LOC)	bāhi/ar 'out(side)' (inter/exteriority)
6.	kehī (Ap) 'for (the sake of)'	(N+INSTR) 'by' (path)
7.	agga, aggẽ (Ap) 'before'	paccha(l)i/e (Ap) 'behind' (ante/posteriority)
8.	samau, sa(h)u, saī /i (Ap) 'with'	viṇu, rahiyu, bāhire (Ap) 'without' (relation)
9.	sammuhu, paḍīva (Ap) 'towards'	majjhẽ (Ap) 'through' (opposing limit)
10.	ãMtar(i) (Ap) 'between'	? 'across' (two limits)
11.	"ãMtar(i) (Ap) 'among'	? 'about' (circumference)
12.	(preverbs *uva-*, *aha-* 'under')	uvari/ī , vari 'over' (inter/superiority)

As shown above, the use of synthetic case (for juxtaposition, movement 'to' versus 'from', location and accompaniment) was more and more limited during the MIA period (the synthetic cases are added in round brackets). The table also shows that MIA continues a number of OIA preverbs, most notably the pair *ud-* 'up' versus *ni-* 'down', *o-* 'off' (< *áva-*), *uva-* and *aha-* 'under' (< *úpa* and *adhás*). The case can be used to differentiate the meaning of the local noun as in *majjhe* (Loc) "into" versus *majjhẽ* (Instr) "through".

3. From Middle to New Indo-Aryan

Some Modern Indo-Aryan languages, such as Hindi, have reduced the number of synthetic case forms to three. Their distribution in masculine nouns is Direct (Sg), Oblique singular, which is formally identical with the Direct plural, and the Oblique plural; in feminine nouns their distribution is different in that the singular forms of the Direct and Oblique are identical:

Table 3. The case system of Hindi

Masc	Sg	Pl	Fem	Sg	Pl
Dir	-Ø/-ā	-e	Dir	-Ø/-ī/-iyā	-iyā̃
Obl	-e	-õ	Obl	-Ø/-ī/-iyā	-iyõ

With personal pronouns the number of distinct case forms can be four in that the oblique form (used with postpositions) is different from the Object form (Acc/Dat):

Table 4. Hindi personal pronouns

	'I'	but	'we'
Dir	maĩ		ham
Obl	mujh		ham
Obj	mujhe		hamẽ
Poss	merā		hamārā

Certain simple (primary) postpositions — *=kā/kī/ke* (Masc/Fem/Pl) 'of'; *=ko* 'to'; *=se* 'from, by'; *=par* 'at, on' and *=mẽ* 'in' — perform functions of the earlier cases (Gen, Dat/Acc, Abl and Instr, and Loc, respectively). One observes two 'mergers' and one 'split' vis-à-vis their OIA functions:

Table 5. OIA cases versus Hindi primary postpositions

		Acc			
=ko	<				
		Dat	Gen	→	=kā

=par			Abl		
	>	Loc		>	=se
=mẽ			Instr		

NIA postpositions are cliticized to the oblique form of the noun. Numerical and gender agreement of the genitive postposition, e.g. *laṛk+e kā kuttā* lit. boy+OBL GEN+M dog 'the boy's dog' *laṛk+e kī kuttī* ... GEN+F dog (f.) 'the boy's dog (f.)', reflects its adjectival ancestry. The earlier Apabhraṃśa forms are *ker+au* (Masc) and *ker+ī* Fem) with *-r* lost in Hindi, but preserved completely in Bengali *er* or Romani *ker+o* (Masc), *ker-i* (Fem), *ker-e* (Pl). The etymology of Apabhraṃśa *ker-au/ī* 'of' is uncertain (the passive participle *kṛta* of the overworked root *kar-* 'do, make' ended up as *ki(a̧)u*; the gerundive *kārya* as *kajja*; the connection with the OIA adjective *kar-á* (Masc), *karī* (Fem) 'doing, working' remains vague but plausible phonologically).

The dative/accusative postposition *=ko* goes back to MIA *kahũ*; its counterpart in Sindhi is *=khe* and in Romani *=ke* (only dative). The latter two postpositions are traceable back to Apabhraṃśa *kehī* 'for the sake of' (formally, the Masc Instr Pl of *ka* 'who'). *kahũ* and *kehī* are perhaps related in the same fashion as *sa(h)ũ* and *saĩ* 'with' (for more details cf. Bubenik 1998: 74–80).

The ablative/instrumental postposition *=se* 'from, with, by' goes back to the MIA *sai/saĩ* ~ *sau, sahu/sahũ* (< OIA *saha* < *sadha* < **sadhā*, cf. 1.3). In certain constructions *=se* expresses the notion of connection/proximity in general and one may end up with a meaning opposite to that of the ablative (e.g. *dillī kalkatte=se dūr hai* 'Delhi is far from Calcutta' vs. *kiśtī balle=se bãdhī hai* 'the boat is tied to the pole'.

Hindi *mẽ* 'in', as we saw in 1.2, goes back to the MIA adverb *majjhe* 'in the middle' (< OIA *madhy+e* middle+LOC 'in the middle'); e.g. *ghar+aho majjh+e* lit. house+GEN middle+LOC 'in the house' > Hindi *ghar=mẽ* 'in the house' (cf. the parallel development in Armenian: Classical *tan mêj+i* lit. house+GEN middle+LOC > Western *tun+i=n meč* lit. house+GEN=ART in 'in the house').

It should be emphasized that we are dealing with a phrasal case (as understood in the configurational syntax) with the postposition attaching only once to the noun phrase, unlike the representation of case on each item in the phrase in Old Indo-Aryan with the synthetic case. This is shown in adjectival agreement in a noun phrase such as 'from the tall boy':

(10)	Sanskrit		vs.	Hindi	
	ucc+ād	kumār+ād		(lãb+e	laṛk+e)=se
	tall+ABL	boy+ABL		(tall+OBL	boy+OBL) from

In Hindi the ablative postposition =*se* 'from' governs the whole noun phrase; nevertheless, the adjective and the noun display adjectival agreement in gender, number and case (both are in the oblique singular case). Matters are more complicated in the plural 'from the tall boys':

(11)	Sanskrit		vs.	Hindi	
	ucc+ebhyaḥ	kumār+ebhya		(lāb+e	laṛk+õ)=se
	tall+ABL/PL	boy+ABL/PL		tall+OBL/SG	boy+OBL/PL from

Sanskrit again displays the typical 'rhyming' agreement of flective languages, while in Hindi we are dealing with 'deflected' agreement within the noun phrase. Put differently, the plural nominal forms are built on the plural oblique form while the adjective remains in the singular oblique form, which in the case of masculine nouns is identical with the plural direct form (in other words, we have to do with 'disagreement' either in number or in case). This state of affairs is rather different from that obtaining in agglutinative languages such as Turkish. Contrast (10) and (11) with (12), where the number and the case are marked only once:

(12)	(uzun	çocuk)	tan		(Turkish)
	(tall	boy)	from		

'from the tall boy'

((uzun	çocuk)	lar)	dan
((tall	boy)	Pl)	from

'from the tall boys'

Typologically speaking, if Sanskrit is a flective (fusional) language and Turkish an agglutinative language, Hindi may be called 'semi-fusional' or 'semi-agglutinative'. We will return to this matter in Romani (Section 4).

Secondary (compound) postpositions in Hindi are those whose adverb is preceded by the oblique form *ke* of the genitive postposition *kā*. This is shown in Table 6:

Table 6. Hindi primary versus secondary (compound) postpositions

us=se	us=ke sāth
he+OBL=from	he+OBL=GEN+OBL with
'from him'	'with him'

ghar=mẽ/par	ghar=ke pās
house=in/on	ghar=GEN+OBL near
'in/on the house'	'near the house'

Secondary postpositions in Hindi can be arranged in binary pairs (numbered 5. - 12. in correspondence with Table 2 for MIA). The pairs in 1. - 4. are realized by primary postpositions (as shown above).

Table 7: Hindi secondary postpositions

5.	=ke bhītar 'in(side)'	=ke bāhar 'outside'	(location)
6.	=ke lie 'for (the sake of)'	=se 'by'	(path)
7.	=ke āge 'before'	=ke pīche 'behind, after'	(ante/posteriority)
8.	=ke sath 'with'	=ke binā 'without'	(relation)
9.	=ke sāmne 'against'	bīc=se 'through'	(opposing limit)
10.	=ke bīc 'between'	ek or=se 'across'	(two limits)
11.	bīc=mẽ, madhy=mẽ 'among'	bāhrī/cārõ or 'about'	(circumference)
12.	=ke nīce 'under'	(=ke) ūpar 'over'	(surface limit)

Perlative =*se* 'by' is actually a primary postposition; it appears in compound forms *bīc=se* 'through' and *ek or=se* 'across' (in 9. and 10.); similarly, the primary locative postposition *mẽ* 'in(to)' is used to form compound postpositions expressing the notion of circumference: *bīc=mẽ* and *madhy=mẽ* lit. centre=in 'among'. The postposition = *ūpar* 'up, over' can be used as either a primary or a secondary =*ke* *ūpar* postposition.

Adverbs and postpositions in *-e* are actually oblique forms of adjectives/nouns:

(13)	nīcā 'low'	→	nīc-e 'under(neath)'
	liyā 'taken' (= PP of *le*- nā 'take')	→	li-e 'for (the sake of)'
	āgā 'front(age), face'	→	āg-e 'before'
	pīchā 'back/hinder part'	→	pīch-e 'behind, after'
	sāmnā 'confrontation, encounter'	→	sāmn-e 'against'

The OIA preverb *ni-* lurks in *nīcā* 'low' (< OIA *nīc-a* 'low' based on the weak root of *ni-áñc* 'downward', lit. bent over). Regarding *āge* 'before', cf. Romani *angl-e*, both from OIA *agra-* 'front; beginning; point, tip, top'. *Pīchā* 'back/hinder part' goes back to OIA *paścā* 'behind, after' (via Pkt *paccha* with apparently some influence from *paśc-ima* 'hinder'). *Sāmnā* 'confrontation' is descended from OIA *sam-ā-na* 'identical, similar' via Apabhraṃśa *samāṇu* 'with' (Hindi *samān* 'identical, similar' is a borrowing from Sanskrit). The development of *par* 'on' and *ūpar* 'over; up' (both from OIA *upári*) is not clear. *bāhar* 'outside' goes back to OIA *bahir* 'outside, out (of)'. Hindi *bīc* 'the middle (part), centre', appearing in the compound postposition *bīc mẽ* 'among', *bīc se* 'through', is somewhat obscure. Its source is probably the weak root of undocumented **vi-añc* i.e. *vi-ic* > *vīc* 'going asunder' (seen in the Vedic rare citation form *vīcyā* 'contradictory' (?), cf. Mayrhofer 1976: 234). There are many other compound adverbs and postpositions such as sanskritizing *madhy mẽ* 'among', and *dvārā* 'through, by means of' (Skt *dvār-ā* lit. by the door → 'by means of, through, by').

The notions of 'two limits' and 'circumference limit' ('across' and 'about') are expressed by means of compound adverbs involving the noun *or* 'direction, side': *ek or=se* lit. one side from (or *dūsrī or=se* another side from) 'across'; *bāhrī or* exterior side or *cārõ or* four+OBL/PL side '(all) around'.

4. Evidence of European Romani

In the following section I would like to discuss these matters from the point of view of one of the most neglected NIA languages, European Romani. Hindi will be used for commenting on certain salient typological similarities and differences between NIA and Romani. Romani data will be taken from one of its Central dialects, namely the East Slovak variety (described by Hübschmannová et al. 1991). To start with the nominal case system, we notice the existence of the contrast between the 'nominative' and the 'accusative' case (from the Indic perspective these are the direct and the oblique case; notice that the ancestral forms of the oblique are the Prākrit genitive forms). The existence of the definite article is one of the most salient features of Romani, setting it apart from all the other IA languages (in spite of its similarity with the Greek article it developed from its own IA source, namely the demonstrative pronoun: OIA *ayam* > MIA *ā(ya)u* > Romani *o*; the other forms are more problematic: Romani Fem Sg *i* and Pl *i* are identical with the Medieval Greek forms, but there are also forms *e* (Fem Sg) and *o* (Pl) where the ultimate MIA source has to be considered: *iyã* (Fem Sg) and ? (only Neuter Pl *āyaĩ* is documented in Apabhraṃśa), see Bubenik, 1996: 95).

Table 8. The case system of Romani nouns and the definite article

Sg Dir	o phral 'the brother'	e phen "the sister"
Acc/Obl	le phral+es	la pheň +a
Pl Dir	o/i phral+a	o/i pheň +a
Acc/Obl	le phral+en	le pheň +en

(Unlike Hindi, Romani preserved the original plural suffix *-a* (< OIA *-āḥ*); but one notices the identity of the singular accusative and the plural nominative with feminine nouns). Further complications appear with adjectives which distinguish the oblique from the accusative case as shown in Table 9:

Table 9. The case system of Romani adjectives

Masc	Sg	Pl	Fem	Sg	Pl
Dir	-Ø/-o	-e		-Ø/-i	-e
Obl	-e	-e		-a	-e
Acc	-es	-en		-a	-en

We notice the skewed relationship of the identical form for the singular oblique and the plural nominative (but also oblique); feminine forms, on the other hand, possess identical forms for the singular oblique and accusative, and (as with masculine nouns) for the plural oblique and nominative. (The existence of the oblique vs. accusative form with adjectives might seem to be a reason to keep the term accusative; however, both *-e* (cf. Hindi) and *-es* go back to the Prākrit genitive form *-as(sa)*. Consequently, one has to distinguish between 'nominal' vs. 'adjectival' oblique case.

Personal pronouns distinguish three case forms in the singular (Nom, Acc, Gen), but only two in the plural (Nom/Acc vs. Gen) with the accusative functioning as the oblique case:

Table 10. Romani personal pronouns

	'I'	but	'we'
Nom	me		amen
Acc	man		amen
Gen	miro		amaro

Primary postpositions of Romani have parallels in various IA languages (these are called 'Layer II inflections' by Masica 1991: 337). In addition to the genitive *=ker+o/i/e* (Masc, Fen, Pl) 'of' and the dative *=ke* 'to' discussed above, there are the locative postposition *=te* 'in', ablative *=tar* 'from' and instrumental *=sa* 'with'. Ablative *=tar* 'from' is normally linked with the OIA comparative suffix *-tar* while instrumental *=sa* 'with' can be traced back to Apabhraṃśa *samāṇu* 'similar' (hence also Old Hindi *=san* 'with'). In various Romani dialects it may appear as *=ha* postvocalically in the singular oblique (*phral+eha* 'with the brother' vs. *phral+en=ca* 'with the brothers') restoring thus the fusional flective typology of OIA (*-ena* vs. *-aiḥ*). The perlative use of the instrumental (*džal drom+eha* 'go by the path') is remarkably archaic; one is reminded of parallel OIA examples (but these are also found in the coterritorial Slavic languages). Locative *=te* has cognates in a number of NIA languages (cf. Masica 1991: 244-5); its ultimate source could be OIA *artha* 'purpose' or *sthā-* 'stand', as suggested by Bloch (1970: 208-9) for Marathi.

As far as adjectival agreement in a noun phrase is concerned, there are two types. Normally, the adjective appears in the oblique adjectival form while the noun is in the nominal adjectival form if followed by the postposition:

(14) (bar+e rakl+es)=ke
(big+OBL boy+OBL)=to

'to the big boy'

(bar+e rakl+en)=ge
(big+OBL boy+OBL/PL)=to

'to the big boys'

In Russian and other Romani dialects it is possible for the adjective to agree completely with its head noun (cf. Wentzel, 1980: 80, for the actually documented examples):

(15) bar+es=ke rakl+es=ke
big+OBL=to boy+OBL=to

'to the big boy'

bar+en=ge rakl+en=ge
big+OBL/PL=to boy+OBL/PL=to

'to the big boys'

Typologically, these dialects restore thus the 'rhyming' agreement of their fusional flective OIA ancestor. The moving force behind this development, however, was the structural influence of the adjacent Slavic languages.

Romani prepositions (called 'Layer III inflections' by Matras (2002: 79) following Masica (1991: 232ff) constitute a (relatively open) set of markers inherited largely from its IA ancestor. Their similarities with MIA and NIA languages are patent from Tables 2 and 7. Their existence is a unique typological feature vis-à-vis all the other NIA languages. It came about in the context of the general shift in word-order typology (SOV Po > SVO Pr) which Romani has undergone during its Early period outside the Indian subcontinent (cf. Matras 2002: 18ff).

Romani prepositions govern the definite/determined noun in the 'nominative' (i.e. the direct case; cf. the situation in Modern Iranian where in Farsi the 'genuine'/basic prepositions are never followed by *ezāfe*). Otherwise, the locative serves as a 'default prepositional case' (Matras 2002: 88) to accompany most local prepositions (e.g. *pre man=de* lit. for I+OBL=LOC 'for me'; *andre phral+es=te* into brother+OBL=LOC 'into a/the brother'). Typologically speaking, we are dealing with 'circumpositions', i.e. the coexistence of both the preposition and the postposition (circumpositions are rare; they are documented in Armenian and Pashto, e.g. *pə-ki* 'at, on', *lə-cxa/na* 'from', etc. cf. Grjunberg 1987). The only two prepositions governing the dative and the genitive are *vaš* 'for' and *bi* 'without', respectively (e.g. *vaš tu=ke* for you=DAT 'for you'; *bi miro* without I+GEN 'without me' ~ *bijal man=de* without I+OBL=LOC 'without me'). Unlike postpositions which are cliticized to the oblique form of the noun, Romani prepositions can host the definite article which is normally procliticized to the noun. This process is clearly observable with prepositions in *-e* which contracts with the vowel of the article: *o* (Masc), *e* (Fem), *o* (Pl).

(16)	o=kher	(andre o=kher)	→	andro kher
	'the house'	'in(to) the house'		
	e=bar	(andre e=bar)	→	andre bar
	'the garden'	'in(to) the garden'		
	o=phrala	(ke o=phrala)	→	ko phrala
	'the brothers'	'to the brothers'		

(Parallel phenomena exist in Modern Greek eis = to N → *s=to* N and German *von=dem* N → *vo=m* N.)

The other way of expressing these notions is by means of postpositions; with the oblique form of the article (*le* Masc, *la* Fem) added unambiguously definite forms result:

(17)	phral+es=ke	vs.	le phral+es=ke
	brother+OBL=DAT		ART+OBL brother+OBL=DAT
	'to a/the brother'		'to the brother'

phral+es=tar	le phral+es=tar
brother+OBL=ABL	ART+OBL brother+OBL=ABL
'from a/the brother'	'from the brother'

(The oblique form of the definite article is above all used with proper names, e.g. *le Jirkas=ke* 'to George', *la Monika=ke* 'to Monica').

The prepositional system of Romani (represented by data from the East Slovak variety of Central dialects, Hübschmannová et al. 1991) is displayed in Table 11.

Table 11. Prepositional system of Romani (East Sloval dialect)

1.	paš 'at'	(N=GEN) 'of'
2.	ke/ko, kija 'to'	andal, khatar/l 'from'
3.	pre/o 'on'	pal 'off'
4.	o/upre 'up'	tel(e) 'down'
5.	andre 'in(to)'	avri 'outside'
6.	vaš 'for'	(N=INSTR) 'by'
7.	angle 'before'	pal 'after'
8.	(N=INSTR) "with"	bi 'without'
9.	angle, mujal 'against'	perdal 'through'
10.	maškar 'between'	prekal 'across'
11.	maškar 'among'	pašal, khatar/l 'about'
12.	tele 'under'	o/upre 'over'

The only two postpositions in this table are the genitive (*=kero*), and the instrumental (*=sa*, implementing the functions of perlative and comitative).

With the exception of *prekal* 'across' (of Serbian origin, cf. Boretzky & Igla, 1994: 381), all the other prepositions can be traced back to Old Indo-Aryan (*pre/o* 'on' in spite of its similarity to Slovak *pre* and Czech *pro* 'for' goes back to OIA *upari* 'over' via *upre*). Vlax *protiv* 'against' (< Serbo-Croatian *protiv*) does not appear in Slovak Romani. In the West there is *mamuj* 'against'; both *mamuj* and *mujal* are derived from *muj* 'face' (OIA/MIA *mukha-* 'face'; cf. *mukham* 'facing/looking towards' used as an adverb).

Synthetic markers of certain postpositional cases are open to the competition from their analytic counterparts: *=ke* (Dat), *=tar* (Abl) and *=te* (Loc) can be replaced by prepositional phrases involving *ke/ko*, *kija* 'to', *andal*, *khatar/l* 'from' and *pre* 'on'. There are considerable dialectal differences in this respect. Vlax varieties tend to realize the dative analytically: *phendem ko raklo* 'I said to the boy', whereas Central dialects do it synthetically: *phend'om rakl+es=ke* lit. boy+ OBL=DAT 'I said to the boy'. Remarkably, as shown in Table 11, the instrumental (perlative "by" and comitative "with") and the genitive are realized only synthetically.

In the Central dialects the ablative may be realized synthetically or analytically: *am+en=dar* we+OBL=ABL 'from us' or *khatar am+en=de* from we+OBL=LOC 'from us'. *Khatar/l* 'from; about' is another preposition whose etymology involves a body part. The second part is apparently the ablative postposition *=tar*; the full form of the first part is *khak* (Fem) 'arm(pit)' (descended from OIA *kakṣā* 'armpit' > *kakkhā* > *khakk(ā)* > *khāk* > *khak*; notice that the expected form in Hindi should be *khak*; one of the reasons for its non-existence could be a homophonic clash with *khāk* 'ashes, dirt' borrowed from Persian *xāq*). More importantly, there may be semantic difference between the synthetic ablative and the prepositional ablative phrase as in *avl'am Praha=tar* 'we returned from Prague' vs. *avl'am pal o Čechi* 'we returned from Bohemia' or *avl'am andal e Anglija* 'we returned from England'; the synthetic ablative is appropriate with a well defined specific source vs. ablative prepositional phrase with a vague source of the whole country (spatial removal from 'inside' vs. 'from the surface'; notice that *pal* is used in the meaning 'off' in *pejl'as pal o skamind* 'he/she fell off the table'). The other ablative preposition, *andar/l* 'from' could have arisen by combining the adverb *andre* 'within' with the ablative suffix *=tar* (so Boretzky & Igla 1994: 380), but it could also be traced back to the OIA ablative form *antar+āt* 'from inside'.

The synthetic locative is used above all with toponyms (*Praha=te* 'in Prague') versus *maškar* 'between' and *andro* 'in(to)' with common local nouns (*bešahas andro/maškar o foros* 'we lived in the city'.)

The final *-e* found in *tele* 'down; under', *andre* 'in(to)', *angle* 'before' corresponds both formally and etymologically to Hindi *-e* representing the oblique case of masculine nouns/adjectives (ultimately from the Apabhraṃśa Loc/Instr suffix *-ahĩ*).

The pair *=sa* 'with' and (preposition) *bi* 'without' is remarkably archaic (cf. Apabhraṃśa *samāṇu* and *viṇu* 'without' < OIA *samāna* and *vi-nā*). Another remarkable archaism is the preposition *vaš* 'for' — without any parallel in Hindi — going back to Prākrit *vaśa* 'on account of' (< OIA *váśa-tas* 'by command/force/will of', an ablative derivative from *váś*-a 'will, wish, desire). *Paš* 'at' (cf. Hindi *=ke pās* 'at') goes back to OIA *pārśva-* 'region of the ribs, side' (> Pāli *passa* > Hindi *pās*). Its case forms were used as local adverbs already in OIA:

(18) pārśv- ā́d (Abl) 'away form; by, through'
pārśv-é (Loc) 'near, beside, at'
pārśv-áyos (Loc Dual) 'on both sides'
pārśva-tás 'beside, aside; from, by'

Another archaic pair is *o/upre* 'up; over' vs. *tel(e)* 'down'/*tele* 'under'. Both Romani *o/upre* and Hindi *ūpar* are descended from OIA *upári*; Romani *tel(e)* goes back to OIA *tala* 'surface; sole (foot); palm (hand)' (another body part used as an adverb/postposition already in OIA; see *tal-e* (Loc) 'at, on, under'). Romani *angle* 'before; against' is closer to the OIA source *agra* 'front; beginning; point, tip, top' than its Hindi counterpart *āge* (several case forms of *agra* were used in the meaning 'before' already in OIA: *agr-am* (Acc), *agr-eṇa* (Instr), *agr-e* (Loc); there was also an adverbial derivative *agra-tás* 'in front; before'). Romani *andre* 'in(to)' (cf. Hindi *=ke ãdar* 'inside') developed from OIA *antara* 'inner; interior' (cf. OIA case forms *antaram* (Acc) 'within', *antareṇa* (Instr) 'between, within', *antar-ād* (Abl) 'out of, after', *antar-e* (Loc) '(with)in', and the adverb *antar-ā́* (with an earlier Instr suffix - *ā́*) 'amidst, between').

A salient derivational suffix of Romani adverbs is *-al* continuing the OIA ablative suffix *-āt* (lateralization *t* > *d* > *l* was a regular Romani diachronic development). This suffix may be attached to prepositions (*tel* 'under' → *tel-al* 'from under', *pal* 'after' (< OIA *pāra-* 'farther back') → *pal-al* '(from) behind' *paš* 'at' → *paš-al* 'about') and all the prepositions/adverbs (*angl-al* '(from) in front', *andr-al* 'from inside', etc.). Many of these adverbial derivatives can be traced back to OIA ablative forms of nouns or adjectives (e.g. OIA *pār+āt* farther bank+ABL > *palal* '(from) behind', *mukhā+t* face+ABL > *mujal* 'against', etc.)

5. Conclusions

At the beginning of the NIA period we find the results of evolution from MIA whose salient points are the following:

(i) The four cases of Late MIA, the syncretic NOM/ACC, syncretic GEN/DAT/ABL, INSTR and LOC were revamped as follows: NOM/ACC > Direct, GEN/DAT/ABL > Oblique, INSTR > relational postpositions, LOC > locative postpositions.

(ii) As we saw in Sections 1 and 2, the indistinctiveness of ablative, locative and instrumental morphology was one of the moving forces towards the analyticity whereby the adpositions supplied unambiguous markers of the notions such as source, location, accompaniment (and others).

(iii) The relatively free phrasal syntax of MIA (AN Po ~ Pr NA) is indicative of an intermediate state of affairs between the non-configurational paradigmatic morphology of OIA and Early MIA, and the configurational phrasal syntax (both nominal and verbal) of NIA.

(iv) NIA languages end up with a fully developed postpositional phrase with the oblique nominal form hosting a score of primary postpositions in the overall 'rigid' SOV syntax. Secondary postpositions are hosted by the oblique genitive form (N+OBL=GEN+OBL).

(v) European Romani differs remarkably from all the other NIA languages in realizing the layer of secondary postpositions as prepositions. More specifically, Romani developed 'circumpositions' combining the primary postpositions with prepositions (contrast Hindi (*baṛī mez)=ke*) *āge* ((big table)=GEN+OBL) 'in front of the big table' with Romani *andre (bar+e skamind+es)=te* into (big+OBL) table+OBL=LOC 'into the big table'. It is important to realize that this typological change in the structure of the postpositional phrase was accompanied by an overall typological shift from SOV to SVO word order.

Primary Literature

Bk	Dhaṇavāla's *Bhavisttakahā*
Hc	Hemacandra's *Siddha-Hema* (Prākrit Grammar)
Pc	Svayaṃbhūdeva's *Paumacariu*
Riṭṭha	Svayaṃbhūdeva's *Riṭṭhanemicariu*
Sc	Haribhadra's *Sanatkumāracarita*
SR	Addahamāṇa's *Saṃdeśa Rāsaka*

References

Beekes, Robert S. P. 1995. *Comparative Indo-European Linguistics. An Introduction.* Amsterdam: John Benjamins.

Bloch, Jules. 1970. The *Formation of the Marāṭhī Language*. Delhi: Motilal Banarsidass.

Boretzky, Norbert & Birgit, Igla. 1994. *Wörterbuch Romani-Deutsch-English für den südosteuropäischen Raum: mit einer Grammatik der Dialektvarianten.* Wiesbaden: Harrassowitz.

Bubenik, Vit. 1996. *The Structure and Development of Middle Indo-Aryan Dialects.* Delhi: Motilal Banarsidass.

____. 1998. *A Historical Syntax of Late Middle Indo-Aryan (Apabhraṃśa).* Amsterdam: John Benjamins.

Bubenik, Vit & John Hewson. (forthcoming). *From Adverbs to Adpositions in Indo-European Languages.* Amsterdam: John Benjamins.

Grjunberg, A. L. 1987. *Očerk grammatiki afganskogo jazyka (pašto).* Moscow: Nauka.

Hübschmannová, Milena et al. 1991. *Kapesní slovník romsko-český a česko-romský.* Praha: Státní pedagogické nakladatelství.

Insler, S. 1993. "The Prakrit ablative in -ahi". *Annals of the Bhandarkar Oriental Research Institute* LXX & LXXIII.15-21.

Masica, Colin P. 1991. *The Indo-Aryan Languages.* Cambridge: Cambridge University Press.

Matras, Yaron. 2002. *Romani. A Linguistic Introduction.* Cambridge: Cambridge University Press.

Mayrhofer, Manfred. 1951, 1956/1963/1976. *Kurzgefasstes etymologisches Wörterbuch des Altindischen.* Heidelberg: Winter.

Tagare, Ganesh V. 1948. *Historical Grammar of Apabhraṃśa.* Poona (Dissertation 5; 1987 ed. Delhi: Motilal Banarsidass).

Wentzel, Tatyana. 1980. *Die Zigeunersprache (Nordrussischer Dialekt).* Leipzig: Enzyklopädie.

WORDS WITH THE MEANING 'FEAR' IN INDO-ARYAN LANGUAGES

TATIANA ORANSKAIA

This paper deals with lexical denotations of FEAR in Indo-Aryan languages. The major aim of the analysis is to show that primarily they are strongly connected with the meaning TREMBLE. The other concepts that underlie the meaning FEAR are BEAT, STRIKE, and SPLIT. They are contiguous and may intersect with the semantic field TREMBLE.

A short presentation of common traits between descriptions of FEAR from the point of view of psychology, on the one hand, and reflection of this emotion in language, on the other hand, forms the background for the linguistic analysis.

The word TREMBLE will be used as the general notion for different types of vibrations of the body. There are a number of verbs with this meaning in Indo-Aryan languages, but only some of them are used in relation to FEAR. Those of them that are relevant for the present discussion are given below (see groups I., II., IV.) together with the words designating FEAR. Similarly, FEAR will for convenience be used as the general notion for the whole range of emotions that humans and animals experience when they find themselves in danger. Also in special literature on psychology, FEAR, which occupies a prominent place in discussion of emotions, usually occurs as the general term for FRIGHT, HORROR, TERROR, DREAD, TO BE FRIGHTENED, TO BE SCARED, etc. (Lewis and Haviland 1993: 511ff.).

Words for different types of trembling have in the Indo-Aryan, as in other languages, different semantic connotations, though they refer to basically the same movement. A native speaker can hardly describe the difference between these words in terms of visual perception or intensity of the action, but relates them unhesitatingly to different sensations.[1]

Two points should be mentioned here. First, words which express 'TREMBLE WITH FEAR' often express also 'TREMBLE WITH

---

[1] I am glad to use this opportunity to express my gratitude to Dr. Bahadur Singh and Mr. Ram Prasad Bhatt, lecturer at the Department of Culture and History of India and Tibet, for advising me on Hindi and Garhwali data, respectively.

COLD'. For most words in which the latter is the basic meaning this coincidence is however not true: 'TREMBLE WITH COLD' is normally not synonymous with 'TREMBLE WITH FEAR'. Second, the meanings FEAR and JOY may, though rarely, find expression in one and the same word. Their coexistence within one word with the etymological meaning TREMBLE is obviously related with somatic reactions to the feelings which typically manifest themselves through vibrations of the body.

Paradoxically, a similarity between FEAR and JOY has deep roots in human psychology. Judging by the cross-cultural popularity of such things as thrillers and horror films or of attractions like the ghost train and roller coaster, humans take pleasure in being frightened, in experiencing FEAR. At some point it becomes impossible to distinguish between FEAR and JOY. Indeed, these emotions are characterised by a number of coinciding traits. Their most obvious typical manifestations are that the person experiencing them trembles and her/his heart beats strongly. Their common ground is novelty of experience (Immelmann et al. 1988: 281).

The author does not intend to analyse these concepts from a psychological point of view, nor will a detailed semantic analysis of lexemes that mean different types of FEAR or JOY or both be made here. The latter would undoubtedly have been useful, but it needs a detailed discussion in a separate work. For the present discussion it is important that similarity in psychological and somatic reactions to acute FEAR and JOY is reflected in a linguistic reality: the same words, based on the meaning TREMBLE, may describe both feelings.

The Indo-Aryan words that have been studied in this paper fall into six groups. In most of the lexemes, the meanings FEAR and TREMBLE coexist in one phonetic form on the synchronic plane (groups I., II., IV., V.); in others this semantic relation is revealed through their etymologies (groups III. and VI. below).

As has already been noted above, the history of some words for FEAR also displays a conceptual contiguity with the notions SPLIT, BEAT, STRIKE. This is in no case to be understood as the FEAR that might be experienced by an object of these actions, a living creature that is being beaten or struck: The relation is based not on the transitive but on the reflexive meaning of the verbs, and can thus be described through the θ-role T h e m e of the grammatical subject.

The semantic link between (TREMBLE with) FEAR, on the one hand, and SPLIT, BEAT, STRIKE, on the other, is supported by the data of Indo-Aryan as well as of other Indo-European languages.

FEAR as a semantic unit belongs to the group of primary emotions which are common to human beings and animals and as such is connected with unintentional somatic reactions. Trembling of the body is presented in descriptions of FEAR in higher animals and in man as its most typical sign, the second significant sign being rapid beating of the heart. A frightened person may also feel cold (Apresyan 1995, II: 368-370). According to the classical description of FEAR given by Darwin "...*terror* causes the body to *tremble*. The skin becomes pale, sweat breaks out, and the hair bristles. ...The heart beats quickly, wildly, and violently..." (cited from: Wolman 1977: 17).

The choice of words in the first sentence of this citation (italicised by this author) presents a convenient opportunity to demonstrate the etymological connection between the described emotional feeling and TREMBLE. The noun *terror* and the verb *tremble* display the relation between the two concepts that is common in Indo-Aryan and is also evident in other Indo-European languages. Engl. *terror* 'dread, great fear' < Lat. *terror* 'dread' is allied to *terrēre* (<**tersēre)* 'to frighten, to scare'; *tremble* 'to shake, usually from fear or cold' < Old French *tremor, tremour* < Lat. *tremoorem* (Acc.) 'a trembling', 'terror', *trembler* 'to tremble', 'to fear'< Lat. vulg. **tremulaare* < Lat. *tremulus* (Barnhart 1988).

Terror and tremble are derived correspondingly from the Indo-European **tres-* and **trem-* that are extensions of the root **ter-* 'to wriggle'/Germ. 'zappeln' (Pokorny 1959). To the former go back also the Old Indic *tras-* 'to tremble, be afraid' and Old Slavic *tręsti: tręsti sę:* 'to tremble (with fear or cold)' (ibid.), s. group V. below. The phonetic structure of this common Indo-European root containing a dental plosive and a thrill is also typical of most Indo-Aryan words meaning TREMBLE with FEAR and is obviously of onomatopoetic nature. It renders the typical manifestation of a strong emotion, first of all of FEAR, in quick oscillatory movements of the body on one plane.

FEAR and JOY are fundamental concepts, and as such defy semantic component analysis. What can be described and analysed is how they manifest themselves. This is the starting point for psychological research and obviously also for semantic development of the corresponding words. Coincidences between psychological descriptions and linguistic evidence, especially in case of FEAR, are fascinating.

Six groups of Indo-Aryan words with the meaning FEAR that have been analysed in this paper will be presented below. They differ in their phonetic form and in some semantic features. Each of the groups contains the nearest cognates. The verbs are presented as stems. The data are restricted to the lexemes in statistically most important languages, to those found in rare editions, and to dialect forms registered by the present author. The second criterion for the choice of the lexemes was diversity of the phonetic forms within one group. For more exhaustive data, in the first place Turner 1966 (*A Comparative Dictionary of the Indo-Aryan Languages)* may be consulted, as well as dictionaries of separate Indo-Aryan languages.

Relations between the semantic features differ from group to group and from language to language. The members of groups I-V are obviously onomatopoetic. All of them combine the meaning of FEAR with the meanings TREMBLE. Some of them may convey, depending on the context, also the meaning of intense JOY.

Group III. contains evidence for a semantic connection between FEAR and SPLIT. The latter forms also the semantic basis for the cognates in group VI. The words in groups III. and VI. do not display this kind of semantic symbiosis on the synchronic plane, but the same correspondences in meaning are found in their etymologies.

I. TO TREMBLE WITH FEAR or JOY, TO FEAR, TO GET FRIGHTENED, TO BEAT (OF THE HEART)

Hindi *dahal-*:

buuRhe jaanvaro˜ ko dekhkar to mai˜ aur ***dahal*** *jaataa huu˜ . lekin ajiib baat hai ki is dahshat ke baavajuud...* (Vaid: 316) 'When I see old animals, I get even more frightened. But strangely enough, in spite of this fear... ' (in the second Hindi sentence, the word for FEAR is *dahshat*);

Punjabi *dahil- /Dahil- / Dahal-* (Singh 1961); Rajasthani *dahal-* (Sakariya and Sakariya 1977); Maithili *dahl-* (Jha 1999);

Garhwali *dahl-* (usually in combination with *dil* 'heart'): *vey ku dil dahliigii* 'His/her heart is beating with fear' or, rarely, 'His/her heart is beating with joy';

Jugi of Hissar, Luli of Samarkand *dahl-* (Oranskiy 1983: 123), cp. Chistoni *dal-* (Oranskiy 1983: 171).

The words in the first group are characterised by a three-consonant structure: The initial is voiced dental plosive (with the exception of the Punjabi, where the retroflex is also possible); the medial is the glottal fricative, and the final is the dental lateral approximant.

In Garhwali, unlike in other languages, the verb is used in combination with the word *dil* 'heart'. The cause of the heart beating is usually FEAR, but it can also be a sudden, unexpected JOY.

In the dialects of the Central Asian Gypsies recorded and described by Oranskiy 1983, the words *dahl-* (Jugi, Luli) and *dal-* (Chistoni) are possibly related: the form *dal-* can be the result of loosing the fricative. Oranskiy 1983, however, relates both *dahl-* and *dal-* with the New Indo-Aryan *Dar* 'FEAR' (s. group III.). This is the most reliable etymology for *dal-*, but not for *dahl-*.

Group I. has no recorded Old Indic ancestors. These lexemes give grounds for reconstruction of an Old Indic **DAHAL*. It may be related to Indo-European **dhel-* 'to tremble'/German 'zittern': Armenian *dołam*, Norwegian, Swedish dial. *dilla* 'to vibrate', 'to swing'/German 'schwingen', Norwegian *dilte* 'to trip'/German 'trippeln' (Pokorny 1959:

246), splitting of the initial aspirated consonant is not an unusual process, cf. e.g. below Punjabi *thar-ak- /tahar-* (group IV.).

II. TO TREMBLE WITH FEAR, EXCITEMENT, or JOY; TO BEAT (of the HEART)

Hindi *dhaRak-* 'tremble', 'beat (of the heart): usually *dil dhaRak-* in contexts describing romantic feelings, love; Punjabi *dhaRak-* 'shudder with fear', *dhaRkaa* 'fright', 'beating of the heart' (Singh 1961); Bengali *dhoR-phoRaani* 'serdtsebeniye'/ 'beating of the heart', 'volneniye'/ 'anxiety' (Loskutov et al. 1974); Garhwali *dhaRak-* 'to experience a sudden joy'.

The roots in group II. have a biconsonantal structure: The initial plosive is, unlike in group I., aspirated and the final is retroflex flap. The verbs in this group are denominative formations; the stems are formed by a noun-building suffix *–(a)k*. Hindi *dhaRak-* is normally used, like *dahal-* in Garhwali, with the noun *dil* 'heart' and has a similar meaning of excitement, inner agitation, which may be caused by fear, joy or anger. Thus it can have both negative and positive connotations. The latter comes forth as a rule in contexts describing romantic feelings: the experiencer of the emotion is nervous and uncertain of the reaction of the object of his/her passion. This verb implies the meaning of FEAR which is coexistent with the dominant semantics of extreme JOY. The semantic domain of this lexeme can be illustrated by a line from a ghazal of Sauda:

Urdu: *dil dhaRaktaa hai ki bedaar karuu˜ yaa na karuu˜* (Matthews and Shackle 1972: 47)

'[My] heart is beating [with excitement mixed with fear (because I apprehend a negative reaction on the side of the beloved)]: should I wake [her] or not?'

III. (TO) FEAR

Words belonging to this group exist in all New Indo-Aryan Languages, e.g. Hindi *Dar-*; European Gypsy dialects *dar-, dar*; *tahr, thar, tar, taar* (Wolf 2002) (cp. group IV.), *dar, dal, dan* (Pott 1845); Chistoni *dal-* (Oranskiy 1983).

Group III. contains the most usual and semantically stable words for FEAR in New Indo-Aryan which do not show any variations in the basic meaning. In the languages on the South Asian subcontinent, their biconsonantal root has initial voiced non-aspirated retroflex plosive and the final flap or trill. In the Gypsy dialects, which have lost the retroflex series, the initial is dental plosive. The Chistoni *dal-* belongs most probably to this group, not to group I. (s. above). The *r/l/n* variation within the same morpheme registered in the data of Pott 1845 is not unusual in Indo-Aryan.

In the Wolf's dictionary of the Gypsy language (2002), the entry *dar-* contains also words with the initial unvoiced aspirated *th-* or non-aspirated *t-*. In the latter case, the root vowel is long *aa*. It is true that devoicing is not infrequent in the European Gypsy dialects, and the voiced and unvoiced members of a pair of plosives lose their meaning distinguishing value, e.g. *dandra / tandra* 'tooth'; *dad/tat* 'father' (ibid.). However, this is hardly the case with *dar-/tahr-/ thar-*. As early as in Pott 1845, the words with the initial *d-: dar, dal, dan* are distinguished from those with the initial *t-/th-*. The latter are given under a separate entry and rightly connected with the Hindi *thar- / tahar-* (Pott 1845) (cp. group IV.). On the synchronic plane, these genealogically different phonetic forms in the Gypsy dialects may be regarded as probable variants of the same word, the lexical merger resulting from the mingling of the phonetic features retroflex/dental, aspirated/non-aspirated and voiced/unvoiced which has been strongly supported by the semantic similarity of the words *Dar-* (group III.) and *thar-* (group IV.).

Next to discuss is the etymology of *Dar-*. This verb goes back to the Old Indic root *dR̥: dara-* with the basic meaning 'to burst', 'to split' which has variants with the final *-r* as well as *-l*. The phonetic distribution reflects the semantic split: The words with the final *-r* in the root have the meanings related both to SPLIT and FEAR, whereas the words with the final *-l* in the root have only the former meaning (Mayrhofer 1986-2001; Turner 1966). In Turner 1966, two semantic derivatives of the root with the final *-l* – SPLIT and QUIVER – are distinguished. The latter belongs to the group of synonyms denoted here by TREMBLE.

Old Indic *dara-, dala-* 'to burst', 'to split'
dar-a-ti 'is frightened'; *dar-dar-ti, dal-a-ti* 'splits'
dara^{1}- 'fear';
dara^{2}-, *dala-* 'piece', *daram* 'a little'
DAL^{1} 'split'; *dal*^{2} 'quiver'.

Both meanings 'to split' and 'to be frightened' are present in the passive *diir-ya-*.

It is tempting to compare the Old Indic *dar-* with the Germanic verbal root * *dræd-* to which Engl. *dread* goes back: *drād-* (Old Saxon *an-drādan*), *trāt-* (Old High German *in-trātan*), *dræd-* (Anglo-Saxon *on-drædan*) 'to fear, be afraid'. These verbs are found only in compounds (Skeat 1968; Barnhart 1988). I have confined myself to the conjecture without attempting an etymological analysis.

IV. TO TREMBLE, TO BE FRIGHTENED, TO BE EXCITED

Hindi *thahar-, thartharaa-* 'to tremble'; Punjabi *tahar-, tharak-* 'to tremble', 'to be excited', 'to wish smth. strongly'; Nepali *thark-* 'to tremble', 'be frightened' (Rabinovich et al. 1968); Old Marathi *tharaar-* 'to tremble' (Tulpule and Feldhaus 1999); European Gypsy *tahr-/thar-/tar-/taar-* (cp. *dar-, daar-*) 'to fear', 'to be frightened'/German 'fürchten, erschrecken' (Wolf 2002); Sanskrit *tharthar(a)-aaya-* 'to swindle', 'to reel'/German 'schwindeln, taumeln' (Böhtlingk 1998);

Old Indic **THAR* (Turner 1966).

The words in this group and in group V. have, unlike those in groups I., II., and III., the initial dental unvoiced plosive. In group IV., the initial consonants are for the most part aspirated, but these words may also have the glottal fricative in the middle as a result of splitting of the aspirated consonant. This suggests the same development in the verbs of group I. The final consonant in the roots with the meaning FEAR is invariably *–r*. The meaning TREMBLE is expressed also by words with the final *–l*, which give sufficient evidence for reconstructing the form **THAL* (Turner 1966).

In this group, the meaning FEAR is comparatively weak and in most languages inseparable on the synchronous plane from the meaning TREMBLE.

V. TO TREMBLE, TO FEAR, TO FRIGHTEN, STRONG EMOTION

V.1. Nepali *tars-/tarch-* 'to be afraid'; Punjabi *traih-* 'to be startled'; Sindhi *Trah-* 'to be frightened'; Pali *tas-* 'to tremble', 'to be afraid'; Prakrit *tas-* 'to fear' < Old Indic *tras-* 'to tremble', 'to be afraid' (Turner 1966: entry 6006).

To this subgroup belong also the words in the European Gypsy dialects *trash-* 'to fear', 'to be frightened'/German '(sich) fürchten', '(sich) erschrecken', *tris-, trias-, tres-* 'to tremble'/German 'zittern, beben' (Wolf 2002), *trasavin* 'shock', 'violent emotion' (Kochanowski 1963) – the same word, the lexical merger resulting from the mingling of the phonetic features.

V.2. Hindi, Gujarati, Bengali *traas* 'fear'; Punjabi *taraah* 'alarm'; Sindhi *Trahu* 'start'; Pali, Prakrit *taasa-* 'trembling, fear' < Old Indic *traasa-* 'fear' (Turner 1966: entry 6013).

Both subgroups V.1. and V.2. are etymologically related with words meaning COLD in Dardic and Nuristani languages: Shina *TSoonu* 'to be cold'; Ashkun *istroos* 'ice' (Turner 1966: entry 6006, 6013). This is another evidence of the parallelism between the somatic reactions to FEAR and their reflection in lexical semantics.

The New Indo-Aryan members of group V. are represented by triconsonantal roots with the initial dental unvoiced non-aspirated plosive, medial dental flap or thrill, and the final dental, palatal or glottal fricative. A number of them have either retained the initial consonant group or borrowed the Sanskrit word.

The Old Indic *tras-* 'to tremble' goes back to IE **tres-*. To the same etymological group belong Old Persian *tars-: tars-a-ti* 'is frightened' and Old Slavic *tręs- : tręs-ti* 'to shake' (Barnhart 1988, Pokorny 1959). In Slavic languages, this root has two variants with ablaut, cf. Russian *trjas-* 'to shake, tremble' and *trus-* 'to fear, 'to behave cowardly', the phonetic split being accompanied by a semantic divergence (Fasmer 1964-1973, IV: 109, 113/Vasmer).

VI. (TO) FEAR

Hindi *bhay*; Lahnda, Punjabi *bhau*; Marathi *bhe˜*; Sinhalese *biya* < Old Indic *bhii-: bhaya-te*, *bhiiya-te* 'fears' (Turner 1966: entry 9390 ff.).

In its phonetic form group VI. is totally different from the other five groups. Its members have the initial labial voiced aspirated plosive and a vocalic member that normally represents front vowels of different grades.

These Indo-Aryan words go back to the Indo-European **bhōi- /bhēi-/ bhī* 'to fear'. Among their cognates are Old Icelandic *bifa,* Old High German *bibēn* (at the end follows **titrōn* 'quiver') > the German *beben* 'tremble with cold, anger or fear' (also 'tremble with joy' – T.O.), Lithuanian *bijoti(s)* 'to fear', and Old Slavic *bojati se˜* 'to fear' (Pokorny 1959: 161,162; Mayrhofer 1986 – 2001, II: 245, 246).

The Protoslavic **bojati sę* 'to fear' and **biti* 'to beat' are genetically related. This relation is evident from the vowel alternation in verbs vs. nouns **biti* (verb) : *bojь* (noun) (Trubachev 1974-, 2: 164). **biti* reflects the Indo-European **bhei(ə)-* that is related to the Indo-European **bheid-* (with the extension *-d-*) 'split'. Old Indic *bhid- /bhind-* 'to split', 'to break' is descended from this root (ibid.: 100). Thus, group VI. demonstrates, like group III., the semantic connection between the concepts FEAR and SPLIT, BEAT that is supported by etymological evidence.

Derivatives of **bheid-* (e.g. English *beat*, Russian *bit'-sja*) are used in a number of languages with the word '*heart*' to express a strong emotion, either FEAR or JOY, in the same way as the verb *dhaRak-* in Hindi or *dahal-* in Garhwali.

The concepts BEAT, STRIKE, and SPLIT in their medio-passive

variant, on the one hand, and TREMBLE, which is the major concept underlying the meaning FEAR, on the other hand, have certain points of contact in their usage and etymologies. Their common semantic features may be roughly interpreted as QUICK ITERATIVE MOVEMENT ON ONE PLANE with the derivative meanings of INSTABILITY and FRAGILITY. This semantic shift, which on the basis of Indo-Aryan data has been presented in group III. above, is also evidenced in other Indo-European languages: cp. English *to shiver* 'to tremble' and *to shiver* 'to break into *shivers* or small pieces' (Skeat 1968); English *to shake* 'to tremble' and *shaky* 'split (of timber)', 'liable to break down' (Barnhart 1988).

To summarize

Most words of Indo-Aryan as well as of other Indo-European languages that express the emotional feeling of FEAR show their genetic relation with the concept TREMBLE. This relation is evident both in their onomatopoetic phonetic forms which are usually characterised by a combination of a dental plosive with a flap or thrill, and in common semantic features.

The concept TREMBLE is semantically and, in some cases, also etymologically related to the concepts BEAT, STRIKE, and SPLIT.

FEAR and JOY may share lexical means of expression that are based on these concepts.

Words that express FEAR and sometimes also JOY are basically descriptions of typical somatic reactions of living things to strong unexpected emotions.

References

Apresyan, Yu D. 1995. *Integral'noe opisanie yazyka i sistemnoe yazykoznanie*. Izbrannye trudy. Moskva: Shkola "Yazyki russkoy kul'tury".

Barnhart, Robert K., ed. 1988. *Chambers dictionary of etymology*. New York: Chambers. First published as *Barnhart dictionary of etymology*.

Böhtlingk, Otto v. 1998. *Sanskrit Wörterbuch, in kürzerer Fassung*. Delhi: MLBD. Reprint. First St. Petersburg Edition 1883-86.

Fasmer, Maks. 1964-1973. *Etimologiceskij slovar' russkogo jazyka*. Perevod s nemetskogo i dopolneniya O. N. Trubaceva. Vol. I-IV. Moskva: Izdatel'stvo «Progress». (Original German edition: Vasmer, Max. 1950-1958. *Russisches etymologisches Wörterbuch*. I-III. Heidelberg: Carl Winter).

Immelmann, Klaus, Scherer, Klaus R., Vogel, Christian, und Schmoock Peter, eds. 1988. *Psychobiologie. Grundlagen des Verhaltens*. Gustav Fischer Verlag / Psychologie Verlags Union.

Jha, Govinda, ed. 1999. *Kalyani Kosh. A Maithili-English Dictionary*. Darbhanga: Maharajadhiraj Kamleshvar Sinh Kalyani Faundeshan.

Kochanowski, Jan. 1963. Gypsy Studies. P. 2. *Shata-Pitaka Series. Indo-Asian literatures, vol. 26*. New Delhi: International Academy of Indian Culture.

Lewis, Michael, and Haviland, Jeanette M., eds. 1993. *Handbook of emotions*. New York – London: The Guilford Press.

Loskutov, V. N., Valuyeva, R. V., and Polyanskiy, B. G. 1974. *Slovar' bengal'skogo yazyka s russkimi ekvivalentami.* Eds. Bykova, E.M. and Bhoumik, Noni. Moskva: Izdatel'stvo "Sovetskaya Entsiklopediya".

Matthews, D. J., and Shackle, C. 1972. *An anthology of classical Urdu love lyrics.* London: Oxford University Press.

Mayrhofer, Manfred. 1986-2001. *Etymologisches Wörterbuch des Altindoarischen.* In 3 Bänden, 32 Lieferungen. Heidelberg: Universitätsverlag C. Winter.

Oranskiy, I. M. 1983. *Tadzhikoyazychnye etnograficheskie gruppy Gissarskoy doliny (Srednyaya Aziya). Etnolingvisticheskoe issledovanie.* Moskva: Izdatel'stvo «Nauka». Glavnaya Redaktsiya Vostochnoy Literatury.

Pokorny, Julius. 1959. *Indogermanisches Etymologisches Wörterbuch.* B. I. Bern: A. Francke AG Verlag.

Pott, A. F. 1845. *Die Zigeuner in Europa und Asien. Ethnographisch-linguistische Untersuchung, vornehmlich ihrer Herkunft und Sprache, nach gedruckten und ungedruckten Quellen.* 2. Teil. Halle: Druck und Verlag von Ed. Heynemann.

Rabinovich, I. S., Korolyov, N. I., and Aganina, L. A. 1968. *Nepal'sko-russkiy slovar'.* Moskva: Sovetskaya Entsiklopediya.

Sakariya, Badri Prasad, and Sakariya, Bhupati Ram. 1977. *Rajasthani-Hindi shabdakosh.* Jaypur: Pancashil prakashan.

Singh, Bhai Maya. 1961. *The Panjabi dictionary.* Patiala: Munshi Gulab Singh and Sons.

Skeat, Walter W. 1968. *Etymological dictionary of the English language.* Oxford: At the Clarendon Press. First edition 1879-1882.

Trubachev, O. N., ed. 1974 - . *Etimologiceskij slovar' slavjanskich jazykov:* praslavjanskij leksiceskij fond. Moskva : Nauka.

Tulpule, S.G., and Feldhaus, Anne. 1999. *A Dictionary of Old Marathi.* Mumbai: Popular Prakashan.

Turner, R. L. 1966. *A comparative dictionary of the Indo-Aryan languages.* London - New York – Toronto: Oxford University Press.

Vaid, Krishna Baldev, s.a. Kaise guzar rahii hai olD ej! *Bahuvacan 1:1. A quarterly journal in Hindi of literature, language, research, and ideas.* New Delhi: Mahatma Gandhi International Hindi University.

Wolf, Siegmund A. 2002. *Großes Wörterbuch der Zigeunersprache. Wortschatz deutscher und anderer europäischer Zigeunerdialekte.* Hamburg: Helmut Buske Verlag (unveränderter Nachdruck der 2.Auflage von 1987).

Wolman, Benjamin B., ed. 1977. *International encyclopedia of psychiatry, psychology, psychoanalysis, & neurology.* New York: Aesculapius Publishers.

CASE, SPLIT NOMINATIVITY, SPLIT ERGATIVITY, AND SPLIT ACCUSATIVITY IN HINDI: A HISTORICAL PERSPECTIVE

ALEXANDER A. SIGORSKIY

Abstract

Evolution of nominativity, ergativity and accusativity from the period of early Hindi up to modern Hindi is traced. Three types of ergative strategies (ES) succeeded each other during the evolution of Hindi: 1) inflectional ES; 2) syntactical ES, and 3) postposition-marked ES, or morphosyntactical ES. There were mixed types of ES also. The evolution of ES is related to the evolution of the case system, or more specifically, to the breaking down of the inflectional case system and the emerging of the postposition-marked case relation system. The evolution of split accusativity in Hindi follows mainly the pattern of the evolution of ergativity with some peculiarities of its own.

Hindi is considered in the broad sense, as standard Hindi with its dialects, or language-dialects, former (literary) languages. Linguistic data from Nepali and Panjabi are also used.

Key words: accusativity, ergativity, nominativity, passive.

1. EC already existed in OIA and MIA languages: in Sanskrit [Ivanov, Toporov 1960: 124-125; Elizarenkova 1967: 124-125]; in Prakrits [Vertogradova 1978/2002: 92-93]; in Pali [Peterson 1996, Abstract in SASSN 1996, 5.2]; in Apabhramsha (Old Western Rajasthani) [Tessitori 1914-1916/1958]. The history of ES in IA languages is similar to its history in Iranian languages [Pireiko 1979]. ES was triggered by introduction of perfect participle forms into the finite verb system. It seems to be an active, not a passive, strategy from the very beginning. There are two major arguments in favor of such an explanation of ES. First, being a part of the finite verb system, ES involves paradigmatic relations with nominative strategy (NS) sentences and so there is syntactic equivalence between them as sentences of active, not passive strategy. Both of them, NS and ES are counterparts of active strategy (AS) opposed to passive strategy (PS). Second, there was a

passive voice in OIA languages. Two passives in one and the same language are too much for its grammar.

The emergence of ES within passive constructions in MIA languages has been traced by P. L. Andersen [1986: 83]; cited and developed in [Bubenik 1996: 172]. The interface between ES and PS (the old inflectional passive) according to both authors is communicative strategy: while an ergative subject conveys old information, a passive subject conveys new information. The only qualification to this very interesting and promising idea is that EC existed already in OIA alongside with PC.

Investigation of grammatical relations in Pali [Peterson 1998; cited from 2001: 207] supports a more traditional point of view. That is "the emergence of an ergative construction in the perfect in Middle Indo-Aryan from an originally resultative construction, noting similarities to the more familiar development of perfect constructions in many West European languages from originally possessive constructions."

It may be considered as a generally recognized fact that the Ergative construction (EC) in Indo-Iranian languages is similar to the periphrastic possessive perfect (*have*-perfect etc) in other Indo-European languages. This differentiation of Indo-European languages between possessive perfect type and possessive EC type is coincident roughly with differentiation between *have*-languages and *be*-languages.

According to Yu. S. Maslov, as early as in the 19th century the similarity between the two types of possessive constructions—in West-European languages and in Russian—has been recognized: *Ich habe das buch – U menya yest' kniga; Ich habe das buch gelesen – U menya kniga prochitana* [Maslov 1948/1984: 224-248].

The problem of the active or passive meaning of EC has been a matter of discussion for a long time. But the idea of the passive meaning of EC is passé. Maslov has treated Russian EC (or syntactic constructions of an ergative type) as active. The idea of possessiveness is reanalyzed and agent does not denote possessor but performer of an action. Thus in the following utterance:

(1) *Na kukhne nel 'zya* *ni na minutku ostavit' nichevo:*
At kitchen [one] can't not for a minute leave nothing:

u koshki uzhe	*stashchena*	*rybina*	(e.g. *koshka stashchila* rybu)
at cat already	stolen	fish	(e.g. cat stole fish).

'One can't leave anything at the kitchen just for a moment: a fish has been stolen by the cat.' (= The cat has stolen a fish / The cat has a stolen fish)

2. Discussions of the passive or active character of the Ergative in

Hindi have been summarized in Ilieva [1997]. According to Ultsiferov [1993: 281-282], the Hindi EC is lexically passive but grammatically active. However this is rather a historical reconstruction because such an ambiguity of EC in Hindi can't be traced even in the earliest stages of Hindi. Nevertheless there remains the problem of the passive nature of the perfect participle. But this problem itself needs more investigation.

Marginal usage of EC with some non-transitive verbs or incompatibility of EC and some transitive verbs have been hypothetically interpreted as remnants of a former active stage (in the IA languages [Zakharyin 1977; 1987: 119-120; Volkhonskiy 1987], in the Iranian languages [Edelman 2001: 141-144]. Lists of such "irregular" verbs in both language families are very similar.

Interrelations of ES, NS and PS in the NIA languages may be presented historically as an opposition of neutral, centripetal and centrifugal strategies, or synchronically as opposition of active (imperfect active and perfect active) and passive strategies.

3. The date of 1000 AD is commonly accepted as the starting point of Hindi; (although some say it is VI-VIII AD). In any case this is a conventional boundary between Apabhramsha and Hindi, or more exactly between the prehistoric and historic periods in the development of Hindi, and the beginning of written texts in early Hindi. At the start of this period the case system is already represented in reduced form. In fact in early Hindi we have already the case system of modern Hindi reduced to DIR and OBL cases plus vocative. But the functions of the cases as well as their endings in early Hindi are not the same as in modern Hindi. The case functions in modern Hindi are even more reduced.

There are at least two more theories of case in Hindi. One is that Hindi basically has reconstructed the OIA system of eight cases. The reconstructed cases are marked by simple postpositions. Close to this is the point of view developed in the case clitic marker theory [Butt, King 1999, 2001; Sharma Devyani 1999]. Case clitics, that is cliticized simple postpositions, are morphologic case markers, or the last step to them. The second theory does not recognize any morphologic cases in Hindi at all, just syntactical case relations [Ultsiferov 1995]. Both theories have one thing in common: they reject the reduced two case system. Hereafter I assume an inflectional two-case system alongside of morphosyntactic cases: NOM, ERG, ACC, DAT, LOC, GEN.

From the historical point of view there are traces of the previous case system in modern Hindi, and simple postpositions retain their syntactic properties, e. g. they govern Oblique case of noun or pronoun including some special "ergative oblique" forms of some pronouns.

One of the functions of the Oblique case of nouns and pronouns as well as Object case of pronouns in early and middle Hindi is that of

Ergative marker. In modern Hindi this function is performed by the postposition *ne*. In early Hindi the postposition *ne* is used randomly.

4.1. I begin my analysis of ES and EC with examples from Dakkhini and Awadhi. For one thing, they demonstrate opposite tendencies of evolution, but another reason is that both of them have been described uniformly by Baburam Saksena [1937/1972; 1952]. Saksena argues that in Dakkhini and Awadhi Direct case and Oblique case as well as Object case of pronouns are not distinguished. All of them are used in the same positions without change of meaning. A. N. Shamatov [1974] follows this point of view (objections in [Zakharyin 1978: 107-109]).

My analysis of materials of the above-mentioned authors as well as of the text corpora of Dakkhini [Shri Ram Sharma 1954] indicates that in both languages these three cases are arranged in complementary distribution: Direct case marks Nominative subject, Oblique and Object cases mark Ergative subject.

Dakkhini

Examples are taken from the above-mentioned anthology of Shri Ram Sharma. In brackets after the translation author, dates of life or manuscript and page are given.

(1) (a) **vo** *meharbaan diyaa jñaan* *baalak kuu˜.*
He NOM mercy gave knowledge boy ACCsp.

'*He* mercifully gave knowledge to the boy.' (Gonda, around 1300-1351, 45)

(b) **aallaa** **taalaa** *kuraan me˜* *farmaayaa hai.*
Allah NOM Koran in said is.

'*Allah* has said in the Koran' (Bandanavaz Gaisudaraz, 1388-1423, 394);

(c) agar **[bandaa]***koii* *nekii kiyaa* ...
If [devotee-NOM] something (someone) good made...

'If a [*devotee*] made something good…' (Or: "If somebody made something good…") (Maula Abdulla, 1623, 401);

(d)	*duniyaa me˜*	***une***	*naam*	*<u>Dubaayaa</u>*
	World in	he OBJ-ERG	name ACCunsp	stained.

'He stained his good name in the world.' (Gonda, 45);

(e)	**hamne**	*<u>kiyaa hai</u>*	*tuphaan*
	I ERG	made is	storm ACCunsp.

'*I* made a storm.' (Gonda, 49)

A peculiarity of Dakkhini is that subject Ergative marking by OBL, OBJ or postposition *ne* does not block its agreement with the predicate. So an Ergative marked subject remains controller of agreement:

(i)	*uske baad* **maarkaaTo˜ ne**	*Dillii ko*	*<u>liye</u>.*
	this after slaughters ERG	Delhi ACCsp	taken.

'After this Delhi was taken over *by slaughters*.' (Mir Asgarali Kazi, 1861, 445)

This feature of Dakkhini is not unique. In modern Hindi the postposition *ko* (the historical synonym of *ne*) behaves itself in the same way in participle clauses:

(3)	*tuu*	**mujhe**	**badlii**	*samajhtaa hai*?
	You	me DAT	changed	thinking is?

'Do you think me changed?' [Ultsiferov 1993: 199]

This complex sentence consists of two clauses: *tuu samajhtaa hai* "You think" and *mai˜ badlii* "I changed". Embedding of the second clause into the first one triggers raising of its subject to the position of direct object of the matrix clause and the predicate of the embedded clause raises to the position of complement (predicative attribute) of the predicate of the main clause. But the trace of the former subject remains. It explains agreement between specific *ko*-marked / object case marked direct object and predicative attribute as a trace of subject-predicate relations. Sentences (2 i) and (3) have one thing in common, namely, transparency in agreement between the subject and the verb, in sentence (3) it is a subject of participle clause.

Hypothetically, Dakkhini conserved the mechanism of the archaic stage of the Ergative when EC preserved its inner form of a possessive construction derived from NC. Subsequently EC became a purely structural phenomenon. Isolated from the mainstream of Northern Hindi,

Dakkhini conserved some archaic features.

The same phenomena – agreement control under postposition or oblique case marking of the head group in some Indian languages – Maithili, Marathi, Nepali and in some Tibeto-Burman languages – have been described in Subbarao 1998: 6-16, also in Oriya [Patnaik 1995].

Awadhi (examples are taken from [Baburam Saksena 1937/1972].

EC: (4) (a) **muninhaa** *kiiratii gaaii.*
Sages OBL-ERG fame sang.

'The sages sang [his] glory.' (Tulsi Das, 1532-1623 [Saksena 1972: 123])

(According to Kellogg the *–nha* ending is common for both Direct and Oblique cases [Kellogg 1875/1955: 124, Table VI].)

(b) *rekhaa* **tinha** *khaa˜cii.*
Line they OBL-ERG draw.

'They draw a line.' (ibid., 172)

(According to Kellogg *tinha* is Accusative-Dative as well as Agentive, that is Ergative [ibid.: 196-197, Table XII].)

NC: (c) **jo** *hamaara dou haatha banaawaa*
Who NOM my/our both hands made.

'*Who* made both my hands.' (Nur Muhammad, 1757 [ibid.: 161])

OBL is used for the subject of a transitive predicate [Liperovsky 1997: 55], but both authors reject ERG in such cases seeing here fusion of case functions. OBL marks the subject not only of perfect participle predicates but of personal verb predicates as well:

(d) **gaïyan** *khaïhaï.*
Cows OBL-ERG will eat (subjunctive in modern Hindi).

'*The cows* will eat.' [Saksena 1937/1972: 128; Liperovsky 1997: 55]

The idea of B. R. Saksena, A. N. Shamatov and V. P. Liperovsky that DIR and OBL cases are not distinguished in Dakkhini and Awadhi reflects the fact that NS and ES do not imply any semantic difference, which in Dakkhini is emphasized by agreement of the ergative subject with the predicate. Nevertheless, the formal opposition of NS and ES is obvious.

Similarity of Dakkhini and Awadhi concerning ergativity exists in the early and middle stages. In the newer period ergativity in Awadhi as well as in other Eastern Hindi languages exists only as remnants of the previous stage. In literary Dakkhini the postpositional, morphological ERG is being strengthened under influence of the emerging standard Hindi. But modern colloquial Dakkhini retains free NS/ES alternation:

NS: (e) **Tu** *tera moo* *khola tou gaalian ati.*
You NOM your mouth opened so curses come

(the feminine perfect participle is not marked by number).

'[Once] you open your mouth curses come.' [Goka 2000, original transcription];

ES: (f) **sarkaar ne** *ismaail ko* *bulaayaa.*
Lord ERG Ismail ACCsp called.

'*The Lord* called Ismail' (I. B. Padyanaman, 1951, in [Shri Ram Sharma 1954: 462]).

(g) **une** *jaisaa bolii vaisaa kartuu˜*
She OBJ-ERG as said so [I] shall do.

'I'll do as she said.' [ibid.: 461]

(The finite verb *kartuu˜* is a fusion of perfect participle *karat* with Aux 1sg *hu˜*. Only 1sg forms are marked in Dakkhini.)

4.2. The situation in early Hindi and Braj is the same as in Dakkhini and Awadhi. The breaking down of the case system decreased the distinctiveness of NS and ES or sometimes eliminated it. Given the fuzziness of case marking, the NS/ES option is determined by contrast of subject and direct object in gender and/or number. If the direct object is marked by the postposition *ko,* the NS/ES option is determined only by the form of the subject and/or its agreement with the predicate.

Khari Boli.

NC: (5) (a) jab **yaar** *dekhaa nain bhar* ...
When friend NOM looked eyes just ...

'When *the friend* just looked in [his] eyes...' (Amir Khusro, cited from [Tivari 1966: 133])

The language of Amir Khusro (1253-1325) is usually considered non-authentic. Recently discovered new riddles of Amir Khusro ['Khusro' Pradip Sharma 2002: 11-13] linguistically do not change anything because the manuscript is of the 18th century AD. An attempt at linguistic reconstruction of the language of that epoch [Shamatov 1978] argues the identity of Khusro's language with the language of his times.)

EC: (b) **logan** *pahine moTe vastra.*
People OBL-ERG worn coarse clothing.

'*People* have worn coarse clothing.' (Banarasidas, 1586-1643, cited from [Malaya 1997])

Unlike Dakkhini the "transparency" of ERG-marked subject for agreement with predicate is not characteristic of Khari Boli so there is object-predicate agreement, not subject-predicate agreement. Free alternation (optionality) of NS and ES is observed also in early Braj.

(6) (a) **raajaa** *snaan* *kiiyo,* **saavaNT ne** *snaan* *kiiyo.*
Raja NOM ablution made, servant ERG ablution made.

'The *Raja* performed his ablutions, the servant made his ablutions.'

(Candbardai, before 1550 AD, cited from [Sinh 1958: 372]).

(b) **gvaal** kahaa
Shepherd NOM said.

'*The shepherd* said.' (Kaviindraacaarya Sarasvatii, *karuNabharaN naaTak,* 1617-1659, cited from [Gupta 1958: 122]);

(c) **un** *kahii*
He OBL-ERG said

(agreement with the zero/elliptical direct object *baat* f. "word", "speech").

'*He* said.' (ibid.)

(d) **riSilogan** *shor* *macaayo.*
Sages OBL-ERG noise made.

'*The sages* made noise.' (*shakuntalaa upaakhaan*, 1680, [Gupta 1958: 136])

5. There are thus 3 types of ERG in the history of Hindi: 1) inflectional, 2) purely syntactical without any inflectional marking, and 3) morphosyntactical, marked by the postposition/clitic *ne*. There are mixed types also. The first type is the most ancient, the successor of the OIA and MIA languages. The second one is an intermediate type. The facts of Dakkhini where the Oblique and Object cases equally mark ERG indicate that ERG in the early and middle Hindi languages is genetically not instrumental, but dative or genitive-dative. The postpositional *ne*-construction which functions at first parallel to the old inflectional ERG and then begins to supplant it, favors this suggestion, because the postposition *ne* is the synonym of the dative-directive postposition *ko*.

Free NS/ES alternation in early and middle Hindi subject ERG marking appeared as a result of elimination of case inflections and it did not result in any semantic changes. This fact argues that EC, historically a possessive construction, was active from the very beginning. The NS > ES switch is purely formal and not semantic (ERG as a structural, not as a lexical case [Davison 2001]. But the configuration:

PS
NS = ES

is not so simple as it seems to be, and needs a special exploration, especially taking into consideration the syntactic behavior of nominative and ergative subjects being transformed not only into passive constructions but indefinite, participle, and converb clauses with both active and passive predicates.

Split ergativity has always existed in the Hindi area; no purely nominative or purely ergative language or dialect is known in the early and middle stages of Hindi. But reduction of the case system resulted in loss of distinctiveness: "...a progressive loss of ergative marking has occurred in varying degrees diachronically in different systems. This process is manifested in two distinct strategies of markedness reduction:

loss of overt subject marking in the nominal domain and loss of marked agreement in the verbal domain" [Deo, Sharma 2002]. A similar situation is observed in one of the modern Iranian languages – Kurdish (Kurmanji) [Pireiko 1963; Taylor 2001]. The situation that emerged gave scope for two possibilities: 1) transformation into a purely nominative language; 2) strengthening the split ergativity (of the nominative-ergative type) on a new basis. Eastern Hindi chose the first way, but inconsistently. Western Hindi chose the second. The process of the strengthening of ES went hand in hand with the formation of standard Hindi. Transition of the Eastern IA languages into a nominative type of language has not been completed and rudiments of ergativeness have remained [Prokofyeva 1987; Amritavalli, Sarma 2002]. According to the Sarma, Assamese is an isolated Nominative-Ergative (purely ergative, not split)-Accusative NIA language among the Eastern NIA languages.

Actually there was no transition from an ergative strategy to a nominative one in the Hindi area languages. Disintegration of the case system has resulted in the two of them coinciding in some cases. Hindi, Dakkhini, Braj, and other Western dialects have restored lost distinctiveness of argument marking by introducing postpositional clitics as case markers. The Eastern dialects, on the other hand, have conserved the previous system with the nominative/ergative strategy almost lost and thus have ended up with some nominative features.

The linguistic material confirms Hoernle's reconstruction that originally ERG had inflectional case marking [Hoernle 1888: 217-218, § 371], that ergative subject was marked by some oblique case.

Origin of the postposition *ne* remains an enigma. New etymologies have been suggested in [Khokhlova 1987; Butt, King 1999, 2001]. But it seems obvious that its source was the area around Delhi, Punjab, the Braj area, Rajasthan and Gujarat. The synonymy of the dative postpositions *ne* and *ko* suggests same origin for both of them. An originally dative meaning of the *ne* postposition is evident from its usage as a synonym of postposition *ko* in old Hindi (up to the 19th century) and its language-dialects, e.g., in Hariani/Bangaru [Sigorskiy 2000]. Here is an example of the dative usage of *ne* in old Hindi correspondence:

(7) *tiisuu~ man* ***nai*** *baDo phikar huvau.*
It from soul DAT big trouble was.

'It troubled him / It was a trouble to him.' (Gupta 1993: 26)

(This letter was written in Kishangarh, now in Jaisalmer district of Rajasthan, in 1825; the language of the letters compiled by the author is according to him a mixture of Khari Boli, Marwari and Braj.)

6. Two ancient types of ERG – 1) dative-possessive, and 2) instrumental – observed as early as in Sanskrit, appear in "greater Hindi". The first type – dative-possessive *ne*-ERG is found in Western Hindi, including "Southern" Hindi – Dakkhini and in Rajasthani dialects. The second type – instrumental ERG marked by the postposition *le* is found in Pahari dialects and Nepali. Both Ergatives are split. Pahari (Kumayuni) examples are given from [Pant 1993].

(8) (a) *Daanjuu*-**l** *bhaat* *khaa*
Danju-ERG rice eaten.

'Danju has eaten rice.' [40]

Instrumental, not ergative usage of *le* is presented in the following utterance:

(b) *mai˜ cashmai*-**l** *caaNauchii˜*
I *glasses-by* was seeing.

'I was seeing through the glasses.' [ibid.]

Double case marking:

(c) *diidi*-**l** *haate*-**l** *diyo* [ibid.]
Didi-ERG hand-by given

'The elder sister has given [it] with [her] hand.'

Similar double marking (*ne*-marking) of subject and indirect object is observed in a Western Hindi dialect, Ahirvati:

(9) (a) *ma˜*-**nai˜** *saab* -**nai˜** *maaryo.* [Yaadav: 208]
I ERG mister DAT beaten.

'I have beaten the Saheb/I have been beaten by the Saheb.' (both translations are possible).

Another variant is also possible, where no ambiguity remains:

(b) *mai˜ saab*-**nai˜** *maaryo* [ibid.]
I mister-ERG beaten.

'I have been beaten by the Saheb.'

(For more detailed discussion of the *ne* postposition in some Hindi dialects see Sigorskiy 2000.)

The situation in Nepali is identical to that in the Pahari dialects. There also exists the split ergativity with ergative subject marked by instrumental postposition *le* "by", which marks an instrumental as well:

(10) (a) haami*i*-**le** *plilim* *henyauu˜*
We ERG film seen.

'We watched a film.' [Hutt; Subedi 1999/2003: 119]

Instrumental use of preposition *le* can be seen in the following utterance:

(b) *haamii* *kaan-**le*** *sunchau˜.*
We ear-INSTR hear.

'We hear with (our) ears.' [Ibid.: 120]

According to S. H. Kellogg, the pattern of subject-predicate agreement in Nepali combines the features of Eastern Hindi dialects, namely, agreement of predicate with subject, and the features of Western Hindi dialects, namely, postpositional marking of subject [1875/1955: 309, § 526]. It means that Nepali is similar in this respect to Dakkhini. In both of them the ergative marker does not block subject-predicate agreement, but while in Nepali such transparency of postposition is regular, in Dakkhini it is an irregular feature (2i) which occurs also in Hindi (3).

In Nepali. the ergative marker *le* is used not only with Perfect forms, but also with the Habitual Past tense. A third type of usage is semantically induced: its function is to emphasize the subject of a transitive verb in the Habitual *Present* tense, i.e.:

(1) "If the sentence says that it is a part of the natural order of things for the subject to perform the verb, and therefore states that this is a role that is specific to the subject" [Ibid.]

(c) *baagh*-**le** *baakhaa* *khaancha*
Tiger ERG goats eats.

'The tiger eats goats.' [ibid.]

(2) "If the sentence is a question asking who or what is the subject of a transitive verb":

(d) *aaj* *kas*-**le** *ciyaa banau˜cha?*
Today who ERG tea will make?

'Who will make the tea today?' [ibid.]

(3) "If the sentence is a response to a question such as those in (2) above, or focuses in any way upon the subject of the verb":

(e) *aaj* *bhaai*-**le** *ciyaa* *banau˜cha*
Today younger brother ERG tea will make.

'Today younger brother will make the tea.' [ibid.]

Old Nepali:

(f) *kaaskilaaii choDi* *gorkaa*-**le** *kaahaa jaanu cha.*
Kaski for left (*converb* = without) Gorkha ERG where go is.

Gorkhaalaaii choDi kaaski-*le* kani kahaa jaanu cha.
Gorkha for left/without Kaski ERG where go is.

'Where will Kaski go without Gorkha? Where will Gorkha go without Kaski?' (rhetoric question).

[Narharinath: 2022/1964; Friendly letter from Gorkha to Kaski, 1747. (The book and the Russian translations of some documents have been kindly given to me by Alexander A. Ledkov.)].

This peculiarity of Nepali seems important, but due to random and occasional occurrence of ergative subject markers with intransitive or imperfect verbs in Old Hindi dialects and to the scarcity of the material available it has till now no rational explanation.

The following Dakkhini example from Vajahi's "Sabras" seems to confirm Hutt-Subedi's rules:

(11) *jahaa˜ Gamza kare Gamze vahaa˜ aashiq* **ne** *kyaa karnaa?*
Where the flirt does flirtings there lover- ERG what to do?

'If a coquette begins to cast amorous glances, what is a lover to do?' [Shamatov 1974: 169.] (Again a rhetorical question).

But this utterance may have another explanation, i.e. a formal contamination of Ergative and Dative case markers in a semantically modal dative clause like in 12 (a and b), and the NP *aashiq ne* is not an Ergative subject but a Dative one in a sentence of obligation modality.

There might have existed some pattern of ES with intransitive/imperfect finite verbs in Early and Middle Hindi dialects like the one presented or conserved in modern Nepali. This would mean that there might have been some semantically triggered ergativity "fluid ergativity") in Hindi dialects as there is in modern Gujarati and Kashmiri [Hook, Modi; Hook, Koul 1998].

Nepali demonstrates a very different pattern of evolution of ergativity. The split ergativity of the early and middle periods demonstrates a tendency to develop into full, non-split ergativity – through expansion of ERG into non-Perfect forms—in modern Nepali [the history of Ergative in Nepali is scrutinized in Aryal 1987]), while the Hindi languages perfected their split ergativity. This peculiarity brings Nepali close to Assamese.

7. The pattern of development of split accusativity is the same as that of the ergative. In early Hindi it is represented by direct case marking for unspecified/indefinite object vs. an inflected form of the noun for specified/definite object. Split accusativity existed in Hindi from the very beginning, at the earliest stage.

<u>Old Hindi</u>.
Unmarked Dir. O.

(12) (a) **ek purukh** *ham dekhaa*
A man ACC-unsp we seen.

'[I] saw *a <u>man</u>*.' [Tiivaarii 1985, Amir Khusro riddle 93, p. 85]

<u>Dakkhini</u>.

(b) *ab mard suu˜* **tuj** *milaauu˜*.
Now man with you ACC-sp introduce.

'Now I'll introduce *you* to a man.' (Gavasii, 17th AD, [Sharmaa 1954: 91]).

<u>Braj</u>.

(c) *tacchan huii dacchin disi, laccha*-**hi** *nahi˜ paavhii*
At that moment became south direction, goal ACCsp no find.

'Right at that moment the southern direction became [covered up (by the monkeys)]' (they] do not find [their] *goal*. [Chandola 1987: 34,

Kesavadasa, 16th century AD (text), 77 (translation)].

<u>Classical Awadhi</u>.
Marked DIR. O.

(d) *piya*-**hii** *rijhaai.*
Beloved ACCsp having pleased.

'Having pleased the beloved.' [Saksena 1972: 122]

In Tulsidas' Ramayana (*raamacaritamaanasa)*, the definite direct object (i.e. pronouns, proper names, and definite common nouns) is marked with *hi/hi˜* :

(e) *tin*-**hi˜** *dekhi*
him-ACCsp having-seen

'Having seen him.' [Tulsidas 1985: 480]

(f) *raam*-**hi˜** *viloki*
Ram-ACCsp having-seen

'Having seen Ram.' [ibid. 482]

(g) *var***hi˜** *viloki*
bride having-seen

'Having seen the bride.' [ibid. 502]

The marked direct object (ACCsp) is much less common in Tulsidas' Ramayana than in MSH. An unmarked direct object in that text is often translated into MSH by a marked direct object, e.g.:

(h) *sataanand tab saciv bulaaye*
Satanand then minister(s) invited(Mpl)

'Then Satanand invited the ministers' [ibid: 479]
[= Hindi tr."tab sataanand *ne* mantriyo˜ *ko* bulaayaa"]

In contrast to the Ergative subject – predicate group Modern Awadhi has developed the common postpositional type of Definite/Specific Accusative:

(i) *lekin tab tak* *raajkumaar* *lakaRiyan* **kaa** *uThaay cukaa rahai*
but by that time prince canes ACCsp lift finished.

'But by that time the prince has lifted *the canes.*' [Liperovsky 1997: 211]

Braj gives unusual examples of object – predicate agreement (this phenomena is described in the works of V. P. Liperovsky. Here I cite his example):

(j) *tai ne˜ tiin jaghai* **mai˜** *kaal pai te* **bacayau uu˜.**
You ERG thrice I death on from saved am.

'Thrice you have saved *me* from death.' [Liperovsky 1988: 199; 2003].

Pronominal Direct Object – predicate agreement in person could be explained historically. *Mai˜* originally is an Oblique form, so it may imply definiteness/specificity marked by Oblique case. But synchronically, in classical Braj *mai˜* functions as Nominative alongside the original Nominative *hau˜*. It is very difficult to suggest any reasonable explanation because of the scarcity of linguistic material of such a type. A similar occurrence of a non-marked 1st sg pronoun direct object is found in Ahirvati example (8b).

Inflectional markers of Accusative, Ergative and Dative in the Early and Middle stages are the same. Distinctiveness has been achieved in the same way as in the case of ergativity, e.g. through introduction of a cliticized marker *ko* (in different phonetic variants) as a marker of definiteness/specificity of the direct object.

Evolution of ergativity and accusativity in "greater" Hindi (strengthening of ergativity in Western Hindi and its remnant status in Eastern Hindi) may be explained by internal factors mainly. But not only are some neighboring IA languages also ergative but some neighboring Iranian languages – Pashto, Balochi, etc—are ergative as well. There is obviously "an ergative linguistic area" present here.

The main difference between the Indo-Aryan and the Iranian ergative constructions lies in the fact that the latter have a split on tense (ergative implying Past tense), rather than on aspect (with ergative implying Perfect aspect). The only exception is Pashto: the "Pashto ergative split is more intricate than has been noted, being determined by both tense and aspect." It is closer to Proto-Iranian than other Iranian languages [Taylor 2001].

"Secondary" ergativity in some NIA languages is explained by

Zakharyin [1978: 107-108] and Khokhlova [1987] as influence of Dardic and Tibeto-Burman languages. But their influence was most likely just a stimulus for conserving split ergativity and preventing transformation into a nominative type in some neighboring IA languages. The same could be said about the accusativity. Internal factors played the main role in that case also.

8. Two notions of subject – canonic (Nominative case and subject-predicate agreement) and non-canonic (multifactoral definition of subject) present two different syntactic models. Thus two interpretations of ES (and not only ES) are equally possible. 1) NS/ES shift involves role shift. Direct object of NC becomes cyclic subject of EC if it is non-marked, otherwise, if marked, a sentence has no subject at all. Such an approach on the basis of relational grammar is developed in Ultsiferov 1993 [op. cit.]. 2) Subject and direct object in both types of constructions remain the same. The NS/ES shift is a shift from unmarked to marked subject. The first approach implicates some uncertainties: a role of former subject and a role of marked, specific direct object is not clear. Assigning to them a role of indirect object seems unnatural.

The two types of subjects may be reduced to a formal subject system vs. a semantic-role subject system.

Hindi has developed an economic and elegant system of coding the two privileged positions of subject and direct object. Historical synonymy of postpositions *ne* and *ko,* still existing in Hariani/Bangaru and some other dialects, is removed. But there is an important difference between the two postpositions. *Ne* implies special forms of some pronouns: oblique case is equal to direct case of: 1st (*mai˜-ne*) and 2nd sg (*tu-ne*) personal pronouns and there is a special, ergative oblique case of demonstrative/personal pronouns 3rd pl (*inho˜-ne, unho˜-ne*). The *ko* postposition on the other hand is always regular in that it takes the regular oblique case of pronouns, but in contrast to *ne* it alternates with inflectional object case (*us-ko/use; ham-ko/hame˜*). These special syntactic properties of *ne* and *ko* set them apart from other postpositions as markers of privileged actants. But this is true only for Modern Standard Hindi (MSH). In old Hindi the compatibility of pronouns with pronouns is not so unified. The forms *tainen* (2 sg) and *unnen* (3 pl.) are common not only in old but in modern Braj. In Dakkhini we find the forms *uno˜kuu˜* OBL + DAT, *uno˜me˜* OBL + LOC, etc.

The NS/ES shift being obligatory is syntactic while definite/indefinite or specific/non-specific object shift is arbitrary and depends on speaker's intention and so is semantic. Argumentation in favor of the second point of view was advanced in Baganz 1983; Mahmood 1985; Zakharyin 1989: 50-51; Ilieva 1997.

I can add some more arguments. Subject/object-predicate agreement in ergative languages is a function of NOM and not an attribute of the predicative relation. In the NC we have a two-way relation between subject and predicate (government and agreement) and a one-way relation in the EC (government only: the predicate demands an ergative-marked subject and does not agree with it). In Dakkhini the subject-predicate relation is a two-way relation in both cases.

Elimination of subject in NC or EC converts these active constructions into passive ones:

(13) (a) *he bhagvaan,yah mere gale* *me˜* **kyaa baa˜dh diyaa hai**!
My God, it my throat in what stuck is!

'My God, what is *stuck* in my throat!' [Raajendra Yaadav 1985: 27].

(b) ... *lekin yaar ek cheez hum understand nahin kar paye*, **yeh itta barka barka speed breaker kahe ko bana diya hai** (he couldn't figure out what is a flyover).
But lad, one thing understand no do could, such a big big speed breaker for what sake built given.

'... but lad I can't get one thing, for what purpose such a big speed breaker is built.' [Bihari Babu – Regional Jokes 1997-2000]

The four Hindi idioms – Khari Boli, Dakkhini, Braj, and Awadhi analyzed here demonstrate some principal differences. (1) Khari Boli, Dakkhini and Braj have developed a new type of ES marked by the postposition *ne*, while Awadhi has conserved the old type of split NS/ES where attrition of case endings seems like transition into a nominative type. It may be explained by the fact that there was no analog to the *ne* postposition in Eastern dialects, or by the fact that Hindi and Braj (with Dakkhini or Southern Hindi under impact of the Northern Hindi) were included in a broader ergative area. (2) Braj and Awadhi in early and middle stages preserve old case endings *–hi*, etc, while Khari Boli (Old Hindi) and Dakkhini seems to have lost these endings in the Apabhramsa period. (3) Hindi (Khari Boli, Dakkhini, Braj and Awadhi) has developed a new type of Accusative, marked by postposition *ko* and its variants.

The evolution of Hindi, particularly of subject – object – predicate structure, demonstrates a cyclic pattern. Morphosyntactic tools being worn out are restored on a new basis. Constants – the domain of semantics, signified, in this case, by split nominativity, split ergativity, and split accusativity—remain as they are, while variables – their material signifiers—are restored in new forms.

Ergativity in Hindi seems to be just a formal, empty morphosyntactic category with no implications for semantics, except for the fact that perfectivity implies ergativity and vice versa. The exception is the intransitive or semi-intransitive verbs of "bodily emissions" [Hoop, Narasimhan, 2003]. Ergative properties of that set of verbs can be explained by a general prototypical implicature of ES: the Actor is considered a possessor of his action, with its results being "moved" in relation to him.

Contrary to ES split accusativeness is a semantic category related to definiteness/indefiniteness or specificity/unspecificity. Split ergativity is an automatic, formal category. But involvement of ES into communicative strategy of a sentence (specific ergative subject opposed to nonspecific as well as specific nominative subject) may be seen in non-trivial usage of ES beyond the Perfective domain.

This last detail is more specific for Urdu (and Hindi of Delhi) than for Hindi generally. I am referring to an alternation of *ne/ko* subject marking in modal infinitival clauses. D. Wunderlich [2000: 8] (following argumentation of M. Butt) considers here willingness and obligation respectively:

(14) (a) *anjum-ne* *xat* *likhnaa* *hai*
Anjum ERG/DAT letter NOM write is.

'Anjum wants to write a letter.'

(b) *anjum-ko* *xat* *likhnaa* *hai*
Anjum DAT letter NOM write is.

'Anjum should write a letter.'

First of all, the *ne* postposition as a subject marker in infinitival modal constructions is obviously an impact of Punjabi (where *ne* is a subject marker of modal constructions with obligation modality [Zograf 1990: 47]. In another version: the subject marker in infinitival modal constructions is not the ERG postposition *ne*; it is the DAT/ACC postposition *nuu˜* [Tolstaya 1960: 45]. So here a contamination of two types of dative construction is present. The same subject marking in the same syntactic constructions is a parametric characteristic in vernaculars surrounding Delhi (where *ne* is a polysemic postposition). Convergence of the two (Hindi-Punjabi) codes resulted in two parallel dative syntactic constructions with modal meaning of obligation (a case of syntactic synonymy). Subsequently differentiation (obligation vs. willingness) developed in their semantics.

There are different types of ERG in Greater Hindi that may be combined in some dialects according their parameter feature:

I. **dative-possessive vs. instrumental**. (The latter type occurs only in Pahari dialects and in their neighbor Nepali.)

II. **syntactic or morphosyntactic vs. morphologic**. (The latter type is limited to Bihari dialects.)

III. **innovated vs. archaic**. (This is an opposition of Western and Eastern dialects.)

IV. **transparency vs. opacity of subject-predicate agreement under ergative subject marking**. (Dakkhini – in the period its autonomous development – and Nepali constitute the former type, while the latter type includes the rest.)

V. **split ergativity vs. unsplit ergativity**. (The latter group is represented by Nepali. Its ergativity history shows expansion of ES towards all the verbal forms. The first group includes the remaining languages, although with sporadic exceptions and violations of split ergativity. But these exceptions may just seem sporadic due to inadequate investigation.)

10. Nominative and Ergative subjects are not the only subjects in Hindi languages. In addition there are Dative, Ablative, Locative and Possessive subjects.

(15) (a) Dative subject (Dakkhini):

... un **kuu˜** *khabar pahu˜cii ke* *yah buzurg* **ko**
You *to* (DAT) news came that this old man *to* (DAT)

kuch khazaanaa milyaa hai.
some treasure obtained is.

'He gained news that this old man has obtained some treasure.' [Sharmaa 1954, 449 (Gausii Daknii, dates unknown)].

(b) Ablative (Source) subject in mediopassive and passive clauses (Dakkhini):

... us **te˜** *nahii˜ rahaa gayaa,* *kuch* kahaa gayaa .
him *from* not was borne, something was said.

'He couldn't bear it, [and] said something.' [Sharmaa 1954, 405

(Vajahii, Sabras, 1636)]

(c) Locative subject (Braj):

Yaahi dekhi yaa shankaa mere man me˜ aavai hai
This seeing this doubt my mind *in* comes.

'On seeing this, this doubt comes into my mind.' [Gupta 1958: 159 (aanand raghunandan naaTak, 1651-1740)]

(d) Possessive subject (Dakkhini).

khudaa **kaa** *hone*	*mangtaa*	*hai...*
Lord's	being	demands...

'It requires the Lord's existence...' [Sharmaa 1954, 412 (Vajahii, Sabras, 1636)].

The question is this: are all these subject types are basic subjects or are there basic and derived subjects? A basic subject is the subject of a basic or prototypical clause, while a derived subject is a subject of a clause derived from the basic one. The last example 14 (d) is by no means a basic syntactic construction. Basic possessive constructions are simple clauses (with *ke paas, kaa, ke* possessive subjects).

Nominative and Ergative constructions might be considered basic (Nominative as more simple/primitive/prototypical) and derivative (Ergative as more complicated) respectively. But this solution implies that perfect aspect is derived from imperfect aspect, which is not natural or reasonable.

Mediopassive and passive (ablative = with *se*-marked subject) sentences are transformed from nominative/ergative sentences by some rules and so are not basic, but derivative. They are more complicated both syntactically and morphologically.

Dative subject is derivative in 13(a) and (b) but basic in 14 (a). In other words the situation is the same as with possessive sentences.

This is also the case with Locative sentences. They are basic only in some types of constructions depending on lexical entries. A basic locative subject is [+animate]; otherwise it would be just a local modifier.

Thus there are constraints on Dative, Ablative, Locative and Possessive subjects as basic. Nominative (naturally in the position of subject) and Ergative subjects are basic subjects without any constraints. In addition, Nominative/Ergative subject (and definite/indefinite direct objects) are indicated by two alternative case forms. These two subject variables – Nominative and Ergative – might be considered as Agent case with two variants. In the same way the two forms of direct object might be taken as two variants of Accusative case.

Agent case is a purely structural case, while other cases exhibit different degrees of semantic properties. The semantic character is minimized with dative and possessive markers and maximized with ablative and local case markers.

Agent case: (1) NOM [+imperfect/non-perfect, -perfect]; (2) ERG [+perfect, -imperfect]; Accusative case: (1) NOM in the function of unspecified ACC; (2) DAT in the function of specified ACC. None of the other cases (syntactic or morphosyntactic, that is; morphological cases are Direct and Oblique + Vocative) combine two alternative forms. All of them are represented by one postposition.

Agent and Accusative cases may be identified as Mega or Hyper cases that are a combination of two simple cases. I define *Megacase* as a case that combines at least two simple cases, in a relation of complementary distribution. Agent (NOM/ERG) is a structural case, ACC (bare ACC and *ko*-marked) is a structural-semantic case (zero/*ko*-marking is determined semantically if it denotes indefiniteness /definiteness etc but sometimes it is determined by syntactic structure – e.g., the presence of a *ko*-marked dative argument which necessitates elimination of *ko*-marking of the direct object. All other cases or case relations are semantic.

Ergativity in NIA languages in general has a set of parameters, different for different languages. They are: (1) ergative / non-ergative (some eastern NIA languages); (2) split ergativity / non-split ergativity (Assami, Kurmali); (3) aspect / tense determined ergativity (some Eastern NIA languages, Kurmali, for instance, [Davison 2002], as well as ergative Iranian languages); (4) subject / object agreement (this parameter is realized in a variety of ways); (5) structural / semantic ergativity (Nepali – in the imperfect domain); (6) dative / instrumental (Nepali); (7) inflectional / morphosyntactic.

Modern standard Hindi is a language that is a first member of oppositions 1, 2, 3, 5, 6 and 7, and the both first and second member of opposition 4: ergative > split (split ergative and split accusative) > aspect-determined or more exactly, transitivity and aspect determined > subject-marked (morphosyntactic type) > object agreement / neutral agreement when object is blocked by postposition *ko,* > structural > historically dative. Opposition 4 is manifested by subject-blocked and split object agreement variant. Historically as well as from the point of view of areal distribution in dialects Hindi shows semantic ergativity, in intransitive/imperfect domain, and subject agreement (with ergative marked subject). The first member of the opposition 7 is represented in

Old Hindi while the second one is a parameter of Modern Hindi.

Exceptions to this model – some transitive and intransitive verbs, deviations in behavior of some *Aktionsart* forms (e.g. iterative aspect "perf. part. + *karnaa*" is non-ergative in spite of the transitivity of the modifier or light verb) – need a special examination. They should be examined together with exceptional usage of ergative in imperfect and future tensed utterances in dialects. ES in these environments may be induced by semantic factors or for historical reasons.

In conclusion I will suggest a definition of split ergative strategy (ES) in Hindi. This definition takes into consideration historical perspective and regional peculiarities of Greater Hindi:

(1) ES is a tripartite syntactic structure "subject – direct object – finite transitive verb predicate".

(2) VP includes the perfect participle of a transitive verb.

(3) The verb agrees with the direct object, or does not agree with any argument if the direct object is marked by a postposition.

(4) Subject – verb agreement is an exception represented only in Dakkhini.

(5) Subject marking is not relevant: it may be inflectional, postpositional or zero marking (bare nominative).

(6) ES is a structural variant in the Perfect domain of NS in the Non-Perfect domain.

S O _ V [+ transitive, + perfect]
AGR

Dakkhini case:

S O V [+ transitive, + perfect]
↘↙
AGR

Summary

At the end of the MIA stage as result of breaking down of the case system, EC in the Hindi languages assumed the form "Subject in Oblique or Object case + Perfective transitive verb". Such an EC is common not only in some Northern NIA languages but also in some Iranian languages. But Oblique case is not always distinct from NOM, so ES came to be mixed up with NS. Two ways were open to Hindi languages: (1) transition into a nominative type of language, (2) restoration of ES/NS distinctiveness. Eastern Hindi has chosen the first way, retaining the older NS/ES system, while Western Hindi preferred the second. Inflectional ergative marking has been changed into postpositional marking. ES became the norm in standard Hindi as well as in Western Hindi dialects. The new type of ES is a differentiating peculiarity not only of Western Hindi, but also of Western and Southern NIA languages.

The same pattern of evolution is traced in direct object marking. Inflectional marking of definite/specific direct object has given way to postpositional (syntactic) marking. A cyclic evolution pattern is traced in the historical development of Hindi. A category of Megacase or Hypercase has developed. There are two megacases/hypercases in Hindi: AGENT (NOM and ERG as two aspectually distributed cases of agent -subject), and ACC (NOM as a indefinite or unspecified direct object and DAT in the function of ACC marking of definite or specified direct object). Both of them mark the privileged arguments: No 1 – agent-subject and No 2 – direct object.

This paper suggests a typology of ergativity in NIA languages as well as in Hindi. A process of optimization of EC in "Greater" Hindi during the course of evolution is considered. A notion of "megacase" is introduced. A new definition of ergativity in Hindi is given.

Abbreviations

ACC accusative
AGR agreement
DAT dative
DIR direct case
DIR. O. direct object
EC ergative construction
ERG ergative case
ES ergative strategy
GEN genitive
IA Indo-Aryan
LOC locative
MIA Middle Indo-Aryan
MSH Modern Standard Hindi
NC nominative construction
NIA New Indo-Aryan
NOM nominative case
NP nominal phrase
NS nominative strategy
OBJ object case
OBL oblique case
OIA Old Indo-Aryan
PS passive strategy
sp specified
non-sp nonspecified

References

Primary Sources

Bihari Babu – Regional Jokes 1997-2000. Online: http://www.jaanproductions.com/humor//regional/bihari.htm

Chandola, Anoop. 1987 (1982). *Mystic and love poetry of medieval Hindi.* With introduction, texts, grammar, notes and glossary. New Delhi: Today & Tomorrow's Printers & Publishers.

Goka, Ajay.2000. *A typical Hyderabadi conversation.* – http://www.reachouthyderabad.com/newsmaker/bs5.htm

Gupt, Mahesh Chandra. 1993. *hindii sadiyo˜ se raajkaaj me˜*. Dilli: Satsahitya Prakashan.
Gupta, Somnath. 1958. *puurva bharatendu naaTak saahitya.* Jalandhar – Ilahabaad: Hindi Bhavan.
Malaya, Yashwant. 1997. *Malaiya on the Death of Akbar*. (malayia@cs.colostate.edu) http://www.groups.google.com/groups? oi=djq&selm=an_261524164
Narharinath, Yogi. 1964. *itihaasprakaashmaa. sandhipatrasangrah. bhaag 2*. Varanasi: Rayal Nepal Ekedemi etc.
Pant, ·Suresh. *Kumaaii (kumaauunii) ke kriyaapad: ek bhaaSaavaijNanik adhyayan.* Dillii: Suurya Bhaaratii Prakaashan, 1993.
Sharma, Shri Ram. 1954. *dakhinii kaa padya aur gadya*. Hyderabad: Hindi Pracar Sabha.
*Sinh, Shivprasad. 1958. *suurpuurva brajbhaaSaa aur uskaa saahitya.* Varanasi.
Tiwari, Bholanath. 1985. *amiir khusro aur unkaa hindii saahitya*. Delhi: Prabhat Prakashan.
Tulsidas. 1985. *gosvaamii tulsii kRt raamacaritamaanasa, shrii vinaayavii Tiikaa sahit:.khaND I.* Bhopal, Madhya Pradesh: Hindi Sahitya Sammelan.
Yadav, Rajendra. 1985 (1951). *saaraa aakaash*. New Delhi: Akshar Prakashan.

Secondary Sources

Andersen, P. L. 1986. Die ta-Partizipialkonstruktion bei Asoka: Passiv oder Ergativ? *Zeitschrift für Vergleichende Sprachwissenschaft.* 99: 75-94.
Amritavalli, R.; Sarma, P. P. 2002. A case distinction between unaccusative and unergative subjects in Assamese. *Snippets.* 5. Online: http://www.ledonline/snippets/
Aryal, B. 1987. Iz istoriyi razvitiya ergativnoy konstruktsiyi predlozheniya v nepal'skom iazyke. (On the history of the development of the ergative construction of the sentence in the Nepali language.) *Aktual'niye problemy yazykov Yuzhnoy Aziyi*: 34-39.
Baganz, Lutz. 1983. Some reflections on a new approach to the notion of subject (in connection with a certain type of ergative and passive constructions in Hindi). *Zeitschrift für Phonetic, Sprachwissenschaft und Kommukationsforschungen.* 36, 1: 15-21.
Bubenik, Vit. 1996. *The structure and development of Middle Indo-Aryan dialects.* Delhi: Motilal Banarsidass.
Butt, Miriam; Deo, Ashwini. 2001. Ergativity in Indo-Aryan. *Kurdica. Magazine for Kurdish language and studies,* 5(3), 47 (Ergativity in Kurdish and Indo-Iranian). Online: http://www.cogsci.ed.ac.uk/~siamakrKurdish/KURDICA/2001/3/ia-erg.html
Butt, Miriam and King, Tracy H. 1999, 2001. The status of case. *Clause structure in South Asian languages.* Eds. V. Dayal, A. Mahajan. Online: http://ling.uni-konstanz.de/pages/home/butt
Davison, Alice. 2001. Ergative case licensing in a split ergative language. Eds. Anvita Abbi; R. S. Gupta; Ayesha Kidwai. *Linguistic structure and language dynamics in South Asia. Papers from the proceedings of SALA XVIII Roundtable.* Delhi, 2001: Motilal Banarsidass, 291-307.
Davison, Alice. 2002. Agreement features and projections of TENSE and ASPECT. *The yearbook of South Asian languages and linguistics 2002.* New Delhi, Thousand Oaks, London: Sage, 27-57.
de Hoop, Helen, Narasimhan Bhuvana. Optimization of case in Hindi. – LSA Meeting, January 2003. http://www.mpi.nl/world/persons/profession/bhuvana.html

Deo, Ashvini; Sharma, Devyani. 2002. An optimality theoretic typology of ergative morphology in Indo-Aryan (Abstract). Stanford University. Online: http://www-linguistics.stanford.edu/sssg/20021203.html

Edelman 2001: K rekonstruktsiyi prairanskogo predlozheniya. (Toward the reconstruction of the Proto-Iranian sentence). *Iazyk i kultura. Fakty I tsennosti. K 70-letiyu IU. S. Stepanova*: 137-145. Moskva: Yazyki Slavianskoy Kultury.

Elizarenkova, T. Ia. 1967. Ergativnaya konstruktsiya v novoindiyskikh yazykakh. (The ergative construction in New Indo-Aryan languages.) *Ergativnaya konstruktsiya v yazykakh razlichnykh tipov*: 116-125. Leningrad: Nauka.

Hoernle, Rudolf. 1880. *A comparative grammar of the Gaudian languages.*

Ilieva, Gabriela Nic. 1997. On the origin of the ergative in Indo-Aryan. *South Asia Graduate Research Journal (SAGAR).* University of Texas. Austin. 4, 2. Online: http://asnic.utexas.edu/asnic/pages/sagar/sagar4.2.html

Hook, Peter E.; Modi, B. 1997. Fluid ergativity in Gujarati. http.//www-personal.umich.edu/~pehook/gujflerg.htnl

Hook, Peter E., and Omkar N. Koul. 1998. Fluid ergativity in Gujarati and Kashmiri and the notion of suspension. *South Asia syntax semantic newsletter (SASSN),* 6. http://www.ling.upenn.edu/sassn/6/node33.html

Hutt, Michael; and Subedi Abbi. 1999/2003. *Teach yourself Nepali.* London: Hodder Headline.

Ivanov, V. V., and V. N. Toporov. 1960. *Sanskrit.* Moscow: Yazyki Zarubiezhnoy Aziyi i Afriki.

Kellogg, S. H. 1875 (1955). *A grammar of the Hindi Language.* London: Routledge and Kegan Paul.

Khokhlova, L. V. 1987. Sintaksicheskaya interferentsiya v dialektakh rajasthani. (Syntactic interference in Rajasthani dialects). *Vestnik MGU. Seriya 13. Vostokovedeniie.*: 65-72.

Khokhlova, L. V. 2001. Ergativity attrition in the history of Western New Indo-Aryan languages (Panjabi, Gujarati and Rajasthani. *The yearbook of South Asian languages and linguistics 2001. Tokyo symposium on South Asian languages. Contact, convergence, and typology.* Ed. Peri Bhaskararao, Karumurti Venkata Subbarao, Chief Ed. Rajendra Singh. New Delhi, Thousand Oaks (CA), London:Sage. 159-184.

Khusro', Pradip Sharma. 2002. "Piitaa huu˜ dhoke Khusarve shiirii˜ sukhan ke paa˜v!" *AAjkal*, farvarii, 11-15.

Liperovskiy, V. P. 1988. *Ocherk grammatiki sovremennogo bradja.* (A grammatical sketch of modern Braj.) Moskva: Nauka.

Liperovskiy, V. P. 1997. *Ocherk grammatiki sovremennogo avadhi.* (A grammatical sketch of modern Awadhi). Moskva: Vostochnaia Literatura.

Liperovskiy, V. P. 2003. Handout. ICON SALILA (ICOSAL 5). Moscow.

Mahmood, Anwer. 1985. *Die Satzbaupläne des Deutscher und des Urdu. Eine Konrastive grammatische Untersuchung im Ramen der Valenztheorie.* Hochschulsammlung Philosophie, Sprachwissenschaft, 5. Freiburg (Breisgau): Hochschulverlag.

Maslov, Yu. S. 1984 (1949). K voprosu proiskhozhdeniia posessivnogo perfekta (On the origin of the possessive perfect). In Maslov, *Ocherki po aspektologii.* Leningrad: Izdatel'stvo LGU. 224-248.

Patnaik, B. N. 1995. On an unnoticed case of verbal agreement in Oriya. *IL*, 56, 1-4.

Peterson, J. 1996. Grammatical relations in Pali and the emergence of ergativity in Indo-Aryan [Dissertation Abstract]. Kiel University, 1996. In: Eds. Veneeta Dayal, Rajesh Bhatt. *South Asia syntax semantics newsletter (SASSN).* 1996, 5, 1-2. Rutgers. http://www.ling.upenn.edu/sassn/5

Peterson, John. 2002. [Regional Reports] Europe. *The yearbook of South Asian languages and linguistics 2002*. Delhi: Sage. 201-217.

Pireiko, L. A. 1963. O narusheniiakh ergativnoi konstrukstii v kurdskom iazyke. *Iranskii sbonik.* Moscow: Izdatel'stvo Vostochnoi Literatury. 150-158.

Pireiko, L. A. 1979. On the genesis of the ergative construction in Indo-Iranian. In F. Plank, ed. 483-488.

Plank, F. Ed. 1979. *Ergativity: towards a theory of grammatical relations* L:ondon: Academic Press.

Prokofieva, I. T. 1987. Ob ergativnosti v vostochnykh novykh indoariiskikh iazykakh. (On ergativity in Eastern New Indo-Aryan languages). *Aktual'nye problemy izucheniia iazykov IUzhnoi Azii.* 143-148.

Saksena, Baburam. 1937/1972. *Evolution of Awadhi (A branch of Hindi),* Delhi, Patna, Varanasi : Motilal Banarsidass, 1972 (reprint of 1937).

Saksena, Baburam. 1952. *dakhinii hindii.* Ilahabad: Hindustani Ekedemi. Tiwari, Bholanath. 1966. *hindii bhaaSaa.* Ilahabad.

Shamatov, A. N. 1974. Klassicheskii dakhini (iuzhnyi khindustani XVII v.). (Classical Dakhini (Southern Hindustani of the 17th century AD). Moskva: Nauka.

Shamatov, A. N. 1978. O lingvisticheskoi podlinnosti proizvedenii Amira Khusro Dehlevi. (On the linguistic authenticity of the works of Amir Khusro Dehlavi). *Indian Linguistics.* Moscow: Nauka. 216-224.

Sharma, Devyani. 1999. Nominal clitics and constructive morphology in Hindi. *Proceedings of the LFG99 conference*. The University of Manchester. Butt M., King T. H. (Eds.), 1999, CSLI Publications. http://www.stanford.edu/-dsharma/hin/1.html

Sigorskiy, Alexander A. 2000. Kategorii ergativnosti i vida v iazyke khindi, v svete dannykh dialektologii I diakhronii. (Categories of ergativity and aspect in Hindi, in the light of dialectology and diacrhony). *Filologicheskie nauki* 2 [17]. Moskva: MGIMO(U) (Moscow State Insitute of International Relations).

Subbarao, K. V. 1998. Linguistic theory and syntactic typology: a proposal for symbiotic relationship. *Vaagbhaaratii.* Proceedings of the international conference on *South Asian languages [ICOSAL] (July 1-4, 1997), M., 1998: 5-23.

Tessitori, L. P. 1958 (1914-1916). *puraanii raajasthaanii,* transl. Namvar Sinh. Kashi: Nagari Pracarini Sabha. (Notes on the Grammar of the Old Western Rajasthani with special reference to Apabhramsa and Gujarati and Marwari. *Indian Antiquary*, 1914,1915,1916).

Taylor, Roberts. 2001. Split-agreement and ergativity in Pashto. *KURDICA: magazine for Kurdish language and studies*. 5(2), 47 (Ergativity in Kurdish and Indo-Iranian).

Tiwari, Bholanath. 1966. *hindii bhaaSaa*. Ilahabad : Kitab Mahal.

Tolstaya, N. I. 1960: *Yazyk pandzhabi*. (The Panjabi langauge). Moskva: Izdatel'stvo Vostochnoi Literatury.

Ultsiferov, O. G. 1993. *Grammaticheskiy slovar'-spravochnik sovremennogo literaturnogo yazyka khindi.* (Grammatical reference glossary of Modern Standard Hindi). Moscow: Moscow State Institute of International Relations.

Ultsiferov, O. G. 1995. Padezh i padezhnye otnoshenia v sovremennom literaturnom yazyke khindi. (Case and case relations in Modern Standard Hindi). *Lingvisticheskiye i metodicheskiye osnovy prepodavaniya inostrannykh yazykov.* Moskva: MGIMO. 137-144.

Vertogradova, V. V. 2002 (reprint of 1978 edition). *Prakrity.* (The Prakrits). Moskva: Nauka. Reprint: Vostochnaia Literatura.

Volkhonskiy, B. M. 1987. O printsipakh klassifikatsiyi glaglolnoy leksiki v indoariyskikh yazykakh. (Concerning the principles of classification of the verbal lexicon in

Indo-Aryan languages). *Aktual'nye problemy izyucheniya yazykov Yuzhnoy Aziyi*: 53-57.

Wunderlich, Dieter. 2000. *Optimal case in Hindi* (preliminary version). http://www.web.phil-fak.uni-diesseldorf.de/~wdl/HindiCase.pdf

Yadav, Ramawatar. 1996/1997. *A reference grammar of Maithili*. 1st ed.: Berlin: Mouton du Gruyter; 2nd ed.: New Delhii Munshiram Manoharlal.

Yadav, Shankar Lal. (n.d.) ahiirvaaTii. (Ahirwati) *hariyaaNaa kii upabhaaSaae~*. (Dialects of Hariyaną). Chandigarh. 193-269.

Zakharyin, B. A. 1977. Genezis ergativnosti v indoariyskikh i dardskikh yazykakh. (The genesis of ergativity in Indo-Aryan and Dardic languages). *Vestnik MGU, Seriya 13.4*: 61-72.

Zakharyin, B. A. 1978. *Vvedenie v istoriyu yazyka khindi*. (Introduction to the history of the Hindi language). Moskva: Izdatel'stvo MGU.

Zakharyin, B. A. 1987. *Tipologiya yazykov Yuzhnoi Aziyi*. (Typology of the languages of South Asia). Moskva: Izdatel'stvo MGU.

Zakharyin, B. A. 1989. *Teoreticheskiya grammatika khindi I urdu*. (A theoretical grammar of Hindi/Urdu). Moskva: Izdatel'stvo MGU.

Zograf, G. A. 1990. *Yazyki Yuzhnoi Aziyi*. (South Asian languages). Moskva: Nauka.

PART II

CROSS-LINGUISTIC AREAL OR TYPOLOGICAL PERSPECTIVES

[Note: Several papers in Parts I and III also involve cross-linguistic perspectives, as noted]

SOUTH ASIA AND TURKIC: THE CENTRAL ASIAN CONNECTION?*

HANS HENRICH HOCK

Introduction

Except for retroflexion, the standard features characterizing the South Asian convergence area recur in Turkish and other Turkic languages: participles (and similar forms, including the Dravidian relative participles), infinitives, verbal nouns or nominalizations, converbs,[1] and quotatives. To these may be added the feature of relative-correlative structures, without embedding of the relative clause into a main clause; see Hock 2001 for discussion and references. Agreement is also found in a few other morphosyntactic features, such as whole-word (re)duplication, which I will henceforth refer to by the Sanskrit term āmreḍita, and echo-reduplication; for these two features see Abbi 1992 as well as the discussion in Hock 1993.

One possible explanation for these similarities has been suggested in Hock 2001, namely that the similarities reflect parallel reactions to a shared typological finite-verb constraint, for which see also Hock 1988, 1989, 1992a, as well as earlier work by Steever (1988). But this explanation would not hold for āmreḍita and echo-reduplication.

A second possibility is the one explored in this paper, namely that the similarities reflect convergence in the Central Asian oases of the early Christian era, with Indo-Aryan Gandhari or Niya Prakrit, East

*This is a revised and shortened version of the paper presented at ICOSAL, 2003. A different version was read at the 2003 South Asia Meeting in Madison, Wisconsin. I am grateful for comments on my paper at both occasions. The responsibility for any errors and omissions, of course, rests with me.

[1] I now prefer the term converb instead of the term absolutive that I have used in earlier publications. None of the many different terms that have been used to designate this class of verbal adverbs in most of the publications on South Asian languages is felicitous. "Absolutive" could be confused with participial constructions such as "Locative Absolutes"; "Conjunctive Participle" similarly fails to distinguish the category from that of the participles; "Gerund" sounds too much like "Gerundive", a very different category. In adopting the term "Converb" I follow Haspelmath and König 1995, as well as the long tradition in Altaic linguistics from which they have accepted the term.

Iranian Sogdian and Saka, Classical Tibetan, Tocharian, and Old Turkic languages and their speakers in intense multilingual contact.

I present evidence that might support this hypothesis, as well as possible counter arguments. The outcome is not a definite conclusion, but a possibility that should be considered as an alternative in future investigations of South Asian convergence.

Relevant structures in Dravidian and Indo-Aryan

An illustration of relevant structures is given in examples [1] through [8], with examples from Tamil and Sanskrit.[2] Where possible, the examples come from the oldest attested stages of the languages, Old Tamil and Vedic Sanskrit. This is important, since in some cases, later changes have obscured the original picture. Thus, Modern Tamil and other southern Dravidian languages require a clitic *-ō* to follow the relative clause in examples of the type [1]; and much of Modern Indo-Aryan has lost quotative marking (type [6]).

---

[2] In these and the subsequent examples, the following abbreviations are used. In most cases, however, forms illustrating a particular category are simply identified by bolding. At the request of the editor, I am giving fuller glosses for the Sanskrit examples.

A	=	accusative
Abl.	=	ablative
CC	=	correlative clause
CP	=	correlative pronoun
D	=	dative
DD	=	cited discourse
Erg	=	Ergative
G	=	genitive
N	=	nominative
I	=	instrumental
impve.	=	imperative
nlzr	=	nominalizer
ptcle	=	particle
pl.	=	plural
poss	=	possessive marker
Q	=	quotative marker
RC	=	relative clause
RM	=	relative marker (uninflected)
RP	=	relative pronoun
sg.	=	singular
VN	=	verbal noun

[1] NON-EMBEDDED RELATIVE-CORRELATIVE STRUCTURES[3]

a. Old Tamil

[minnitai naṭunkuṅ kaṭaippeyal vāṭai	ekkāl varuvat(u)	enri]$_{RC}$
	RP	Verb

[akkāl varuvar en-k kātalōr-ē]$_{CC}$
CP

'My lover will come at the time that you say the cold wind will come.'

b. (Vedic) Sanskrit

[tváṁ	táṁ	deva	jihváyā	bādhasva	duṣkṛ́tam]$_{CC}$
you.sg.N	CP	O God	tongue.sg.I	tie.sg.2impve.	evil-doer.sg.A

[márto	yó	no	jíghāṁsati]$_{RC}$ (RV 6.16.32)
mortal.sg.N	RP	us-clitic	slay.sg.3present.desiderative

'You, O God, tie down with your tongue that evil-doer who, a mortal, tries to slay us.'

---

[3] Throughout this paper I draw on the following general data sources. Individual sources will be referred to only when they provide specific interpretations or arguments.

Burushaski: Berger 1998, vols. 1 and 2
Classical Tibetan: Jäschke 1883, Beyer 1992
Chang: Hutton 1929/1987
Newari: Grierson 1909
Gandhari Prakrit: Brough 1962
Hindi: Abbi 1992
Sanskrit: Hock 1975, 1982, 1984, 1988, 1989, 1992b, 1993, 1996, 2001 (w. references)
Tocharian: Krause & Thomas 1960, Thomas 1964
Modern Persian: Lazard 1992
Khotanese: Leumann 1936, Emmerick 1989
Ossetic: Abaev 1964
Pamir languages: Payne 1989
Tamil: Beythan 1943, Steever 1988, 1998
Old Tamil: Lakshmi Bai 1985, Lehmann 1998, Ramasamy 1981
Turkic languages in general: Deny et al 1959 (with various contributions, indicated where appropriate)
Turkish: Lewis 1967/1988, Kornfilt 1987
Chwarezmian Turkic: Eckmann 1959a
Old Turkic: von Gabain 1959
Classical Armenian: Jensen 1959

[2] PARTICIPIAL STRUCTURES

a. Tamil

nā<u>n</u> **pōkira** vīṭṭukku nī varavēṇṭām

'You must not come to the house (to which) I (am) going.'

b. (Vedic) Sanskrit

yuñjánti	bradhnám	aruṣáṁ	**cárantam**	pári
yoke.pl.3	stallion.sg.A	ruddy.sg.A	moving.sg.A	around

tastúṣaḥ
standing.pl.A

'They yoke the ruddy stallion that moves around those who stand/stay in place.'

Lit.: 'They yoke the ruddy stallion, moving around the standing ones.'

[3] INFINITIVES[4]

a. Tamil

mīṇ **piṭikka** ārampi<u>n</u>ārkaḷ

'They began to catch fish.'

b. (Vedic) Sanskrit

hávāmahe	tvā	**úpagantavā́**	u (RV 10.160.5)
invoke.pl.1	you.sg. A	come.inf.	ptcle

'We invoke you to come/so that you will come.'

---

[4] Infinitives, verbal nouns, and nominalizations are included in this survey of features for several reasons. There is a common assumption that what characterizes the Dravidian (and other "strict" OV) languages is not just the use of converbs and quotatives, but a general constraint against more than one finite verb per sentence; see e.g. the survey of literature in Steever 1988. This constraint, then, is considered to motivate a general use of non-finite verb constructions for embedded propositions, including converbs, infinitives, verbal nouns, and nominalizations. The constraint is formulated and justified more explicitly in Steever 1988, with subsequent modifications by Hock (1988, 1989, 1992a). Note in addition the discussion further below, regarding the close historical relationship between verbal nouns, infinitives, nominalizations, and converbs.

[4] VERBAL NOUNS AND NOMINALIZATIONS

a. Old Tamil

kuvalai …	**malar-tal**	aritu
	VN, sg. N	

'It is rare for the kuvalai flower to blossom.'

b. (Vedic) Sanskrit

purā́	**sambādhā́d**	abhy	ā́vavṛtsva	no … (RV 2.16.8)
before	oppression	to	turn-to.sg.2.impve	us.clitic
	VN.sg. Abl.			

'Before we get oppressed (lit. before (our) oppression) turn to us.'

[5] CONVERBS

a. Tamil

nāṉ atai-c **ceytu muṭittu**-p pōṉēṉ

'Having done that, having finished, I went away.'

= 'I did that, finished, and went away.'
Or: 'After I had done that and finished I went away.'

b. (Vedic) Sanskrit

punardā́ya	brahmajāyā́ṁ	**kṛtvī́**	devaír	nikilbiṣám |
give-back.conv.	b's-wife.sg.A	do.conv.	God.pl.I	expiation.sg.A

ū́rjam	pṛthivyā́	**bhaktvā́ya**	urugāyám	úpāsate (RV 10.109.7)
vigor.sg.A	earth.sg.G	partake.conv.	far-goer.sg.A	respect.pl.3

'After they have returned the brahmin's wife, accomplished expiation through the Gods, and partaken of the earth's vigor, they pay their respects to the far-striding one.'

Lit.: 'Having returned the brahmin's wife, having accomplished expiation through the Gods, having partaken of the earth's vigor, they pay their respects to the far-striding one.' (RV 10.109.7)

[6] QUOTATIVES

a. Tamil

nāṉ	[avaṉ iṉkē vantāṉ]	**eṉṟu**	niṉaikkiṟēṉ
		Q	

'I think [(that) [he has come here].'

c. (Vedic) Sanskrit

nákir	vaktā́	[ná	dād]	**íti** (RV 8.33.15)
no-one.sg.N	say.sg.N	not	give.sg.3.subjunctive	Q

'No one is about to say [He shall not give].'

[7] AMREDITA

a. Tamil

oṉṟu-v-**oṉṟu**

'one by one'

b. (Vedic) Sanskrit

páñca pañca (RV 3.55.18)

'five by five, five each'

[8] ECHO-REDUPLICATION

a. Tamil

pustakam-**ki**stakam

'books and the like'

b. Hindi

caai-vaai

'tea and the like'

Relevant structures in Turkish and Old Turkic

Let me now turn to a demonstration that these features have counterparts in Modern Turkish and also in Old Turkic; see examples [1c] - [8c] below. The fact that most of the features are found even in Old Turkic is important, for it establishes the presence of these features for a much earlier time (at least around the 8th century AD) and in a location much closer to South Asia, namely in Central Asia.

A special comment is required regarding category [4]. As suggested by the glosses, Modern Turkish seems to differ from Old Turkic in the morphosyntax of nominalization. Old Turkic appears to have been of the type represented by Tibetan (see further below), as well as Korean (see e.g. Yoon 2002), where the internal structure of nominalized propositions takes "ordinary" clause syntax, including nominative case for the subject. The subordinate status of the nominalized proposition is indicated merely by a post-clause (and post-finite-verb) nominalizer, followed by case marking appropriate to the structure of the main proposition. Modern Turkish, by contrast, shows what may be called a higher degree of nominalization, with genitive marking of the subordinate subject (as well as other features, such as possessive marking intervening between the nominalizer and the case suffix that is assigned by the main proposition).

[1] NON-EMBEDDED RELATIVE-CORRELATIVE STRUCTURES

c. <u>Turkish</u>

[**ne** kadar yukarıdan	inerse]RC
RP	sg.3conditional
[**o** kadar derine	girer]CC
CP	sg.3

'From whatever extent high it (= the pile driver) descends, to that extent low it enters.'

= 'The greater the height it falls from, the deeper it goes down.' Or: 'If the height is greater …'

c' <u>Old Turkic</u>

[kim	**qorq-sar]**RC	[yorïŋlar]CC
RP	conditional	

'Who may be/is afraid should go away.'

[2] PARTICIPIAL STRUCTURES

c. Turkish

gülem adam çıkarıldı

'The man (who was) laughing was thrown out.'

c'. Old Turkic

yazïn-mïs yazuq

'The sinned sin.' (i.e., 'the sin that has been committed')

[3] INFINITIVES

d. Turkish

çalısmak istiyor

'He wants to go.'

c'. Old Turkic

uc-qalï bat-γalï bolurlar

'They can fly and dive.'

[4] VERBAL NOUNS AND NOMINALIZATIONS

c. Turkish

yürümeğe	başladık
VN, sg. D	

'We began to walk.'

[Ahmed-in	**ben-i**	**sev-diğ-in] -i**	biliyorum
Ahmed (sg.G)	me (A)	love-nlzr-poss.-A	I know

'I know that Ahmet loves me.' (Kornfilt 1987)

c'. Old Turkic

[qan	**aq]-mïs-ïn**	körti
blood (N)	flow-nlzr.-A.	saw

'She saw the flowing of the blood/the blood flow(ing).'
= 'She saw that the blood was flowing.'

[5] CONVERBS

c. Turkish

alkıp gittik

'Having risen we went.' = 'We rose and went.'

c'. Old Turkic

bo savïγ **isid-ip** incä **tip** tidi

'Having heard this word, speaking thus, he spoke'
= 'He heard this word and spoke thus.'

[6] QUOTATIVES

d. Turkish

[kim bunu yaptı]	**diye**	düşünüyordum
	Q	

'I was wondering [Who has done this?]

c'. Old Turkic

[amraqlartïn adïrïlγuluq ämgäk bolmu-zun ärti]	**tip** qorqar män
	Q

'I was afraid (that) [the suffering arising from being separated from loved ones might arise]'

ci-nakkä	**in-cä**	**tip**	**ayttï** [DD]	**tip**
	thus	speaking	said	Q

'… he said to Chandaka [DD]'

[7] WHOLE-WORD REDUPLICATION OR AMREDITA

c. Turkish

bir bir

'one by one'

c'. Old Turkic

miŋ miŋ

'thousands after thousands'

[8] ECHO-REDUPLICATION

d. Turkish

burada kutu **mutu** yok

'There is no box or the like here.'

Relevant structures in Tibeto-Burman, Burushaski, Tocharian, Iranian

In order to examine whether these features can be attributed to Central Asian convergence, I will now focus on the existence of similar structures in Tibeto-Burman, Burushaski, Tocharian, and various Iranian languages (both Middle and Modern).

Relative-correlatives are found in Old Iranian languages and have survived, in one form or another, in much of Modern Iranian; see the selected examples in [9 a-c]. Modern Persian, just like Indo-Aryan Hindi, to be sure, also permits embedded relative clauses, as in the second example under [9c]; but this is an innovation.

Relative-correlatives also occur in Tocharian and Burushaski; see [9d-e].[5] Tibetan has somewhat similar constructions, employing, like Burushaski and Tocharian (as well as Dravidian), an interrogative pronoun in what appears to be relative-pronoun function, at last

[5] Burushaski requires the relative clause to be followed by a generalizing particle (*ke*) — an intriguing parallel with the post-RC marker *-ō* of southern Dravidian. This parallelism at first sight raises interesting questions about possible relationships. However, since the modern southern Dravidian phenomenon is a relatively recent innovation and restricted to the southern languages (Hock 1988, 2001, Lehmann 1998), the idea of a common innovation, or of convergence or subversion seems to be precluded.

optionally [9f]. However the relative clause is always followed by a nominalizer and, in the present example, this is followed by a case suffix marking agreement with the antecedent in the main clause. The similarity to the other languages, thus, is a rather superficial one and may merely reflect similarities in the use of interrogative pronouns as indefinites.[6] Tibeto-Burman Chang, spoken in the far eastern part of Nagaland, has structures that more strongly resemble the common South Asian — and Turkic — pattern [9g].

[9] RC-CC in Iranian, Central Asia, etc.

a. Rosanī (Pāmir):

[uf qalam-ēn-um tā-re	**ca**	dācūg]RC
	RM	
[unde-n	vid]CC	
here-pl.3		

'Those pens that I gave you were here.'

b. Ossetic

[sæ xistær	**ci** w**ɨ**d]RC	[w**ɨ**y zaɣta]CC
	RP	CP

'Who was the oldest of them, (he) said'

c. Modern Persian

[man	ketāb-i-rā	did-am]CC	[**ke** Hasan dār-ad]RC
			RM

'I saw the book that/which Hasan had.'

[man	ketāb-i-rā	[**ke** Hasan dār-ad]RC	did-am]MC
		RM	

'I saw the book that/which Hasan had.'

---

[6] At the same time, as Beyer (1992) notes, the use of such structures is relatively more common in translations of Sanskrit relative-correlative constructions, which may suggest at least some degree of convergence or subversion.

c. Tocharian (A)

[tu wäṣpā krant pñi yāmte paṁ]CC
[**kus-ne** wsā-ci caṁ kāpñe]RC
RP

'Then indeed you made = acquired good merit which gave to you this dear (thing/one)' (Maitreyasamiti-Nāṭaka)

d. Burushaski

[**ámin** daúċkuin imánimi]RC	**ke**
RP	ptcle

[íne buáa ćhap … oóścói]CC
CP

'Whoever has become a hunter, does not eat beef'

e. Classical Tibetan

saṅs-rgyas	[(**gaṅ**)	dgon-pa-la	bzugs]-**pas**
Buddha-Erg.	who	monastery-in	lives-nlzr-Erg.
tshos	bsad		
dharma	taught		

'The Buddha [who lives in the monastery] taught the dharma.'

f. Chang

[**au-e**	ngou	**kokkeji**]RC
RP	gayal	stole-subjunctive
[nge	khwoto	ngampe]CC
I	CP	beat

'I beat the man who stole the gayal.'

Participial structures are likewise in widespread use in the Iranian languages, Tocharian, and Burushaski, just as they are in most of the Eurasian languages. In the interest of limiting this paper to manageable size I will forgo giving examples.

Non-finite verb forms have a tendency to "cross over" from one category to another. For instance, the converb suffix *-tvā* of Sanskrit is related to the infinitive suffix *–tu-* (in Ved. *-tavai, -tos*, and later Vedic/Classical *-tum*) and to the Latin supines in *-tu* and *-tum*, all of which are frozen case forms of a verbal noun.[7] Many of the Turkish converbs are derived from participles or verbal nouns, and the infinitive is closely related to verbal nouns (Lewis 1967/1988: 174, 167).

What further complicates matters is that in addition to — or instead of — verbal nouns and infinitives, a number of area-relevant languages employ a strategy of subordination by means of a clause-final nominalizer. And, as suggested by the difference between, say, Classical Tibetan and Modern Newari, such nominalized structures may turn into verbal-noun constructions and the like.

It is therefore convenient to treat infinitives, verbal nouns, nominalizations, and converbs together.

Let me begin with a few selected examples of infinitives [10a-b], followed by examples of verbal nouns/nominalizations [11a-b]. Note especially the difference — and presumable historical relationship — between the pure nominalizations of Classical Tibetan and the infinitives of Modern Newari, as well as the fact that the latter are still quite transparently marked as datives, thus betraying their verbal-noun origin.

[10] INFINITIVES

a. Newari

ão chha-na kãe **dhãe-ke** jogya ji ma ju-la

'Now I am not worthy to call your son.'

b. Burushaski

huyés **uyáras** éikhinimi

'He taught him to herd small livestock.'

[11] VERBAL NOUNS/NOMINALIZATIONS

a. Classical Tibetan

[bla-mas	**bgegs**	**btul]-sa**	ri-la	yod
Lama	demon	tame-nlzr	mountain-on	is

'[The place where the Lama tamed the demon] is on the mountain.'

[7] For recent, rather different discussions of the relationship between verbal nouns and infinitives in Indo-European, see Disterheft 1980 and Gippert 1978.

(Classical Tibetan has a large number of such nominalizers, in various functions. Some of these, such as *-sa*, seem to be derivable from nouns, e.g. *sa* 'earth, land, place'; Beyer 1992: 300, with 294-350 for general discussion.)

b. Burushaski

śurayeéś **étasće** duúnuman
VN, sg. Adessive

'They began to be happy (lit. to make happiness).'

Since converbs are considered especially important in studies of South Asian convergence, I give a broader listing of examples in [12a-g]. Note that the interpretation of the Classical Tibetan example [12c] is a bit doubtful, since its suffix *-zin* is described as a coordinating conjunction by Beyer (1992); its function, however, seems to be entirely the same as that of the converb affixes in the other languages.

[12] CONVERBS

a. Modern Persian

ū-rā **borde** rū-ye nīmkat x^{v}ābānīdand
("gérondif"; related to the past participle)

'Taking him they laid him on the couch.'
= 'They took him and laid him on the couch.'

b. Ossetic

Xævdɨn…sær riwɨl **ærwadzgæyæ**…donɨ bɨl-tɨl ratsu-batsu kodta

(Abl. of the "participle-gerund")

'Xævdɨn, lowering his head to his chest … paced along the bank of the river.'

c. Classical Tibetan (?)

rmal-ziṅ bkal-bkal (|) bkal-ziṅ bzu-bzu (|) bzu-ziṅ …
"&" "&" "&"

She plucked it "and" kept spinning it. She spun it "and" ≈ Having spun it, she kept making thread. She made thread "and"
≈ Having made thread …'

d. Newari

tho-te thao kāe-yā khā **ne-nāo** babā-mha-sẽ thao seoka-panista dhā-la …

'**Hearing** such words from his son, the father said to the servants …'

e. Chang

nyak	**shā'n**	loko
rice	having eaten	will come

'(After) having eaten the rice I will come.'

f. Burushaski

ne giráśar duúnimi, **nikíratin** … ġaríṅ étimi …

'He began to dance; having danced he … sang songs …'

g. Tocharian A

[tämne tāṣ āṣānik] **wewñūräṣ** tmäṣ ānand kuntis-tsekānac **kakmuräṣ** träṅkäṣ

'["Thus it may be, O honorable one."] Saying (this) then Anand, going to the potter, says …'

(Converb = Abl. of preterit participle; for the grammar see Thomas 1964: 23, with Krause & Thomas 1960: 185)

There is clear evidence of some kind of **quotative** marking on the northern periphery of South Asia, including Classical Tibetan and various Tibeto-Burman languages as far east as Chang, as well as in Burushaski; see [13a-d]. Certain complications, however, suggest that in contrast to Modern Newari, Classical Tibetan did not have full quotatives but rather what I have called quotativals (Hock 2001).

Quotatives are also found in Gandhari Prakrit, which was used in the Central Asian area and in some Iranian languages; see [13e-f]. We also find such markers in Middle East-Iranian languages [13g], but coexisting with a number of other marking strategies; see e.g. Emerick 1989, Heston 1976, Leumann 1936, Sims-Williams 1989a,b. Quotative marking thus is only weakly established in Middle East-Iranian.

Tocharian B, too, has some attestations of quotatives, in some cases clearly as a translation of Sanskrit *iti*, as in the last example of [13h].

There is some question, however, as to how native this construction is in Tocharian.

[13] QUOTATIVES

a. Classical Tibetan

des-na [dge-bai tshos-rnams] **ses** byao
Q

'Therefore they are called [virtuous elements].'

b. Newari

chha-mha seoka-yā-ta sala-tāo, [DD] **dha-ka** ne-na
Q

'Calling a servant, he asked, [DD].'

c. Chang

[Besang	masu	kokke]	**to-go**	nge	lenke
Besang	cow	stole	Q	I	said

'I said that [Besang had stolen a cow].' (Hutton 1929/1987: 47, w. 41, 49)

d. Burushaski

… íne ćága … ééói ke [be qísume máa uṣúçóon] **nusénin**
Q

'He said (lit. made a narration) to them … [How do you eat them?]'

[hamza] **nusénin** hin murtazabáatum śuá híran bam
Q

'There was a certain [Hamza] (by name), a fine man from Murtazabad.'

séi	bái ke [kyot bésan baláan maními]	**nusénin**	**ité**	qhiáalulo	bam
said	ptcle	Q	thus	thought	

'He said, […], thus he thought.'

e. Gandhari Prakrit

[brammaṇo] **di** pravucadi
Q

'He is called [brahmin].'

f. Ossetic

[kædæm lidzɨs] **zægɨgæ** yæ færsɨ Wɨrɨzmæg
Q

'[Where are you running] Wɨrɨzmæg asked.'

(Abaev 1964: 133; Q = "participle-gerund" of 'say, speak')

g. Khotanese

ṣei [bōdhisatvə] **tta** hvīnde
Q (?)

'He is called a [Bodhisattva]' (Leumann 1936, text 7: 45)

h. Tocharian B

[nesäṁ] **te mant** (Thomas 1964: 69, with Krause & Thomas 1960: 167)

'[It is] (unquote).' (Translates Skt. *iti*; lit. 'this so')

[rūp] **te** $k_u$se ste (Thomas 1964: 68)

'What is [form]?'

[upekṣasmṛtipariśuddhaṁ caturthaṁ dhyānaṁ upasaṁpadya viharati] **te mant** '[upeksaṣmṛtiparisuddhaṁ caturthaṁ dhyānaṁ upasaṁpadya viharati] (unquote)' (a Sanskrit citation, meaning 'he remains, having brought about the fourth dhyāna that is purified of indifference and recollection')

According to Abbi (1992), **āmreḍita** constructions are a hallmark of South Asian convergence, and structures with iterated finite or non-finite verbs characterize the core of the convergence area.

As it turns out, āmreḍita is also found on the northern periphery of South Asia, including structures with finite or non-finite verbs [14a-c]. As Heston (1980) has shown, āmreḍita also occurs in Old, Middle, and Modern Iranian languages. In fact, both Modern Persian and Ossetic have non-finite verb iteration; see [14d-g], especially [14f] and [14g]. Tocharian, too, has āmreḍita [14h]; however, I am not aware of any verb iteration. Finally, Classical Armenian, far removed from Central Asia but relatively close to (transplanted) Ossetic, also has āmreḍita [14i].

[14] AMREDITA

a. Classical Tibetan

byeu sñi-ñul-du **soṅ-soṅ**

'The little birds kept going (lit. went-went) into the snare.'

b. Chang

… saunyüe mesiau **shauko shauko** lobu

'… the tiger kept eating (lit. came eating-eating) the animals.'

c. Burushaski

guchárimi-guchárimi

'He went-went = he kept going.'

d. Avestan

narəm narəm

'man by man'

e. Bartangi (Pamir)

ðawī (ðawī)

'two each'

f. Ossetic

raxæts-raxæts

'pulling-pulling'

g. Persian

kas-ān (kas-ān)

'(while) pulling'

h. Tocharian A

koṁ-koṁ

'day by day'

i. Classical Armenian[8]

luṙ luṙ

'very quiet'

mi mi

'one each'

Finally, **echo-reduplication** has counterparts in Modern Iranian languages [15a-b], as well as in Burushaski [15c] and Classical Armenian [15d]. Interestingly, as in Turkish, in all of these languages the initial consonant of the second part of the compound is the labial nasal. The *v-* of the Hindi type *cāy vāy* agrees at least in labiality. The Dravidian type, however, with its velar initial, is quite different (see [8a] above). Should this difference be considered significant? And if so, of what?

[15] ECHO-REDUPLICATION

a. Persian

cāi-māi

'tea and the like'

baqqāl-maqqāl

'grocers and the like'

---

[8] In addition to cases of clear whole-word duplication, Armenian also has a type with inflectional endings only added at the end of the entire compound and/or with *-a-* inserted after the first member. For the latter compare *gund-a-gund* 'in droves', coexisting with *gund gund* in apparently the same meaning. Since a similar alternative pattern, with inserted *-a-* is found in echo reduplication, it seems safe to consider this second type of duplication to be a genuine alternative variant of āmreḍita. Note that this particular type can also be made from verbs, as in *kar-kar-em* 'run back and forth'. (See Jensen 1959: 45-46, 76.)

b. Ossetic

k'ædz-**m**ædz'

'curved, crooked'

c. Burushaski

gúsan-**m**úsan

'woman and the like'

d. Classical Armenian

aɫx-a-maɫx

'goods and the like'

A Central Asian Connection?

In his pioneering study of structural similarities in South Asia and beyond, Masica (1976: 184-185) notes striking structural similarities between Altaic and South Asia, and in this regard makes the following interesting remarks:

> Contacts between India and Central Asia, particularly in the sense of migrations, have been important since very early times. Migrations can involve the kind of intimate mingling of people that seems to be required. It is conceivable that the six-hundred years of Turkish rule in India also had more profound effects than Turkish rule in the Balkans, involving a moving in and settling down of larger numbers of people. Turkish rule was over the North, however, and the greatest affinity is between Altaic and the languages of the South... This clearly must go back to a period long before the Muslim invasion of India. *(For whatever reason or combination of reasons, it is worth noting that the hiatus between India and the Perso-Turkish Middle East — as distinct from the Semitic Middle East — is much less profound than that between India and Southeast Asia. In fact, there is no hiatus, but rather an allied border zone, with gradual transitions.)* [emphasis added]
>
> There is no reason, of course, why we must seek a single explanation for the "Indo-Altaic" configuration. A succession of factors may account for its present shape…

The evidence of echo-reduplication, with its contrast between southern, Dravidian velar replacement and northern as well as extra-

South Asian labial replacement, might argue for a relatively recent interaction between Turkish and northern South Asia, excluding the Dravidian south — possibly reflecting Turkish rule in northern South Asia. However, the other features considered here seem to go back much farther in time and thus would require a much earlier period of contact. Moreover, note that echo-reduplication with labial replacement is already attested in Classical Armenian, roughly contemporary with Old Turkic, but much farther to the west. This raises interesting questions about where the feature originated. Could it have arisen in the Caucasus area and spread from there, possibly via Iranian, to Central and northern South Asia? The uneven nature and chronology of the sources may make it impossible to ever give a satisfactory answer.

What, then, about the other features?

One possibility would be to return to the argument in Hock 1975, modified and updated in Hock 1984, that Proto-Indo-European may have been a (peripheral) member of a large, prehistoric Indo-Altaic convergence area,[9] and that many of the structural similarities may therefore date back to a very early, prehistoric period.

Another possibility would be the suggestion mooted in Hock 1984 and elaborated with specific reference to South Asia in Hock 2001, namely that the typological similarities in syntax may be independent manifestations of a shared constraint on finiteness which is found in many other verb-final languages, including Luiseño and several varieties of Quechua.

In the remainder of this paper I consider a third possibility, namely that the similarities between Turkic and South Asia may have arisen in the Central Asian oases of the early Christian era, with Indo-Aryan Gandhari or Niya Prakrit, East Iranian Sogdian and Saka, Classical Tibetan, Tocharian, and Turkic languages and their speakers in intense multilingual contact.

In addition to textual evidence for the presence of these languages in the oases of Central Asia (Winter 1984: 14), there is a fair amount of evidence in terms of lexical borrowings, beginning at least around 700 AD, but possibly going as far back as the beginning of the Christian era. Borrowings into Turkic come from Chinese, Iranian, Tocharian, later also Sanskrit. There is also evidence that in the 8th century, Turfan was attacked by the Tibetans. And, according to Winter, there may have been 'an international, Iranian-Prakrit-Turkish vocabulary in this domain'. (See Winter 1984: passim.)

Tibetan participation in this area may further be suggested by the fact that Tocharian A is the only Indo-European language to make a distinction between 'I (masc.)' and 'I (fem.)', namely *näṣ : ñuk*. Only

---

[9] I.e., projecting Masica's "Indo-Altaic" convergence area into a much earlier period.

one other language known to have been in the general area makes such a gender distinction for the first person pronoun, namely Tibetan, which has *ṅa* (unmarked) beside *kho-bo* (masc.): *kho-mo* (fem.), with the usual suffixal gender marking (Beyer 1992: 213). Note that Tocharian A and Classical Tibetan further share the restriction that the gender marking is found in the first person pronoun, but not in the second person.[10]

There is thus a large amount of evidence that, in principle, might make it possible to explain Turkic-South Asian similarities in terms of multilingual contact in Central Asia, with East Iranian Saka/Sogdian and/or Tocharian as the vector.

However, the details cause difficulties

For instance, Classical Tibetan has sentential nominalization, without change of subject case. The Indo-Aryan, Iranian, and Tocharian languages, as well as Burushaski, instead have verbal nouns requiring change of subject case.[11] Modern Turkish presents yet a different type, which retains the "internal syntax" of the embedded proposition, except for the fact that it assigns genitive case to its subject; see [4c] above. Modern Turkish, thus, can be considered to be somewhere midway between the sentential nominalization found in Classical Tibetan and the verbal nouns of the Indo-European languages and Burushaski. What is more difficult to assess is the Old Turkic situation. The only two examples cited in von Gabain 1959 (see e.g. example [4c']) might suggest that Old Turkic is more similar to Classical Tibetan, by not changing the subject's case. However, it is difficult to be certain on the basis of just two examples. Even if this interpretation of Old Turkic should be correct, however, would this justify the assumption of Tibetan-Turkic convergence, especially since Tibetan appears to have been quite peripheral as far as Turkic is concerned and since Tocharian, with which Tibetan shares the feature of gender-marked first person singular pronouns, does not have nominalizations of this type?[12]

In the area of relative clauses, most area-relevant languages use relative-correlative structures that are similar to the Turkic and general South Asian type. But on this count Tibetan, with its nominalized relative clauses, is quite different. Moreover, relative-correlatives seem to be inherited in both Indo-European and Dravidian (Hock 1992a,

---

[10] At the same time, Classical Tibetan can add the plural marker to the gender-marked first-person plural, while Tocharian A makes no gender distinction in the first person plural.

[11] In addition, of course, to verbal adjectives (participles), and/or infinitives and converbs derived from verbal nouns and adjectives.

[12] The "relative participle" of Dravidian (see e.g. [2a] above) is similar to the Tibetan type of sentential nominalization, in that the subject of the embedded proposition does not change case (compare the nominative *nāṉ* in [2a]). But Dravidian is geographically far removed from Old Turkic.

Lakshmi Bai 1985, Ramasamy 1981, Steever 1988) and thus are not likely to reflect convergence between these two language families (Hock 2001). This would still leave the possibility that Old Turkic and the Turkic languages in general acquired the feature through contact with the Indo-Aryan, Iranian, and Tocharian languages of Central Asia. But the apparently independent origin of relative-correlatives in Dravidian and Indo-European suggests that the feature could just as well be an independent development in Turkic too — unless it dates back to the prehistoric Indo-Altaic convergence area suggested by Hock (1984).

As for echo-reduplication, all the languages or language families have this type, except Tibetan.[13] The agreement of Turkish with Ossetic (originally East Iranian) and Burushaski in the choice of *m-* as the normal replacement consonant might be considered to favor a Turkic connection. But the prehistory of Burushaski is uncertain. The *m-* of Ossetic, as mentioned earlier, might be a regional Caucasus feature, as shown by its presence in Classical Armenian. Most important, at this point it is not clear whether the feature was already present in Old Turkish. If nevertheless the shared *m-* should be relevant, it would align Turkic more closely with Burushaski and, possibly, with East Iranian.

As far as converbs and most of the other features are concerned, all the languages have something along these lines, with of course considerable differences in detail. None of these features help single out one or another language as especially important.

Finally, the case of Turkic quotatives is rather difficult to explain as the result of Central Asian convergence. True, Gandhari/Niya Prakrit has a quotative marker (inherited from Sanskrit), but the evidence of the other area-relevant languages is much more tenuous. Tibetan seems to have had quotativals, rather than a robust pattern of quotative marking. The situation in the Eastern Middle Iranian languages is quite complex, but the use of postposed cited-discourse markers is rare. And the use of quotative marking in Tocharian is extremely rare, and possibly not native. By contrast, quotative marking, using a converb of the verb *ti-* 'speak, say', is robustly present throughout the history and geographical spread of Turkic. It is difficult to see how the robustness of this feature in Turkic could be attributed to subversion by the rather tenuous quotatives or quotativals in most of the other languages of the Central Asian oases.

---

[13] Unless we want to compare the type *glan-glen*, with change in the vowel, rather than the initial consonant—on this count note the Panjabi type *khānā khūnā* 'food and the like' (Abbi 1992: 20).

Conclusion

All in all, then, the possibility of a Central Asian connection in the early Christian era is certainly intriguing and should be considered seriously in future discussions of South Asian convergence and its possible connections to the outside. To become convincing, however, the case would have to be supported by evidence strong enough to warrant abandoning what I consider the most likely alternative, namely independent developments, in response to a shared finiteness constraint. As noted earlier, the latter seems to be a common tendency in verb-final languages, including such languages as Quechua and Luiseño, for which a South Asian — or Turkic — connection would be preposterous.

References

Abaev, V. I. 1964. *A grammatical sketch of Ossetic*, transl. by Steven P. Hill. Bloomington/The Hague: Indiana University/Mouton

Abbi, Anvita. 1992. *Reduplication in South Asian languages: An areal, typological, and historical study.* New Delhi: Allied Publishers

Bazin, Louis. 1959. Structures et tendances communes des langues turques (Sprachbau). In: Deny et al. 1959: 11-19

Berger, Hermann. 1998. *Die Burushaski-Sprache von Hunza und Nager*. 3 volumes. Wiesbaden: Harrassowitz

Beyer, Stephan V. 1992. *The Classical Tibetan language*. New Delhi: Sri Satguru Publications

Beythan, Hermann. 1943. *Praktische Grammatik der Tamils*prache. Leipzig: Harrassowitz

Brough, John. 1962. *The Gāndhārī Dharmapada.* (London Oriental Series, 7.) Repr. 2001, Delhi: Motilal Banarsidass

Deny, Jean, Kaare Grønbech, Helmuth Scheel,, and Zeki Velidi Togan (eds.). 1959. *Philologiae turcicae fundamenta.* Aquis Mattiacis [Mainz]: Steiner

Disterheft, Dorothy. 1980. *The syntactic development of the infinitive in Indo-European.* Columbus, OH: Slavica

Eckmann, János. 1959a. Das Chwarezmtürkische. In: Deny et al. 1959: 113-137

____ 1959b. Das Tschaghatische. In: Deny et al. 1959: 138-160

Emmerick, Ronald E. 1989. Khotanese and Tumshuqese. In: Schmidt 1989: 204-229

Gippert, Jost. 1978. *Zur Syntax der infinitivischen Bildungen in den indogermanischen Sprachen. Europäische Hochschulschriften, Reihe 21, Linguistik,* 3. Frankfurt: Lang

Grierson, George A. 1909. *Linguistic Survey of India, Vol. 3, Parts 1 and 2.* Repr. 1967, Delhi: Motilal Banarsidass

Haspelmath, Martin, and Ekkehard König, eds. 1995. *Converbs in cross-linguistic perspective: Structure and meaning of adverbial verb forms — adverbial participles, gerunds.* Berlin: Mouton de Gruyter

Heston, Wilma L. 1976. Selected problems in fifth to tenth century Iranian syntax. Philadelphia: University of Pennsylvania Ph.D. dissertation in Oriental Studies.

____ 1980. Some areal features: Indian or Indo-Iranian? *International Journal of Dravidian Linguistics 9:* 141-157

Hock, Hans Henrich. 1975. Substratum influence on (Rig-Vedic) Sanskrit? *Studies in the Linguistic Sciences 5:2.*76-125

____ 1982. The Sanskrit quotative: A historical and comparative study. *Studies in the Linguistic Sciences 12:2*.39-85

____ 1984. (Pre-)Rig-Vedic convergence of Indo-Aryan with Dravidian? Another look at the evidence. *Studies in the Linguistic Sciences 14*: 1.89-108

____ 1988. Review article: Finiteness in Dravidian. (Steever (1988): The serial verb formation in the Dravidian languages.) *Studies in the Linguistic Sciences 18:2*.211-231

____ 1989. Conjoined we stand: Theoretical implications of Sanskrit relative clauses. *Studies in the Linguistic Sciences 19*:1.93-126

____ 1992a. Reconstruction and syntactic typology: A plea for a different approach. In: *Explanation in historical linguistics*, ed. by G. W. Davis & G. K. Iverson, 105-121. Amsterdam & Philadelphia: Benjamins

____ 1992b. Review of Tikkanen (1987): The Sanskrit gerund: A synchronic, diachronic, and typological analysis. *Kratylos 37*.62-68

____ 1993. Review of Abbi (1992): Reduplication in South Asian languages: An areal, typological, and historical study. *Studies in the Linguistic Sciences 23:1*.169-192

____ 1994. Discourse linkage in Sanskrit narratives with special emphasis on the story of Nala. In: *Papers from the Fifteenth South Asian Language Analysis Roundtable 1993*, ed. by A. Davison and F. M. Smith. Iowa City, IA: South Asian Studies Program, 117-139

____ 1996. Pre-Ṛgvedic convergence between Indo-Aryan (Sanskrit) and Dravidian? A survey of the issues and controversies. In: *Ideology and status of Sanskrit: Contributions to the history of the Sanskrit language*, ed. by J. E. M. Houben, 17-58. Leiden: Brill

____ 2001. Typology vs. convergence: The issue of Dravidian/Indo-Aryan syntactic similarities revisited. In: *Tokyo symposium on South Asian languages: Contact, convergence, and typology*, ed. by Peri Bhaskararao and K. V. Subbarao, 63-99. (= *The Yearbook of South Asian Languages and Linguistics, 2001*)

Hutton, J. H. 1929/1987. *Chang language: Grammar and vocabulary of the Chang Naga Tribe*, revised and edited by Satkari Mukhopadhyay. Delhi: Gian Publishing

Jäschke, H. A. 1883. *Tibetan grammar*. 2nd ed. London: Trübner

Jensen, Hans. 1959. *Altarmenische Grammatik*. Heidelberg: Winter

Kornfilt, Jaklin. 1987. Turkish and the Turkic languages. In: *The world's major languages*, ed. by Bernard Comrie, 619-644. New York: Oxford University Press

Krause, Wolfgang. 1955. Tocharisch. In: *Handbuch der Orientalistik, 4:3*. Leiden: Brill

Krause, Wolfgang, and Werner Thomas. 1960. *Tocharisches Elementarbuch, vol. 1*. Heidelberg: Winter

Lakshmi Bai, B. 1985. Some notes on correlative constructions in Dravidian. In: *For Gordon H. Fairbanks*, ed. by V. Z. Acson & R. L. Leed, 181-90. Honolulu: University of Hawaii Press

Lazard, Gilbert. 1992. *A grammar of contemporary Persian*, transl. by Shirley A. Lyon. Costa Mesa/New York: Mazda Publishers/Bibliotheca Persica.

Lehmann, Thomas. 1998. Old Tamil. In: Steever 1998: 75-99

Leumann, Ernst. 1936. *Das nordarische (sakische) Lehrgedicht des Buddhismus*, posthumously ed. by Manu Leumann. (Abhandlungen für die Kunde des Morgenlandes, 20.) Leipzig.

Lewis, G. L. 1967/1988. *Turkish grammar*. Oxford/New York: Oxford University Press. (1st ed. 1967; Repr. with corrections, 1988)

Masica, Colin P. 1976. *Defining a linguistic area: South Asia*. Chicago/London: University of Chicago Press.

Payne, John. 1989. Pāmir languages. In: Schmidt 1989: 417-444

Ramasamy, K. 1981. Correlative relative clauses in Tamil. *Dravidian syntax*, ed. by S. Agesthialingom & N. Rajasekharan Nair, 363-80. Annamalainagar: *Annamalai University Publications in Linguistics, 73*

Schmidt, Rüdiger (ed.). 1989. *Compendium linguarum iranicarum*. Wiesbaden: Reichert

Sims-Williams. 1989a. Eastern Middle Iranian. In: Schmidt 1989: 165-172

____ 1989b. Sogdian. In: Schmidt 1989: 173-192

Steever, Sanford B. 1988. *The serial verb formation in the Dravidian languages*. Delhi: Motilal Banarsidass

____ 1998. (ed.) *The Dravidian languages*. London/New York: Routledge

Sundermann, Werner. 1989. Westmitteliranische Sprachen. In: Schmidt 1989: 106-113

von Gabain, Annemarie. 1959. Das Alttürkische. In: Deny et al. 1959: 21-45

Thomas, Werner. 1964. *Tocharisches Elementarbuch, vol. 2*. Heidelberg: Winter

Winter, Werner. 1984. *Studia tocharica: Selected writings—Ausgewählte Beiträge*. Poznań: Uniwersytet Im. Adama Mickiewicza

Yoon, James. 2002. What the Korean copula reveals about the interaction of morphology and syntax. In: *Japanese/Korean Linguistics* 11: 34-50

RESULTATIVE CONSTRUCTIONS WITH OVERT AGENT/POSSESSOR IN HINDI-URDU AND WESTERN NIA LANGUAGES

L. V. KHOKHLOVA AND CHARANJIT SINGH

Action and process verbs usually form special syntactic constructions to denote *the explicit result of a previous action or process*. They are called resultatives. Such a process passes through 3 stages – *a, b* and *c*: the process itself (*a*); natural completion of the process and beginning of the resulting state (*b*); and the resulting state (*c*). Stage *b* denotes the perfect, whereas *c* is the resultative (Kholodovich 1979: 139-140; Nedyalkov & Yakhontov: 1983: 8). It has been shown by typologists (Comrie 1981: 67-78, Nedyalkov & Yakhontov 1983) that in most cases resultative constructions denote the state of either the subject (S) of an intransitive action or that of the object (O) of a transitive action: X went > X is gone. Hindi-Urdu *vah gayaa huaa hai* (He is away); X broke the chair> the chair is broken. Punjabi *kursii TuTTii hoii hai* (The chair is broken).

The third less frequent type - resultatives with overt Agent/Possessor - usually implies the second participant of the situation. In most cases it describes the state of the Agent (A) of the previous transitive action like Russian *u neë uroki vyucheny* 'She has her lessons learnt' (lit. with her lessons learnt). In some cases the second participant is a possessor of the result of a previous action. It may be or may not be the Agent. In the above given Russian resultative *u neë uroki vyucheny* 'She has her lessons learnt' Agent and Possessor are coreferential, while the Russian construction *u Mashi kvartira ubrana* 'Masha has her flat cleaned' may mean either that Masha has cleaned her flat herself or that somebody else did it for her.

The third type of resultative implies the existence of the second, and the existence of the second presupposes the existence of the first type. (Nedyalkov & Yakhontov 1983: 17).

Resultatives are usually formed from telic verbs, resultatives from atelic verbs are very rare (Nedyalkov & Yakhontov 1983: 59; Plungyan 2001: 50-88).

A comprehensive study of all types of resultatives used in Hindi-Urdu as predicates, adjectives and adverbs is available in Dashchenko

1987. Several Hindi grammarians discussed selected syntactic and semantic properties of past participle phrases in their works on Hindi syntax (Kachru 1966: 153-157, Kachru 1980: 72; 80-81, Subbarao 1984: 167-185), etc. A comparative study of the structural types of resultative constructions in Modern Western NIA is given in Khokhlova 1999: 91-112.

This paper will focus on common and distinct features of resultatives with overt Agent/Possessor in four Modern Western NIA languages: Hindi-Urdu (H-U), Punjabi (P), Gujarati (G) and Marwari (M). These types of resultatives have been chosen here as up till now they attracted less attention of NIA grammarians and because in comparison with widely used one-valency structures like 'He is gone' or 'The chair is broken' two-valency resultatives show more structural and semantic divergencies in various Western NIA languages. We shall concentrate on resultatives used as predicates, only selected cases of divergencies in the adverbial usage of the resultative construction will be discussed in this paper.

It will be shown below that contrary to common belief that Hindi-Urdu and Punjabi have very similar grammars, with regard to resultatives Punjabi has structural and semantic divergences from other Western NIA languages. At the same time, Punjabi resultatives have some common features with Slavic languages like Russian which are relatively distant genetically.

Examples used in this paper have largely been taken from information provided by native speakers and from literary sources. Fabricated examples have been painstakingly checked and cross-checked with native speakers. References to literary sources have, however, been given only in borderline cases or in cases where the constructions are being described for the first time.

Resultative constructions in Modern Western NIA languages are formed by combination of the stative participle of the main verb with the auxiliary verb *to be*. In Hindi-Urdu stative participles are formed analytically by combination of the past participle from the main verb with the past participle of the verb 'be' . In Punjabi and (rarely) in Hindi-Urdu the past participle of the auxiliary verb 'be' may be replaced by the past participle of the verb 'lie, fall': H-U. *paRaa*, P. *piaa*. The latter is used as a substitute of the past participle of the verb *'be'* – mostly in cases when the resultative denotes a visible stationary condition.[1] However, replacement of the past participles of the verb 'be' by the past

---

[1] A visible stationary condition is preferable, but not obligatory for replacement of the past participles of the verb 'be' by the past participle of the verb 'fall'. Compare (1) and (2) with the following sentence: *khaaNaa khatam hoiaa piaa hai* "The food is finished"

participle of 'fall' is possible only in case of one-valency resultatives. Compare correct (1) and (2) with ungrammatical (3) and grammatical (3a):

(1) P.	*ciTThii*	*likhii*	*hoii/paii*	*hai*
	letter	write+PP+F/Sg	be/fall+ PP+F/Sg	is

'The letter is written.'

(2) P.	*uh*	*bistre*	*te*	*leTiaa*	*hoiaa/piaa*	*hai*
	he	bed	in	lie+ PP+M/Sg	fall+PP+M/Sg	is

'He is lying in bed.'

(3) P.**munDe*	*ne*	*daaRhii*	*rakhii*	*paii*	*hai*
boy	Erg	beard-F/Sg	keep+PP+F/Sg	fall+PP+ F/Sg	is

'The lad has a beard.' (lit. has beard kept)

(3a) P. *munDe*	*ne*	*daaRhii*	*rakhii*	*hoii*	*hai*
boy	Erg	beard-F/Sg	keep+PP+F/Sg	be+PP+ F/Sg	is

'The lad has a beard.' (lit. has beard kept)

Marwari and Gujarati have special synthetic forms of stative participle with the suffix *=yoR=* in Marwari (4) and *=el=* in Gujarati (5).

(4) M.	*buuRhii*	*Dokriyaa˜*	*chii˜Taa˜*	*raa*	*ghaaghraa*
	old	old ladies+F/Pl	printed cloth	of+M/PL	long skirt+M/Pl

pai'r=i=yoR=ii	*hai*
wear+stativePP+F	be+Pres/3/Sg=Pl

'Old ladies are wearing printed long skirts.'

(5) G. *aa cor*	*ej*	*poliisvaalaae*	*pakR=el=o*	*che*
this thief-M/Sg	this very	policeman+Instr	catch+stativePP+M/Sg	is

'This thief is caught by this very policeman.'

Two types of resultatives with overt Agent are common for all the languages under review:

I. O-type: The stative participle of a transitive verb refers to an Object in the Nominative case, controlling verbal agreement. The Agent is in the Genitive (Hindi-Urdu, Punjabi, Marwari) or Instrumental case (Gujarati). This construction is normally used when the Agent is the focus of the sentence. The Object in most cases is inanimate.

(6) H-U.	*yah*	*kaam*	***us=ii***	***kaa***	*kiyaa*	*huaa*	*hai*
	this	work-M/Sg	he/Obl+**Emph**	**Gen**	do+PP+M/Sg	be+PP+M/Sg	is

'This work is done by him (not anyone else).'

(7) P.	*ih*	*ramesh*	***dii***	***hii***	*racii*	*hoii*	*kheD*	*hai*
	this	Ramesh	**Gen**	**Emph**	create+PP+F/Sg	be+ PP+F/Sg	game F/Sg	is

'This is the handiwork of Ramesh (not anyone else).'

(8) G.	*aa navalkathaa ramanlaal*	***desaaii=e=j***	*lakh=el=ii*	*che*
	this novel-F/Sg Ramanlal	Desai+Instr+Emph	write+stativePP+F	is

'This novel is definitely written by Ramanlal Desai.'

A Gujarati Agent expressed by 1st person pronouns may be Genitive, not Instrumental:

(9) G.	*aa*	*patr*	***maaro-j***	*lakh=el=o*	*che*
	this	letter-M/Sg	my-M/Sg-**Emph**	write+stativePP+M/Sg	is

'This letter is written by me, nobody else.'

Some Hindi-Urdu and Punjabi speakers including one of the authors of this paper reject human Objects with agent process verbs[2] in this type of construction:

(10) H-U.	***?yah cor***	*raam*	*ka*	*hii*	***pakRaa***	*huaa*	*hai*
	this thief-M	Ram	Gen	Emph.	**catch**+PP+M/Sg	be+PP+M/Sg	is

'This thief is caught by Ram himself.'

However, when put in a proper context resultatives with a human Object are accepted by many Hindi-Urdu and Punjabi speakers as well as

---

[2] A description of the main classes of state predicates in Hindi based on Chafe's classification is given in Abbi 1980: 3-17.

by the speakers of Gujarati and Marwari (see Gujarati (5) above)[3]. A human Object is more acceptable in all the languages under review in resultatives with agent process experiencer verbs:

(11) H-U. ***yah bacca*** *ramesh kaa hii* ***bigaaRaa*** *huaa hai*
this child-M/Sg Ramesh-Gen Emph **spoil**+PP+M/Sg be+PP+M/Sg is

'This child was spoiled by Ramesh, nobody else.'

(12) P. ***zafar*** *jasvindar daa hii* ***uksaaiaa*** *hoiaa hai*
Zafar-M/Sg Jasvinder of Emph **instigate**+PP+M/Sg be+PP+M/Sg is

'Zafar is instigated by Jaswinder, nobody else.'

Verbs with the meaning 'to know', 'to find out' are avoided in O-type resultatives:

(13) H-U. **yah baat usii kii jaanii (maaluum kii) huii hai*
this fact-F/Sg he/Obl+Emph of know+PP+F known make+PP/F be+PP/F is

'This fact has been found out by him, nobody else.'

However, the verb 'to recognize' that belongs to the same 'information' sphere is quite acceptable:

(14) H-U. *yah cor usii gavaah kaa pahcaanaa huaa hai*
this thief-M/Sg this/Obl+Emph witness of recognize+PP+M/Sg be+PP+M/Sg is

'This thief is recognised by this very witness.'

---

[3] According to Y. Kachru (1980: 72) resultatives with the animate object are not used adjectivally. The author gives examples of ill-formed phrases like *raam kaa pukaaraa huaa laRkaa andar aayaa* 'The boy called by Ram came *in'* ; *manjuu kaa piiTaa huaa baccaa ro rahaa hai* 'The child hit by Manju is crying'; *uskii saraahii huii laRkii khush ho gaii* 'The girl admired by him became happy.' These sentences may be rejected by native speakers for some other reasons: in all of them Agent is not in a focus position and the past participles are not formed from telic verbs. Aside from that it is not clear from Y. Kachru's description whether resultatives with human objects cannot be used as noun modifiers or cannot be used as predicates as well.

The Agent may not retain its focus position in idiomatic expressions like (15):

(15) H-U.	*yah*	*aadmii*	*meraa*	*jaanaa*	*pahcaanaa*	*hai*
	this	man	my	know+PP+M/Sg	recognise+PP+M/Sg	is

'This man is known to me.'

II. A-type. The stative participle of a transitive verb refers to the Agent of a previous transitive action and/or the Possessor of its results.

Descriptions of these types of resultatives in various genetically and geographically unrelated languages like Nivkh [= "Gilyak"] (Nedyalkov & Otaina 1983: 84), Evenk (Nedyalkov 1983: 130), Georgian (Machavariani 1983: 140), Arabic (Khrakovskiy 1983: 170), Armenian (Kozintseva 1970: 290-307) etc. demonstrate that they are used with similar semantic classes of verbs such as 'put on' and other verbs related to wearing clothes, ornaments and cosmetics, verbs denoting action involving parts of the body, verbs denoting action on body parts, ingestive verbs, some cognitive verbs etc. Most of them form resultatives in Modern Western NIA. However, in the languages under review resultatives of this type are used with an even wider range of verbs.

In most cases Agent and Possessor in this type of resultatives are coreferential. However, it is not always so. For example, (16) is ambiguous, as somebody else, not the boy himself, could put the hat on his head.

The following types of Agent/Possessor case marking and verbal agreement are attested in the languages under review:

1. Nominative Agent, default agreement (fixed uninflected form of the past participle in = e): standard Hindi-Urdu (16)

(16) H-U.	*yah*	*laRkaa*	*sundar*	*Topii*	*pahne*
	this	boy-Nom/M/Sg	beautiful	hat-F/Sg	wear+PP in=e
	hue		*hai*		
	be+PP in = e		is		

'This boy is wearing a beautiful cap.'

2. Ergative Agent; verbal agreement controlled by Object: colloquial Hindi-Urdu (17), Punjabi (18)

(17) H-U.	*merii*	*beTii*	*ne*	*itihaas kaa*	*imtihaan*
	my	daughter	Erg	history of	exam-M/Sg

paas kiyaa	*huaa*	*hai*
pass do+PP+M/Sg	be+ PP+M/Sg	is

'My daughter has passed her exam in history', i.e. 'she has done history.'

(18) P.	*uhne*	*paise*	*chupaa ke*	*rakkhe*	*hoe*	*han*
	he-Erg	money-M/Pl	having hidden	keep+PP+M/Pl	be+ PP+M/Pl	are

'He has his money hidden.'

The past participle of the verb 'be' may be omitted in H-U, but not in Punjabi. Omission of the verb 'to be' in Punjabi turns the resultative construction into a perfective.

3. Instrumental Agent, verbal agreement controlled by Object: Gujarati (19)

(19) G.	*gopale*	*kaalii*	*Topii*	*paherelii*	*che*
	Gopal-Inst	black	hat-F/Sg	wear+stativePP+F	is

'Gopal is wearing a black cap.'

4. Nominative Agent controlling verbal agreement: Marwari (20); several idiomatic expressions in Gujarati (21), (22)[4]:

---

[4] Interestingly, (21) and (22) with Nominative instead of typical for Gujarati Instrumental Agent marking belong to the group of verbs that form stative participles used as attributes. There is a general rule that stative participles from transitive verbs cannot be used as attributes:

H-U	**bahut*	*mehnat*	*kiyaa*	*huaa*	*aadmii*
	much	work	do+PP+M/Sg	be+PP+M/Sg	man

"The man who did a lot of work"

However, there are several verbs that are exception to this rule. Their list varies in different NIA and may be different even in different idiolects of the same language, but it usually includes verbs denoting changes in appearance or inner state of the agent; compare possible in Hindi-Urdu (1) and (2) with impossible (3) and (4):
(1) *hindii siikhaa huaa rajesh* "Rajesh who has learned Hindi', i.e. Rajesh who has acquired more knowledge and perhaps can get a better job or better understanding of events
(2) *sharaab piyaa huaa ramesh* 'Ramesh who has drunk wine', i.e. drunk Ramesh.
(3) **paanii piyaa ramesh* 'Ramesh who has drunk water'
(4) **nayaa hindii shabd siikhaa rajesh* 'Rajesh who has learned a new Hindi word'

(20) M.	*gomtii*	*haath*	*me˜*	*kelo*	*pakRiyoRii*	*hai*
	Gomti-Nom/F	hand	in	banana-Nom/M/Sg	hold+stativePP+F	is

'Gomti is holding a banana in her hand.'

(21) G.	*rajesh*	*gujaratii*	*shikhelo*	*che*
	Rajesh-M/Sg	Gujarati	learn+stativePP+M/Sg	is

'Rajesh has learned Gujarati.'

(22) G.	*ramesh*	*to*	*piidhelo*	*che*
	Ramesh	Emph.	drink+stativePP+M/Sg	is

'Ramesh is drunk.'

Agent may be expressed not only by **animate nouns** that are typical for this position but sometimes **also by inanimate** - in case of **personification** (23):

(23) P.	*ik*	*vaDDii*	*caTTaan*	*ne*	*jive˜*	*aapNe*	*kaleje*	*vic*	*uh*
	one	large	rock	Erg	as if	self's	heart	in	that

mandar	*rakkhiaa*	*hoiaa*	*sii*
temple-M/Sg	keep+PP+M/Sg	be+ PP+M/Sg	was

'As if a large rock had that temple in its heart.' [Amrita Pritam, Uh Admi, p. 28];

Or, in case of **metonymy** (24):

(24) P.	*thiieTraa˜ ne*	*vaDDe vaDDe posTar*	*laake*	*baRii*	*rauNak*
	theaters Erg	big-big posters	having brought	grand	ambience

baNaaii	*hoii*	*sii*
make+PP+F/Sg	be+PP+F/Sg	was

'Theatres had created a grand ambience by hanging large-sized posters' [Amrita Pritam, *Uh admi,* p. 22]

In Punjabi and some Hindi idiolects (perhaps influenced by Punjabi), but not in Marwari and Gujarati, resultatives may also be used to express

---

Two latter sentences do not describe serious changes in the Agent, that is why stative participles from transitive verbs cannot be used in them as attributes.

meanings that may not be limited to denoting the result of a recent action. Rather, they may express experience in a given field of activity.[5]

(25) P.	*asii~*	*ih*	*vii*	*kiitaa*	*hoiaa*	*hai*
	we	this-M/Sg	also	do+PP+M/Sg	be+ PP+M/Sg	is

'We have done it before', i.e. 'We have experience in this field as well'

(26) P.	*jasbiir*	*ne*	*hal*	*vaahiaa*	*hoiaa*	*hai*
	Jasbir	Erg	plough-M/Sg	plough+PP+M/Sg	be+ PP+M/Sg	is

'Jasbir has ploughed earlier', i.e. 'He knows how to plough'

(27) P.	*usne*	*kaii tarah*	*de*	*imtihaan*	*paas*	*kite*	*hoe*	*han*
	he/Obl+Erg	several types	of+M/Pl	exam	pass	do+PP+M/Pl	be+PP+M/Pl	are

'He has passed exams of various types', i.e. 'He knows how to pass exams'

(28) H.	*usne*	*ghaaT*	*ghaaT*	*kaa*	*paanii*	*piyaa*
	he/Obl-Erg	river bank	river bank	's	water-M/Sg	drink+PP+M/Sg
	huaa	*hai*				
	be+ PP+M/Sg	is				

'He has drunk the water at many river banks', i.e. 'He knows the world thoroughly', 'He is very experienced'.

(29) H.	*mai~*	*shaakaahaarii*	*huu~,*	*lekin*	*mai~*	*ne*	*murgaa*	*bhii*
	I	vegetarian	am	but	I	Erg	chicken-M/Sg	also
	khaayaa	*huaa*	*hai*					
	eat+PP+M/Sg	be+ PP+M/Sg	is					

'Although I am a vegetarian, I have had chicken too.'

Apart from telic verbs used in (25-29) above, the meaning of experience in a given field of activity may also be expressed in Punjabi with atelic verbs:

---

[5] In fact this meaning of the resultative construction is very close to that of present perfect. Interestingly, resultatives in some Russian dialects formed with suffixes -***shi***, -vshi have a very similar meaning: *vy poyezdivshi, povidavshi lyudey* "You have travelled a lot and seen many people' (Kuzmina 1971: 133).

(30) P.	*mai˜*	*us*	*kuRii*	*nuu˜*	*cummiaa*	*hoiaa*	*hai*
	I	that/Obl	girl	Acc	kiss+PP+M/Sg	be+ PP+M/Sg	is

'I have kissed that girl', i.e. 'Once I had this experience.'

(31) H.	*yah*	*khel*	*mai˜*	*ne*	*khelaa*	*huaa*	*hai*
	this	game-M/Sg	I	Erg	play +PP+M/Sg	be+PP+M/Sg	is

'I have played this game', i.e. 'I know all these tricks.'

When used adverbially, the described resultatives have different structures in the languages under review: Hindi-Urdu (32) employs the fixed uninflected form of the past participle in =*e*:

(32) H-U.	*raam*	*haath*	*me˜*	*kitaab*	*liye*	*khaRaa*	*thaa*
	Ram	hand	in	book	take+PP in = e	standing	was

'Ram was standing with a book in his hand.'

Gujarati employs the conjunctive participle (33):

(33) G.	*atul*	*haath*	*maa˜*	*sundar*	*ful*	*no*	*guccho*
	Atul	hand	in	beautiful	flower	of+M/Sg	bunch
	laiine		*ubho*		*hato*		
	take+CP		standing		was		

'Atul was standing with a beautiful bunch of flowers in his hand.'

In Marwari the past participle may agree with its subject (34), though in most cases it is used in a fixed form in = aa˜ (35) – i.e. on the Hindi-Urdu model:

(34) M.	*wii˜nNii*[6]	*nhaavaN-ghar*	*suu˜*	*sinaan kar*	*haat*	*me˜*
	daughter in law-F/Sg	bathroom	from	having taken bath	hand	in
	giilaa	*gaa'baa*	*liyoRii*	*baarai*	*nikLai*	
	wet+M/Pl	clothes+M/PL	take+stativePP+F	out	appears	

'Daughter in law after taking bath comes out of the bathroom with wet clothes in her hand.' [Narayandatt Shrimali, *Binni*: 141]

---

[6] Although this transcription may seem phonologically odd, we are here merely transliterating the spelling found in the original text. The initial B is dotted, hence our W.

(35) M.	*ekaN*	*kaanii*	*suu~*	*laalraaj*	*haath*	*me~*	*pyaalau*	*liyaa~*	*aavai*
	one	side	from	Lalraj	hand	in	cup	take+CP	comes

'From one side comes Lalraj holding a cup in his hand.' [Shaktidan Kaviya, *Virmati:*42]

Punjabi adverbial resultatives are formed using the conjunctive participle in *=ii* (36), (37):

(36) P.	*narindar*	*baTuaa*	*phaRii*	*baiThii sii*
	Narindar	purse	take+CP	sitting was

'Narinder was sitting holding a purse.'

(37) P.	*jasbiir*	*mu~h*	*kholii*	*baiThaa*	*sii*
	Jasbir	mouth	open+CP	sitting	was

'Jasbir was sitting with his mouth open.'

Unlike the resultatives of the first (O) and second (A) types, common to all the Western NIA, the P-type resultatives described below exist only in Punjabi. In Punjabi too, these constructions have a limited usage and that too predominantly in colloquial speech. These constructions are most typical for the Malwai dialect region of eastern Punjab from where they have spread to modern literary Punjabi.

III. There are three main varieties of P-type resultatives. In both of them the Possessor is marked by the Genitive postposition in the fixed Masculine Oblique case form:

1. The stative participle of a transitive verb refers to the Object of a previous action. This property is shared with the O-type resultatives. In contrast to the O-type resultatives where the second argument marked by Genitive or Instrumental is always the Agent of previously completed action, and similar to the A-type resultatives, where the role of the second argument is ambiguous, the second argument in the first variety of P-type resultatives may or may not be the Agent of a previous action. The verb agrees with the Object:

(38) P.	*bishne de*	*ciTTii*	*pagg*	*te*	*khaddar*	*daa*
	Bishna Gen	white+F/Sg	turban-F	and	khaddar	of

sajraa	*kurtaa*	*paaiaa*	*hoiaa*	*sii*
clean+M/Sg	kurtaa+M/Sg	put on+PP+M/Sg	be+PP+M/Sg	was

'Bishna was wearing a white turban and clean kurta made of khaddar.' [Gurdial Singh, 2].

The marking of the Possessor in these constructions is similar to the Possessor marking in constructions denoting inalienable possession:

(39) P.	*rajindar singh de...*	*ikk*	*muNDaa*	*sii*
	Rajinder Singh Gen+M/Obl	one	son	was

'Rajinder Singh had a son.' [Raam Saruup Anakhi, 22]

These constructions have different ranges of acceptability. Most acceptable, typical for all types of resultatives, are descriptions of appearance with verbs like *paauNaa* 'to put on', *rakhNaa* 'to keep', *ta˜gNaa 'to tie'*, etc:

(40) P.	*harjiit*	*de*	*kirpaan*	*Ta˜gii hoii*	*hai*
	Harjit	of	dagger-F/Sg	tie+PP+F/Sg	is

'Harjeet is wearing a dagger.'

(41) P.	*munDe*	*de*	*daaRhii*	*rakhii*	*hoii*	*hai*
	boy	of	beard-F/Sg	keep+PP+F/Sg	be+PP+F/Sg	is

'The lad has a beard.'

The meaning of constructions (38), (40), (41) is very close to those of the A-type with Ergative Agent: see (16) above. The difference is that in (16) the focus of communication is the Agent/Possessor, while in (38), (40), (41) the focus of communication is the Object. Both in (16) and in constructions like (38), (40), (41) Agent and Possessor may or may not be coreferential.

A raising transformation results in Agent/Possessor promotion in case of A-type resultatives (42) and in Object promotion in case of P-type resultatives (43).

While a raising transformation of P-type resultatives implies retaining of the basic form of the conjunctive participle in *=ii* (43), the raising transformation of A-type resultatives changes the *=ii* form into the *=iaa˜* form (42):

(42) P.	*kartaarii nuu˜*	*lishkve˜ kapRe*	*paaiaa˜*	*vekhke*
	Kartari Acc	shining clothes	wear+CP	having seen

nuuraa˜	*saR gaii*
Nooraan	felt jealous

'Nooraan felt very jealous on seeing Kartari in shining clothes.'

(43) P.	*bhagte*	*de*	*caTak pagg*	*phabii*	*vekhke*
	Bhagta+Obl	Gen	bright turban	adorn+CP	having seen

biiraa	*baRaa*	*khush*	*hoiaa*
Bira	very	happy	felt

'Bira felt very happy on seeing a bright turban adorning Bhagta.'

The same *=iaa˜* form is used in syntactic constructions where the subject of the main verb is not coreferential with the subject of the conjunctive participle:

(44) P.	*tainuu˜*	*paise*	*udhaar*	*liaa˜*	*kai*	*saal*	*ho gae han*
	you+Dat	money	loan	take+CP	several	years	passed

'Several years passed since you borrowed the money.'

2. The stative participle of an intransitive verb refers to the Object of a previous action. Among the most frequent intransitives are *bajhNaa* 'to be tied', *Ta˜gNaa 'to hang'*, *sajjNaa* 'to be decorated' etc.

(45) P.	*giitaa*	*de*	*cangii*	*saaRii*	*bajjhii*	*hoi*	*hai*
	Gita	of	good	saree-F/Sg	tie+PP+F/Sg	be+ PP+F/Sg	is

'Geeta is wearing a good saree.'

(46) P.	*kuRiiaa˜*	*de*	*suhNiiaa˜*	*saahRiiaa˜*	*sajjiiaa˜*	*hoiiaa˜*
	Girls	of	beautiful	sarees	put on+PP+F/Pl	be+ PP+F/Pl

han
are

'Girls had beautiful sarees on them.'

P-type constructions may be used to express not only directly visible features of appearance but also constant features, compare (47) and (48) below:

(47) P.	*bacce*	*de*	*ainak*	*paaii*	*hoii*	*hai*
	child	of	spectacles-F/Sg	put on+PP+F/Sg	be+PP+F/Sg	is

'The small child is wearing spectacles.' (present situation)

(48) P.	*oh de*	*ainak*	*laggii*	*hoii*	*hai*
	he of	spectacles-F/Sg	attach+PP+F/Sg	be+PP+F/Sg	is

'He wears spectacles.' (constant feature)

The role of Agent/Possessor in this variety of P-type resultative is also ambiguous. In some contexts the Agent interpretation of the Genitive NP is excluded (49):

(49) P.	*ciitte*	*de*	*golii*	*laggii*	*hoii*	*hai*
	leopard	Gen+M/Obl	bullet-F/Sg	attach+PP+F/Sg	be+PP+F/Sg	is

'The leopard has been shot.'

3. The stative participle refers to the Subject of a previous intransitive action. The overt Possessor marked by a fixed form of the Genitive postposition is somehow connected with the results of the previous action.

(50) P.	*uh de*	*bhaiN*	*aaii*	*hoii*	*hai*
	he Gen+M/Obl	sister-F/Sg	come+PP+F/Sg	be+PP+F/Sg	is

'Sister is visiting him.'

(51) P.	*sante de*	*praahuNaa*	*baiThiaa*	*hoiaa*	*hai*
	Santa of	guest-M/Sg	sit+PP+M/Sg	be+ PP+M/Sg	is

'A guest is sitting at Santa's.'

There is a striking similarity between the form and meaning of resultatives with promoted possessor in Punjabi and in some Slavic languages. Constructions of this type have been described by Russian typologists as 'possessive resultatives'. In literary standard Russian 'possessive resultatives' are formed by using the passive participles of transitive verbs. The Possessor is marked by the possessive preposition *u*+Gen case and the predicate agrees with the direct Object. This model is similar to the first variety of P-type resultatives in Punjabi:

(52) R.	*u*	*neë*	*byli*	*otbeleny*	*volosy...*
	at-Gen prep	her-Gen	were	bleach-PP/Pl	hair-Pl

'Her hair was bleached... ' [Astafiev, *Tsar'-ryba*]

Cf. similar constructions denoting possession with Genitive marking of Possessor: *U Mashi mnogo druzey* 'Masha has many friends'.

Both Russian and Punjabi resultatives have a noun in Genitive case, which often has an ambiguous role of the Agent/Possessor: the Possessor NP may be or may not be coreferential with the Agent of the previous action. In (53) below, Masha could have tidied the flat herself or somebody else could have done it. The same ambiguity is true of Punjabi (54):

(53) R.	*u*	*Mashi*	*kvartira*	*ubrana*
	at	Masha-Gen	flat-nom/f/sg	tidy-PP/f/sg

'Masha's flat has been tidied up.'

(54) P.	*bacce*	*de*	*cange*	*kapRe*	*paae*	*hoe*	*han*
	child- M/Sg/Obl	Gen	good	clothes	wear+PP+M/Pl	be+PP+M/Pl	are

'The child is well dressed.'

This ambiguity shows that in 'possessive resultatives' the Agent is not significant. Significant is the fact that the Possessor NP acquires the result of a previously performed action. In comparison to Punjabi constructions with promoted possessor Russian 'possessive resultatives' have a much wider range of acceptability.

The Russian vernacular and dialects have constructions similar to the third variety P-type resultatives in Punjabi:

(55) R.	*u neë*	*sestra*	*priyekhavshi*
	at her	sister	come+stative CP

'Her sister has come to visit.'

Interestingly, both in Punjabi and Russian (but not in the other Western NIA under review) constructions with promoted possessor are used not only in the resultatives, but also with finite verbal forms:

(56) P.	*uh*	*de*	*beTaa*	*hoiaa*	*hai*
	he	Gen	son	be+PP+M/Sg	is

'A son has been born to him.'

(57) R. *u nas* *moloko* *skislo*
at us-Gen milk soured.

'As for us, our milk has turned sour.'

(58) P. *kuRii* *de* *saaRii* *phab* *rahii* *hai*
girl Gen sari-F/Sg suit remain-PP/F/Sg is

'The sari suits the girl.'

(59) R. *u nikh* *vsë* *blestit* *i* *sverkayet*
at them-Gen everything shine-pres/3Sg and sparkle- pres/3Sg

'As for them, everything is sparkling and glittering.'

Conclusion

There are three types of resultative structures found in four Modern Western NIA languages: Hindi-Urdu, Punjabi, Gujarati and Marwari. Of these, O-type structures referring to the object of a previous transitive action and A-type structures referring to the Agent of a previous transitive action and/or Possessor of its results, are found in all the languages under review. The second participant of the situation in O-type resultatives is always the Agent, in A-type resultatives it may be both the Agent of a previous action and/or the Possessor of its results. Agent and Possessor may or may not be coreferential. The main models of case marking and verbal agreement in O-type and A-type resultatives have been discussed in the paper as well as semantic constraints on their usage. At the same time it has been shown that in Punjabi, A-type resultatives are used with a wide range of verbs including atelic verbs and may denote not only the result of an action, but also the general experience of having indulged in a certain type of activity.

When used adverbially A-type resultatives have different structure in the languages under review. Punjabi is the only language among Western NIA that has two fixed uninflected verbal forms for A-type adverbial resultatives.

Unlike O-type and A-type resultatives, P-type resultatives are found only in Punjabi. These constructions have come into standard Punjabi relatively recently from the Malwai dialect region of eastern Punjab. The main distinctive feature of P-type resultatives is that their Possessor is marked by the Genitive postposition in the fixed Masculine Oblique case form.

A raising transformation results in Agent/Possessor promotion in case of A-type resultatives and in Object promotion in case of P-type resultatives.

While a raising transformation of P-type resultatives entails retention of the basic conjunctive participle in *=ii*, the raising transformation of A-type resultatives changes the *=ii* form into the form of conjunctive participle in *=iaa˜*.

There are three main varieties of P-type resultatives. In the first two the stative participle refers to the Object of previous action. The stative participle is formed from transitive (first variety), or from intransitive (second variety) verbs. In the third variety of P-type resultatives, the stative participle refers to the Subject of a previous intransitive action.

In the first two varieties of P-type resultatives the role of Possessor is ambiguous: it may and may not be coreferential with the Agent. There are cases when Possessor can not be identified with the Agent. In the third variety of P-type resultatives Possessor can never be interpreted as the Agent.

There is a striking similarity between the form and meaning of P-type resultatives with promoted possessor in Punjabi and in some Slavic languages like Russian. Both Russian and Punjabi resultatives have a noun in Genitive case, which often has an ambiguous role of Agent/Possessor: the Possessor NP may be or may not be coreferential with the Agent of the previous action. This ambiguity shows that in 'possessive resultatives' the Agent is not significant. Significant is the fact that the Possessor NP acquires the result of a previously performed action.

In both Punjabi and Russian, constructions with promoted Possessor are used not only with the resultatives, but also with finite verbal forms.

References

Abbi, Anvita.1980. *Semantic grammar of Hindi. A study in reduplication.* New Delhi: Bahri Publications.

Comrie, Bernard. 1981. *Aspect and voice: some reflections on perfect and passive.* – In: *Tense and aspect. Syntax and Semantics 14.* New York: Academic Press.

Dashchenko, G. M. 1987. *Rezul'tativnye prichastiya v yazyke urdu* (Resultative participles in Urdu). Moscow: Moscow University publication.

Kachru, Yamuna.1966. *An introduction to Hindi syntax.* Urbana, Illinois: University of Illinois publication.

____ 1980. *Aspects of Hindi grammar.* New Delhi: Manohar Publications.

Khokhlova, L. V. 1999. *Stative participles in Western NIA languages* – In: *Vidyopaasanaa: Studies in honour of Harivallabh C. Bhayani.* Mumbai: Image Publications, pp. 91-112.

Kholodovich, A. A. 1979. *Problemy grammaticheskoy teorii* (Problems of Grammatical Theory). Leningrad: Nauka.

Khrakovskiy, V. S. 1983. *Rezultativ i passiv v arabskom yazyke* (Resultative and passive in Arabic) – In: *Tipologiya rezul'tativnykh konstruktsiy* (The typology of resultative constructions), ibid.

Kozintseva, N. A. 1970. *Zalogovyye znacheniya i sintaksicheskiye funktsii rezul'tativnogo prichastiya v sovremennom literaturnom armyanskom yazyke* (Perfective/ imperfective meaning and syntactic functions of the resultative participle in the modern Armenian literary language) – In: *Lingvisticheskiye issledovaniya* (Linguistic studies). Leningrad: Nauka. Kuzmina, I. B. 1971. *Predikativnoye upotrebleniye prichastnykh form* (Participial forms used as predicates) – In: Kuzmina, I. B., Nemchenko E. V. *Sintaksis prichastnykh form v russkikh govorakh* (Syntactic properties of participles in Russian dialects). Moscow: Nauka.

Machavariani, M. V. 1983. *Stativ, rezul'tativ, passiv i perfekt v gruzinskom yazyke* (Stative, resultative, passive and perfective constructions in Georgian) – In: *Tipologiya rezul'tativnykh konstruktsiy*, ibid. pp. 133-142.

Nedyalkov V. P, Yakhontov S. E. 1983. *Tipologiya rezul'tativnykh konstruktsiy* (The typology of resultative constructions) – In: *Tipologiya rezul'tativnykh konstruktsiy* (The typology of resultative constructions), ibid. Chapter 1, pp. 3-41.

Nedyalkov, V. P. and Otaina. 1983. *Rezul'tativ i kontinuativ v nivkhskom yazyke* (Progressive and resultative in the Nivkh language) – In: *Tipologiya rezul'tativnykh konstruktsiy*, ibid. pp. 80-89.

Plungyan, V. A. 1983. *K opredeleniyu rezul'tativa (universal'na li svyaz' rezul'tativa i predel'nosti?)*. (Defining the resultative (Is the link between resultatives and termination universal)? In: *Voprosy yazykoznaniya* 1983, N6, pp. 55-63.

____ 2001. *Antirezultativ: do i posle rezul'tata* (The antiresultative: before and after the result) – In: *Glagol'nyye kategorii. Issledovaniya po teorii grammatiki* 1. (Verbal categories. Studies in grammatical theory 1. Moscow: Russkiye slovari, pp.50-88.

Subbarao K. V. 1984. *Complementation in Hindi syntax*. Delhi: Academic Publications.

Quoted literary sources

Anakhi, Ram Sarup. 2003. *Dulle di dhaab*. Chandigarh: Lokgeet Prakashan (in Punjabi)

Astafiev, V. P. *Tsar' ryba*. At http://www.fro196.narod.ru/library/astafiev/astafiev.htm (in Russian)

Kaviya, Shaktidan. 1966. *Virmati*. In: Rajasthani Ekanki, Bhandari G. Ch.(Ed.). Udaipur: Rajasthan Sahitya Akademi, pp. 35-48. (in Marwari)

Pritam, Amrita. 2003. *Uh admi*. Delhi: Shilalekh Prakashan (in Punjabi)

Shrimali, Narayandatt. 1966. *Binni*.- In: Rajasthani Ekanki, ibid., pp. 35-48. (in Marwari)

Singh, Gurdial. 1970. *Anhoe*. Delhi: Navyug Publishers (in Punjabi).

THE COMPOUND VERB IN CHINESE AND HINDI-URDU AND THE PLAUSIBILITY OF THE INDO-TURANIAN LINGUISTIC AREA

HSIN-HSIN LIANG AND PETER E. HOOK

0. Overview

In his pioneering 1976 study Masica used the "explicator compound verb" as one of the features whose geographic distribution across the Eurasian landmass defines South, Central, and Northeast Asia as a single gigantic linguistic area. In it the absence of the compound verb in the languages of China and Southeast Asia bundles with a number of other typological isoglosses to demarcate the eastern boundary of this "Indo-Turanian" Linguistic Area (Masica 1976: 181). However, in a more recent study Masica reverses his position and counts Mandarin Chinese among those languages that do have a compound verb construction (2001: 250-52). During the past several years a number of writers (Butt, Butt and Scott, Maisak) have presented discussions of verb-verb sequences across Asia including data from Hindi-Urdu and Mandarin. In these studies parallels are stressed and differences largely ignored. The co-authors of this paper examine the putative compound verbs of Chinese and attempt to determine more precisely the extent to which they are formally and functionally similar to those found in the languages of South Asia. We conclude (at least as a *pūrvapakṣa*) that the Chinese "compound verb", less productive and less systematic than its Hindi-Urdu counterpart and possessing a radically different syntax and semantics, does not show sufficient parallels in form and function to justify Masica's change in position. Data from Lahu and Karen provide an additional reason for preferring the analysis and map in Masica 1976.

1. What is a compound verb?

"Compound verb" is not a given or self-evident category. On the basis of its shared properties in the languages of South Asia and Central Asia the compound verb may be defined as a sequence of two verbs AB (main verb A plus auxiliary or "vector" verb B) that alternates with main verb A with very little difference in meaning translatable into languages which do not have compound verbs (such as Sanskrit or English). Throughout this paper we will refer to concatenations meeting this minimal definition as "compound verbs" (CV's) or "Vv's" or "verb-verb sequences". In this pair of examples from Hindi-Urdu the SV [or "simple verb"] *aataa* alternates with the CV *aa jaataa*:

(1a)	*raat*[1]	*ko*	*yahãã*	*roz*	*paanii*	*pii-ne*	***aataa***	*hai*
	night	Dat	here	daily	water	drink-Inf[2]	come	is

'Every night he comes here to drink water.' (*Godan* 86, line 5)

(1b)	*kabhii.kabhii*	*dopahar*	*mẽ*	*bhii*	***aa***	***jaataa***	*hai*
	sometimes	afternoon	in	also	come	GO	is

'Sometimes he comes in the afternoon, too.' (*Godan* 86.6)

Though the meaning of the non-Vv (or simple verb) *aataa* in (1a) is not the same as that of the corresponding Vv *aa jaataa* in (1b), the difference in their meanings is not one that is easy to articulate or to translate into English. Certainly the meaning of the vector *jaa* 'GO' whatever it may be in (1b) is not the same as the meaning of the full lexical verb *jaa* 'go' in this example taken from a *ghazal* by Dagh (2):

---

[1] The transcription system used here for displaying data from Hindi-Urdu is the one commonly found in the linguistics literature on modern South Asian languages. In it doubling of a symbol indicates contrastive length; use of capital letters, retroflexion. The digraphs /ai/ and /sh/ are used to represent the front low vowel and the palatal fricative. Chinese data are given in Pinyin.

[2] Abbreviations include the following:

Abl.	ablative	Loc.	locative
Acc.	accusative	Masc.	masculine
CP.	conjunctive participle	MW.	measure word
Caus.	causative	Neut.	neuter
CS.	Change of Status	Nom.	nominative
CV.	compound verb	Obl.	oblique
Dat.	dative	Part.	participle
Def.	default	Pass.	passive
Emp.	emphatic particle	Perf.	perfect
Erg.	ergative	Pfv.	perfective
Fem.	feminine	Prtcl.	particle
Fut.	future	PP.	past participle
Hab.	habitual	Pst.	past tense
Indic.	indicative mood	Sbjn.	subjunctive
Inf.	infinitive	SV.	simple verb
		Top.	topic particle

(2)	*thake*	*sab*	*payaamii*	*vahãã*	***jaate-jaate***	*yahãã*
	tired	all	messengers	there	going-going	here

	aate-aate
	coming-coming

'All the messengers were exhausted going there, coming here.'

Indeed, the presence (without its creating contradiction) in (1b) of an auxiliary which (were it a full lexical verb) would be an antonym of the main verb *aa* 'come' is an unmistakable sign of grammaticalization.

Another pair, this from the Central Dravidian language Gondi, also exhibits both the criterial features of semantic bleaching and relative omissibility of the vector [= *haTTur* 'WENT' in (3b)]:

(3a)	*oor*	*tecchi*	*apnoo*	*daadaa-naa*	*muTTis*	***taak.tur***
	he	rising	his.(own)	father-Gen	near	went

'He got up and went to his father.' (Grierson 4: 489-90)

(3b)	*cuDur*	*marri*	*lakk*	*deesh*	***taak-si***	***haT.Tur***
	young	son	distant	country	go-CP[3]	went

'The younger son ... went to a faraway place.' (Grierson 4: 489)

In (3b) the use of vector *haT* 'GO' homophonous with a full lexical verb itself synonymous with the main verb *taak* 'go' without creating redundancy in itself indicates a high degree of semantic bleaching.

---

[3] In most South and Central Asian languages the compound verb is formed using the conjunctive participial form (CP) of the main verb. Among the exceptions are Hindi-Urdu and Panjabi where what appears to be the main verb's bare stem is used instead. However, in Hindi-Urdu the CP itself may appear as a bare stem. Compare the zero CP of example (a)'s ***kar aayaa*** with the full CP *kar-ke* in (b)'s ***kar-ke aayaa***:

(a)	*donõ*	*caacaaõ*	*ke*	*ghar*	*jaa-kar*	*raam-raam*	***kar***	***aayaa***
	both	uncles	's	home	go-CP	"Ram-Ram"	do	came

'I came back from going and saying "hello" to both uncles.' (*Godan* 213.34)

(b)	*aisaa*	*lajjit*	*thaa*	*maanõ*	*hatyaa*	***kar-ke***	***aayaa***
	so	ashamed	was	as.if	murder	do-CP	come

'He was so ashamed as if he'd just come back from murdering someone.'
(*Godan* 188.43)

2. The geographic distribution of compound verbs in Asia

With the exception of the isolate Burushaski examples of compound verbs in alternation with non-compound verbs can be adduced from at least some members of each South Asian language family as well as from many languages spoken in Central, NW, and NE Asia[4]. Northeast Asia may be represented by this pair of examples from Japanese:

(4a) *sake-wa* *boku-ga* ***non-da***
rice.wine-Topic I-Nom drink-Pst

'I drank the sake.'

(4b) *sake-wa* *boku-ga* ***non-de*** ***shimat-ta***
rice.wine-Topic I-Nom drink-CP PUT.AWAY-Pst

'I drank up the sake.' (adapted from Mizutani 1977: 188)

The pair (5a-b), from the Caucasian language Avar, attests to the existence of the compound verb in the west-by-northwestern lobe of the Indo-Turanian linguistic area:

(5a) *c'a*[5] ***suna***
fire went.out

'The fire went out.' (Charachidze 1981: 127)

(5b) *c'a* ***sun*** ***an.a***
fire go.out WENT

'The fire went out.' (Charachidze 1981: 127)

The Altaic languages of Central Asia all have Vv sequences that are compound verbs satisfying the minimal definition given in section 1. The Orkhon Inscriptions, the earliest attestation of Altaic, provide examples of the compound and non-compound forms of the verb *uc* 'fly; die':

(6a) *kyl* *tigin* *qon'* *jıl-qa* *jiti* *jegirmi-kae* ***uc.dı***
Kul Tigin Sheep Year-in seven twenty-in flew

'Prince Kul died on the 17th day of the Sheep Year.'
(Tekin KT NE:1)

---

[4] Compound verbs alternating with non-compound counterparts are also found in the languages of northern Australia. See Wilson (1999: 82-3) and Merlan (1994).

[5] In transcriptions of data from Avar the apostrophe represents ejective articulation of stops and affricates.

(6b)	*[qaγan*	*ı]t*	*jıl*	*onun'c*	*a*[i]	*altı*	*otuz-qa*
	kagan	Dog	*Year*	tenth	month	six	twenty-in

	uc-a	***bar.dı***
	fly-CP	WENT

'[The Kagan] died the 26th day of the 10th month of the Dog Year.' (Tekin BK S: 10)

Though much less frequent than those found in Indo-Aryan and Altaic, Tibetan[6] has compound verbs. In (7b) the perfect participle of the verb *'jog* 'put, place' serves as an omissible vector:

(7a)	*khö*	*kyēmɛn*	*daŋ*	*pūgu*	*tsʰāŋma*	*yūk*	*soŋ*
	he.Erg	wife	and	children	all	throw	Pst
(7b)	*khö*	*kyēmɛn*	*daŋ*	*pūgu*	*tsʰāŋma*	*yūk*	***shak***
	he.Erg	wife	and	children	all	throw	PUT
	soŋ						
	Pst						

'He abandoned his wife and children.'

3. Verb-verb sequences in Chinese

As functional equivalents of the compound verb in South Asian and Central Asian languages there are two candidates in Chinese: Main verb plus either a resultative or a directional auxiliary. Since the former category includes items like *bái* 'white', *míngbai* 'clear', *bǎo* 'full', *zuì* 'drunken', etc. which correspond to adjectives in most South Asian languages, we will not consider them here. Some of these may be comparable to vector verbs; while others [eg, *míngbai* in *nòng míngbai* 'make (something) clear' → 'realize'] clearly do not meet the criterion of relative omissibility:

---

[6] High tone in (7a-b) is shown by macrons on vowels. Thanks to Nicolas and Tseyang Sihle for providing this evidence for the existence of compound verbs in colloquial Tibetan of Lhasa. Abbi also notes the use of *shak* as vector (2004: 11). Vv sequences of the South Asian type are also found in West Tibetan (Balti: cf Read 1934: 60, 70, 102), the Kiranti languages of East Nepal (Driem 1987: 118-132, Ebert MS), and in Dzongkha, the national language of Bhutan (Driem 1992: 236-46).

(8)	*xiàn.zài*	*wǒ*	*nòng*	***(míng.bai)**	*le*
	now	I	do	CLEAR	CSPrtcl

'Now I understand.'

In order to delimit our set of putative compound verbs to those sequences in which the second element is not a stative verb or adjective (*bái* 'white', *míngbai* 'clear', *zuì* 'drunken', etc.), we will exclude all items that can occur as complements of the adverb *hěn* 'very'.[7]

The verb *zǒu* as a main verb means 'move', 'walk' or 'depart'. As a vector it optionally combines with verbs that express manner of motion such as *fēi* 'fly', *pǎo* 'run', *tiào* 'hop', *táo* 'flee', *pá* 'crawl; slither', *chuī* 'blow', etc. to express motion away:

(9a)	*lǎo.yīng*	***fēi***	***zǒu***	*le*
	eagle	fly	MOVE	Pfv

(9b)	*lǎo.yīng*	***fēi***	*le*
	eagle	fly	Pfv

'The eagle flew away.'

(10a)	*fàn.rén*	***táo***	***zǒu***	*le*
	prisoner	flee	MOVE	Pfv

(10b)	*fàn.rén*	***táo***	*le*
	prisoner	flee	Pfv

'The prisoner escaped.'

Depending on the semantic and syntactic environment vector *zǒu* alternates with its absence. In the progressive aspect, for example, it cannot occur:

(9c)	*lǎo.yīng*	*zài*	***fēi***	***(*zǒu)***
	eagle	is.at	fly	MOVE

'The eagle is flying.'

---

[7] If a putative vector can co-occur with *hěn* it is excluded as too close to the adjectival pole. This test is somewhat "over-exclusive": For instance, polysemous items with both a verbal and an adjectival meaning (such as *haǒ* 'be finished' and 'good') on the basis of their adjectival meaning will not pass it.

(10c)	*fàn.rén*	*zài*	*táo*	*(*zǒu)*
	prisoner	is.at	flee	MOVE

'The prisoner is escaping.'

Compare Hindi-Urdu in which the progressive also disprefers the occurrence of a vector[8]:

(11)	*ciil*	*uR*	*(*jaa)*	*rahaa*	*hai*
	hawk	fly	GO	-ing	is

'The hawk is flying.'

(12)	*qaidii*	*bhaag*	*(*jaa)*	*rahaa*	*hai*
	prisoner	flee	GO	-ing	is

'The prisoner is escaping.'

4. Parallels between Hindi-Urdu Vv's and Chinese Vv's

In this section we present and illustrate additional ways in which the compound verb in Hindi-Urdu is similar to its counterpart in Chinese. (In section 5 we will look at ways in which they differ.)

4a. In Hindi-Urdu vectors may be used to create pairs of compound verbs alike in every respect except their orientation. For instance in the following pair the use of vector *de* GIVE as opposed to vector *le* TAKE with the main verb *rakh* 'put; keep' accords with the intention to put something out **for others** versus the desire to keep something **for oneself** hidden away from others:

---

[8] The Hindi-Urdu compound verb does very occasionally occur in the progressive aspect:

(a)	vo	*is-tarah*	*bhaag-aa*	***jaa***	*rahaa*	*thaa*	*maanõ*
	he	this-manner	flee-Perf.Msg	GO	-ing	was	as.if
	piiche	*dauR*	*aa.rahii*	*ho*			
	behind	stampede	coming	were			

'He was racing along as if a stampede were right behind him.' (*Godan*, 135.46)

Note the difference in morphology of main verb *bhaag* from that seen in non-progressive compound verbs. For further discussion of progressive CV's see Hook 1974: 258-260.

(13)	*tab-tak*	*thoRaasaa*	*bhuusaa*	*nikaal-kar*	***rakh***	***do***
	then-until	a.little	straw	take.out-CP	put	GIVE

'In the meantime, put out a little straw (for Bholā).'
(*Godan* 23.23)

(14)	*gaaR-kar*	***rakh***	***lo***	*to*	*kaun*	*dekh-taa*	*hai*
	bury-CP	put	TAKE	then	who	see-Hab	is

'If you bury it (keep it underground), then who will see it?'
(*Godan* 219.28)

In Chinese a similar contrast is possible using the outwardly versus inwardly directed vectors *diào* 'drop, fall' versus *xià* 'descend[9], come down':

(15)	*bǎ*	*fáng-zi*	***zū***	***diào***	*ba*
	Acc	house	rent	DROP	prtcl

'Rent (out) the house (for others to live in).' (Teng 1977: 16)

---

[9] The antonymy of *diào* versus *xià* is not so easy to see as that of *de* 'GIVE' versus *le* 'TAKE'. While both *diào* and *xià* mean 'descend' or 'fall' the descent denoted by *diào* is typically **away from** the subject, the topic, or the speaker [cf., the hair in (a)] while that denoted by *xià* is typically **toward** the subject, topic, or speaker [cf., the rain in (b)]:

(a)	*tóufa*	*dōu*	***/ diào //***	****xià /***	*le*
	hair	all	fall.away	fall.toward	Pfv

'All his hair fell out.'

(b)	*yǔ*	*yǐ.jīng*	***/ xià //***	****diào /***	*le*
	rain	already	fall.toward	fall.away	Pfv

'It's already rained.'

If the situation itself is atypical, the characteristic directionality can sometimes be canceled or reversed by using a vector verb:

(c)	*huī.chén*	*dōu*	***diào***	***xià***	*le*
	dust	all	fall.away	FALL.TOWARD	Pfv

'All the dust fell down (towards me or toward the person dusting).'

In other cases, reversing the typical orientation of an action may require two vectors:

(d)	*yǔ*	***xià***	***xià***	***qù***	le
	rain	fall.toward	FALL.TOWARD	GO	Pfv

'It rained down away (from me - standing on a cliff above the clouds).'

(16)	*bǎ*	*fáng-zi*	***zū***	***xià***	*ba*
	Acc	house	rent	DESCEND	Prtcl

'Rent the house (for yourself to live in).' (Teng 1977: 16)

The feasibility of arranging vectors in sets and subsets on the basis of the semantic properties of the full lexical verbs with which they are homophonous depends on the distance they have traveled along an imagined path to grammaticalization. The more easily they can be put into such sets and subsets, the more they retain the semantics of their full lexical counterparts and the less grammaticalized they are.

4b. Both in Hindi-Urdu and in Chinese the unmodified (or the non-compound) Accomplishment[10] verb may be subject to non-completive or conative interpretation as in this song from the film *Bārādarī*:

(17)	*tasaviir*	***banaa-taa***	*hũũ;*	*tasaviir*	*nahĩĩ*	***ban-tii***
	picture	make-Hab	am	picture	not	be.made-Hab

'I try to picture (her) but the picture won't form.'

Use of *banaa le* the compound verb corresponding to *banaa* precludes a conative interpretation[11]:

---

[10] We are assuming that the reader has some familiarity with the Aristotelian-Vendlerian classification of verbs by their inherent aspectual properties as States, Activities, Achievements and Accomplishments. For discussions of these categories see (among others) Dowty (1979) and Van Valin (1990).

[11] The meaning of completeness inherent in the compound verb is responsible for SV/CV pairs that occasionally correspond to lexically distinct pairs of verbs in languages like English. Thus, *DhũũRh le* 'find' expresses the successful outcome of the action *DhũũRh* 'search for':

(a)	*ek.baar*	*us-ne*	*us shiishii-ko*	***DhũũRhaa***	*bhii*	*thaa*
	once	he-Erg	that bottle-Dat	searched	also	Was
	par	*nahĩĩ*	*milii*			
	but	not	turned.up			

'Once he had even looked for that bottle but it wasn't to be found.' (Bhandari 1979: 127)

(b)	* *ek.baar*	*us-ne*	*us shiishii-ko*	***DhũũRh liyaa***	*bhii*	*thaa*
	once	he-Erg	that bottle-Dat	search TOOK	also	Was
	par	*nahĩĩ*	*milii*			
	but	not	turned.up			

'Once he had even found that bottle but it was not to be found.' (contradiction)

(18a)	*tasaviir*	***banaa-ii***	*lekin*	*tasaviir*	*nahı̃ı̃*	***ban-ii***
	picture	make-Pst	but	picture	not	be.made-Pst

'I tried to picture (her) but the picture wouldn't form.'

(18b)	*tasaviir*	***banaa-lii***	*(*lekin*	*tasaviir*	*nahı̃ı̃*	***ban-ii)***
	picture	make TOOK	but	picture	not	

'I pictured (her) (*but the picture wouldn't form).'

In Chinese the tendency of an unmodified Accomplishment verb to be interpreted conatively is, if anything, even stronger[12] than it is in Hindi-Urdu.

(19a)	*wǒ*	***huà-le***	*huà*	*kěshì*	*méi*	*huà*	***hǎo***
	I	paint-Pfv	picture	but	not	picture	done

'I tried to paint a[13] picture but the picture wouldn't paint.'

(19b)	*wǒ*	***huà***	***hǎo**-le*	*huà*	*(*kěshì*	*méi*	*huà*	***hǎo)***
	I	paint	done-Pfv	picture	but	not	picture	done

'I painted a picture (*but the picture wouldn't paint).'

Recent work by Pederson (in press) on Tamil suggests that the susceptibility of non-compound forms of Accomplishment verbs to conative interpretation follows from inferences made by the language learning child who interprets each part of the compound verb as referring to a discriminate phase of telic events. However, as we show below (in §

---

[12] In fact, according to Ross (1990: 64) to avoid conative interpretation all Accomplishment verbs in Chinese must be compounded.

[13] The susceptibility of particular instances of *huà* 'paint' to conative interpretation depends also on properties of its object:

(a)	*wǒ*	*huà*	*le*	*liǎng-fu*	*huà*	*(*kěshì*	*méi*	*huà*	*haǒ)*
	I	paint	Pfv	two-Cl	pictures	but	not	pictures	be.done

'I painted two pictures (but the pictures didn't get done).'

However, the point we wish to make is that a conative reading of the non-compound form is under at least some conditions possible. For the effect of classifiers on the interpretability of an Accomplishment verb as conative see Soh and Kuo (cyberspace).

5d), Chinese and Hindi-Urdu differ markedly in the extent to which the vector in and of itself expresses the *telos* of an action.

4c. In Hindi-Urdu the compound versus non-compound alternation is suppressed in the phasal verb construction. Complements of verbs of phase (*V-ne lag-* 'begin to V', *V-taa rah-* 'keep V-ing', 'continue to V', *V-naa choR-* 'stop V-ing') cannot appear in compound form:

(20)	***mazduurõ-ne***	***divaar***	***gir-aa***	***dii***
	workers-Erg	wall	fall-Caus	GAVE

'The workers knocked down the wall.'

(21)	*mazduur*	*divaar*	***gir-aa***	***(*de)***	***-ne***	*lage*
	workers	wall	fall-Caus	GIVE	-Inf	began

'The workers began to knock down the wall.'

In Chinese depending on the class of the main verb phasal meaning is managed in various ways. With Activity and Ektelic[14] verbs the "change-of-status" particle *le* or vectors[15] are used to indicate phase. However, with verbs of Accomplishment full phasal predicates (eg., *kāishǐ* 'begin to V') may be used:

(22)	*gōng.rén*	***zá***	***dǎo***	*le*	*qiáng*
	workers	knock	FALL	Pfv	wall

'The workers knocked down the wall.'

(23)	*gōng.rén*	*kāi.shǐ*	***zá***	***(*dǎo)***	*qiáng*
	workers	begin	knock	FALL	wall

'The workers began to knock down the wall.'

If one thinks of the compound form of an Accomplishment verb as expressing an inherently complex situation comprised of two-phases, a prefatory Activity followed by the Achievement of a new State, then it follows that phasal verbs like *lag* and *kāishǐ* 'begin' may select only that

---

[14] Ektelic verbs are those whose *telos* or limit precedes (rather than follows a prefatory) activity: *flee, leave (behind), keep,* etc. Karen Ebert (p.c.) suggests "initiotransformative".

[15] For instance, the two-part lexicalized sequence *xià-qù* DESCEND, GO DOWN may be used with Activities in the sense of 'continue':

(a)	*nǐ*	*shuō*	***xià***	*qù*	'Go on talking!'
	you	speak	DOWN	GO	(from Teng 1977: 21)

part of the compound verb that most clearly refers to the prefatory Activity. For this reason phasal verbs, refusing compound verbs as infinitival complements, take their non-compound counterparts instead.

4d. In Hindi-Urdu there is a marked (if not absolute) preference for CV's in clauses that are complements of the conjunction *jab tak* 'until':

(24)	*yahãã*	*tab-tak*	*ruko*	*jab-tak*	*vo*	*darvaazaa*
	here	then-till	stop	when-until	they	Door
	khol	*na*	***dẽ***			
	open	not	GIVE			

'Wait here until they open the door.'

In Chinese the facts are more nuanced: Both compound and non-compound are possible depending on the situation. In (25a) the door-openers have yet to arrive. In (25b) they are present but have not yet succeeded in opening the door:

(25a)	*děng*	*zài*	*zhèr*	*zhí.dào*	*tā.men*	***kāi***	*mén*
	wait	at	here	until	they	open	door

'Wait here until they (come and) open the door.'

(25b)	*děng*	*zài*	*zhèr*	*zhí.dào*	*tā.men*	***kāi***	***kāi***
	wait	at	here	until	they	open	OPEN
	mén						
	door						

'Wait here until they open the door.'

4e. In both Hindi-Urdu and Chinese complements of expressions of fear and anxiety prefer use of Vv's:

(26a)	*ham*	*Dar-rahe the*	*kahĩĩ*	*qaidii*	***bhaag***	*na*	***jaa.e***
	we	fear-ing were	lest	prisoner	flee	not	GO

'We were afraid the prisoner might escape.'

(26b)	*wǒ.men*	*pà*	*nà.ge*	*fàn.rén*	*huì*	***táo***	***zǒu***
	we	fear	lest	prisoner	could	flee	MOVE[16]

'We were afraid the prisoner might escape.'

Expressions of fear seem to focus attention on the (unwanted) results of action. This may explain the preference encountered for a CV in negative (as opposed to positive) imperatives and warnings:

(27a)	*bié*	*bǎ*	*qiáng*	***zá***	***dǎo***	*le*
	don't	Acc	wall	knock	FALL	Pfv

'(Make sure you) don't knock down the wall!'

(27b)	*bǎ*	*qiáng*	***zá***	*le*
	Acc	wall	knock	Pfv

'Knock down the wall!'

The data in both these subsections (4d and 4e) indicate that the alternation of compound with non-compound verb in both Hindi-Urdu and Chinese has acquired at least some ability to express aspectual contrast of the "view-point" sort. Compare the reactances of perfective vs. non-perfective forms to the corresponding environments in Russian (Forsyth 1970: 259; Rassudova 1984: 174-75, 190-92; Hook 2001: 112).

5. Ways in which the Hindi-Urdu and Chinese verb-verb sequences differ

5a. The vector verbs in Hindi-Urdu are highly grammaticalized; those of Chinese, less so. At times the elements in a Chinese Vv sequence express sequential components of a complex action (28); at other times they express synchronous components (29):

(28)	*gōngrén*	*bǎ*	*qiáng*	***zá***	***dǎo***	*le*
	workers	Acc	wall	knock	FALL	Pfv

'The workers knocked down the wall!'

---

[16] Notice the dispreference for the compound verb in the negative counterpart of (26b):

(a)	*wǒ.men*	*pà*	*nà.ge*	*fàn.rén*	*bú*	*(huì)*	*táo*
	we	fear	lest	prisoner	not	could	flee

'We were afraid the prisoner might not escape.' [i.e. We wanted him to escape.]

(29)	*tā*	*cóng*	*chē.zhàn*	***zǒu***	***kāi***	*le*
	he	from	station	walk	OPEN	Pfv

'He walked away from the station.' (Teng 1977: 12)

Clearly componential compound verbs are also found in Hindi-Urdu:

(30)	*dhaniyaa-ko*	*to*	*vo*	*zabardastii*	***khĩĩc***	***laa***
	Dhaniya-Dat	Topic	he	by.force	pull	BRING
	saktaa-hai					
	can-3sgPres					

'… but Dhaniya he can drag (here) by force.' (*Godan* 47.41)

However, their frequency of occurrence is lower than it is in Chinese.

5b. Phrasal constituents may interrupt the components of a compound verb in Chinese (with vectors *lái* COME and *qù* GO):

(31)	*tā*	***qí***	*dān.chē*	***lái***
	he	ride	bicycle	COME

'He rides a bike (in this direction).'

(32)	*zǒu*	***jìn***	*jiào.shì*	***lái***
	walk	enter	classroom	COME

'Enter the classroom.' (from Lu 1984: 84)

In Hindi-Urdu only adverbial particles like *hii* 'only; indeed', *bhii* 'also, even', *to* (concession), *na* or *nahII* 'not', *hii kyõ na* 'why not just', and the like may separate a main verb from its vector.

(33)	*aur*	***le***	*bhii*	***lũũ***	*to*	*ghar.vaalii*
	and	take	even	TAKE.Sbjnc	then	Wife
	mujhe	*jiitaa*	*choR-egii ?*			
	me	alive	leave-Fut			

(*Godan* 206.26)

'And even if I did take it, would my wife leave me in peace?'

Unlike in Chinese[17], full nouns or other lexical phrases in Hindi-Urdu rarely if ever intervene.

5c. Perhaps as a consequence of being less grammaticalized, the vector verbs of Chinese are much more numerous than those of Hindi-Urdu. Even setting aside the quasi-adjectival vectors like *hǎo* 'GOOD' (whose functions and reactances are similar to the more clearly verbal vectors like *zǒu* 'MOVE') the list is longer than Hindi-Urdu's. (See appendices A & B.) Less grammaticalized vectors harmonizing more closely with the meanings of their main verbs necessarily occur with more limited sets of them. For example, in Hindi-Urdu the vector *le* TAKE occurs with centripetal main verbs belonging to a number of different subsets: verbs of perception (*dekh* 'look; see', *sun* 'listen; hear', etc.); verbs of consumption (*khaa* 'eat', *pii* 'drink', etc.), verbs of mental action (*soc* 'think', *samajh* 'understand', etc.), and prehension (*pakaR* 'catch', *chiin* 'snatch', etc.). In Chinese for each one of these subsets there is a different vector, one that is more complexly and specifically linked with the main verbs in the set:

(34) ***tā kàn jiàn le yì-zhī dà.xiàng (*diào***
he look SEE Pfv one-MW elephant DROP

dào *zhù)
ARRIVE STAY[18]

'He saw an elephant.'

(35) ***tā hē diào le yì-píng jiǔ (*jiàn***
he drink DROP Pfv one-MW wine SEE

[dm]dào *zhù)
ARRIVE[19] STAY

'She drank up a whole bottle of wine.'

(36) ***tā rèn.shì dào nà-ge wèn.tí (*jiàn***
he recognize ARRIVE that-MW problem SEE

****diào *zhù)***
DROP STAY

'He came to recognize the problem.'

---

[17] Different classes of V-v sequences in Chinese have different degrees of separability.

[18] This vector does occur with *kān* (note the different tone) in the sense of 'guard'.

[19] The superscript "dm" indicates a 'different meaning'. The sequence *hē dào* means something like 'managed to find a way to drink'. This might be said of someone who found a source of alcohol in, say, Arabia.

(37)	*bǎ*	*qì.chē*	***tíng***	***zhù***	***(*jiàn***	****diào***	***^{dm}dào)***[20]
	Acc	car	stop	STAY	SEE	DROP	ARRIVE

'Stop that car!'

Unlike Hindi-Urdu's *le* TAKE, in Chinese there is no single general vector which can be used with all the members of these four subsets[21].

5d. Vector verbs in Mandarin can be negated independently of main verbs. Not so in Hindi:

(38)	*wǒ.men*	***shēng***	*bù*	***zháo***	*huǒ*
	we	light	Neg	ATTACH	fire

'We (try to) light the fire but it won't light.'

(39)	*ham*	*aag*	*nahĩĩ*	***lag-aa-***	***(*de-)***	-te	hãĩ
	we	fire	Neg	light-Caus	GIVE	Habitual	Pres

'We don't light the fire.'

To express lack of success despite effort Hindi-Urdu uses a very different construction in which a transitive expresses the attempt and the corresponding intransitive is negated to express failure:

(40)	*ishq*	*hai*	*vo*	*aatish*	*ki*	***lagaa-e***	*na*	***lage***
	love	is	that	fire	that	light-PP	not	lights

'Love ... is ... the fire ... that doesn't light no matter how hard you (try to) light it ...' (Ghalib)

The reason that the construction in (40) is the one that compares[22] more closely with the use of Vv's to express incapacity in Chinese is that it clearly divides the action of lighting a fire into two parts: (1) the activity of the agent, and (2) its result. The construction in (38) and the

---

[20] With *dào* the sense *of tíng* shifts to 'park' and requires a location phrase as its complement.

[21] The subsets themselves are internally coherent vis-à-vis vector choice: 1. *tīng jiàn* 'hear', *qiáo jiàn* 'stare at'; 2. *chī diào* 'eat up', *yòng diào* 'use up'; 3. *xiǎng dào* 'think of', *zhù.yì dào* 'notice'; 4. *dǎi zhù* 'capture', *wò zhù* 'clutch', etc.

[22] See discussion of Thai and Mandarin "success verbs" in Thepkanjana and Uehara (2004a, section 3).

one in (40) allow the negative particle to apply to just that second component of the action, in effect to single it out for negation, whereas the vector in the Hindi-Urdu compound verb [see (39)], while it does express completeness in the representation of a complex action, does not itself express a discrete element or component of that action. Hence, it cannot be separately negated.

5e. Unlike in Hindi-Urdu where there is normally harmony in the valency of main and vector in a compound verb, in Chinese the vector is almost always intransitive. (See Liu 2003, section 5.2). While the intransitive main verbs in both languages take intransitive vectors, transitive main verbs in Hindi-Urdu (*phẽk* 'throw', *uThaa* 'pick up', *dekh* 'look', *bec* 'sell', *bataa* 'tell', etc.) commonly take one or the other of two transitive vectors: *le* TAKE (for reflexive or centripetal action: see section 5c) or *de* GIVE (with other polyvalent main verbs). Transitive main verbs in Chinese take intransitive vectors (with the exception of those taking *jiàn* SEE; MEET). Contrast and compare (41) with (42):

(41)	*jhuniyaa-ne*	*Topii*	*utaar-kar*	*phẽk*	***dii***
	Jhuniya-Erg	cap	doff-CP	throw	GAVE

'Jhuniya took off her cap and threw it away.' (*Godan* 210.17)

(42)	*bǎ*	*mào.zi*	*tuō.le*	*rán.hòu*	***rēng***	***diào***	*le*
	Acc	hat	doffed	then	throw	DROP	Pfv

'(She) took off her hat and threw it away.'

In (41) the outward orientation of the subject's action determines the choice of the vector *de*. In (42) the choice of the intransitive *diào* DROP as vector reflects the motion imparted to the object of main verb *rēng*. Thus, while the subject of the vector verb in Hindi-Urdu is the same as the subject of the main verb, the subject of the vector verb in Chinese is usually the object of the main verb (assuming the main verb is transitive). If intransitive vectors are used with transitive main verbs in Hindi-Urdu, they refer either to the situation as a whole or to the subject. They never refer to the object. Thus, in (43) if the vector *gayaa* WENT indicates any actual physical displacement at all[23], it is the motion of the subject *vo* 'he', not that of *asar* 'impression':

---

[23] The vector *jaa* GO when used with transitive main verbs may indicate a psychological rather than a physical movement. But even so the psychological movement is presented as something pertaining to or having its source in the subject, not the object.

(43)	*horii*	*par*	*na miTnevaalaa*	**asar**	*choR*	***gayaa***
	Hori	on	Neg erasable	impression	leave	WENT

'(He) left an indelible impression on Hori.' (*Godan* 356.05)

This may be the most important difference between the Hindi-Urdu and the Chinese compound verb. In Hindi-Urdu the vector acts as a kind of semantic diacritic on the situation represented by the clause as a whole. In Chinese the scope of the vector is narrower: It denotes a conceptually distinct component of a complex situation or event, one which usually follows temporally and logically as a consequence or result of the action denoted by the main verb.

By this difference not only is South Asia distinguished from China but Northeast Asia and most of Central Asia are, too. Note the transitive vectors *de* and *kure,* homophonous with full verbs meaning 'give' in Hindi-Urdu (44) and Japanese (45), versus the intransitive *chū* and *chut* EMERGE in the corresponding Mandarin (46) and Cantonese (47):

(44)	*us-ne*	*apnii*	*qaabiliyat*	dikhaa	***dii***
	she-Erg	his	ability	show	GAVE

'She showed her ability.'

(45)	sukoshi	*yuuki-o*	***mise-te***	***kure[24]-ta***
	a.little	courage-Acc	show-CP	GIVE-Pst

'(He) showed a little courage.'

(46)	*tā*	*xiǎn.shì*	***chū***	le	*qiánlì*
	he	reveal	EMERGE	Pfv	potential

'He showed his potential.

(47)	*ta*	*him.shì*	***chut***	liao	*chim.le*
	he	reveal	EMERGE	Pfv	potential

'He showed his potential.

(Cantonese[25] of Heng Xian village, Zhuang-zu)

[24] Using *kure* implies the beneficiary is the first person or belongs to the "inner" group.
[25] Thanks to Mr. Teng-pong Liang for the Cantonese data.

The CVs in (44) and (45) may be said to exhibit 'componential valency harmony'. Those in (46) and (47) do not[26] have valency harmony.

Text counts of Premchand's novel *Godān* show that in Hindi-Urdu compound verbs over 90% of transitive main verbs are accompanied by etymologically transitive vectors; whereas a count of Vv sequences in a text in Mandarin (Lü 1999) shows at most 25% of transitive main verbs are followed by transitive vectors. Even among that 25% most of the transitive vectors are labile items such as *kāi* OPEN, whose etymological sources are indeterminate with respect to their inherent valency.

The abstract structure[27] of the Chinese Vv or compound verb is different from its South, Central, Northwest, and Northeast Asian counterparts. It is a reduction or compression of a two-clause structure:

(48) X did J to Y and Y K'ed. => X, Y (J) > Y (K)
[where J is the cause of K and K is a (plausible) effect of J]

This structural compression allows Chinese to render certain situations more succinctly than languages in South, Central, Northwest,

---

[26] Is *chū* in these examples really intransitive? It is essential to our demonstration of the syntactic difference between Hindi and Chinese compound verbs to establish that vectors like *chū* correspond not to a transitive, but to an intransitive main verb. While *chū* as a main verb does have some transitive uses they are limited to fixed expressions such as *chū shū* 'publish', *chū chéng.guǒ* 'produce results', *chū lì* 'contribute energy', *chū qián* 'provide the money', etc., or to clauses in which the subject is a (promoted or "ascended") location or experiencer of an emergent event but not its agent:

(a) *haí.zi chū má.zhěn le*
child emerge measles CS

'The child came down with measles.'

chū in (46) does not belong to either of these two sets of non-canonically transitive uses:

(b) * *ta chū qiánlì.*
he emerge potential

'He has potential.'

There is no fixed expression *chū qiánlì* 'have potential' nor can the subject of (b) be interpreted as the non-agentive location or source of potential. We are grateful to Colin Masica for calling our attention to the need to demonstrate the basic valency of *chū*.

[27] If we adopt the concept and terminology of the "syntactic pivot" (Dixon 1994, Bickel 2004), we can characterize the difference succinctly: In the languages of South Asia the vector verb operates on a Subject-Agent (or "nominative") pivot while in Chinese its pivot is Subject-Object ("absolutive"). The only exception in the languages of South Asia are the "vector adverbs" of southern Rajasthan and eastern Sind which (as far as gender and number agreement is concerned) operate on a Subject-Object pivot. See fn 34 below.

and Northeast Asia can. Contrast the brevity of *yǎo sǐ* in (49)[28] and *qí sǐ* in (51) with their lengthier (and heavier) Avar and Hindi counterparts *`xánc`un ch`wan réxxana* in (50) and *dauRaa-ke maar Daalaa* in (52):

(49)	*lǎo.hǔ*	***yǎo***	***sǐ***	*le*	*tā*
	tiger	bite	die	Pfv	him

'The tiger bit and killed him.'

(50)	*`gázhdarahay-all'*	***`xánc`-un***	***ch`wa-n***	***réxx-ana***
	dragon-Erg	bite-CP	kill-CP	THROW-Pst

'The dragon bit (him) and killed (him).' (Charachidze 1981: 192)

(51)	*tā*	***qí***	***sǐ***	*le*	*mǎ*
	he	ride	DIE	Pfv	horse

'He rode the horse to death[29].' (Li 1990)

(52)	*raaste-bhar*	***dauR-aa-ke***	***maar***	***Daalaa*** . . .
	road-full	run-Caus-CP	kill	THROW.Pst

'(You've) / run me to death… // run me ragged…/' (*Godan* 87.11)

When X = Y (ie, where J is a non-stative intransitive verb) the schema in (48) reduces to a structure that looks like it is parallel to the compound verb of the non-Chinese type:

(53) X did J (to itself) and K'ed => X (J > K)
[where J is the cause of K and K is a (plausible) effect of J]

---

[28] Dumi, a Kiranti language spoken in eastern Nepal, has a similar construction but one which, owing to Dumi's complex systems of agreement, reveals its biclausal identity more clearly than its Mandarin counterparts. Compare (a) with (49) and (51):

(a)	*ımma-?a*	*hammıl*	***sid-ini-ka***	*ham-**mits-a***
	beer-Erg	they.Nom	intoxicate-2/3Pl-CP	3Pl-die-2/3

'The beer got them roaring drunk.' (from Driem 1993: 228; glossing normalized)

[29] In its idiomatic meaning of 'excessively' vector *si* DIE is one of the few in Chinese able to modify either the object or the subject. Thus, according to Li (1990), the sequence *qí sǐ le mǎ* in (51) can also mean that the horse's rider has ridden himself 'to death'.

In Mandarin the presence of a vector even has the power to increase valency:

(54) X (J) > K (Y) => X did J and Y K'ed => X, Y (J) > Y (K)
[where J and K are lexically intransitive]

In comparing lexical intransitive *lèi* 'get tired' in (55) with its contextually transitive counterpart in (56) notice the two sentences[30] are identical except for the presence in (56) of the vector *sǐ* DIE:

(55)	*tā*	***lèi***	*(*wǒ)*	*le*
	he	tire	(me)	Pfv

'He got tired.' [Including *wǒ* does not yield the meaning 'He tired me.']

(56)	*tā*	***lèi***	***sǐ***	*wǒ*	*le*
	he	tire	DIE	me	Pfv

'He tired me to death.' [See (54) and compare (56) with (49) and (51).]

In no South Asian language does the presence of an intransitive vector verb have the ability (through a kind of "inverse operation"[31]) to induce an increase in the valency of an intransitive main verb. Nor, given the absence in South Asia of models like those in (49) and (51), should we expect to encounter analogical extensions of them like the one seen in (56).

6. Macrolinguistic areas in Asia

In his most recent study, Masica poses the question: "...are the 'resultative' verbs of Chinese, Thai, Burmese, etc., essentially the same phenomenon as the explicator verbs of South Asia?" (2001: 250). If we consider only intransitive verb + intransitive verb combinations, as in examples (9a) through (12), there seems to be no reason not to regard them as representing a single phenomenon that has diffused throughout South, Central, Northwest, Northeast, East, and non-Malay Southeast Asia (as indicated by Masica in Figure 11 of his 2001 paper: see Appendix D). However, when we examine verb-verb combinations that

[30] See Chang (1998: 83) for further discussion of this kind of alternation in valency.
[31] See Harris (1968: 95-99) for the notion of the "inverse operation".

involve transitive main verbs we find distinct differences in syntax and semantics that divide East and Southeast Asia from South, Central, Northwest, and Northeast Asia: The East and Southeast Asia group as a rule have transitive-intransitive sequences (Thepkanjana and Uehara, 2004b); the South, Central, Northwest, Northeast group, as a rule do not. Furthermore, one or two exceptions apart, languages in East and Southeast Asia do not have transitive-transitive sequences; whereas in South, Central, Northwest, and Northeast Asia transitive main verbs are normally followed by transitive vectors.

This line of division corresponds closely to the VO versus OV isogloss that separates the same areas from South, Central, Northwest, and Northeast Asia. In other parts of the world verb-verb sequences of the South Asian type are associated with OV languages like Quichua (Hook 1987) while those of the Chinese (and Southeast Asian) type are found in Atlantic Creoles (Schiller 1995) and VO languages spoken in West Africa (Crowley 2002). Of special interest are Sino-Tibetan languages like Lahu and Karen which find themselves on the western side of the OV/VO typological divide and exhibit both kinds of verb-verb sequences simultaneously:

(57)	*nga*^{21}*.hi*[32]	*ga*	*qo?*^{21}	***chi***^{54}	***to?***^{54}	***pi***^{54}	*ve*
	we	must	again	lift	EMERGE	GIVE	Indic

'We had to lift (it) out again for (them).'

(Lahu, Matisoff 1973: 200)

The line separating VO languages to the east from OV languages to the west runs near the Myanmar-Thai border. Although Lahu belongs to the Sino-Tibetan language family, most of whose non-Tibetan members are (or were) VO, it is spoken in an area lying to the west of the OV/VO isogloss and is now itself an OV language (Matisoff 1973: 40). However, it retains remnant features of word order more typical of VO languages, such as the preverbal placements of the modals *ga* 'must' and *qo?*^{21} '(do) again' that are visible in (57). Lahu also retains the Sinitic kind of compound verb in which a transitive primary (such as *chi*^{54} 'lift') is followed by an intransitive secondary (*to?*^{54} 'emerge') which modifies the object rather than the subject of the clause. In fact, except for the absence of any component answering to Lahu's vector *pi*^{54}, the order of verbal elements in (57) is identical to the order that is found in the corresponding Mandarin sequence *deǐ zài qǔ chū*:

[32] Matisoff's transcription of Lahu data has been modified for typographical convenience. The double numbers represent tonal distinctions based on a five-part range. See Matisoff (1973: 22) for definition and discussion.

(58)	*wǒ.men*	*deǐ*	*(weì*	*bìng.rén)*	*zài*	***qǔ***
	we	must	for	patient	again	Extract
	chū		*(yí-ge*	*zhǒng.liú)*		
	EMERGE		(one	tumor)		

'We have to take (the tumor) out again (for the patient).'

In (57) Lahu differs from Mandarin in its addition of the "South Asian" style vector *pi*[54] 'GIVE' which has closer parallels in Hindi-Urdu and other languages of South Asia than it does in Mandarin[33]:

(59)	*hamẽ*	*tyuumar*	*phir.se*	***nikaal***	***de-****naa*	*paRegaa*
	us.Dat	tumor	again	extract	GIVE-Inf	must.Fut

'We'll have to remove the tumor again.'

Our conclusion, then, is that Masica (1976) with its categorization of East and Southeast Asian verb-verb sequences as distinct from those of South[34], Central, and Northeast Asian, adheres more closely to the typological and geographical facts, and is preferable to Masica (2001). Indeed, Masica's earlier view accommodates (and is supported by) the co-existence of the two kinds of verb-verb sequences observed in the border area between South and Southeast Asia in languages like Lahu and Karen (Solnit 1997).

---

[33] Mandarin and other forms of Chinese do have a grammaticalized form of a main verb GIVE, but like *bǎ* HOLD, *zài* BE AT (a place), and other "coverbs", this form is used as a preposition, not as an auxiliary verb:

(a)	*tā*	***geǐ***	*wǒ*	*dǎ*	*le*	*yí.ge*	*diàn.huà*
	he	GIVE	me	strike	Pfv	a	telephone

'He made a phone call **for me**.'

[34] In the pattern of their agreement the "absolutive adverbs" of southern Rajasthan and eastern Sind are an exception. Concord is either with the intransitive subject or with the transitive object in all tenses and moods. [See Hook & Chauhan (1988).]

(a)	*uena*	***tehsan***	*pug-aaw*	***ri***	from Ashok Kumar,
	her.Dat	station	arrive-Caus	AWAY.FemSg	Thar Parkar, Sind

'Deliver her to the station.' (from Hook's 1989 field notes on Thari, aka Dhatki)

7. Relativizing linguistic areas

The Indo-Turanian Linguistic Area proposed in Masica (1976) is to our knowledge the largest one ever proposed (unless we take the discussion and charts in Masica (2001) as the basis for an even larger one incorporating China and Southeast Asia). Since bilinguals operating in a bilingual or multilingual environment are regarded as providing the mechanism for the creation of linguistic areas, we must assume that the Indo-Turanian Linguistic Area (if it is a linguistic area) is the result of chains of bilingual encounters affecting the structures of a broad mosaic of different languages over a period of many thousands of years. In the absence of direct contact between Japanese and Marathas or between Koreans and Tamils, we must suppose the convergence between the languages of South Asia and Northeast Asia to have been mediated by the diffusion of linguistic features along the links of smaller chains of social, political, and economic relations lasting over enormous spans of space and time. This network of change would have to persist despite the presence of competing networks radiating from different directions. The more extended these supposed chains are, the more fragile they become; and the more susceptible to influence (or interruption) from new sets of social, political, and economic relationships with speakers of typologically different languages, relationships that over such long periods of time and enormous distances must inevitably emerge. In this particular instance, we are confronted with groups of languages having different holistic typologies: the OV languages of South, Central, Northwest, and Northeast Asia (as well as Myanmar) and the VO languages of East and Southeast Asia. By merging differing kinds of Vv sequences into a single type, Masica's 2001 chart makes it more difficult to identify and understand the ways in which languages of divergent typologies have interacted and, by further inflating an already mammoth linguistic area, makes it less likely that it actually is a linguistic area in the full historical and sociolinguistic sense of the term[35].

References

Abbi, Anvita. 2004. The typology of 'manner' in verb sequences in South Asian languages. *Indian Linguistics* 65: 1-29.

Bhandari, Mannu. 1979. *aap kaa baNTii*. 4th edition. New Delhi: Akshar Prakashan.

Bhaskararao, P., and K. V. Subbarao, Eds. *South Asia yearbook 2001: Papers from the*

---

[35] While the co-authors of this paper have exchanged views with Masica on its contents and the conclusions it reaches, many areas of disagreement remain: "...one would expect there to be differences in origin of converging constructions where the underlying syntax is different." (personal communication). We are grateful to him, to Timur Maisak, and to Karen Ebert for their careful reading and comments. The usual disclaimers apply.

symposium on South Asian languages: contact, convergence and typology. Delhi: SAGE Publications.

Bickel, Balthasar. 2004. Syntax of experiencers in the Himalayas. In Bhaskararao & Subbarao, Eds. *Non-nominative Subjects.* Amsterdam: J. Benjamins. pp. 77-111.

Butt, Miriam. 2003. *The Light Verb Jungle.* In G. Aygen, C. Bowern, and C. Quinn (eds.) *Harvard Working Papers in Linguistics, Volume 9: Papers from the GSAS / Dudley House Workshop on Light Verbs.* pp. 1-49.

Butt, Miriam, and Biljana Scott. 2002. *Structuring events: The role of light verbs and directionals.* Paper presented at the Autumn 2002 Meeting of the Linguistics Association of Great Britain, University of Manchester.

Butt, Miriam, and Wilhelm Geuder. 2003. Light Verbs in Urdu and Grammaticalisation. In Eckardt et al. (eds). pp. 295-350

Chan, Alice Yin Wa. 2002. Syntactic structure of Chinese serial verb construction. *Journal of Chinese Linguistics* 30: 16-38.

Chang, Claire Hsun-huei. 1998. V-V compounds in Mandarin Chinese. In Packard, Ed. pp. 77-102.

Charachidze, Georges. 1981. *Grammaire de la langue avar* . Éditions Jean-Favard.

Crowley, Terry. 2002. *Serial verbs in oceanic: a descriptive typology.* Oxford University Press.

Dixon, R. M. W. 1994. *Ergativity.* Cambridge University Press.

Dowty, David. 1979. *Word meaning and Montague Grammar: the semantics of verbs and times...* Dordrecht: Reidel.

Driem, George van. 1992. *The Grammar of Dzongkha* Thimphu: Dzongkha Development Commission.

_______. 1987. *A Grammar of Limbu.* Berlin and New York: Mouton.

_______. 1993. *A Grammar of Dumi.* Berlin and New York: Mouton.

Ebert, Karen H. MS. *Functions of compound verbs in Kiranti languages.*

Eckardt, Regine, Klaus van Heusinger & Christoph Schwarze (eds): 2003. *Words in Time. Diachronic Semantics from Different Points of View.* Berlin: Mouton.

Forsyth, James. 1970. *A grammar of aspect: usage and meaning in the Russian verb.* Cambridge: Cambridge University Press.

Grierson, George A., Ed. 1919. *Linguistic survey of India.* Govt. of India. (1967-68 MLBD reprint.)

Harris, Zellig. 1968. *Mathematical structures of language.* New York: Interscience Publishers.

Hook, Peter E. 2001. Where do compound verbs come from? And where are they going? In Bhaskararao and Subbarao, Eds. pp. 101-30.

_______. 1987. Linguistic areas: getting at the grain of history. In *Festschrift for Henry Hoenigswald, on the occasion of his seventieth birthday.* George Cardona and N. H. Zide, Eds. Tuebingen: Gunter Narr Verlag. 155-168. Reprinted in *International Journal of Dravidian Linguistics* 16: 220-237.

_______. 1974. *The compound verb in Hindi.* Ann Arbor: University of Michigan, South & Southeast Asian Studies.

Hook, Peter E., and M. M. Chauhan. 1988. The Perfective Adverb in Bhitrauti. In *WORD* 39, 3: 177-186.

Joseph, B., and A. Zwicky. 1990. *When verbs collide: Papers from the 1990 Ohio State Mini-Conference on Serial Verbs.* Columbus: Ohio State University.

Kang, Seung-man. A comparative analysis of SVCs and Korean V-Vs. http://fccl.ksu.ru/issue001/conf_gen.97/kang.pdf

Lefebvre, C. (Ed). 1991. *Serial verbs: grammatical, comparative and cognitive approaches* Amsterdam: J. Benjamins.

Liang, H-h. MS. *The directional verb in Mandarin Chinese.*

Li, C., and S. A. Thompson. 1981. *Mandarin Chinese: A functional reference grammar*. Berkeley: University of California Press.

Li, Yafei. 1990. On V-V compounds in Chinese. *Natural language and linguistic theory* 8: 177-207.

Liu, Haiyong. 2003. *Complex predicates in Mandarin Chinese: three types of* bu-yu *structures.* UCLA PhD dissertation.

Lu, Jianji. 1984. Directional complement: A pedagogical view. *Journal of Chinese Language Teachers' Association* 19: 79-94.

Lu, John H-T. 1977. Resultative verb compounds vs. directional verb compounds in Mandarin. *Journal of Chinese Linguistics* 5: 274-313.

Lü, Xiao-xin. 1999. *mào nián yì wǎng (Recalling the past while in my eighties).* Taiwan: published by the author.

Maisak, Timur. 2003. *Auxiliary verbs as perfectivizing devices.* Presented at ALT-V Conference, Cagliari (Sardegna).

______. 1999. Multiple periphrastic perfectives: Another case of "bounder perfectivization" In *Language Typology: Proceedings of Electronic Conference.* At http://fccl.ksu.ru/winter.99/lang_typ/ogl.htm.

Masica, Colin P. 2001. The definition and significance of linguistic areas. In Bhaskararao & Subbarao, Eds. pp. 205-67.

______. 1976. *Defining a linguistic area: South Asia.* University of Chicago Press.

Matisoff, James. 1973. *The grammar of Lahu.* Berkeley: University of California Press.

Merlan, F. C. 1994. *A grammar of Wardaman.* Berlin: Mouton de Gruyter.

Mizutani, Osamu and Nobuko. 1977. *An introduction to Modern Japanese*. Tokyo: Japan Times.

Packard, Jerome L., Ed. 1998. *New approaches to Chinese word formation.* Berlin: Mouton de Gruyter.

Pederson, Eric. In Press. Event realization in Tamil. In M. Bowerman and P. Brown, Eds. *Crosslinguistic perspectives on argument structure: Implications for learnability.* Mahwah, NJ: Lawrence Erlbaum.

Pořízka, Vincenc. 1967-69. On the perfective verbal aspect in Hindi. *Archív orientálni* 35: 64-88, 208-231; 36: 233-251; 37: 19-47, 345-364.

Premchand. 1936. *godaan (Gift of a cow).* Allahabad: Saraswati Press.

Rassudova, O. P., 1984. *Aspectual usage in modern Russian.* Moscow: Russkij Jazyk.

Read, A. F. C. 1934. *Balti grammar.* London: Royal Asiatic Society.

Ross, Claudia. 1990. Resultative Verb Compounds. *Journal of the Chinese Language Teachers Association* 25: 61-83.

Schiller, Eric. 1989. On the phrase structure of serial verb constructions. *CLS 25.*

Scott, Biljana. 1996. *Aspectogenesis and the Categorisation of Directionals in Chinese.* Oxford University PhD diss.

Soh, Hooi Ling, and Jenny Yi-Chun Kuo. *Perfective aspect and accomplishment situations in Mandarin Chinese*. Cyberspace: USC Chinese linguistics website.

Solnit, David. 1997. *Eastern Kayah Li: Grammar, texts, glossary.* Honolulu: University of Hawai'i Press.

Suh, Yongwhan. 2000. Study of the auxiliary verb construction and verb serialization in Korean. Seoul: Hankuk.

Tekin, Talât. 1968. *A grammar of Orkhon Turkic.* Bloomington: Indiana University.

Teng, Shou-hsin. 1977. A grammar of verb particles in Chinese. *Journal of Chinese linguistics.* 5: 1-25.

Thepkanjana, K., and S. Uehara. 2004a. Grammaticalization of Directional Verbs into Success Markers in Thai. *CLS 38* (proceedings of the main session). Chicago Linguistic Society. pp. 649-664.

______. 2004b. Semantic types of resultative predicate in transitive-based resultative constructions in Thai. In Somsonge Burusphat (ed.), *SEALS 11*: 731-747.

Tempe: Program for SE Asian Studies, Arizona State University.

Thompson, S. 1973. Resultative verb compounds in Chinese: A case for lexical rules. *Language* 49: 361-79.

Van Valin, Robert. 1990. Semantic parameters of split intransitivity. *Language* 66: 221-260.

Wang, Chun-Chih. *Delimitation: evidence from Mandarin.* Cyberia: USC Chinese Linguistics Website.

Wilson, Stephen. 1999. *Coverbs and complex predicates in Wagiman.* Stanford: CSLI

Xing, Zhiqun. 2003. Grammaticalization of verbs in Mandarin Chinese. *Journal of Chinese Linguistics* 31: 101-144.

Appendix A: Table of Chinese vectors with glosses (in caps) of their lexical sources and examples of them used concretely and then more abstractly.

vector	gloss						
qù	GO	*shū*	*nǐ*	*kě.yǐ*	*ná*	***qù***	
		book	you	may	take	go	
		'You may take (away) the book.'					
	abstract	*yù.suàn*	*jiǎn*	***qù***	*le*	*yí-bàn*	
		budget	shrink	GO	Pfv	one-half	
		'The budget was cut in half.'					
lái	COME	*qǐng*	*kuài*	*huí*	***lái***		
		please	fast	return	come		
		'Please hurry back (here).'					
	abstract	*kàn*	***lái***	*wèn.tí*	*bú*	*dà*	
		look	COME	problem	not	big	
		'It seems not to be much of a problem.'					
dǎo	FALL	*shù*	*beì*	*chuī*	***dǎo***	*le*	
		tree	Pass	blow	fall	Pfv	
		'The tree was blown down.'					
	abstract	*nǐ*	*nán*	***dǎo***	*wǒ*	*le*	
		you	difficult	FALL	me	Pfv	
		'You've stumped me (with that one).'					

diào	DROP (intr)	*bǎ*	*jiù*	*bào.zhǐ*	*rēng*	***diào***
		Acc	old	newspaper	throw	drop

'Throw away the old newspapers.'

	abstract	*niú.naǐ*	*yǐ.jīng*	*huài*	***diào***	*le*
		milk	already	spoil	DROP	Pfv

'The milk's already gone bad.'

kāi	OPEN (intr)	*tā*	*qīng.qīng.de*	*tuī*	***kāi***	*mén*
		she	quietly	push	open	door

'She quietly pushed the door open.'

	abstract	*qǐng*	*ràng*	***kāi***
		please	yield	OPEN

'Please move over.'

xià	DESCEND	*tā*	*fàng*	***xià***	*bào.zhǐ*
		he	put	descend	newspaper

'He put down the newspaper.'

	abstract	*qǐng*	*liú*	***xià***	*nǐ.de*	*dì.zhǐ*
		please	leave	DESCEND	your	address

'Please leave your address.'

zǒu	MOVE (intr)	*tā*	*bǎ*	*hái.zi*	*dài*	***zǒu***	*le*
		she	Acc	child	take	move	Pfv

'She led the child away.'

	abstract	*wǒ*	*cāi*	***zǒu***	*le*	*nǐ.de*	*dá.àn*
		I	guess	**MOVE**	Pfv	your	answer

'Ha, ha! I guessed your answer!'

dào	ARRIVE	*qiú*	*dǎ*	***dào***	*wǒ.de*	*tóu*
		ball	hit	arrive	my	head

'The ball hit me on the head.'

abstract	*SARS*	*yǐng.xiǎng*	***dào***	*lǚ.yóu*	*yè*
	SARS	affect	ARRIVE	tourism	trade

'SARS affects tourism.'

zhù	STAY	*zhàn*	***zhù***
		stand	stay

'Freeze!'

abstract	*xiān*	*wěn*	***zhù***	*mín*	*xīn*
	first	stabilize	STAY	people	heart

'First appease public opinion.'

sǐ	DIE	*yān*	***sǐ***	*le*	*hěn*	*duō*	*lǎo.bǎi.xìng*
		drown	die	Pfv	very	many	people

'Many people were drowned.'

abstract	*wǒ*	*máng*	***sǐ***	*le*
	I	busy	DIE	Pfv

'I am extremely busy.'

duàn	BREAK (intr)	*tā*	*bǎ*	*shù*	*kǎn*	***duàn***	*le*
		he	Acc	tree	chop	break	Pfv

'He chopped down the tree.'

abstract	*bié*	*dǎ*	***duàn***	*wǒ.de*	*huà*
	don't	beat	BREAK	my	word

'Don't interrupt me while I am talking.'

jiàn	SEE; MEET	*wǒ*	*kàn*	***jiàn***	*le*	*dàxiàng*
		I	look	see	Pfv	elephant

'I saw an elephant.'

abstract	*wǒ*	*tīng*	***jiàn***	*tā.de*	*shēng.yin*
	I	hear	SEE	his	voice

'I hear(d) his voice.'

chū EMERGE

xuésheng	*zǒu*	***chū***	*jiàoshì*
student	walk	emerge	classroom

'Students walk out of the classroom.'

abstract

tā	*xiǎnshì*	***chū***	*qiánlì*
he	reveal	EMERGE	potential

'He showed his potential.'

shàng ASCEND

hóu.zi	*pá*	***shàng***	*le*	*shù*
monkey	climb	ascend	Pfv	tree

'Monkeys climbed up a tree.'

abstract

tā	*ài*	***shàng***	*xiǎo*	*lǐ*
he	love	ASCEND	little	Li

'He falls in love with Little Li.'

zháo ATTACH

huǒ	*shaō*	***zháo***	*le*	*dào.cǎo*
fire	burn	attach	Pfv	straw

'The straw has caught on fire.'

abstract

wǒ	*zhǎo*	***zháo***	*le*	*shǒu.biǎo*
I	search	ATTACH	Pfv	watch

'I found the watch.'

diū LOSE

zài rén.qún-lǐ	*wǒ*	*bǎ.tā*	*gēn*	***diū****-le*
Loc crowd-in	I	him	follow	lose-Pfv

'I lost him in the crowd.'

abstract

hái.zi	*zǒu*	***diū***	*le*
child	walk	LOSE	Pfv

'The child wandered off.'

Appendix. B: List of ten[36] most common Hindi-Urdu vectors with glosses of their lexical sources and examples of them used first concretely and then more abstractly.

jaa	GO	*mirzaa*	*bhii*	*baahar*	*nikal*	***gae***	
		Mirza	too	outside	exit	went	

'Mirza also went out.' (*Godan* 169.2)

abstract	*12*	*bajte-bajte*	*vo*	*shuruu*	*ho*	***gayaa***
	12	striking-2	it	begin	happen	WENT

'It began on the stroke of 12.' (*Godan* 143.43)

de	GIVE	*tamaakhuu*	*hai*	*ki*	*laa*	***dũũ***
		tobacco	is	that	bring	give.Sbjn

'Have I any tobacco to bring & give you?'(*Godan* 109)

abstract	*kyõ*	*na*	*cheR.chaaR*	*shuruu*	*kar*	***de***
	why	not	teasing	begin	do	GIVE

'Why not start teasing (him)?' (*Godan* 141.45)

le	TAKE	*us-ne*	*ããcal*	*sir-par*	*khĩĩc*	***liyaa***
		she-Erg	border	head-on	pull	took

'She pulled the sari's edge over her head.'
(*Godan* 303)

abstract	*log*	*hãs-ẽge*	*hãs*	***lẽ***
	people	laugh-Fut3pl	laugh	TAKE.Sbjn

'People will laugh, let them laugh.' (*Godan* 191.17)

Daal POUR Concrete use of *Daal* as a vector not available.

abstract	*us-ne*	*khet.baarii*	*sab*	*bec-baac*	***Daalii***
	he-Erg	fields	all	sell-Echoic	POURED

'He had sold off his farm and all.' (*Godan* 363.31)

---

[36] There are an additional dozen or so less common vector verbs in Hindi-Urdu: *choR de* RELEASE, *maar* STRIKE, *mar* DIE, *nikaal* TAKE OUT, *nikal* EMERGE, etc. These are so rarely used that even a 350-page novel like Premchand's *Godan* may not afford instances of them. For discussion and examples see Hook 1974 (120-144).

rakh	PUT	*tere-lie*	*muus*	*pakaR*	***rakhaa***	*hai*	
		you-for	mouse	catch	put	is	

'For you we've caught (& kept) a mouse.' (*Godan* 43.41)

use	*gaay*	*hii*	*samajh*	***rakhaa***	*thaa*
it	cow	Emp	consider	PUT	was

'(I) had taken it to be a cow.' (*Godan* 317.22)

baiTh	SIT	*us vaqt*	*jhuniyaa*	*jaag-kar*	*uTh*	***baiThii***
		that time	Jhuniya	wake.up-CP	rise	sat

'At that moment Jhuniya awoke & sat up.' (*Godan* 342.21)

abstract	*krodh-mẽ*	*mãĩ*	*kyaa*	*kar*	***baiThũũ***
	anger-in	I	what	do	SIT.Sbjn
	na	*kah*	*saktii*		
	not	say	can		

'I can't say what I'd do if I got mad.' (*Godan* 306.29)

paR	FALL	*punnii*	*dhakkaa*	*khaa-kar*	*gir*	***paRii***
		Punni	shove	eat-CP	topple	fell

'Punni was shoved and fell down.' (*Godan* 34.7)

abstract	*ye*	*kah-te*	*kah-te*	*vo*	*muskaraa*	***paRii***
	this	say-ing	say-ing	she	smile	FELL

'While saying this, she smiled.' (*Godan* 189.17)

uTh	RISE	*horii*	*kaa*	*xuun*	*khaul*	***uThaa***
		Hori	's	blood	boil	rose

'Hori's blood boiled.' (*Godan* 48.41)

abstract	*maalatii*	*adhiir*	*ho*	***uThii***
	Malati	impatient	become	ROSE

'Malati became impatient.' (*Godan* 82.45)

aa	COME	***mũh***	*mẽ*	*paanii*	*bhar*	***aayaa***	
		mouth	in	water	fill	came	

'His mouth watered.' (*Godan* 217.9)

abstract	*ããkhẽ*	*sa-jal*	*ho*	***aayii***	*thĩĩ*
	eyes	with-water	become	CAME	were

'His eyes became wet (with tears).' (*Godan* 347.26)

cal	MOVE	*aaie*	*lauT*	***calẽ***
		come	return	move.Sbjn

'Come. Let's go back (together).' (*Godan* 294.22)

abstract	*use*	*kuch-kuch*	*raaj.niitik*	*gyaan*
	him	some-some	political	Knowledge
	ho	***calaa***	*hai*	
	be	MOVE	is	

'He's become a bit politically aware.' (*Godan* 203.18)

Appendix C. Distribution of explicator–compound verbs and analogous phenomena. Map after Masica 1976 (p. 151).

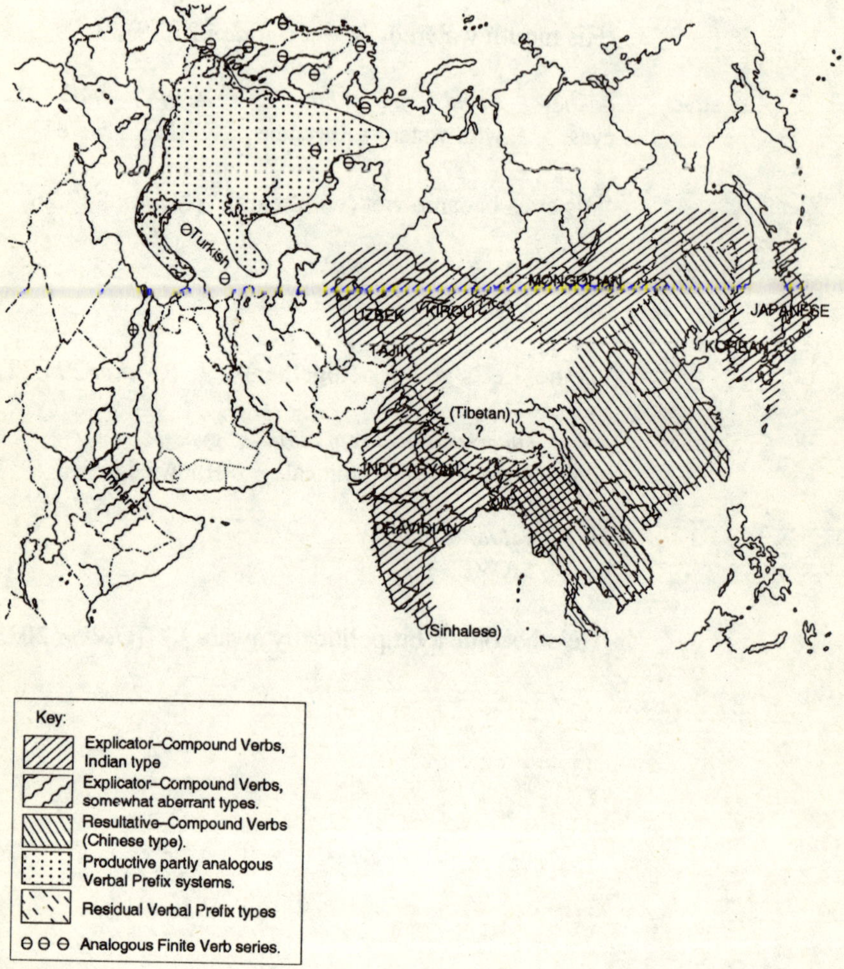

Appendix D. Explicator and resultative compound verbs (versus other verb-specifying devices). Map after Masica 2001 (p. 251).

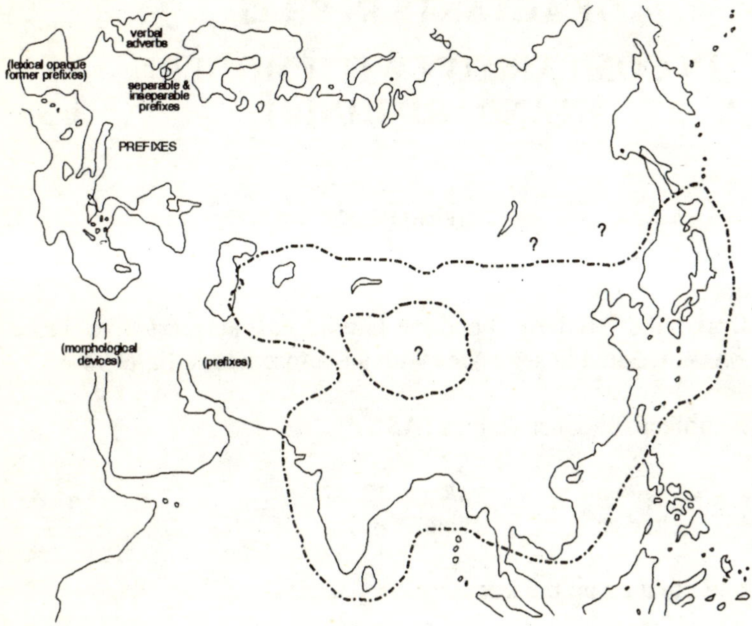

NOTES ON THE MARKING OF ACTANTS IN BRAJ (IN COMPARISON WITH MODERN STANDARD HINDI)

V. P. LIPEROVSKY

Modern Braj, like Modern Standard Hindi, has at least five basic constructions embodied in sentences with an autosemantic finite verb:

(1) Active-subjectival constructions (ASC):

(a) *raajaa* *peR pai* *caRhyau* (S, 87)
raja-M tree-on climb-Pfv-Msg

'The raja climbed up the tree.'

(b) *bhai˜siyaa* *duudh* *dai˜tii* (S, 49)
buffalo-F milk give-Impfv-Fsg

'A female buffalo used to give milk.'

(c) *kauRiyaa gulaam* *apane* *bhaiyanu* *kuu˜* *bhautu*
'cowrie slave-M his-own-Mpl brother-obl-pl DAT/ACC much

caahatu *o* (D,23)
desire-Impfv-M be-Past-Msg

'The slave holding a shell was very fond of his brothers.'

(d) *uu˜T* *na* *maanyau* (S, 109)
camel-M not agree-Pfv-Msg

'The camel did not agree.'

(2) Active-objectival constructions (AOC):

(a)

sipaahiin	*ne˜*	*raanii*	*pakari*	*laii*...(S, 135)
soldier-obl-pl	ERG	ranee-F	seize-CP	take-Pfv-Fsg

'The soldiers seized the ranee.'

(b)

bvaane˜	*raajaa*	*apane paas*	*bulaayau* (S, 84)
he-obl ERG	king-M	him(self) near	call-Pfv-Msg

'He called the king.'

(c)

logan	*ne˜*	*ii˜T-patthar*	*uThaaye*... (P, 94)
people-obl-pl	ERG	bricks-stones-M	pick up-Pfv-Mpl

'The people picked up bricks and stones...'

(3) Active-neutral constructions (ANC):

(a)

gaurii	*nai˜*	*syaam kuu˜*	*dekhyau* (P, 33)
Gauri-F	ERG	Shyam DAT/ACC	see-Pfv-Msg

'Gauri saw Shyam.'

(b)

sakaTuaa	*nai*	*aakaas maauu˜*	*nihaarau* (M, 34)
Saktua	ERG	sky-in	look-Pfv-Msg

'Saktua looked at the sky.'

(c)

raavan	*kuu˜*	*raam*	*ne*	*cau˜*	*maaryau?* (P, 48)
Ravana	DAT/ACC	Rama	ERG	why	kill-Pfv-Msg

'Why did Rama kill Ravana?'

(4) Inactive-objectival construction (IOC):

(a)

...holii me˜	*ii*	*dRIshya*	*ghar ghar me˜*	*dekhyau*
...Holi-in	this	scene-M	house house-in	see-Pfv-Msg

jaay	*hai* (B, 26)
go-Subj-3sg	be-Pres-3sg

'...in the festival of Holi this scene is seen in each house.'

(b)

udaaharaN ke	*taa˜i*	*kachu pad*	*die*	*jaai*
example-of	for the sake	some couplets-M	give-Pfv-Mpl	

rahe	*hai˜* (B, 85)
go-CP remain-Pfv-Mpl	be-Pres-3Pl

'Some couplets are being cited as an example.'

(c)

saath hii	*harek*	*saal*	*naii naii*	*caupaii*	*gaRhii*
also	each	year	new new	chaupais-F	create-Pfv-F

jaa˜y	*hai˜*...(B, 27)
go-Subj-3pl	be-Pres-3pl

'At the same time new chaupais are created every year...'

(5) Inactive-neutral construction (INC):

(a)

pyaas ke	*maarai˜*	*un*	*suu˜*	*khaayau*	*ii*
thirst-of	because	they-obl	INSTR/ABL	eat-Pfv-Msg	even

naa˜y	*jaay*	*rahau*	*o* (D,26)
not	go-CP	remain-Pfv-Msg	be-Past-Msg

'Owing to thirst they were not able even to eat.'

(b)

...*mahaabhaarat ke*	*kathaanakan*	*kuu˜*	*kathyau*
...«Mahabharata»-of	story-M-obl-pl	DAT/ACC	tell-Pfv-Msg

jaay	*hai* (B, 37)
go-Subj-3sg	be-Pres-3sg

'...the stories of the «Mahabharata» are told.'

(c)

...*yaa*	*parva*	*kuu˜*	*lokotsav ke*	*ruup me˜*
...this-obl-sg	feast-Msg	DAT/ACC	folk festival-of	form-in

manaayau	*jaay*	*hai* (B, 47)
celebrate-Pfv-Msg	go-Subj-3sg	be-Pres-3sg

'...this feast is celebrated as a folk festival.'

These constructions are discerned by taking into account: (1) the voice of the verb (active : inactive); consequently a construction can be either active or inactive; (2) agreement or non-agreement of the verb with one of those actants which are considered to be relevant for syntactical structures, namely: (a) *A* – a nominal (noun or pronoun) which denotes the subject of an action denoted by a transitive verb, (b) *S*

– a nominal which denotes the subject of an action denoted by an intransitive verb, (c) *P* – a nominal which denotes the object of an action (denoted of course by a transitive verb); consequently a construction can be either subjectival or objectival, or it can be neutral, i.e. with the verb form equal to the form of the third person masculine singular.

The following shared properties are noteworthy:

1. *A/S* of the ASC and *P* of the AOC and of the IOC are bound to be direct case nominals (cf. *raajaa, bhai˜siyaa, kauRiyaa gulaam, uu˜T* in (1); *raanii, raajaa, ii˜T-patthar* in (2), *dRIshya, pad, caupaii* in (4)).
2. *A* of the AOC and of the ANC (also *S* of the ANC in some instances with anomalous verbs) is an oblique case nominal marked (coded) with a special postposition analogous to *ne* which, as far as Hindi is concerned, should be treated as the agentive postposition, and this kind of marking (cf. *sipaahiin ne˜, bvaane˜, logan ne˜* in (2); *gaurii nai˜, sakaTuaa nai, raam ne* in (3)) is associated with the perfective form of the verb.
3. *P* is not an obligatory item in the ASC, ANC and INC, because the verb in these constructions is not necessarily transitive. At the same time being associated with a transitive verb *P* appears in the ANC and in the INC in the oblique case marked with the dative-accusative postposition analogous to *ko* of Hindi (cf. *syaam kuu˜, raavan kuu˜* in (3); *kathaanakan kuu˜, parva kuu˜* in (5)). In the ASC, *P* is either an oblique case nominal with the just mentioned postposition (cf. *bhaiyanu kuu˜* in (1)) or a direct case nominal displaying a "null instance of case marking" (cf. *duudh* in (1)).
4. The instrumental-ablative postposition analogous to *se* of Hindi can be used as a marker for *A/S* of the INC (cf. *un suu˜* in (5)) and presumably for *A* of the IOC.

Such are the properties shared by Braj (modern) and Hindi in the marking of actants. Nevertheless Braj has its own peculiarities which seem to be deviations from what Braj and Hindi have in common within the frame of the above-mentioned constructions.

I. The postposition that is generally used to mark *A* (in the AOC and ANC) is also used to mark *P* in different positions, e.g.:

(a) *mai˜ tau aa˜khi-macaunii ke* ***daavan nai*** *(P) tau jaanuu˜ huu˜...* (M, 82)

'As for me, I know the **tricks** of blind-man's-buff...' (cf. **mai˜ to aa˜kh-micaunii ke* ***daa˜vo˜ ne*** *to jaantaa huu˜...*).

(b) *mantrii dvai **sevakan nai** (P) laike bhiitar maauu˜ bhaagau* (M, 84)

'The secretary having taking two **servants** ran inside.' (cf. **mantrii do* ***sevako˜ ne*** *lekar bhiitar ko bhaagaa*)

(c) *[biraamman]* ***binne˜*** *(P) bulaaibe aayau so binne˜ (A) bauhauterii naa˜ii˜ karii pari bu na maanyau* (S, 5)

'...[the Brahmin] came to call **them** [to partake in meal], they stubbornly refused but he did not accept their excuses.' (cf. **...[braahmaN]* ***unne*** *bulaane ko aayaa...*)

It is to be noted that there is no formal distinction between *P* of the first clause and *A* of the second clause of the last example. On taking into consideration this kind of marking *P* in Braj one can assume the lack of a formal distinction between *P* and *A* within the ANC like, for instance, in Bangaru, e.g. *mannai sohan nai maaryaa* 'I beat Sohan' or 'It was Sohan who beat me' being dependent on the context (Ambaprasad 'Suman' 1966. *hindii aur uskii upabhaaSaao˜ kaa svaruup.* Prayag: Hindi Sahitya Sammelan: pp. 125-126), or in Kauravi, e.g. *ek bandar ne us ne dekh liyaa* 'A monkey saw it' (from a specimen of Vernacular Hindostani spoken in District Muzaffarnagar. G. A. Grierson. *Linguistic Survey of India. Volume IX. Part I*, p. 231).

II. The oblique plural of a noun appears in the capacity of *A* or *P* <u>without any postposition</u>, e.g.:

(a) ***coranu*** *(A) sabu maalu asbaabu nikaari liiyau* (S, 56)

'The **thieves** took out the whole luggage.' (cf. ***coro˜ *sab maal-asbaab nikaal liyaa*)

(b) *kuttaa un* ***coranu*** *(P) dekhi rahyau* (S, 56)

'The dog caught sight of those **thieves**.' (cf. **kuttaa un coro˜ dekh rahaa*)

III. There are cases when the postpositional marking of *P* does not preclude the agreement of the perfective form of a transitive verb with a given noun or pronoun, e.g.:

(a) *raajaa ne* ***maitarii kuu˜*** *(P)* bulaaii (G. A. Grierson. *LSI. Volume IX. Part I*, p. 355)

'The king called the **charwoman**.' (cf. **raajaa ne* ***mehtaraanii ko*** bulaaii)

(b) *yaa baat kuu sun vaakai khasam ne* ***vaa kuu*** *(P) bauhat* maarii ii (D, 53)

'On having heard this, her husband had beaten **her** severely.' (cf. **is baat ko sunkar uske khasam ne* ***us ko*** *bahut* maarii thii)

(c) *unho˜ ne...* ***mo kuu*** *(P) khuub* maarii, *mai˜ dukhiyaarii raat bhar rotii rahii* (D, 54)

'...he...beat **me** severely. I, poor, kept weeping all night.' (cf. **...unho˜ ne...* ***mujh ko*** *khuub* maarii...)

These examples reveal, as can be noted, verb agreement in number (singular) and gender (feminine), while agreement in person is not evident. In these examples, a property of the AOC (verb agreement with a *P*-noun/pronoun) is combined with a property of ANC (the postpositional marking of *P*).

IV. One can not fail to be puzzled on seeing an example like the following:

(a) *aur thore dinaa˜ paache lohare* ***beTaa ne*** *(S) sigarau dhan ik-Thaurau karikai duur desan ku˜* calyau (G. A. Grierson. *LSI. Volume IX. Part I*, pp. 271-273)

'And a few days later the younger **son** collected the whole wealth (literally 'having collected the whole wealth') and went far to a strange land.' (cf. **...choTe* ***beTe ne****...* calaa...)

It is striking that *S* is marked with the postposition which is bound to mark *A* in the AOC and ANC. Is *calyau* a neutral perfective form or is it affected by agreement with a masculine noun? What would be correct for "the younger daughter went": *loharii beTii ne calyau* or *loharii beTii ne calii?* In other words, is the construction presented here neutral or subjectival?

V. The locative postposition *pai (pe)* analogous to *par* of Hindi is generally used instead of the instrumental-ablative postposition analogous to *se* of Hindi for marking *A* of the IOC and *S* (presumedly *A* as well) of the INC, e.g.:

(a) ***jaa pai*** *(A) paanii naa˜y uThaayau jaatu* (S, 114)

'**She** is not able to lift water.' (cf. ****is par*** *paanii nahii˜ uThaayaa jaataa*)

(b) *chorii ke* ***baap pai*** *(A) apanaa naam uu baRau sau naa˜y dharau gayau* (M, 40)

'Even his own name was not exalted by the girl's **father**.' (cf. **laRkii ke* ***baap par*** *apnaa naam bhii baRaa saa nahii˜ dharaa gayaa).*

(c) *jab* ***mo pai*** *(A) maaru na sahii gaii*... (D, 40)

'When **I** became unable to endure beating...' (cf. **jab* ***mujh par*** *maar na sahii gaii...*)

(d) ***...ham pai*** *(S) paayan na calyau jaaigo* (D, 36)

'...**I** shall not be able to go on foot' (cf. **...* ***ham par*** *paidal na calaa jaaegaa*).

VI. In Braj (unlike in Hindi), the direct case form of personal pronouns (and of demonstrative pronouns used for the third person) in the capacity of *P* can be cooccurrent with the perfective verb form, e.g.

(a) *taine˜ tiin jaghai* ***mai˜*** *(P) kaal pai te* bacaayau uu˜ (S, 139)

'Thou hast saved **me** from death on three occasions.' (cf. **tuu ne tiin jagaho˜ par* ***mai˜*** *kaal par se* bacaayaa huu˜)

(b) *mahaaraaj* ***mai˜*** *(P) raajaa ne˜ saat taare bhiitar* muu˜di raakhii huu˜ (S, 34)

'O, my lord, the raja has been confining **me** under seven locks.' (cf. **mahaaraaj,* **mai˜** *raajaa ne saat taalo˜ ke bhiitar* muu˜d rakhii huu˜).

(c) ***ham*** *(P) jaaii ne˜* bacaae ai˜ (S, 163)

'It is he who saved **us**.' (cf. ****ham usii ne*** bacaaye hai˜)

(d) ***tuu** (P) mere maalik ne˜* yaadi kiiyau hai (S, 29)

'My lord has recalled **thee**.' (cf. ****tuu** mere maalik ne* yaad kiyaa hai)

(e) *bvaane˜ roTiin kuu˜ ii **tuu** (P)* bhejii hai (S, 125)

'He has sent **thee** just for the cakes of bread.' (cf. **usne roTiyo˜ ke liye hii **tuu*** bhejii hai)

(f) ***tum** (P) raajaa saab ne* yaad kiye hau (S, 76)

'The king has remembered **you**.' (cf. ****tum** raajaa saahab ne* yaad kiye ho)

(g) *baadshaah jaade ne˜ **bu** (P) apane ghoRaa pai baiThaari laii…* (S, 80)

'The prince helped **her** on to his horse.' (cf. [?]*baadshaahzaade ne **vah** apne ghoRe par* baiThaa lii...)

The verb agrees with *P*-pronouns in number, gender and person. So in Braj the AOC proves to be more capacious (or the ergative construction more consistent) than in Hindi (that is, Modern Standard Hindi).

VII. The perfective feminine form (in singular) of some verbs (of saying, thinking, feeling, etc.) is used widely (more frequently than in Hindi) in sentences, when a syntactic position of *P* or *S* can be ascribed to a feminine noun (presumedly *baat* 'matter', 'thing', 'point'), which is not expressed overtly, e.g.:

(a) *syaam ne **dekhii** kai baa habelii ke kamaraan me˜ te sabarau saamaan kahuu˜ aur calyau gayau. baane˜ dhanapat te **puuchii**. dhanapat ne˜ **kahii** – "bhaiyaa, ham logan ke bhaag me˜ aaraam tau hai naa˜y"* (P, 50)

'Shyam **noticed** that all the goods had disappeared somewhere from the rooms of the mansion. He **asked** Dhanpat [about it]. Dhanpat **said**: «Oh brother! Repose is not in store for us».'

(b) *...par vaa choraa ne˜ naa˜y **maanii*** (S, 141)

'...but the boy did not **agree**'.

(c) *raajaa ke beTaa ne˜* ***puu˜chii*** *kai yaar toi kaise* ***maalim parii*** *ki ji peDu giraigau?* (S, 138)
'The king's son **asked:** «Oh friend, how **did** it **come** to your **knowledge** that this tree would fall?».'

VIII. The AOC (presumedly the ANC as well) has to get rid of *A*, if no definite doer of a given action is meant in narrative contexts, e.g.

(a) *bindaaban me˜ uu kraantii kau sankh baj uThyau. gobindjii me˜ ek gupt miiTing bhaii. baa me˜ sabare kaaryakarttaa ikhaTTe bhaye.* <u>*sab kuu˜ alag-alag kaam sau˜p diye*</u> (P, 83)

'The appeal for uprising rang out in Brindaban too. A clandestine meeting was held in the Gobind temple, and all the activists gathered together at it. <u>Everybody was charged with a separate task.</u>' (literally 'To all separate-separate tasks having charged given'; *diye* 'given' – plur. masc. according to *kaam* 'tasks')

As *A* is not evident, *sau˜p diye* may be conceived here as a semantic equivalent of the inactive verb form – *sau˜p diye gaye.*

In conclusion, Braj, not being a standard idiom of the Hindi-speaking area, does not display, as compared with Modern Standard Hindi, a tendency to get rid of non-functional differentiation of grammatical phenomena.

Sources

Dani, Baijnath. 1959. *braj kii lok kahaaniyaa˜*. Mathura: Elora Publishing House.

Gosvami, Sharanbihari. 1965. *puu˜charii kau lauThaa*. Brindaban: Rashtravani Prakashan.

Satyendra, Shri (ed.). Samvat 2004. *braj kii lok kahaaniyaa˜*. Mathura: Braj Sahitya Mandal.

Sharma, Mohan Lal. 1969. *braj-vaarttaa*. Kosikalan: Braj-Bhasha Prakashan.

Suman, Shyamsundar. 1968. *manasukhaa*. Mathura: Shri Suman Sahitya Prakashan Mandir.

Abbreviations Used in References in Text

B – Sharma, Mohan Lal.. *braj vaarttaa...* [see above]
D – Dani, Baijnath. *braj kii lok kahaaniyaa˜...* [see above]
M – Suman, Shyamsundar. *manasukhaa...* [see above]
P – Gosvami, Sharanbihari. *puu˜charii...* [see above]
S – Satyendra, Shri. *braj kii lok kahaaniyaa˜...* [see above]

THE ROLE OF PARTICLES AND CLITICS IN DISAMBIGUATION IN SOUTH ASIAN LANGUAGES*

KARUMURI V. SUBBARAO

1. The purpose of this paper is to demonstrate that there are similar or identical phenomena across South Asian languages in disambiguating a sentence. Such disambiguation plays an important role in conveying the intended information with proper interpretation. We shall show that the occurrence of particles or verbal clitics, the process of copying the head, and the presence vs. absence of reduplicated forms are some of the processes that block a specific interpretation and facilitate the other intended interpretation. We argue that the notion of syntactic dependency domain helps in sentence processing and enables us to explain the two different interpretations of specific sentences. Further, it also enables to explain why the occurrence of some specific particles facilitates one interpretation while the occurrence of some others does not. Our analysis demonstrates that reduplication is not just a phenomenon restricted to the area of morphology alone but it has syntactic implications to the extent that it can help disambiguate a sentence.

Discussion of ambiguous sentences played a very important role in transformational-generative grammar. Sentences such as (1) and (2) are ambiguous while sentences such as (3) and (4) and (5) and (6) are not.

1. *Flying planes can be dangerous*
2. *Visiting relatives can be a nuisance*
3. *Flying planes are dangerous*
4. *Flying planes is dangerous*
5. *Visiting relatives are a nuisance*
6. *Visiting relatives is a nuisance*

A sentence such as (7) can only be disambiguated by adding some

---

*Presented also at: SYNTAX OF THE WORLD'S LANGUAGES (SWL1), Leipzig, (Germany), 5-8 August, 2004

thematic arguments as in (8) and (9).

7. *The chickens are ready to eat*
8. *The chickens are ready for the kids to eat*
9. *The chickens are ready to eat their grains*

It is the verbal agreement in (3)-(6) that eliminates the ambiguity in sentences (1) and (2) whereas it is the addition of arguments *for the kids to eat* in (8) and *their grains* in (9) that resolves the ambiguity. We wish to demonstrate that although a disambiguation process in a language might appear to be language specific, some of the processes in general are similar in different languages – at least in different South Asian languages.

In section 2 we shall discuss the role of particles in disambiguation and discuss its implications.

2.1. The role of the emphatic particle in Hindi-Urdu and Punjabi

In Hindi-Urdu Punjabi and in almost all South Asian languages the conjunctive participle performs several functions. Conjunctive participles are typical of Indian languages where a verbal form devoid of the *phi* (person, number and gender) features links the main clause and the subordinate clause (cf. Masica 1976, Abbi 1984, Davison 1981, Kachru 1981, Subbarao 1996). The conjunctive participial bound morpheme in Hindi-Urdu is *kar/ ke* which is a nonfinite form and is added to the right of the verb stem. For example *sun kar/sun ke* 'having heard' or *khaa kar/khaa ke* 'having eaten'. One of the primary functions that the conjunctive participle performs is to denote sequential actions. It also occurs as a manner adverb, in *even though* clauses and in *in spite of* clauses in association with the negative morpheme. In Hindi-Urdu it also imparts the aspectual meaning of "certainty" when the matrix verb is *rah* 'be'. For example: (10) is ambiguous between sequential interpretation and aspectual meaning.

10.

ham	*dillii*	*jaa*	*kar*	*rahenge*
we	Delhi	go	Cpm	will stay

(i) 'We will go to Delhi and stay (sequential interpretation).'

(ii) 'We will definitely or certainly go to Delhi (aspectual interpretation)'.

However, the occurrence of the emphatic clitic *hii* to the right of the conjunctive participle imparts only the modal/aspectual meaning and the sequential meaning in (i) is not conveyed.

11.

ham	*dillii*	*jaa*	*kar*	***hii***	*rahenge*
we	Delhi	go	Cpm	Emph	will stay

(i) '*We will go to Delhi and stay (sequential interpretation).'
(ii) 'We will definitely or certainly go to Delhi (aspectual interpretation).'

In Hindi-Urdu and in some other South Asian languages the conjunctive participle and the verb *rahnaa* 'to be' imparts the aspectual meaning of definiteness[1]. The form *hii* is an emphatic particle. Hence, it adds to the degree of definiteness without disturbing the adjacency of the constituents V + conjunctive participle and the verb *be*. If there occurs an intervening particle such as *bhii* 'also' or *to* 'as for', adjacency between the constituents is disturbed and hence, the aspectual meaning is lost.

12.

ham	*dillii*	*jaa*	*kar*	***bhii***	*rahenge*
we	Delhi	go	Cpm	also	will stay

(i) '*We will certainly go to Delhi and stay.'
(ii) 'We will even go to Delhi and stay.'

---

[1] Telugu (Dravidian) has a similar construction in which the conjunctive participle of a verb and the verb *tiir* 'finish' is used as the matrix verb and this imparts an aspectual interpretation.

meemu	*Dilli*	*weLL-*	*i*	*tiiru*	*taamu*
we	Delhi	go	Cpm	become	will

'We'll certainly go to Delhi.'

While Hindi-Urdu the matrix verb *rah* 'be' occurs with a nominative subject, the verb *tiir* requires a Dative Subject when it occurs as the main predicate.

(ii)

aame	*ki*	*aakali*	*tiirindi*
she	DAT	appetite	fulfilled/satisfied

'To her appetite is fulfilled.' (literal translation)
'She is not hungry.'

13.

ham	*dillii*	*jaa*	*kar*	*to*	*rahenge*
we	Delhi	go	Cpm	even	will stay
lekin	*kisii*	*se*	*nahii~*	*mil*	*paayenge*
but	anybody	with	not	meet	will be able

(i) '*We will certainly go to Delhi and stay.'
(ii) 'We will of course go to Delhi and stay but we won't be able to meet anybody.'

As far as the sequential interpretation is concerned, adjacency is not a requirement and hence, the two constituents *jaa kar* and *rahenge* can freely be scrambled.

14.

[aagre	*se*	*jaa*	*kar]*	*ham*	*dillii*	*rahenge*
Agra	from	go	Cpm	we	Delhi	will stay

'We will go from Agra and stay in Delhi.'

15.

ham	*[aagre*	*se*	*jaa*	*kar]*	*dillii*	*rahenge*
we	Agra	from	go	Cpm	Delhi	will stay

'We will go from Agra and stay in Delhi.'

In the aspectual interpretation the conjunctive participial form of the verb *jaa* 'go' and the verb *rah* 'be' together belong to the same VP and the sentence has a monoclausal structure whereas in the sequential interpretation the conjunctive participial clause and verb *be* belong to two different clauses and hence, it has a biclausal structure.

An explanation in terms of sentence processing can also be provided. In a sequential interpretation the two elements are independently processed while in the aspectual interpretation the two elements are compositionally processed. Thus, in the aspectual interpretation both the elements depend on each other for interpretation while in the sequential interpretation there is no such dependency at all and the elements are not even losely 'tied together'.

To explain the occurrence of an emphatic particle we invoke the concept of *syntactic dependency domain*. When two elements are adjacently placed and are required to be adjacent for their interpretation, we can label such occurrence as a syntactic dependency domain. The syntactic dependency domain is not affected if a particle that intensifies the meaning occurs and the particle is in line with the projected semantic content of the compositional whole. In other words, the clitic that is added should be in consonance with the total meaning that is being projected compositionally by the individual units. That is why the occurrence of the emphatic particle is permitted in sentences with aspectual meaning in Hindi-Urdu.

Punjabi too exhibits a similar pattern. (16) is ambiguous between a sequential adverbial interpretation and a modal interpretation just as in Hindi-Urdu.

Punjabi (Indo-Aryan):

16.

mai~	*o~the*	*jaa*	*ke*	*reyaa~gaa*
I	there	go	Cpm	will stay

(i) 'I will certainly go there.'
(ii) 'I will go there and stay.'

(Ramakant Agnihotri & Chandar Singh, pc)

When the emphatic clitic *–i* occurs to the right of the conjunctive participle, the sentence has only the aspectual interpretation and not the sequential interpretation just as in Hindi-Urdu.

17.

mai~	*o~the*	*jaa*	*ke-*	*i*	*reyaa~gaa*
I	there	go	Cpm	Emph	will stay

(i) 'I will certainly go there.'
(ii) '*I will go there and stay.'

Note that there are other similar syntactic dependency domains in Hindi-Urdu. In (18) the phrase *kar dikhaana* has the interpretation of 'demonstrate' or 'show' and the elements *kar* and *dikhaanaa* are verbs and have their independent meaning. However, in (18) they can be interpreted if and only if they occur adjacent to each other and no other element intervenes between the two as (19) shows.

Hindi-Urdu:

18.

meraa	*dost*	*yah*	*kaam*	*ek*	*minaT*	*me~*	*kar*	*dikhaayegaa*
my	friend	this	work	a	minute	in	do	will show

'My friend will demonstrate this work (by doing it) in one minute.'

19.

*?*meraa*	*dost*	*yah*	*kaam*	*kar*	*ek*	*minaT*	*me˜*	*dikhaayegaa*
my	friend	this	work	do	a	minute	in	will show

On the other hand, there is a construction in Hindi-Urdu where the conjunctive participial form of the verb *kar*, the stem form of *karnaa* 'to do' and *dikhaanaa* 'to show' occur in a sequence as in (20). This sequence has a sequential interpretation and the conjunctive participle and the matrix verb are not syntactically dependent and hence, do not constitute a syntactically dependent domain. Hence, this sequence can permit an intervening adverb of time or place as (21) or (22) show.

20.

meraa	*dost*	*yah*	*kaam*	*ek*	*minaT*	*me˜*	*kar*
my	friend	this	work	one	minute	in	do

ke	*dikhaayega*
Cpm	will show

'My friend will do this work in a minute and show it to you.'

21.

meraa	*dost*	*yah*	*kaam*	*ek*	*minaT*	*me˜*	*kar*
my	friend	this	work	one	minute	in	do

ke	*abhii*	*dikhaayegaa*
Cpm	right now	will show

'My friend will do this work in a minute and show it to you right now.'

22.

meraa	*dost*	*yah*	*kaam*	*abhii*	*kar*	*ke*
my	friend	this	work	right now	do	Cpm

yahii˜	*dikhaayegaa*
here	will show

'My friend will do this work right now and show it to you right here.'

The above discussion clearly shows that the notion of syntactically dependent domain plays a crucial role in sentence processing. This notion is crucially dependent on constituent structure and the consequences that take place due to scrambling and the occurrence and nature of intervening elements.

2.2. The conjunctive participle and particles

The second case concerns the occurrence of the emphatic particle with the conjunctive participle in Hindi-Urdu (Indo-Aryan), Manipuri (Tibeto-Burman) and Telugu (Dravidian) and in almost all the other South Asian languages. A sentence such as (23) in Hindi-Urdu has two interpretations. In interpretation (i) the scope of the negative is on the matrix verb while in (ii) it is on the conjunctive participle *le kar* 'having taken' in the embedded clause. That is, in (ii) the effect of the negative percolates down to the embedded clause from the matrix clause while in (i) it does not.

Hindi-Urdu:

23.

ravi	*rishwat*	*le*	*kar*	*kaam*	*nahii˜*	*kartaa*
Ravi	bribes	take	cpm	work	not	do

(i) 'Ravi takes bribes and does not do the work.'
(ii) 'Ravi does not take bribes but (still) does the work.'

However, if an inclusive particle *bhii* 'also' occurs to the right of the conjunctive participle of the embedded clause, the sentence has only the interpretation in (i) and the negative cannot percolate down to the embedded clause.

24.

ravi	*rishwat*	*le*	*kar*	***bhii***	*kaam*	*nahii˜*	*kartaa*
Ravi	bribes	take	Cpm	also	work	not	do

(i) 'Ravi takes bribes too and does not do the work, i.e., Ravi does not do the work even though he takes bribes.'
(ii) '*Ravi does not take bribes and still does the work.'

The embedded clause in (24) is an adverbial clause and the entire adverbial clause can freely 'float' and the sentence still retains its ambiguity as (25) and (26) show.

25.

ravi	*kaam*	*nahii~*	*kartaa*	*[rishwat*	*le*	*kar]*
Ravi	work	not	do	bribes	take	Cpm

26.

[rishwat	*le*	*kar]*	*ravi*	*kaam*	*nahii˜*	*kartaa*
bribes	take	Cpm	Ravi	work	not	do

(i) 'Ravi takes bribes and does not do the work.'
(ii) 'Ravi does not take bribes but (still) does the work.'

Since the embedded clause is an adverbial clause, it does not form a syntactically dependent domain with the constituents of the matrix clause. The question that now arises is: Why is the percolation of the negative to the embedded clause blocked and hence, the ambiguity? Our contention is that the occurrence of the inclusive particle with the embedded participle blocks the percolation of the negative to the embedded clause and the embedded clause forms a syntactic island.

Let us now look at the occurrence of two other particles in such constructions. The emphatic particle *hii* alone, or together with the focus particle *to*, blocks the percolation of the negative to the embedded clause.

27.

ravi	*rishwat*	*le*	*kar*	***hii***	*(to)*	*kaam*	*nahii~*	*kartaa*
Ravi	bribes	take	Cpm	Emph	as for	work	not	do

(i) 'Ravi takes bribes alright but does not do the work, i.e., Ravi does not do the work even though he takes bribes.'
(ii) '*Ravi does not take bribes and still does the work.'

However, the occurrence of the focus particle *to* the right of the conjunctive participle does not block the percolation of the negative to the embedded participle.

28.

ravi	*rishwat*	*le*	*kar*	***to***	*kaam*	*nahii˜*	*kartaa*
Ravi	bribes	take	Cpm	as for	work	not	Do
lekin	*vaise*	*hii*	*kar*	*letaa hai*			
but	like that	just	do	takes			

(i) 'Ravi does not take bribes but he (some how) does the work.'
(ii) '*Ravi takes bribes but he (some how) does not do the work.'

Recall that the occurrence of the inclusive particle *bhii* 'also, too' stops the percolation of the negative to the embedded clause.

24 (repeated)

ravi	*rishwat*	*le*	*kar*	***bhii***	*kaam*	*nahii~*	*kartaa*
Ravi	bribes	take	cpm	too	work	not	do

(i) 'Ravi takes bribes too but does not do the work. i.e., Ravi does not do the work even though he takes bribes.'
(ii) '*Ravi does not take bribes and still does the work.'

In Manipuri (Tibeto-Burman) also, similar ambiguity obtains with the embedded conjunctive participle and the negative in the matrix clause.

Manipuri (Tibeto-Burman):

29.

tomba	*paysa*	*ca-*	*raga*	*thabak*	*tau-*	*de*
Thomba	money	eat	Cpm	work	do	not

(i) 'Thomba takes bribes and does not do the work.'
(ii) 'Thomba does not take bribes and (still) does the work.'

When an inclusive particle *su* 'also' occurs to the right of the conjunctive participial form of *ca* 'eat', that is, *ca raga* 'having eaten', the sentence is no longer ambiguous and it has the interpretation as in (i) of (30).

30.

tomba	*paysa*	*ca-*	*raga*	***su***	*thabak*	*tau-*	*de*
Thomba	money	eat	Cpm	also	work	do	not

(i) 'Thomba takes bribes too and does not do the work, i.e., Thomba does not do the work even though he takes bribes.'
(ii) '*Thomba does not take bribes and still does the work.'

(Subbarao & T. Sarju Devi ms., Sarju Devi, in preparation)

In Telugu too similar ambiguity obtains with the embedded conjunctive participle and the negative in the matrix clause.

Telugu (Dravidian):

31.

ravi	*lancaalu*	*tiisu-*	*kon-*	*i*	*pani*	*ceyyaDu*
Ravi	bribes	take	self ben	Cpm	work	does not do

(i) 'Ravi takes bribes and does not do the work.'
(ii) 'Ravi does not take bribes and (still) does the work.'

When an inclusive particle *kuuDaa* 'also, too' occurs to the right of the conjunctive participle, the negative does not percolate down to the embedded clause because the particle blocks it.

32.

ravi	lancaalu	tiis-	i	kon-	i	***kuuDaa***	*pani*	*ceyyaDu*
Ravi	bribes	take	cpm	self ben	Cpm	also	work	does not do

(i) 'Ravi takes bribes too and does not do the work. i.e., Ravi does not do the work even though he takes bribes.'
(ii) '*Ravi does not take bribes and still does the work.'

Just as in Hindi-Urdu, the occurrence of the focus particle *ayitee* 'as for' to the right of the conjunctive participle does not block the percolation of the negative to the embedded participle.

33.

ravi	*lancaalu*	*tiis-*	*i*	*kon-*	*i*	***ayitee***	*pani*	*ceyyaDu*
Ravi	bribes	take	Cpm	self ben	Cpm	as for	work	does not do

(i) 'Ravi does not take bribes but he (some how) does the work.'
(ii) '*Ravi takes bribes but he (some how) does not do the work.'

The blocking of the negative by the emphatic particle is also observed in Kokborok, Boro (Tibeto-Burman) and Ho (Munda) and in other Indo-Aryan and Dravidian languages too.

2.3. The occurrence of the verbal clitics

The third case concerns the occurrence of the verbal clitics that block long-distance binding. These include verbal anaphors (reflexives and reciprocals), self-benefactive or other-benefactive clitics with the matrix or embedded verb.

2.3.1. Verbal clitics and long-distance binding

There are many South Asian languages such as Mizo, Hmar, Boro, Angami (Tibeto-Burman), Telugu, Tamil, Kannada (Dravidian) in which there occurs a nominal as well as a verbal anaphor while there are languages such as Mundari, Ho, Santali (Munda) in which there is only a verbal anaphor. The verbal anaphor in all the aforementioned languages functions also as a self-benefactive and an inchoative marker (Lust et al 2000).

Let us first consider the Telugu examples. In sentnence (34) the nominal anaphor *tana koosam* 'for self' is coindexed with the matrix subject and the embedded verb does not carry any verbal anaphor.

Telugu (Dravidian):

34.

ashook$_i$	*sarita*$_j$	*ni*	*tana koosam*$_{i/*j}$	*Tii*	*ceeyya*	*m-ani*	*ceppeeDu*
Ashok	Sarita	ACC	self for	tea	do(imp)	Quot	said-Msg
(male)	(female)						

'Ashok asked Sarita to make some tea for himself (Ashok)/*herself.'

The verbal anaphor/self-benefactive in Telugu is *kon*. If the self-benefactive *kon-* occurs with the embedded verb, the nominal as well as the verbal anaphor are coindexed with the embedded subject PRO which in turn is coindexed with the matrix object *sarita* 'Sarita'.

35.

ashook	*sarita*$_j$	*ni*	*[PRO*	*tana koosam*$_{*i/j}$	*Tii*	*ceesi*	*kona*$_{*i/j-i}$
Ashok	Sarita	ACC		self for	tea	do	self ben
(malc)	(female)						

m-ani]	*ceppeeDu*
Quot	said-Msg

'Ashok$_i$ asked Sarita$_j$ to make tea for himself$_{*i}$/herself$_j$.'

When the other benefactive *peTT-* occurs with the embedded verb, the anaphor unambiguously refers to the matrix subject *ashok* 'Ashok' alone.

36.[2]

ashook$_i$	*sarita$_j$*	*ni*	*[PRO*	*tana koosam$_{i/*j}$*	*Tii*	*ceesi*	*peTTa*
Ashok (male)	Sarita (female)	ACC		self for	tea	do	other ben

m-ani]	*ceppeeDu*
Quot	said-Msg

'Ashok$_i$ asked Sarita$_j$ to make tea for (him)self$_{i/*j}$.'

In Hindi-Urdu too the nominal anaphor (only the reflexive and not the reciprocal) in (37) may either be coindexed with the embedded subject PRO which in turn is coindexed with the matrix indirect object or with the matrix subject. The former is an instance of local binding and the latter an instance of long-distance binding.[3]

Hindi-Urdu:

37.

ashok$_i$	*ne*	*lalitaa$_j$*	*se*	*[PRO$_j$*	*apne liye$_{i/j}$*	*caay*
Ashok	ERG	Lalita	with		for self	tea

---

[2] The verb *cepp-* 'tell' requires the indirect object to be dative Case-marked by *ki* in a simple clause as (i) illustrates:

(i)

nenu	*mamata*	***ki***	*ii*	*sangati*	*ceppeenu*
I	Mamata	DAT	this	news	told

'I told Mamata this news.'

The occurrence of the accusative Case marker in place of the dative Case marker is not permitted as (ii) illustrates.

(ii)

**nenu*	*mamata*	***ni***	*ii*	*sangati*	*ceppenu*
I	Mamata	ACC	this	news	told

However, when an embedded sentence occurs as the complement of the verb *cepp* 'tell', the indirect object is accusative case-marked as in (35) and this in our opinion deserves an explanation as in 36. Telugu appears to have backward control of the indirect object too where the embedded subject 'controls' the matrix indirect object and hence, the matrix indirect object is a null element (see Subbarao ms. For a detailed discussion of the backward control of the subject in Telugu). The embedded subject in turn gets accusative case-marked due to exceptional case marking in the sense of the government and binding framework. The details of the construction are being worked out. See Bhaskararao & Subbarao, in preparation.

[3] (Subbarao 1971) was the first to discuss the phenomenon of long-distance binding.

banaane	*ko*	*kahaa*
make	to	asked

'Ashok$_i$ asked Lalita$_j$ to make tea for himself$_i$/ herself$_j$.'
(Subbarao1971, Davison 2001)

However, if a self-benefactive *le* 'take' occurs with the embedded verb, then the nominal anaphor *apne liye* 'for self' can be coindexed only with PRO, the local subject which in turn is coindexed with the matrix indirect object.

38.

ashok$_i$	*ne*	*lalitaa$_j$*	*se*	*[PRO$_j$*	*apne liye$_{i/j}$*	*caay*
Ashok	ERG	Lalita	with		for self	tea

banaa	*lene*	*ko]*	*kahaa*
make	self ben	to	asked

'Ashok$_i$ asked Lalita$_j$ to make tea for *himself$_i$/ herself$_j$.'

If the other benefactive clitic *denaa* 'to give' occurs with the embedded verb, the nominal anaphor permits long-distance binding and no coindexing with the local antecedent is permitted. Hence, in (39) the anaphor *apne liye* corefers with *ashok* 'Ashok' and not with *lalitaa* 'Lalita'.

39.

ashok$_i$	*ne*	*lalitaa$_j$*	*se*	*[PRO$_j$*	*apne liye$_{i/j}$*	*caay*
Ashok	ERG	Lalita	with		for self	tea

banaa	*dene*	*ko]*	*kahaa*
make	other ben	to	asked

'Ashok$_i$ asked Lalita$_j$ to make tea for himself$_i$/herself$_{*j}$.'

It is interesting to note that if the anaphor is scrambled to the left of the matrix object, the binding possibilities change. In (40) - (42) below the letter ***t*** stands for the trace of the moved element and the subscript denotes the coindexing relation.

40.

ashok$_i$	*ne*	*apne liye$_i$*	*lalitaa$_j$*	*se*	*[PRO*	*t_i*	*caay*
Ashok	ERG	for self	Lalita	with	for self		tea

banaane	*ko]*	*kahaa*
make	to	asked

'Ashok$_i$ asked Lalita$_j$ to make tea for himself$_i$/herself$_{*j}$.'

The binding possibilities however do not change when the self-benefactive or the other-benefactive clitics occur with the embedded verb. E.g., with the self-benefactive clitic:

41.

ashok$_i$	*ne*	*apne liye*	*lalitaa$_j$*	*se*	*[PRO*	*t$_i$*	*caay*
Ashok	ERG	for self	Lalita	with	for self		tea

banaa	***lene***	*ko]*	*kahaa*
make	**self ben**	to	asked

'Ashok$_i$ asked Lalita$_j$ to make tea for *himself$_{*i}$/herself$_j$.'

With the other-benefactive clitic:

42.

ashok$_i$	*ne*	***apne liye$_{i/*j}$***	*lalitaa$_j$*	*se*	*[PRO*	*t$_i$*	*caay*
Ashok	ERG	for self	Lalita	with	for self		tea

banaa	***dene***	*ko]*	*kahaa*
make	other ben	to	asked

'Ashok$_i$ asked Lalita$_j$ to make tea for himself$_i$/herself$_{*j}$.'

The reason why scrambling does not affect binding possibilities is due to the occurrence of the self-benefactive clitic, which is 'subject-oriented' and 'clause-bound' and in contrast, the other-benefactive clitic, which is not 'subject-oriented' and not necessarily 'clause-bound'.

The next case concerns long-distance binding in Mizo, Boro, and Ao (Tibeto-Burman). A simplex nominal anaphor in the embedded clause in Ao can have either the embedded subject or the matrix subject as its antecedent provided the embedded verb does not carry either the self-benefactive or the other-benefactive clitic. The subscript $_k$ referes to discourse antecedent.

Ao (Tibeto-Burman):

43.

akumla	*nA*	*arenla$_j$*	*tangko*	*[pa$_{i/j/k}$*	*tomAka*	*sAnga*	*yanglu-*
Akumla	NOM	Arenla	for	self	for	tea	make

ang]	*ta*	*sa*
Imp	Comp	said

'Akumla $_i$ asked Arenal $_j$ to make some tea for himself/for herself$_{i/j/k}$.'

However, the occurrence of the verbal reflexive (vr) or other-benefactive clitic blocks long-distance binding and the anaphor can only be coindexed locally.

44.

akumla$_i$	*nA*	*arenla$_j$*	*tangko*	*[pa*	*tomAka*	*sAnga*	*yanglu-*
Akumla	NOM	Arenla	for	self$_{*i/j/*k}$	for	tea	make

ang	*bi]*	*ta*	*sa*
Imp	Other Ben	Comp	said

'Akumla $_i$ asked Arenla $_j$ to make some tea for self$_{*i/j/*k}$'
(Pangarsenla 2004)

2.3.2. Long-distance binding and the morphological nature of the anaphor

Another aspect that is crucial in long-distance binding is the morphological nature of the anaphor. South Asian languages have simplex and complex forms of the anaphor and in many cases the complex anaphor is a reduplicated form of the simplex form (Subbarao & Lalitha Murthy, 2000 for Telugu, Lust et al 2000 for other South Asian languages). It is significant that in all South Asian languages a reduplicated form does not permit long-distance binding while it is the simplex form that permits long-distance binding. In Subbarao & Lalitha Murthy 2000, Sarju Devi & Subbarao 2003 we have demonstrated that the complex anaphor in many South Asian languages is the result of reduplication of the anaphor and Case Copying of the subject case marker onto one of the elements of the bipartite structure of the complex anaphor. Let us look at the following data from Hindi-Urdu. In Hindi-Urdu the complex anaphor *apne aap* + case marker does not permit long-distance binding (45) while the simplex form *apne*+ case marker does (46). The subscript k refers to discourse antecedent. '*apnee áap* has only a local antecedent, but *apne* is ambiguous [that is, it permits long-distance binding.-KVS].' (Davison 2000: 424).

Hindi-Urdu:

45.

mantrii $_i$	*ne*	*raajaa $_j$*	*se*	*[PRO $_j$*	*apne aap $_{*i/j/*k}$*	*ko*	*doS*
minister	ERG	king	with		self (complex)	DAT	blame

na	*dene*	*ko]*	*kahaa*
not	give	to	said

'The minister$_i$ told the king$_j$ not to blame himself (king)/* him (minister).'

46.

mantrii $_i$	*ne*	*raajaa$_j$*	*se*	*[PRO$_j$*	*apne$_{i/j/*k}$*	*ko*	*doS*
minister	ERG	king	with		self (simplex)	DAT	blame

na	*dene*	*ko*	*kahaa*
not	give	to	said

'The minister$_i$ told the king$_j$ not to blame him (minister)$_i$ / himself (king)$_{j/}$'

In Telugu too a simplex anaphor permits long-distance binding while a complex anaphor does not. The complex anaphor is formed by the reduplication of the simplex anaphor and Case Copying (Subbarao & Lalitha Murthy 2000).

Telugu:[4]

47.

karuNa$_i$	*sarita*	*ni$_j$*	*tana$_{i,j}$*	*miida*	*ciraaku*
Karuna	Sarita	ACC	self	on	irritation

paDa	*vaddu*	*ani*	*andi*
fall	not (Imp)	Quot	said

---

[4] Telugu has a form of the negative *waddu* 'don't' that occurs only in imperative sentences and it cannot occur in affirmative sentences. Though (48) and (49) are sentences in indirect speech with the quotative as the complementizer, the negative *waddu* 'don't' that occurs only in imperative sentences occurs in such sentences. This is due to the absence of a clearcut distinction between the direct and indirect speech in South Asian languages unlike in most European languages. For details, see Subbarao (in press) and Sigurdsson (2004).

'Karuna$_i$ asked Sarita$_j$ not to get irritated at herself (Karuna/Sarita$_{i,j}$.)'

48.

karuNa$_i$	*sarita*	*ni$_j$*	*tana*	*miida*	*tanu$_{*i/j}$*	*ciraaku*
Karuna	Sarita	ACC	self	on	self	irritation

paDa	*vaddu*	*ani*	*andi*
fall	not (Imp)	Quot	said

'Karuna$_i$ asked Sarita$_j$ not to get irritated at herself$_{*i\ (Karuna)/\ j\ (Sarita)}$.'

It is the process of reduplication of the anaphor that disambiguates sentence (48) and this disambiguation process in Telugu is in consonance with similar processes in other South Asian languages.

Recall that a verbal anaphor blocks ambiguity and hence, long-distance binding is not permitted when a verbal anaphor occurs in the embedded clause. There are some predicates in Telugu and in other Dravidian languages that require a verbal anaphor. Hence, (49) and (50) are unambiguous irrespective of the nature of the nominal anaphor, whether it is simplex or complex, due to the presence of the verbal anaphor in the embedded clause.

49.

maalati$_i$	*mamata$_j$*	*ni*	*tana*	*ni*	*tanu$_{*i/j}$*	*poguDu*	*kona$_{*i/j}$*
Malati	Mamata	ACC	self	ACC	self	praise	Vr

vaddu	*ani*	*ceppindi*
not-Imp	Quot	said

'Malati$_i$ told Mamata$_j$ not to praise herself$_{*i\ (Malati)/j\ Mamata)}$.'

50.

maalati$_i$	*mamata$_j$*	*ni*	*tana*	*ni$_{*i/j}$*	*poguDu*	*kona$_{*i/j}$*
Malati	Mamata	ACC	self	acc	praise	Vr

vaddu	*ani*	*ceppindi*
not-Imp	Quot	said

'Malati$_i$ told Mamata$_j$ not to praise her$_{*i\ (Malati)/j\ Mamata)}$.'

We have pointed out earlier that a verbal clitic blocks long-distance binding. If our claim is correct, a language that has only verbal anaphors and no nominal anaphors must permit only local binding and not long-distance binding. Our claim gets support from Munda languages such as Ho and Mundari in which there is only a verbal anaphor and hence, no long-distance coindexation of the anaphor with the matrix subject is permitted.

2.3.3. Copying/Repetition of a noun as a disambiguating device

We shall now show how the repetition of a noun or noun phrase effects the interpretation of a sentence. In internally-headed relative clauses in Mizo a sentence in (51) is ambiguous. The sentence becomes unambiguous, if the head noun is repeated in the matrix clause as in (52).

Mizo (Tibeto-Burman):

51.

nimin-ah	*chang*	*changurna*	*a-*	*lei-*	*na*	*cu*
yesterday	bread	bakery	3sg	bring	nozr	def

ϕ	*a-*	*hlui*
	3sg	old

(i) 'The bread that she brought yesterday is old.'
(ii) 'The bakery from which she brought the bread is old.'

In (52) the noun *changurna* is copied in the main clause as a result of which the sentence in no longer ambiguous.

52.

nimin-ah	*chang*	*changurna*	*a-*	*lei-*	*na*
yesterday	bread	bakery	3sg	bring	nozr

cu	*changurna*	*a- hlui*
def	bakery	3sg old

(i) '*The bread that she brought yesterday is old.'
(ii) 'The bakery from which she brought the bread is old.'

(Om Prakash & Subbarao 2004), Om Prakash (in preparation)

Thus, the native speaker of Mizo uses copying of the head noun phrase as a principled device to disambiguate a sentence.

In Sema (Tibeto-Burman) an internally-headed relative clause occurs in direct object, indirect object and oblique object (except the comitative) positions. An ablative PP can head an internally-headed relative clause if and only if the NP is repeated as the internal head as well as the external head subject to the following conditions:

(i) the external head should not carry the generic possessive marker.
(ii) no lexical case marker other than the nominative occurs with the NP occurring in the position of the external head.

Sentence (56) can have only the DO as head and not the ablative PP. Thus, it gives the interpretation that 'the water is dirty' and not 'the well is dirty.'

Sema (Tibeto-Burman):

53.

nO -	*nO azIkhikhi*	*lOnO*	*azI*	*sIle -*	*keu ti*	*- ye*	*miThe*	*mO*
you	[+trm]well	from	water	brought	NOZ	that [-trm]	clean	neg

(i) *'The well from which you brought the water is dirty.'
(ii) 'The water which you brought from the well is dirty.'

Thus, in (53) though the NP *azIkhikhi* 'well' occurs with an ablative case marker, it cannot head the internal relative clause though it fulfills both the requirements of case and word order. Though the DO *azI* 'water' or *azIkhikhi* 'well' can potentially be the heads of the internal relative clause, it is the DO that is interpreted as the head in (53) and not the ablative PP *azIkhikhi lOnO* 'well from'. To make an ablative PP the head of an internal relative clause there is a specific strategy that Sema adopts. Under this strategy the head noun is partially **repeated** in the matrix clause. It occurs to the right of the definite marker *-u* in a position ear-marked for the head noun in an externally headed relative clause. Sentence (54) below is illustrative:

54.

nO - nO	***azIkhikhi***	*lOnO*	*azI*	*sIle – keu*	***zIkhIkhI****- ye*	*miThe*
you [+trm]	well	from	water	brought NOZR	well [-trm]	clean

(i) 'The well from which you brought the water is dirty.'
(ii) *'The water which you brought from the well is dirty.'

(Subbarao & Kevichusa 2005, Kevichusa in preparation, Achumi in preparation)

The repetition of the noun phrase *azIkhikhi* 'well' as *zIkhikhi* is only partial and as *a-*, the generic possession marker is not repeated. The generic possession marker in many Tibeto-Burman languages is used with kinship terms and with objects that are very intimate to the possessor such as 'well' or 'home' etc. (cf. Subbarao & Sarju Devi, ms.).

The data from Hindi-Urdu, Mizo and Sema clearly demonstrate that reduplication or repetition plays an important role in disambiguation.

2.3.4. The Role of Clitics in Scope Disamiguation

In this subsection section we discuss how the occurrence of a clitic/particle permits or blocks wide scope interpretation. In Narrow Scope a question word occurring in an embedded complement may have its scope limited to the same clause while in Wide Scope the question expression has its scope extended to the matrix clause.

There are six parameters, amongst others, that affect the scope of a question expression (cf. Subbarao 2001). We present here one of the parameters.

2.3.4.1. With matrix predicates *anukonu* 'think', *vinu* 'hear' the question expression occurring in a complement clause has Wide Scope reading in Telugu (Dravidian).

In Telugu, unlike in Bengali (Bayer 2001), both wide and narrow scope readings are permitted with a verb such as *think.* (55) is an example of a question word with a wide scope reading. Note that in (55) neither an *yes/no* question marker nor the clitic *–ō* is present.

Wide Scope reading

55.

mīru	*[[paarṭī*	*ki*	*evaru*	*vastaar(u)-*	*ani]*	*anukonṭunnaaru*
you	party	DAT	who	will come	Quot	are thinking

'Who do you think will come to the party?'

The Wide Scope reading is blocked and the sentence has Narrow Scope reading (56) below:

(i) when the marker *-oo* which is generally termed as a dubitative marker (dub mkr) or complementizer (Krishnamurti & Gwynn 1985: 361) occurs to the right of the embedded verb, or
(ii) when an *yes/no* question marker occurs.

It is due to the presence of these markers that Wide Scope reading is blocked.

Narrow Scope reading

Telugu (DR)

56.

mēmu	*[[paarṭī*	*ki*	*evaru*	*vastaar(u)-*	*aa/*
we	party	DAT	who	will come	qm

oo]	*ani]*	*anukonṭunnāmu*
dub mkr	Quot	are thinking

'We were thinking/wondering who would come to the party.' (Narrow Scope)
'*Who do you think will come here?' (Wide Scope)

3. In this paper we attempted to demonstrate that particles, clitics, the occurrence of complex forms in contrast to simplex forms play an important role in disambiguation and help the speaker in conveying the intended information. Though the data presented in support of our hypothesis are basically from South Asian languages, we believe that our hypothesis may be found to have cross-linguistic validity. This paper also highlights the syntactic role that reduplication plays and demonstrates that it cannot simply be restricted to the domain of morphology alone.

Acknowledgements

We are thankful to R. K. Agnihotri, T. Bhattacharya, Bahadur Singh, R. Bhatt, N. Sharma, Om Prakash, T. J. Koh, Pawan Kumar, Shashi Misra, Chander Singh and many others whose judgements have been helpful in this study. Special thanks are due to Peter Hook for his valuable comments.

Abbreviations

ACC: accusative, Cpm: conjunctive participial marker, DAT: dative, Emph: emphatic marker, Def: definite marker; ERG: ergative, Fut: future, Imp: imperative, NOM: nominative marker, NOZR: nominalizer, Other Ben: other benefactive, Self Ben: self benefactive, pl: plural, Quot: quotative, sg: singular, trm: transitive marker, Vr-verbal reflexive.

References

Abbi, A. 1984. The conjunctive participle in Hindi-Urdu. *International Journal of Dravidian Linguistics.*

Achumi, R. In preparation. *Aspects to Sema Syntax.* Doctoral dissertation, University of Delhi.

Bayer, J. 2001. Two grammars in one: Sentential complements and complementizers in Bangla and other South Asian languages. In: Bhaskararao, Peri & Karumuri Venkata Subbarao (eds.).*The Yearbook of South Asian Languages 2001.* New Delhi. Thousand Oaks. London: Sage Publications.

Davison, A. 1981. 'Syntactic and semantic indeterminacy resolved'. In P. Cole, ed. *Radical Pragmatics.* Academic Press, New York.

____ 2000. Lexical anaphors and pronouns in Hindi-Urdu. In: Lust et al. (2000).

Kachru, Y. 1981. 'On the syntax, semantics and pragmatics of the conjunctive participle in Hindi-Urdu'. *Studies in the Linguistic Sciences 11:2.*

Kellogg, S. H. 1938. *A grammar of the Hindi language.* Oriental Reprint. Delhi: Oriental Books Reprint Corporation.

Kevichusa, M. In preparation. *Aspects of Angami syntax.* Doctoral Dissertation, University of Delhi.

Krishnamurti, Bh. & J. P. L. Gwynn. 1985. *A grammar of Modern Telugu.* Delhi: Oxford University Press.

Masica, C. P. 1976. *Defining a linguistic area: South Asia.* Chicago: The University of Chicago Press

Lalitha Murthy, B. 1994. *Participial constructions: A cross-linguistic study.* Doctoral thesis. Delhi: University of Delhi.

Lalitha Murthy, B. & K. V. Subbarao. 2000. Lexical anaphors in Mizo. In: Lust et al. (2000).

Lohse, B, J. A. Hawkins, T. Wasow. 2004. Domain minimization in English verb-particle constructions. *Language* 80.2.

Lust, B. J. Gair, K. Wali and K. V. Subbarao (eds.). 2000. *Lexical anaphors and pronouns in selected South Asian languages.* Berlin: Mouton de Gruyter.

Om Prakash. In preparation. *Subordination in Mizo.* Doctoral Dissertation, University of Delhi.

Om Prakash & K. V. Subbarao 2003. Internally-headed relative clauses in Mizo. Paper presented at the Himalayan Languages Conference, CIIL, Mysore.

Pangarsenla, A. Lexical Anaphors in Ao. ms. University of Delhi.

Sarju Devi, T. In preparation. *Embedded Clauses in Manipuri.* Doctoral Dissertation, University of Delhi.

Sigurdsson, H. 2004. The syntax of person, tense, and speech features. To appear in: *Italian Journal of Linguistics / Rivista di Linguistica* 16,1, 2004.

Subbarao, K. V. 1971. Reflexivization in Hindi. *Studies in the Linguistic Sciences* 3.2. Urbana-Champaign: University of Illinois.

____ 1996. Conjunctive participles in South Asian languages: Paper presented at the Indo-French Seminar, University of Hyderabad.

Subbarao, K. V. 2001. Complementation in South Asian languages. Paper presented at South Asian Languages Analysis Conference, University of Konstanz, Germany.

____ ms. Tense and agreement in backward control. Paper presented at the Seminar on Control Verbs at ZAS, Berlin, Germany.

____ (in press). Typological characteristics of South Asian languages. In: *Language in South Asia.* (Eds.) Kachru, B. B. & S. N. Sridhar. Cambridge University Press.

Subbarao, K. V. & M. Kevichusa. 2005. Relative clauses in Sema. In: Tanmoy Bhattacharya (ed.). *The year book of South Asian Languages and Linguistics* 2005. Berlin: Mouton de Gruyter.

Subbarao, K. V. & Lalitha Murthy, B. 2000. Lexical anaphors in Telugu. In: Lust et al. 2000.

Subbarao, K. V. & T. Sarju Devi. ms. *A grammar of Manipuri.* University of Delhi.

PART III

OLD AND NEW DESCRIPTIVE PERSPECTIVES ON PARTICULAR LANGUAGES

SYNTACTIC DUALITY IN CLASSICAL TAMIL POEMS

JEAN-LUC CHEVILLARD

"Since the punctuation of compounds is my own responsibility, it is no doubt up to me to try to justify the practice. [...] So far as the grammatical analysis itself is concerned, I am anxious not to give the impression of imagining that experienced Sanskritists stand in the same need of it as an aid to interpretation as I do myself. One might nevertheless urge its merits as a simple convenience to all readers, like word-division, the use of which does not imply that scholars would be unable to separate the words out for themselves. However my case rests on quite different grounds, those supplied by Hertel to justify word-division itself, namely that its use provides the simplest form of running commentary. To justify his choice of readings, an editor must make clear how he construes his own text."

(M. Coulson, *Mālatīmādhava*, introduction, p. liii)

When one attempts to make a linguistic description of a dead language, some limitations have to be kept in mind:

- **Limitation 1 :** one works on a finite set of data (a closed corpus of texts), and that text has to be handled by the methods of philology[1] (and it can have variants).
- **Limitation 2 :** one cannot check that data with native speakers and obtain feedback, and great parts of the data may be poorly understood (or not at all).

If that language has possessed at one point in time an indigenous grammatical, lexicographical and/or commentatorial tradition, the second limitation may seem to be partly overcome, because a one-way flow of information can be established with a, hopefully, native source of linguistic knowledge, provided one is aware of another limitation:

- **Limitation 3 :** the perspective of a traditional grammarian, or lexicographer, or commentator, does not necessarily coincide with that of a modern descriptive linguist.

  If, additionally, the texts one studies are literary/poetical texts, there appears a supplementary difficulty which could be

[1] For sharing with me her insights concerning many points discussed here and for reading several successive versions of this paper, I would like to express here my special thanks to my philologist colleague, and learned friend, Eva Wilden. All errors are of course mine.

formulated thus:

Limitation 4 : Can a language used in literary/poetical texts be said to have had native speakers? and should it be recognized as a natural language or as an artificial creation?[2]

Defining perfect guidelines for avoiding all the pitfalls which are the consequences of these four limitations is beyond the scope of this paper, which solely concerns itself with one case study concerning such a language, namely Classical Tamil. However I shall try to keep them in mind.

Classical Tamil: the language of a corpus

Many present-day speakers of Tamil would probably be shocked to see Classical Tamil described as a "dead language" : one often meets with statements that Tamil is at the same time a living and a classical language. Their perception is shaped by the fact that a sizeable part of the vocabulary of Classical Tamil is still in use in the H (or formal) variety of Modern Tamil, and also probably by the fact that memorizing of some CTamil texts (like the *Kuṟaḷ*), at least partly, is traditionally done in schools. Moreover, a number of bridges between the past and the present exist, some of them being commentaries, glosses, translations from CTamil to more recent varieties, and some of them being scholars who have been specially trained in reading the ancient texts and their ancient commentaries, having received their knowledge from earlier scholars. Nevertheless, it is improbable that there has been a perfect continuous line of transmission of the understanding of classical texts, and even traditional scholars cannot play the role of quasi-native speakers for Classical Tamil (henceforth CTamil), although some of them can certainly compose poetry in neo-classical Tamil.

The CTamil texts which we shall examine here, are poems which were composed at dates difficult to determine. The main vehicles through which these poems have been handed down to us are anthologies, compiled at dates which are also not well known.[3] One of the problems that face us is to determine whether some anthologies are, as a whole, later than others. Another problem, which has possibly been examined less often, is to examine whether inside each anthology there is linguistic homogeneity. An improvement of our knowledge in this respect might be

---

[2] That language could possibly be described as a creative extension of a natural language, obeying a set of constraints, that differs [in a dual/parallel way] from those for another language with which it is in symbiotic relation in a diglossic situation. For the Tamil diglossia, see Britto [1986]. For other perspectives on diglossia, see the volume edited by Bh. Krishnamurtti [1986] *South Asian Languages: structure, convergence and diglossia.*

[3] For a discussion of the chronology, see Wilden [2002] [WZKS, XLVI (105-133)]

a way of improving also our grasp on their internal chronology. With these objectives in mind, a program of systematic observations of the linguistic characteristics of several CTamil anthologies is currently being conducted[4] and concentrates for the time being on a set of 3 early anthologies of love poetry: the *Kuṟuntokai* (KT, 401 short poems, 4 to 8 lines), *Naṟṟiṇai* (NA, 400 poems, 9 to 12 lines) and *Akanāṉūṟu* (AN, 400 long poems, 13 to 31 lines). The results presented here will mainly be drawn from 4 corpora, listed here by ascending number of lines.

- CK [152 lines] (a subset of KT): the 38 poems having 4-lines inside the KT
- NE [658 lines] (a subset of AN) consisting of the 40 *neytal* poems[5]
- KT [2504 lines] (the complete anthology)
- NA [4180 lines] (the complete anthology)

A dual Syntax: M-syntax vs. U-syntax

The main point which I would like to emphasize in this study, is that there is a duality in the syntax of these texts contrasting two poles, which I shall characterize as a **marked syntax** (or M-syntax) opposed to an **unmarked syntax** (or U-syntax), and that most of the poems that belong to the corpus bear traces of these two syntaxes, in ways which I shall try here to quantify. The roots of that phenomenon probably lie in the diglossic situations that have been existing at the various periods when the poems were composed: M-syntax is probably rooted in the "vernacular speech" that was in use at that time, although the poetical constraints certainly restricted/filtered the spectrum of what was put inside the mould; on the other hand, U-syntax would draw its strength/impetus/efficiency from the poetical craft of learned men vying with (or emulating) each other in the use (and the enrichment) of a stock of formulae, where the use of what traditional CTamil grammar calls *tokai* (or *tokuti*), usually translated as "compounds", is frequent.

The terminology which I shall use in describing the CTamil texts is ultimately based on the one found in the oldest preserved CTamil grammar, the *Tolkāppiyam* (T), subsequently reworked by later grammars like the *Naṉṉūl* (N), and partly adapted into western languages

---

[4] This effort, by my colleague E. Wilden and myself, is itself part of a wider Pondicherry "Sangam Project", that has the ambition to cover the whole of CTamil literature.

[5] The *neytal* poems are devoted to the sea-shore setting. A critical edition and translation project is currently underway (Wilden & Chevillard, forthcoming). A full edition and translation of the 400 poems of AN [totalling 7151 lines] is also planned.

(Latin, English, etc.) by missionaries (most notably Beschi) who had acquainted themselves with traditional grammars. As seen through that terminology, there are in CTamil, to begin with, two main inflected parts of speech, the noun (*peyar*) and the verb (*viṉai, toḻil*),[6] but that basic terminological dichotomy allows for the presence of other categories. For instance, the forms that we could consider as predicative adjectives, are treated by the T as occurrences of special verbs, called *kuṟippu viṉai* "suggestive verbs", morphologically defective with respect to the expression of tense.

My description of M-syntax will be quite incomplete. The reason is that it is much more complex than U-syntax. I shall in fact concentrate on those features in M-syntax which have a dual feature in U-syntax. One such area, in the case of the verbal paradigm, is the use of the two main types of *peyar-eccam* "relative participles", designated here as V^{PE1} and V^{PE2}, which is echoed in U-syntax by constructions using plain verbal roots, designated here as V^0, which could be considered as an unmarked relative participle. Both will be presented, in a preliminary fashion, in the next paragraph.

Argument positions around a relative participle

The *peyar-eccam* forms are so called because they are (syntactically) "incomplete" (*eccam*) forms, which have to be completed by a *peyar* "noun", which immediately follows it. We shall refer to this noun, N_1, as the "head noun" and shall consider it as the most prominent syntactic argument for the participle. Many relative participles have other arguments, N_2, N_3, etc., standing on the left, and a typical template for these constructions can be represented as:

$$\{((\ldots N_3) \ldots N_2)V^{PE}N_1\} \text{ (where } V^{PE} \text{ could be } V^{PE1} \text{ or } V^{PE2})$$

The difference between the V^{PE1} and V^{PE2} types is temporal (or aspectual) but syntactically they behave in the same way, although we shall see later that the most frequent semantic roles for their arguments are not the same. I shall give a first series of examples with the verbs *utirtal* "to fall" and *aṭutal* "to kill". Their PE1 forms are *utirum* "which-falls" and *aṭūum*[7] "which kills". Their PE2 forms are *utirnta* "which-fell" and *aṭṭa* "which-killed". The English translations given here are approximations, because the head noun can have various roles with

[6] In their main occurrences in non-technical literature, *viṉai* is "action" and *toḻil* "activity".

[7] There is another variant : *aṭum*.

respect to the PE, as shall be seen in some of the following examples, where the head noun is underlined

- *utirnta **kaṉi*** (fall^{PE2} ripe-fruit) "**fruit** which fell" [AN 380-4/5]
- *utirum ... **malar*** (fall^{PE1}flower) "**flowers** which fall" [AN 199-2/3][8]
- *aṭṭa **mallar*** (kill^{PE2} warriors) "**warriors** which killed" [KT 34-5]

I shall refer to such examples as instances of $\{V^{PE1}N\}$ or $\{V^{PE2}N\}$ constructions. These examples, which are "real" examples extracted from the CTamil corpus, are simply the most elementary ones, inside a class of examples where we most often find more than one nominal argument, as in the following two examples, which are instances of, respectively, $\{N_2V^{PE2}N_1\}$ and $\{N_3...N_2V^{PE1}N_1\}$ constructions.[9]

- *kāy$_{N2}$ utirnta **[paiṅ kulai]**$_{N1}$* (unripe-fruit fall^{PE2} green bunch) "**green bunch** from which unripe fruits have fallen" [AN 21-20][10]
- *[puli ēṟṟai]$_{N3}$ ... kaḷiṟu$_{N2}$ aṭūum ... **verpu**$_{N1}$* (tiger male elephant-bull kill^{PE1} mountain) "**the mountain** where the male tiger kills the elephant-bull" [NA 36-1/4]

It should also be noted here that, although the inflectional paradigm of the noun is primarily described in terms of case by traditional CTamil grammarians, the multiple nominal arguments N_1, N_2, N_3 that appear in these examples are not morphologically marked and this is quite typical of the language of that corpus, where case morphemes are not at all frequent.[11]

This information being given, I shall now give parallel examples for the *viṉait tokai* "verbal compound", which results, as already noted, from the combination of a verbal root V^0 and of a noun. In the case of the verbs *utirtal* and *aṭutal*, the V^0 are *utir* and *aṭu* and we can see them used in the following examples, combined with a noun,

---

[8] In order to keep this initial presentation simple, the other specifiers of *malar* "flower" are not reproduced here.

[9] I have used square brackets to indicate those nominal arguments that are themselves complex, like *[paiṅ kulai]* and *[puli ēṟṟai]*. It has also to be noted that, even though the examples are more complex than the preceding ones, they are simplified, as can be seen from the use of "...".

[10] The head noun has for its referent the starting point of the action of falling.

[11] In the real picture of noun morphology in CTamil that emerges from a corpus-based study, the most important distinction is the one between the unmarked and the oblique forms.

- *aṭu pōr* (kill^{V0} war) "deadly battle" (NA 39-9)
- *aṭu piṇaṉ* (kill^{V0} corpse) "killed corpse" (NA 329-2)
- *utir vī* (fall^{V0} flower) "flowers that drop" (AN 99-7)

Just like the V^{PE1} and V^{PE2}, the V^0 (or plain verbal root) is often found with two arguments, like what we have in the following example, which I shall describe as an instance of $\{N_2V^0N_1\}$:

- *ikal aṭu* ***muṉpiṉ*** (enmity^N kill^{V0} strength$^{N\text{-obl.}}$) "[tusks having the] **strength** to kill enemies" (AN 172-9)

Analysis of a two-lines sample text

In order to explain more precisely what I refer to when talking about a dual syntax, I shall start with the analysis of a 2-lines passage extracted from a 15-lines poem in the AN anthology. This will also serve as an illustration of the difficulties inherent in dealing with classical poetry, and this is why I shall first give it in its metrical form, accompanied by an unpublished English gloss going back to the late V. M. Subramanya Ayyar (henceforth VMS).

mutumarat tuṟaiyu muravuvāy mutupuṭ
katumeṉak kuḻaruṅ kaḻutuvaḷaṅ karaināḷ [AN 260, 12-13]

"At midnight when the demons start to roam about, the old rock-horned owl which has a broken beak and is always residing in the old tree, ..., suddenly cries." (VMS)

If we separate the metrical feet into words and additionally dissolve the sandhi, while keeping as an information the fact that there was originally a sandhi change[12], we obtain a text, which is the following, in which I have isolated 14 strings.

mutu marattu{S^{aut}} *uṟaiyum*{S^{aut}} *muravu vāy mutu puḷ*{$S^{?sign}$}
katum-eṉa{S^{aut}} *kuḻarum*{S^{aut}} *kaḻutu vaḷaṅku*{S^{aut}} *arai-nāḷ*

---

[12] This information must not be lost, because it can have consequences on how one must interpret the syntactical relations. However, many sandhi rules can be described as "automatic", and they shall be indicated here by {S^{aut}} but these "automatic" sandhi rules are most of the time not applied by modern editors, which might give the impression to the reader that they are optional. The significant sandhis shall be indicated by {S^{sign}} or by {$S^{?sign}$} (when there is a doubt).

Using as exponents grammatical tags, intended as short-cuts[13] into the morphology of Tamil and soon to be explained, and giving the meanings, the 14 strings reduce to 12 items, because *katum-e<u>n</u>a* can be analysed as an ideophonic expression, containing the particle *e<u>n</u>a* as a constituent, (see Chevillard 2004: 416) and because *arai-nāḷ* "midnight" is best treated as an unanalysable idiom, although *arai* "half" and *nāḷ* "day" could exist as stand-alone nouns. The 12 items are as follows:

<u>old$^{\text{A0}}$ tree$^{\text{N-OBL}}$</u> reside$^{\text{V-PE2}}$ <u>broken^{D} beak^{N} old$^{\text{A0}}$ bird^{N}</u>
suddenly$^{\text{ideoph-ena}}$ cry$^{\text{V-PE2}}$ <u>demons^{N} roam$^{\text{V0}}$ midnight^{N}</u>

For reasons which are ultimately rooted in the traditional grammatical analysis of CTamil "compounds", three phrases inside the text have been underlined. They constitute what I designate as the domain of U-syntax (unmarked syntax), and I shall call them "U-components". A further step in their analysis, which shall shortly be explained, can be accomplished by adding some punctuation marks, adapted from Coulson [1989]:[14]

- (old$^{\text{A0}}$:TREE) "old tree"
- ((broken^{D}:beak^{N})-(old$^{\text{A0}}$:BIRD^{N})) "old bird with a broken beak"
- ((demon^{N}-roam$^{\text{V0}}$):MIDNIGHT^{N}) "at midnight, when the demons roam about"

For each of the three U-components, the last item, which has been marked here by small capitals, is designated as "the head" of the U-component. When we replace inside the original text each of the U-components by its head, the three heads being "tree", "bird" and "midnight", we obtain a reduced text, which is:

---

[13] Among the tags that appear as exponents, those starting by V (resp. A or N) indicate forms belonging to a verbal (resp. adjectival or nominal) paradigm. The items with a "D" tag are isolated items which cannot easily be ascribed to a regular verbal, adjectival or nominal paradigm, but which are in the position of determiners. A more thorough examination of CTamil lexicon might however possibly provide ground for considering them as belonging to the paradigms of defective verbs, nouns or adjectives. This is to say that "D" is also a "waiting-room" grammatical category.

[14] In this system (Coulson [1989] pp.l-li), "A;B" is a co-ordinative compound (*dvandva*), "A:B" is a descriptive compound (*karmadhāraya*) and "A-B" is a dependent compound (*tatpuruṣa*), both descriptive and dependant compound being considered as "determinative compound" (the wider acceptation of *tatpuruṣa*). Additionally, another type of compound, the *bahuvrīhi* type, can be formed on top of these 3 types and is noted by an underlining : "A<u>;</u>B", "A<u>:</u>B" and "A<u>-</u>B". Finally, there is special notation "A B" for prepositional compounds (*avyayībhāva)*, a special type of exocentric compound.

tree^{OBL} reside$^{\text{V-PE2}}$ bird^{N} suddenly$^{\text{ideoph-eṉa}}$ cry$^{\text{V-PE2}}$ midnight^{N}

This reduced text constitutes what I designate as the domain of M-syntax (marked syntax) and it can be translated thus:

"at MIDNIGHT, when the BIRD that resides in the TREE suddenly cries".

The pivotal elements, in the building of the reduced phrase with "marked syntax", are, in this case, 2 verbal forms, *uṟaiyum* "reside$^{\text{V-PE1}}$" and *kuḻaṟum* "cry$^{\text{V-PE1}}$" which are the *peyar eccam* ("relative participles") of the *ceyyum* type of the verbs *uṟaital* "to reside" and *kuḻaṟutal* "to howl" (see above).

If we now combine the domains of these two syntaxes, we obtain the full text, where the head nouns are in capitals:

"at MIDNIGHT-when-the-demons-roam-about, when the old-BIRD-with-a-broken-beak that resides in the old-TREE suddenly cries."

Compounds in CTamil: the building blocks of U-Syntax

Lest my presentation of U-syntax and M-syntax might appear as an arbitrary decision of mine, I shall now try to briefly explain the standard "theory" on the compounds which is found in the native CTamil grammars, starting with T.[15] The basic idea, which was certainly adapted from the Sanskrit grammarians' concept of *samāsa,* is that one can meet with 6 types of complex items called *tokai*-s[16] (see TC412c) which "have the behaviour of a single [inflected] word *(oru col)*" (TC420c), although they contain several components (see TC419c). However, the author (or the authors) of T, which is the most ancient CTamil grammar, seem(s) to have been hesitant to make precise statements on the nature of the

---

[15] For a detailed exposition, the interested reader who reads French can consult Chevillard [1996] (pp. 491-513).

[16] The word *tokai* itself could be explained in two ways. As Cēṉāvaraiyar, one of the commentators of T puts it: "Les maîtres sont de deux partis : **a.** ceux qui disent que [les composés] sont [appelés] *tokai* «composés-[à-élision]» du fait que s'élide *(tokutal)* un morphème casuel *(vēṟṟumai ~urupu)*, un morphème de comparaison *(uvama ~urupu)*, [la particule coordinative] *um*, une finale verbale *(viṉai+-col= īṟu)* ou une finale de mot de qualité *(paṇpu+-col= īṟu)*; et ceux qui disent que [les composés] sont [appelés] *tokai* «composés-[somme]» du fait que sur une [unique] valeur, deux ou plusieurs mots, étant perçus comme une unité *(oṟṟumai+ paṭutal)* sans qu'il y ait fissure *(piḷavu-paṭutal)*, sont liés *(iyaital)* entre eux." (TC412c, as translated in Chevillard [1996]). According to Cēṉāvaraiyar, the correct interpretation is the second one.

components to be found inside a *tokai*,[17] although devoting 10 sūtra-s to a presentation of the 6 types of tokai which he/they recognize(s) and of their properties. The traditional list of *tokai* found in sūtra TC412c, is the following:

1. *vēṟṟumait tokai* "case compound" (characterized in TC413c),
2. *uvamat tokai* "comparison compound" (characterized in TC414c),
3. *viṉaiyiṉtokai* (later called *viṉait tokai*) "verbal compound" (lit. "action compound") (characterized in TC415c),
4. *paṇpiṉ tokai* (later called *paṇput tokai)* "adjectival compound" (lit. "quality compound") (characterized in TC416c),
5. *ummait tokai* "copulative compound" (lit. "compound" [with] *ummai* [for its value], where *ummai* designates the coordinating clitic *-um*) (characterized in TC417c),
6. *aṉmoḻit tokai* "compound [with] a non-word"[18] (characterized in TC418c)

We have to rely on the commentators for illustrations, because none are found in the T itself, which contains only characterizations and enumerations. I shall not however reproduce here all the examples they give, but shall also draw examples, as far as possible, from the CTamil corpus and concentrate my efforts on the three types of *tokai*-s most frequently met with, which are the 4th, 3rd and 1st in this list.

One fairly frequent and simple type of *tokai* is the *paṇput tokai* "adjectival compound".[19] A standard example given by commentators is *karuṅ kutirai* (TC410i) "black horse". In the sample text which we have examined, this type was represented in *mutu marattu* (old^{A0}:TREE$^{N\text{-}OBL}$) and *mutu puḷ* (old^{A0}:BIRD^{N})). The head (or second element) is a noun. The first element can be a plain adjectival root, here tagged A^0; it can also often be an adjectival form with an *–m* or an *–um* ending.[20] I shall punctuate them with a colon, imitating Coulson's representation of Sanskrit descriptive determinative compounds. The example *karuṅ kutirai* (black^{Aum}:horse^{N}) will thus be seen as an instance of A^{um}:N.

---

[17] The commentators excuse him by saying that the T does not deal with the topic of *oru-moḻip puṇarcci* "internal sandhi".

[18] These are usually identified with the Sanskrit *bahuvrīhi*-s. The Sanskritized grammar *Vīracōḻiyam* even calls them, in a direct loan translation, *pala nel camācam*-s (Vi_45).

[19] I have already studied that topic in Chevillard [1994].

[20] The class of adjectives is not completely homogeneous. The most convenient way of describing the typical adjectives seems to be to consider them as defective verbs, uninflected for tense.

Another very frequent type of *tokai* is the *viṉait tokai* "verbal compound". A standard example given by commentators is *kol yāṉai* (kill^{V0}:elephant^{N}) "murderous elephant". The head (or second element) is a noun. The first element is a plain verbal root, tagged V^0. The template is thus $\{V^0{:}N\}$, where I use the same punctuation as for *paṇput tokai*. In the sample text which we have examined, there is indeed a V^0, but it is found in combination with 2 nominal arguments, in ((demon^{N}-roam^{V0}):MIDNIGHT^{N}) "at midnight, when the demons roam about". It could thus be said to be an instance of a $\{(N_2\text{-}V^0){:}N_1\}$ template. The commentators of T quote one example that seems to fit into this template; however they do not do so while explaining *viṉait tokai*, but in connection with a T *sūtra* about ambiguous verbal constructions (TC95c). The example given is *puli kol yāṉai* [(tiger^{N}-kill^{V0}):elephant^{N}], which, according to them, can have two interpretations: "elephant which killed a tiger" and "elephant which a tiger killed". A corpus based examination reveals that V^0 forms are in fact used more frequently in $\{(N_2\text{-}V^0){:}N_1\}$ constructions than in $\{V^0{:}N\}$. We shall come back to these constructions later. I shall refer to them as "extended verbal compounds".

The third type of *tokai* which we shall present here is the *vēṟṟumait tokai* "casal compound", in which a head noun N_1 combines with another noun N_2 in a $\{N_2\text{-}N_1\}$ template. Commentators give series of 6 illustrations for this type of *tokai*, and explain that there is a casal relationship between the two nouns, and that the underlying case can be any case between the 2nd (accusative) and the 7th (locative). I punctuate them with a hyphen, following Coulson's representation of dependant determinative compounds. An example for the 6th case (or genitive), which is probably the most frequent, is *yāṉaik kōṭu* (elephant^{N}-tusk^{N}) "the elephant's tusk, elephant tusk".

2nd-degree expressions: $\{(A^0{:}N_2)\text{-}N_1\}$ constructions (*vaṇṇac ciṉaiccol*)

Before going back to the exploration of the relative importance of U-syntax and M-syntax in the various domains of the CTamil corpus, it seems important to mention a type of construction which is quite frequent in the corpus, and which seems to result from a combination of a *paṇput tokai* with a head noun. That construction is dealt with by TC26c, [21] and

[21] *Aṭai ciṉai mutal eṉa muṟai mūṉṟu um mayaṅkāmai // naṭai peṟṟu iyalum vaṇṇac ciṉaic col*

"Ne pas brouiller l'ordre des trois: (1b) / épithète, membre et principal; (1a) / C'est ainsi qu'ils ont la possibilité de s'employer, (2a) / Les mots à couleur et membre (2b)." (Chevillard, 1996). Although the sūtra only mentions "colour" for the adjectival component, other qualities are possible, as seen in the examples provided by the

the standard examples are:

- *ceṅ kāl nārai* ((red$^{A\text{-}m}$:foot^{N})-heron^{N}) "red-footed heron"
- *perun talaic cāttaṉ* ((big$^{A\text{-}um}$:head^{N})-Proper_Noun^{N}) "big-headed Cāttaṉ"

The sūtra describes a situation where 3 components combine in a specific order and become what is called a *vaṇṇac ciṉaic col:* inside it, the first element is called *aṭai* "adjunct", the second is called *ciṉai* "part" and the third is called *mutal* "whole".

Quantifying the proportions: the notion of U-density

Since I intend to define some tools for comparing the stylistic characteristics of different poems, I shall now introduce some numerical parameters to be used for making these comparisons possible. They are the following:

- **u** is the number of U-components (in this case, u = 3)
- **U** is the total number of items in the U-components (in this case, U = 9)
- **R** is the number of items in the reduced text (in this case, R = 6)
- **T** is the total number of items in the full text (in this case, T = 12)

Since the heads of the U-components are counted when determining both R and U, it should be clear that we always have:

$$\mathbf{T = U + R - u}$$

Finally, in order to be able to compare texts which do not have the same length, we shall define the U-density and the R-density, in the following way:

- U-density = U/T (in this case, U-density = 9/12 = 75%)
- R-density = R/T (in this case, R-density = 6/12 = 50%).

The sum of the R-density and of the U-density for a given text is usually greater than 100%: there is some overlapping, due to the fact that the heads of the U-components are ruled by both the U-syntax and the M-syntax.

---

commentators.

U-density variations inside the CK corpus.

We now turn back to data exploration and examine the CK corpus. This is the smallest of the corpora considered for this study: an exhaustive study of some of its features is therefore easier. As already stated, it consists of 38 poems containing 4 lines each, and I shall now proceed to expose how the parameters previously defined can be applied to it. Even with a very small corpus like this, it is of course not possible to justify here every step that leads to the results found as was done earlier in the case of the 2-lines sample text. For each poem inside the corpus, the following procedure was applied:

- determine T (not counting the 3 clitic particles -*ē*, -*ō* and –*um*).
- determine U, u and R
- compute the U-density

After making the computation for each poem, the results were ordered from lowest to highest, and the mean value was computed, and found to be close to 35%. The results can be seen in the following chart.

Chart 1: U-density in the CK corpus

U-Density	Poem Number	Adjectives (number of)	V^0 (number of)	Additional remark
0%	{KT 102}	nil	nil	s = 4
0%	{KT 120}	nil	nil	s = 3
0%	{KT 20}	nil	nil	
0%	{KT 399}	nil	nil	
0%	{KT 4}	nil	nil	s = 3
0%	{KT 97}	nil	nil	s = 4
15%	{KT 17}	nil	1	s = 4
16%	{KT 42}	1	nil	IL feature (*nāṭa*)
18%	{KT 6}	(1 D item :	nil	s = 4
19%	{KT 44}	*naṉam*)		s = 3
19%	{KT 93}	1	1	
		2	nil	
24%	{KT 137}	2	nil	
26%	{KT 124}	1	1	
26%	{KT 63}	2	1	
28%	{KT 135}	1	1	
33%	{KT 33}	2	nil	
33%	{KT 96}	1	nil	IL feature (*nāṭaṟku*)
35%	{KT 371}	0	1	IL feature (*nāṭaṉoṭu*)
38%	{KT 166}	2	1	

U-Density	Poem Number	Adjectives (number of)	V^0 (number of)	Additional remark
38%	{KT 186}	2	1	IL feature (*nāṭaṟku*)
40%	{KT 157}	1 (*tūu* ?)	2	
40%	{KT 188}	2	1	
40%	{KT 37}	2	nil	s = 3
42%	{KT 122}	3 ?	nil	s = 3 (or 4 ?)
45%	{KT 171}	2	nil	
47%	{KT 369}	1	1	
47%	{KT 3}	3	nil	IL feature (*nāṭaṉoṭu*)
50%	{KT 227}	2	nil	
55%	{KT 315}	2	3	IL feature (*nāṭaṉ*)
55%	{KT 39}	3	2	
55%	{KT 71}	3	2	? IL feature
57%	{KT 384}	3	2	(*kāṉavar*)
59%	{KT 68}	3	1	
60%	{KT 47}	4	1	
62%	{KT 109}]	2	2	
62%	{KT 116}]	3	2	IL feature (*tuṟaivaṉ*)
78%	{KT 119}	4	1	
80%	{KT 1}	3	1	

As can be seen on the chart, there is a wide range of value for the U-density parameter, and special attention will be given to the extremes. We can notice for instance that the highest U-density is seen in poem KT1, which is in fact, as noted by E. Wilden, probably the original *Kaṭavuḷ vāḻttu* ("invocation to God") of the KT anthology, and, as such, probably later than the other poems. On the other hand, we have a set of 6 poems for which the computed U-density is 0%, which means that they do not contain any *tokai*, and for 4 of these 6, I have indicated that the s parameter is greater than 1. This means that they contain more than one sentence, a non-written rule of CTamil poetry (disobeyed in their case) being that a poem should consist of a single sentence. Another feature which has been indicated in this chart is the IL (or "Interior Landscape" feature) which shall be explained later.

Before examining more in detail one of the complex poems, it seems useful to give other statistical information on this small corpus. For instance, the number of adjectives and of *paṇput tokai*-s (or adjectival compounds) which is found in these 38 poems is 62. The distribution is of course irregular because 9 poems do not contain any adjectives whereas some contain 4. These adjectival compounds can themselves be part of more complex constructions like those following the $\{(A^0{:}N_2)\text{-}N_1\}$ template which occurs 14 times in this small corpus. Another possibility is to have a combination of 2 adjectives with one noun, like for instance in *neṭu veḷ nilavu* ((long^{A0};white^{A0}): moonlight^{N})[22] (KT 47).

As far as verbal compounds and extended verbal compounds are concerned, it is to be noted that there are 24 V^0 forms in this corpus. Since the corpus has 152 lines, this means that the V^0-density is 16%. This can be compared with the characteristics of longer corpora, like KT and NA, in which we find, respectively, 710 and 1564 V^0 forms,[23] which gives us V^0-densities of 28% and 37%. These differences could have several explanations. One important parameter is that the NA corpus consists of poems which have a number of lines comprised between 9 and 12, whereas the poems in the KT corpus have between 4 and 8 lines. Since the CK corpus is simply the subset of the shortest poems in the KT, we could try to state an observation that

"the longer a poem is, the higher its V^0-density will be".

This observation might also be continued the following way:

"the longer a poem is, the more it has to draw on the resources of U-syntax, in which V^0 forms are an essential component"

The building elements of M-Syntax: verbal morphology

Before continuing our exploration of the CTamil corpus, the traditional classification of verbal forms will be briefly summarized here: there is first a dichotomy between forms which are described as (syntactically) complete (*muṟṟu*), i.e. the finite verbal forms, and forms which are described as incomplete (*eccam*), and there is even a relatively marginal group of in-between forms, considered as both *muṟṟu* and *eccam* (ME).[24] As far as *eccam* "incompletes" proper are concerned, they are further subdivided into the subgroup of the *viṉai eccam* (VE), ad-verbal participles (or "converbs"), that can be completed by a verb, and the subgroup of the *peyar eccam* (PE), "ad-nominal (or relative) participles", that can be completed by a noun. Further subdivisions inside PE and VE are made by mentioning the corresponding forms in the paradigm of *ceytal* "to do". To sum up, we have:

---

[22] This example will be commented on when I examine poem KT47. The use of ";" imitates Coulson's notation for *dvandvas*.

[23] These figures are based on indices kindly communicated to me by Eva Wilden.

[24] Concerning these *muṟṟ(u)-eccam* forms, see Steever [1988] p. 45 & p.51.

Chart 2: CTamil verbal paradigm

Main Groups in the verbal paradigm	Subgroups	Frequent English Equiv.	Statistics for the NE corpus	
			occur.	Distinct items (vocabulary)
PE (*peyar eccam*) "relative participle"	PE1 : *ceyyum* PE2 : *ceyta*	non-past (imperf.) past (perfective)	**86** **140**	**70** **100**
V^0 (plain verbal root)			**215**	**116**
VE (*vinai eccam*) (several types of converbs)	**VE1 : *ceytu*** VE2 : *ceyyū/(ceyyā)* VE3 : *ceypu* VE4 : *ceytena* VE5 : *ceyyiyar* VE6 : *ceyyiya* VE7 : *ceyin* **VE8 : *ceya***	absolutive absolutive absolutive conditional "infinitive"	**200** 2 8 4 1 2 15 **183**	**129** 1 7 4 1 2 13 **92**
VM (*vinai murru*) "finite verb"	inflected for PNG and tense		not computed	not computed
ME (*murr-eccam*)	inflected for PNG and tense		not computed	not computed
VAP (*vinaiyāl aṇaiyum peyar*) "participial noun"	inflected for PNG, tense and case.		not computed	not computed
TP (*tolir peyar*) verbal noun	inflected for case		not computed	not computed

Inside this (incomplete) list of forms that together constitute the verbal paradigm it must be noted that the V^0 type, which we have already mentioned in connection with the "unmarked syntax" is not considered by the CTamil grammarians as a stand-alone form but is mentioned only as a constituent of the *vinait tokai* "verbal compound".

Syntactic depth: the case of a poem with high U-density: KT 47

We now examine a slightly more complex poem from the CK corpus, which has a U-density of 60%. Although the U-density is a useful parameter for a first exploration, it has to be completed by other parameters. My purpose shall now be to show that the U-syntax elements can not only be frequent in a poem, but that they can also be used, to some extent, recursively, and that the degree of complexity reached varies from poem to poem.[25] That degree notion was already in fact implicit when I wrote that the $\{(A^0{:}N_2)\text{-}N_1\}$ template was used to build second degree expressions. The text of the poem will be directly given with grammatical tags and punctuation, without going through the stage of undoing the sandhi, as was done for the first text sample examined.

[((((karum$^{\text{A-um}}$:kāl^{N})-vēṅkai^{N})-vī^{N})-uku$^{\text{V0}}$):tuṟukal^{N}]
[(irum$^{\text{A-um}}$:puli^{N})-kuruḷaiyiṉ$^{\text{N-obl.}}$] tōṉṟum$^{\text{V-pel}}$ kāṭṭu$^{\text{N-obl}}$ iṭai$^{\text{Postp.}}$
elli^{N} [26] varunar$^{\text{N-vap}}$ kaḷaviṟku$^{\text{N-dat.}}$
nallai$^{\text{A-2nd -sing.}}$ allai$^{\text{neg.2nd-sing.}}$ [(neṭu$^{\text{A0}}$;veḷ$^{\text{A0}}$) : nilavu^{N}] ē$^{\text{voc.}}$

[((((black$^{\text{A-um}}$:foot^{N})-Tree(spec.)^{N})-flower^{N})-fall$^{\text{V0}}$):ROCK^{N}]
[(big$^{\text{A-um}}$:tiger^{N})-CUB$^{\text{N-5th.case}}$] appear$^{\text{V-pel}}$ forest$^{\text{N-obl}}$ through$^{\text{Postp.}}$
night^{N} come$^{\text{V-agent}}$ secret$^{\text{N-dat.}}$
good$^{\text{A-2nd -sing.}}$ not$^{\text{neg.2nd-sing.}}$ [(long$^{\text{A0}}$;white$^{\text{A0}}$) : MOONLIGHT^{N}] *ē*$^{\text{voc.}}$

The first line in the poem is the description of a rock and boils down to one item in the reduced sentence. The noun "rock" is the head of an extended verbal compound which has for its other argument a case compound. The first component of that case compound is itself a 2nd-degree expression. This makes the line into a fifth-degree U-expression, that can be translated as:

"ROCK(S), on which fall the flower(s) of the black-footed *Vēṅkai* [tree]"

The second line contains a 2nd-degree expression which has its head in the 5th case (the case used for comparisons):
"like [the] CUB(S) of [a] big tiger"

The last line contains the U-expression "long white MOONLIGHT" which

---

[25] The hope that it should be possible to quantify precisely the syntactic complexity of CTamil poems, and that this might be useful for clarifyying their chronology has been entertained by me ever since I read in Renou[1956] the following, about Sanskrit compounds: "comment la langue est-elle passée d'un état ancien – celui que reflète the Rgveda – où les composés étaient brefs et relativement peu nombreux, à l'état que l'on connaît par la littérature classique, où le procédé a pris un développement que J. Bloch qualifiait justement de « monstrueux » *(Indo-aryen*, p. 106) ?"

[26] The status of *elli* is not absolutely clear. Instead of seeing it as a noun (as was tentatively done here), it could be considered as the *viṉai eccam* (VE1) of an impersonal verb *ellutal* "to-be-night, to-become-dark". In that case, *elli varunar* would mean "those who come when it is night/when it becomes dark". CTamil is not a well-understood language!

was already mentioned and which must have appeared as striking because the poet's real name was forgotten and he is only mentioned in the anthology as "He-of-the-long-white-moonlight-[formula]".[27]

The reduced sentence is:

ROCK^{N} CUB$^{\text{N-5th.case.}}$ appear$^{\text{V-pel}}$ forest$^{\text{N-obl}}$ through$^{\text{Postp.}}$
night^{N} come$^{\text{V-agent}}$ secret$^{\text{N-dat.}}$
good$^{\text{A-2nd -sing.}}$ not$^{\text{neg.2nd-sing.}}$ MOONLIGHT^{N} *ē* ^{voc}

That sentence itself starts with the description of a wilderness/forest. The noun "forest" is the head of a relative participle which is also connected with 2 more arguments, which happen to be the heads of the first 2 U-expressions we have just described. This gives us:

"Through [the] forest where ROCK(S) appear like CUB(S)"

The successive embeddings strategy which was seen in the U-components is also seen in the reduced sentence, although it is under the rule of the M-syntax. This is a consequence of the (generally observed) constraint that poems should consist of one single sentence. One could, as a consequence, try to define a degree of embedding for reduced sentences also. A full translation of the reduced sentence is easier to read in English if all the components are inverted:

"Ô MOONLIGHT! you are not good, for the secrecy, of those who come at night, through [the] forest where ROCK(S) appear like CUB(S)."

A full translation of the poem is obtained by replacing the 3 words in small capitals by the translations of the corresponding U-expressions.

Interior Landscape (IL) feature: use of a pivotal *uṭaip peyar*

While examining the U-density of the 38 poems in the CK corpus, it was stated that 7 (or 8) of them had a special feature which I designated as the "Interior Landscape" (IL) feature. What I was referring to is the fact that in these poems, we find a word in a syntactically pivotal situation, connecting two apparently independant discourses, although one is often reinforcing the other, in an allusive way (through some *uḷḷurai uvamai*). The first discourse is a description of a lansdcape and the second one is the description of a love situation. The pivotal word syntactically

27 "Long white moon" probably means "white moon that shines for too long".

connects the two. Typical examples are *nāṭaṉ*, *tuṟaivaṉ*, *ūraṉ*, *veṟpaṉ*, *cērppaṉ*. CTamil grammatical commentators consider these terms as *uṭaip peyar*-s "nouns of possession" and they analyze them as combining a place noun (*nāṭu* "country", *tuṟai* "ghat, harbour", *ūr* "town", *veṟpu* "mountain", *cērppu* "shore") with a suffix *–aṉ* which brings the meaning "He who possesses that place" (cf. TC114c & TC165c).

As a typical example, I shall present a simplified extract from KT186

... mullai mel koṭi ... mukaiyum nāṭaṟku-t tuyil tuṟantaṉa ... em kaṇ...
(mullai^{N}-(mel^{A0}: koṭi^{N})) mukaiyum$^{V\text{-}pe1}$ nāṭaṟku$^{N\text{-}dat}$ tuyil^{N} tuṟantaṉa^{Vvm3PlNt} em$^{N\text{-}obl}$ kaṇ^{N}
(Jasmine^{N}-(soft^{A0}: creeper^{N})) bud$^{V\text{-}pe1}$ country-He$^{N\text{-}dat}$ sleep^{N} renounce^{Vvm3PlNt} I$^{N\text{-}obl}$ eye^{N}

"For Him, of the country where the soft jasmine creeper is budding, my eyes have renounced sleep."

Seen from the point of view of the interior (or embedded) landscape description, the most important element in *nāṭaṉ* "He-of-the-country" is *nāṭ(u)* "country". Seen from the point of view of the main sentence, the head, however is the pronominal ending *–aṉ*. The landscape description is here, as is very often the case, anchored onto *nāṭ(u)* thanks to *mukaiyum* which is a relative participle, which acts as the main predicate for the embedded sentence and which has two main arguments: *koṭi* and *nāṭu*. The kernel of the embedded description is thus:

koṭi^{N} *mukaiyum*$^{V\text{-}pe1}$ *nāṭu*^{N}
creeper^{N} bud$^{V\text{-}pe1}$ land^{N}

"country where a creeper is budding."

Statistics on the distribution of relative participles and verbal roots

One of the main obstacles to the correct primary[28] understanding of a CTamil poem, provided one is familiar with its vocabulary, is to determine how the words are syntactically connected. As far as the U-components are concerned, the absence of marks can be compensated by

[28] We shall not be concerned here with understanding the allusions, but shall only be concerned with understanding the syntax, that *axis mundi*.

a familiarity with a stock of formulae. As far as M-syntax is concerned, the marks which are found on a number of items (but not on all) clear the way for construing the reduced sentence, but there are cases of long-distance relationships between items, which may not appear at the first glance.

In this respect, since the relative participles (V^{PE1} and V^{PE2}) and the verbal roots (V^0) play the pivotal role of a verbal kernel connecting several arguments, it has seemed useful to give here some statistics on the most frequent roles that these arguments play with respect to the kernel. Additionally, since the use of V^0 form is characteristic of U-syntax, whereas the use of V^{PE1} and V^{PE2} forms is typical of M-syntax, this exploration, which remains of course a preliminary one, should throw some light on the global economy of the system.

We first start with some statistical figures concerning the total number of such forms in the two biggest corpora that were examined for this study. These figures, which are collected in the following 2 charts,[29] are mostly based on the extensive data collected by Eva Wilden (forthcoming publication) for her critical editions (and translations) of two CTamil anthologies, the *Kuṟuntokai* (KT) and the *Naṟṟiṇai* (NA) totalling respectively 4180 and 2504 lines, in most editions.[30]

Chart 3a: distribution of V^0, V^{PE1} and V^{PE2}
inside *Naṟṟiṇai* (400 poems)

NA (4180 lines) (9 to 12 lines poems)	V^0 (verbal root)	V^{PE1} (*ceyyum* "which does")	V^{PE2} (*ceyta* "which did")
occurrences	1564	583	853
vocabulary (distinct items)	343	261	361
Density	37.4 %	13.9 %	20.5 %

[29] The figures contained in these charts should not be considered as precise to the last digit, because these texts abound in variants. Moreover, and more importantly, the figures given for V^0 are higher than what should be given for V^0N constructions only, because the occurrences of V^0V^{aux} serial constructions have not been factored out. Still, it seemed useful to give them because what matters mostly in them at this stage is their order of magnitude. The presence of V^0 does remain a massive fact.

[30] Because of variants, these numbers should be taken as indicative only. The KT contains 399 poems with lengths comprised between 4 and 8 lines (and 2 exceptional 9-lines poems) and the NA contains 400 poems with lengths comprised between 9 and 12 lines (plus seven "exceptional" 13-lines poems).

Chart 3b: distribution of V^0, V^{PE1} and V^{PE2} inside *Kuṟuntokai* (401 poems)

KT (2504 lines) (4 to 8 lines poems)	V^0 (verbal root)	V^{PE1} (*ceyyum* "which does")	V^{PE2} (*ceyta* "which did")
occurrences	710	361	423
vocabulary (distinct items)	227	193	225
density	28%	14.4 %	17.5%

The first bit of information which can be gathered from these two charts is that the use of V^0 forms is a massive phenomenon in CTamil poetry. This is a testimony to the pervasiveness of U-syntax. The massive presence of V^0 forms is all the more impressive since they do not seem to be used in the other varieties of Tamil with which I am familiar (Modern Tamil, spoken or written, H or L, medieval prose Tamil).

A CTamil grammarian's position on argument roles

We shall now take a closer look at the $\{((N_3)... N_2)V^{PE}N_1\}$ and at the $\{(N_2)V^0N_1\}$ syntactic templates which have been presented at the beginning of this exploration and with which we have met quite often. We shall tentatively do it this time from a semantic role point of view, which will be adapted from a CTamil grammarian's conception which is presented several times in the T and illustrated by the commentators. There is indeed a canonical list, first mentioned in TC112c, which consists of 6 prerequisite for an activity to take place; they are the following: P1 *nilaṉ* "place", P2 *poruḷ* "object (patient)", P3 *kālam* "time", P4 *karuvi* "instrument", P5 *viṉai-mutal* "agent", P6 *viṉai* "action". This list resembles the Pāṇinian *kāraka* list but is not identical with it. It appears a second time in TC234c,[31] in connection with the *peyar eccam* characterization. The commentators enumerate on that occasion two series, respectively, of $\{V^{PE1}N_1\}$ and $\{V^{PE2}N_1\}$, where the N_1 element takes successively the six values. The examples are:

- P1 : *vāḻum il* "the house where one lives"
- P2 : *kaṟkum nūl* "the book that one studies"
- P3 : *tuyilum kālam* "the time when one sleeps"
- P4 : *vaṉaiyum kōl* "the stick with which [the potter] fashions [the pot]"

[31] See Chevillard [1996: 362-365].

- P5 : *ōtum pārppaṉ* "the brahmin who recites"
- P6 : *uṇṇum ūṇ* "the eating one eats"
- P1 : *pukka il* "the house one has entered"
- P2 : *uṇṭa cōṟu* "the rice one has eaten"
- P3 : *vanta nāḷ* "the day one has come"
- P4 : *veṉṟa vēl* "the spear with which one has vanquished"
- P5 : *āṭiya kūttaṉ* "the dancer who has danced"
- P6 : *pōyiṉa pōkku* "the going one went"

Among these 6, the last one, P6, is probably slightly mysterious to some readers. What seems to be at stake is the fact that inside a verb expressing some activity, the process itself is accessible to some syntactic transformations like relativization.[32]

In the case of V^0, the T, which does not state anything specific regarding the formation of the *viṉait tokai*, could not be expected to give any similar details. However, its commentators do indeed give a list similar to the ones found for V^{PE1} and V^{PE2}. The list is the following:

- P1 : *āṭu araṅku* (dance^{V0} stage) "dancing stage"
- P2 : *cey kuṉṟu* (make^{V0} hill) "artificial hill"
- P3 : *puṇar poḻutu* (unite^{V0} day) "day of uniting"
- P4 : *ari vāḷ* (cut^{V0} blade) "cutting blade"
- P5 : *kol yāṉai* (kill^{V0} elephant) "murderous elephant"
- P6 : *cel celavu* (go^{V0} going) "the going one goes"

Statistics on argument roles for V^0 constructions

The universal classification proposed by the CTamil grammarians (for the semantic role of the head of a relative participle or of a verbal root) is of course partly a theoretical one, but since it was proposed by, possibly, native masters of that poetical language, it seems useful to examine how it fits the data which it is supposed to describe. The present examination is based on a subcorpus of the NE corpus, which consists of the 22 first *neytal* poems, totalling 344 lines, in which I could identify 78 V^0 forms, 39 of them being found in $\{V^0N_1\}$ constructions and 39 in $\{N_2V^0N_1\}$ constructions. The global V^0-density is thus 23%, higher than the one found for the CK corpus. It should however be noted that the distribution

---

[32] When clarifying the meaning of the sixth prerequisite (while commenting on TC112c), the commentator explains that whatever the verb used in a sentence, one can always use the DO verb to ask "what is he DOING ?". The process itself appears thus as the internal object of some DO verb. To eat is to DO the action of eating.

is a very irregular one[33]: an extensive examination of a still wider corpus would certainly be called for.

For the 39 {V^0N_1} examples, the first impression obtained while examining them one by one is that it seems possible in a number of cases to use the labels provided by CTamil grammarians: for instance a *vel*^{V0} *vēl*^{N} (win^{V0}:spear^{N}) "victorious spear" (AN60-12 & AN70-13) is indeed a "spear **with which** one (can) win" and can appear as a good P4 example. However, in a greater number of cases the choice seems arbitrary. One can indeed attribute agentivity to the sea (*kaṭal*) and consider *muḻaṅku kaṭal* (roar^{V0}:sea^{N}) "roaring sea" (AN220-12) as an example of P5. But what about *ōṅku ciṉai* (rise-high^{V0}:branch^{N}) "high-rising branch(es)" (AN20-5) and *paṭu ciṉai* (lean-downwards^{V0}:branch^{N}) "lowering branch(es)" (AN210-12) ? It seems arbitrary to categorize the branch as an agent or as a patient. A more promising direction in that particular case might be to examine these 2 examples in their wider context, where the tree to which the branches belong is mentioned.[34] And we could ask similar questions for the greater part of the 39 examples. It should be added that the main difficulty in attributing the labels (P1 to P6) to the head noun is of course the minimality of the syntagm. It is somehow easier to attribute semantic roles when there is more than one argument, as will be seen when we examine the {$N_2V^0N_1$} examples. When the only argument for the V^0 is the head noun, and especially if the phenomenon is seen through the lenses of a language like English (or French), the impression obtained, and probably useful from a pedagogical point of view, is that CTamil only has a small stock of *real* adjectives, but it can use plain verbal roots as quasi-adjectives. These verbal roots no longer refer to actual events or to actual descriptions (in as much as what appears in a poem can be said to be actual!), but they then express aptitudes, permanent states, etc.

Turning now to the 39 {$N_2V^0N_1$} examples, it seems somehow easier to attribute semantic role labels to the two arguments N_1 and N_2. However, it often still seems impossible to be very precise in assigning the labels, especially when we try to distinguish between a P5 ("agent") and a P2 ("object, patient"). A more general label like "participant in the process", which could also include P4 ("instrument") seems easier to use. Grouping together P1 ("place") and P3 ("time") under a more general "Locator" label, and renaming P6 ("action") as "Process", I have

[33] For instance, the global number of V0 forms oscillates between 0 (for AN10) and 8 (for AN190).

[34] The syntactic treatment of whole-part relationships is a complex area. One interesting feature in this field is the existence of double subject constructions, which seem to have already been a topic of concern for CTamil grammarians themselves (cf. for instance TC61c in Chevillard [1996: 137-139]).

tentatively assigned 25 among the 39 examples to the squares of a double entry chart, to be found below.

Chart 4: distribution of N_2V^0 N_1 syntagms (in the NE corpus)

↓N_2(V)N_1→	Locator	Participant	Process	Total
Locator		5		5
Participant	12	6	2	20
Total	12	11	2	25

As already emphasized, what makes it easier to attribute significant semantic roles to the arguments in {$N_2V^0N_1$} examples, is the fact that there are more than one. This can first be illustrated by the examples where I have labelled one of the arguments as "Locator" and the other one as "Participant". This gives us 2 possible types: {$N^{Participant}V^0N^{Locator}$} and {$N^{Locator}V^0N^{Participant}$}. The first one is illustrated by examples like:

- *pū nāṟu parappiṉ* (flower^{N} smell^{V0} expanse$^{N\text{-}obl}$) (AN 130-8) "in the vast stretch perfumed by flowers"
- *tirai payil aḻuvam* (wave^{N} be-frequent^{V0} sea-expanse^{N}) (AN 210-5) "the sea expanse where there are many waves"
- *curumpu ār kaṇṇi* (bee^{N} be-full^{V0} wreath^{N}) (AN 180-6) "the garland on which bees were humming"

The second one is illustrated by examples such as:

- *vicumpu aṇi villiṉ* (sky^{N} adorn^{V0} bow$^{N\text{-}obl}$) (AN 210-4) "like a rainbow"
- *viḻavu aṇi makaḷir* (festival^{N} adorn^{V0} women^{N}) (AN 70-12) "women adorning themselves at time of festivals"

In the cases where both arguments are labelled as "Participants", i.e. ({$N^{Participant}V^0N^{Participant}$}), we can observe a polarity between an agent and a patient, as in:

- *koṇṭal iṭu maṇal* (East-Wind^{N} place^{V0} sand^{N}) (AN 20-7) "Sands heaped by the East Wind"
- *viḷi aṟi ñamali* (call^{N} recognize^{V0} dog^{N}) (AN 140-9) "dogs that recognize (familiar) voices [and bark on strangers]"

The label "Process" appears in several configurations. One possibility is seen in the example *[tuṇai puṇar uvakai]-y-ar* (AN 30-3), which should be analysed in two stages. Firstly, a {$N^{Participant}V^0N^{Process}$} element is formed:

- *tuṇai puṇar uvakai* (companion^{N} unite^{V0} rejoicing^{N}) "rejoicing in the uniting with companions"[35]

Secondly, a pronominal suffix is added to the extended compound giving as a meaning: "those who rejoice in uniting with companions".

There are however types of examples where the Locator/Participant/Process grid does not seem appropriate for characterizing the N_1 and N_2 arguments. Among those, 2 deserve special mention. The first one is the case where the 2 arguments are in a relation of meronymy (see Chart 5a). The second is the case the 2 arguments are in a relation of comparison (see Chart 5b).

Chart 5a: distribution of N_2V^0 N_1 syntagms in the NE corpus (whole-part relationship)

↓$N_2(V^0)N_1$→	Part (meronym)	Whole (holonym)	Total
Part (meronym)		2	2
Whole (holonym)	2		2
Total	2	2	4

As a comment to Chart 5a, the {$N^{Whole}V^0N^{Part}$} template can be illustrated by

tāḻai vīḻ kayiṟṟu (fragrant_screwpine^N fall^{V0} rope^N) (AN 20-6) "aerial roots of the fragrant screwpine" (VMS translation)

The {$N^{Part}V^0N^{Whole}$} template can be illustrated by
taḻai aviḻ tāḻai (sprout^N release^{V0} fragrant_screwpine^N) (AN 90-3) "fragrant screwpine of loosening sprouts"

[35] As an additional argument for explaining that this type of analysis is not an invention by me but is in line with a traditional analysis by a grammatical commentator, let me quote a similar example drawn from the *Kalittokai* anthology and given by Cēṉāvaraiyar under TC234c : "Lorsqu'il est dit: *niṉ-mukaṅ kāṇu-maruntiṉē ṉ-eṉṉum-āl* «s'il dit: J'ai pour remède [que] de voir ton visage» (*Kali* 60_19) étant donné que [le poète] appelle «remède» (*maruntu*) le fait de voir (*kāṭci*), l'expression *kāṇu-maruntu* «remède [que] de voir» a pris [pour sa construction] le nom de l'action *(viṉaip-peyar)*." (Chevillard [1996, p. 364].

Chart 5b: distribution of $N_2V^0 N_1$ syntagms in the NE corpus (comparisons)

↓$N_2(V^0)N_1$→	*upamāna* (comparable object)	*upamēya* (object compared)	Total
upamāna		2	2
upamēya	2		
Total	2	2	4

As a brief comment on chart 5b, I shall give only one example:

kaṇ pōl neytal (eye^N resemble^{V0} Neytal-[flower]^N) (AN 170-4) "eye-like Neytal flower"

The Semantic spectrum of a Syntactic template

As a global comment on this tentative classification of $\{N_2V^0N_1\}$ constructions, it is noticeable that there is a clear dominance of some role sets for the N_1 **and** N_2 positions. That role set will be referred to as the semantic spectrum of the $\{N_2V^0N_1\}$ construction. According to our statistics for this short sample, the most prototypical $N_2V^0N_1$ U-component is of the type $\{N^{Participant}V^0N^{Location}\}$ (12 items). This type of U-component is more frequent than the $\{N^{Participant}V^0N^{Participant}\}$ type (6 items), which itself is more frequent than the $\{N^{Location}V^0N^{Participant}\}$ type (5 items). Of course, these figures are too small. The spectral analysis that these tentative results provide has to be verified in the future against those for larger corpora. It could be useful for scrutinizing the homogeneity of corpora. In the following section, I shall try to compare very briefly this spectrum with those for $N_2V^{PE1}N_1$ and $N_2V^{PE2}N_1$ constructions (and for larger ones). It will be only a brief sketch because such constructions can have a larger number of arguments and can span several lines each. A full description of M-syntax cannot be short.

Statistics sketch for argument roles in $\{(... N_3) ... N_2 ...V^{PE}N_1\}$ constructions

I shall now briefly present the results of two preliminary explorations done on the NE corpus, targetting the V^{PE2} and the V^{PE1} occurrences. My first remark is that whereas in $N_2V^0N_1$ items there is a balance in weight between N_2 on the left and the head noun N_1 on the right, the situation is usually much more dissymmetrical between the two sides of a V^{PE2} or of a V^{PE1}: combined with what stands on its left, the V^{PE} is the last element in a relative clause which can be quite long and which draws on most of the resources of M-syntax. For that reason, it is difficult to fit the various possibilities inside the squares of a double entry chart (as was done in charts 4, 5a and 5b). It often seems possible to recognize semantic roles for the noun arguments, but the establishment of the spectrum would require the use of charts with a number of dimensions greater than 2. Even if possible, this would exceed what can be accomplished here. Moreover, because of the dissymmetry between the two sides of a V^{PE}, the priority seems to be to establish the statistics for the head noun N_1 itself. This is what was done on a subset of the NE corpus, and the results are as follows:

- For the V^{PE1} (i.e. non-past) relative participle, the head noun is more frequently a locator than a participant.
- For the V^{PE2} (i.e. past) relative participle, the head noun is more frequently a participant than a locator.
- Examples where the head noun can be categorized as "Process" (or P6) seem to be quite rare but at least one example was found with a V^{PE1} (in KT37).

In order to illustrate the complex way in which all these forms are used, it has seemed to me that the best method would be to give a "real-life" example, which shows most of them. This is what the next section will be devoted to.

Multi-level Syntactic analysis of a 14-lines poem (AN 320)

The poem chosen is a *neytal* (sea-shore setting) poem, AN320, from the *Akanāṉūṟu* anthology, and I shall first give its complete syntactical analysis, without however going through the preliminary stage of undoing the sandhi. Because of the high level of intricacy brought about by the successive embeddings, it has appeared necessary to use distinct sets of paired delimiters, in the following way:

- "{" and "}" are used for level 0 of M-syntax
- "[" and "]" are used for level 1 clauses in M-syntax
- "<" and ">" are used for level 2 clauses in M-syntax
- "{{" and "}}" are used for level 3 clauses in M-syntax
- "(" and ")" are used for U-syntax

Inside a zone/clause delimited by a pair of delimiters, the nominal arguments are distinguished by numerical indices as before, but these indices are flanked by a lower case letter which is a unique identifier for the delimited zone. For instance N_{4b} , alias *mīṉ* "fish", is the 4th argument inside "clause b" which describes its street-selling. In case a noun is the head of a relative participle and is a nominal argument for another participle, it will as a consequence be attributed two indices. The same *mīṉ* "fish" can also be referred to as N_{1a} in the clause that describes its capture by fishermen.

{ [<(ōṅku$^{\text{V0}}$:tirai^{N})-parappiṉ$^{\text{N-obl}}$>$_{\text{N(3a)}}$
<(vāṅku$^{\text{V0}}$:vicai^{N})-koḷīi$^{\text{V-VE1}}$>$_{\text{(a)}}$
<timilōṉ^{N}>$_{\text{N(2a)}}$
<tanta$^{\text{V-PE2}}$**>**$_{\text{(a)}}$
<(kaṭum$^{\text{A-um}}$: kaṇ^{N})-(vaya^{D}: **mīṉ**)^{N}> $_{\text{N(1a)}}$] $_{\text{N(4b)}}$
[((taḻai^{N}-aṇi$^{\text{V0}}$):alkul^{N})- (celva^{D}:taṅkaiyar^{N})]$_{\text{N(3b)}}$
[(viḻavu^{N}-ayar$^{\text{V0}}$): maṟukiṉ$^{\text{N-obl}}$] $_{\text{N(2b)}}$
[vilai^{N} eṉa$^{\text{V_VE8}}$]
[pakarum$^{\text{V-PE1}}$**]**$_{\text{(b)}}$
[((kāṉal^{N} am$^{\text{incr.}}$ ciṟukuṭi^{N}) (peru$^{\text{A0}}$:nīr^{N}) **cērppu**^{N})] $_{\text{N(1b)}}$ –a$^{\text{Pro-N-voc}}$}$_{\text{(c)}}$
{ [(((((malar^{N}-ēr$^{\text{V0}}$):(uṇ$^{\text{V0}}$:kaṇ^{N})) -(em$^{\text{N-obl}}$-tōḻi^{N}))–evvam^{N})-
alar$^{\text{V0}}$):vāy^{N}] $_{\text{N(1d1)}}$
[nīṅka$^{\text{V-VE8}}$**]**$_{\text{(d1)}}$
[nī^{N} aruḷāy$^{\text{V-ME-neg-2nd.Sg}}$ poyppiṉum$^{\text{V-concessive}}$]$_{\text{(d2)}}$}$_{\text{(c)}}$
{ [< {{(neṭum$^{\text{A-um}}$:kaḻi)^{N}}} $_{\text{N(2e)}}$ **{{tuḻaiiya**$^{\text{V-PE2}}$**}}**$_{\text{(e)}}$ {{(kuṟum$^{\text{A-um}}$: kāl^{N})-
aṉṉam ^{N}}} $_{\text{N(1e)}}$ >$_{\text{N(4f)}}$
<(aṭumpu^{N}-amar$^{\text{V0}}$): ekkar>$_{\text{N(3f)}}$
<(am^{D}: ciṟai)> $_{\text{N(2f)}}$
<uḷarum$^{\text{V-PE1}}$**>** $_{\text{(f)}}$
<((((taṭavu^{D}:nilai^{N}) - puṉṉai)- tātu^{N})- aṇi$^{\text{V0}}$):(perum$^{\text{A-um}}$:
tuṟai^{N})> $_{\text{N(1f)}}$]$_{\text{N(3g)}}$
[< {{(naṭuṅku$^{\text{V0}}$:ayir^{N})}} $_{\text{N(2h)}}$ {{**pōḻnta**$^{\text{V-PE2}}$}}$_{\text{(h)}}$ {{(koṭuñci^{N}-
(neṭum$^{\text{A-um}}$: **tēr**^{N}))}} $_{\text{N(1h)}}$> $_{\text{N(2i)}}$
<(vaṇṭal^{N} -pāvai^{N})> $_{\text{N(1i)}}$
<citaiya$^{\text{V-VE8}}$**>** $_{\text{(i)}}$] $_{\text{(g)}}$
[vantu$^{\text{V-VE1}}$] $_{\text{(g)}}$
[nī^{N}] $_{\text{N(2g)}}$
[tōḷ^{N} putitu$^{\text{A-VE1}}$ **uṇṭa**$^{\text{V-PE2}}$] $_{\text{(g)}}$
[ñāṉṟai^{N}**]** $_{\text{N(1g)}}$ }$_{\text{N(c)}}$
{cūḷ^{N} –um}$_{\text{(c)}}$
{poy^{N} -ō }$_{\text{(c)}}$

{kaṭal^{N} (aṟi^{V0} :kari)^{N} –ē}$_{(c)}$

This poem consists of a single main sentence, but several sub-clauses are embedded in the main clause, and a short description can be made in the following way:

- Clause (a) describes the capture of a fish (*mīṉ*) [head-noun for (a)]
- It is embedded in clause (b) describing the selling of the fish, that takes place in the coastal area (*cērppu*) [head-noun for (b)]
- The word (*cērppu*) is the base, in an interior landscape construction, for a pivotal word *cērppa* (Vocative "Ô, Lord of the sea-shore"), addressed to the hero, which belongs to the main clause (c).
- The embedded clauses (d1) and (d2) are part of the discourse addressed to him
- Clause (f) is a second landscape description with head-noun *tuṟai* ("ghat") and it contains an embedded clause (e) describing the activity of a bird.
- That ghat (*tuṟai*) is also the locator in a clause (g) describing, in a flash-back, how the hero took the virginity of the heroine, and containing an embedded clause (i) describing the arrival of his chariot
- The head-noun for clause (g) is a temporal locator in the main clause (c)
- The remaining words are the end of the discourse addressed to the hero.

I conclude this section with a word-for-word gloss and a translation of the poem:

{ [<(rise_high^{V0}:wave^{N})-expanse$^{N\text{-obl}}$>$_{N(3a)}$
<(bend^{V0}:speed^{N})-cause_to_take$^{V\text{-}VE1}$>$_{(a)}$
<boat_man^{N} >$_{N(2a)}$
<give$^{V\text{-}PE2}$>$_{(a)}$
<(fierce$^{A\text{-}um}$: eye^{N})-(strong^{D}: **fish**)^{N}> $_{N(1a)}$] $_{N(4b)}$
[((leaf^{N}-adorn ^{V0}):hip^{N})- (pet^{D}:younger_sisters ^{N})]$_{N(3b)}$
[(festival^{N}-celebrate^{V0}): street$^{N\text{-obl}}$] $_{N(2b)}$
[price^{N} Quotative$^{V\text{-}VE8}$]
[announce$^{V\text{-}PE1}$]$_{(b)}$
[((grove^{N} (adj.suffix)$^{incr.}$ hamlet^{N}) (big^{A0} :water^{N}) **sea_shore**^{N})] $_{N(1b)}$ –
(pron.suffix)$^{Pro\text{-}N\text{-}voc}$}$_{(c)}$

{ [(((((flower^{N}-resemble$^{\text{V0}}$):(be$^{\text{V0}}$:eye^{N})) -(we$^{\text{N-obl}}$-female_friend^{N}))
–suffering^{N})-gossip$^{\text{V0}}$):mouth^{N}] $_{\text{N(1d1)}}$
[avoid$^{\text{V-VE8}}$]$_{\text{(d1)}}$
[you^{N} grace$^{\text{V-ME-neg-2nd.Sg.}}$ deny$^{\text{V-concessive}}$]$_{\text{(d2)}}$}$_{\text{(c)}}$
{ [< {{(long$^{\text{A-um}}$:back_water)^{N}}} $_{\text{N(2e)}}$ **{{stir$^{\text{V-PE2}}$}}**$_{\text{(e)}}$ {{(short$^{\text{A-um}}$: leg^{N})-**swan**^{N}}} $_{\textbf{N(1e)}}$ >$_{\text{N(4f)}}$
<(Veg.Spec.^{N}-reside$^{\text{V0}}$): sand_dune>$_{\text{N(3f)}}$
<(beauty^{D}: wing)> $_{\text{N(2f)}}$
<adjust$^{\text{V-PE1}}$> $_{\text{(f)}}$
<((((curvedness^{D}:stand^{N}) – Veg.Spec.)- pollen^{N})- adorn$^{\text{V0}}$): (big$^{\text{A-um}}$: **ghat**^{N})> $_{\text{N(1f)}}$]$_{\text{N(3g)}}$
[< {{(tremble$^{\text{V0}}$:sand^{N})}}$_{\text{N(2h)}}$ {{**cut**$^{\text{V-PE2}}$}}$_{\text{(h)}}$ {{(Ornament_Sp.^{N}-(long$^{\text{A-um}}$:**chariot**^{N}))}} $_{\text{N(1h)}}$> $_{\text{N(2i)}}$
<(Game_Sp.^{N} -doll^{N})> $_{\text{N(1i)}}$
<destroy$^{\text{V-VE8}}$> $_{\text{(i)}}$] $_{\text{(g)}}$
[come$^{\text{V-VE1}}$] $_{\text{(g)}}$
[you^{N}] $_{\text{N(2g)}}$
[shoulder^{N} new$^{\text{A-VE1}}$ **eat**$^{\text{V-PE2}}$] $_{\text{(g)}}$
[day^{N}] $_{\text{N(1g)}}$ }$_{\text{N(c)}}$
{oath^{N} –Coord.part.}$_{\text{(c)}}$
{lie^{N} -Interrog.part. }$_{\text{(c)}}$
{sea^{N} (know$^{\text{V0}}$:witness)^{N} –Emphat.part.}$_{\text{(c)}}$

"Chief of the maritime tract having small hamlets surrounded by sea-shore groves where the petted sisters, who wear on their waist a garment of leaves, sell in the streets where festivals are celebrated the ferocious and strong fish caught [by their brothers] in their boats, dragging the fishing nets with great force in the expanse of the rising waves in the ocean! Even if you become unfaithful to your word by not bestowing your grace on my friend, who has eyes that are as beautiful as flowers and that are taking in collyrium, to remove her distress and the scandal of the village folk,

Is the oath that you swore on that day when you had first union with her, coming in your tall chariot having a part resembling lotus bud, cutting the loose fine sand so as to destroy the doll made of sand during play, in the big ghat which was made beautiful by the pollen of the *puṉṉai* tree (mast wood tree) of curved stature, where the swan of short legs adjusts its feathers with its beak and dries them (eating the fish) after stirring the long back-water (for fish), sitting on the mound of sand on which the creeper of *aṭumpu* is resting, also false, for which the sea bore a witness?" (V. M. Subramanya Ayyar)

The limits of the distinction between U-syntax and M-syntax

After explaining for a number of pages that there is a dual syntax in CTamil, I must also now mention several facts that might appear as contradicting the thesis I have been defending. These facts all have to do with the "opacity" (or non-opacity) of the U-components. According to what I have illustrated by a number of examples, the only element in a U-component which should be eligible for syntactic relationships with the elements that belong to what I called the "reduced sentence" should be the head of the U-component. But if that principle holds good, we might possibly have to extend the list of what may be accepted in a U-component. The elements we have considered so far were:

- adjectives (plain root or suffixed form: $A^0/A^{um}/A^m$)
- verbal root (V^0)
- nouns (base form N, but possibly also oblique form N^{obl})[36]
- apparently uninflected items tagged D ("determiners")[37]

In this setup, the only element inside a U-component that can bear a mark is the head noun. However, we might have to extend this list to V^{VE1} forms (the 1st type of converb, see above), because it seems that in some cases, V0 elements can be specified by a V^{VE1} form, as in the following (simplified) example drawn from KT
((vārntu$^{V\text{-}VE1}$-ilaṅku^{V0}):(vai^{A0} : eyiṟṟu^{Nobl})) (KT 14-2)
((be_regular$^{V\text{-}VE1}$-shine^{V0}):(sharp^{A0} : tooth^{Nobl})) (KT 14-2)
"[girl with] sharp teeth, that shine regularly"

Although such examples do not seem to be frequent, we have to define a consistent position in order to deal with them:

- either extend the list of what can be met with in a U-expression (and find out precisely how frequent such cases are).
- or characterize this example as exceptional and find some (possibly chronological) reasons for its being exceptional.

Another difficulty which can be met with if we maintain that there is a

---

[36] A full treatment of that question is outside the scope of this study, because it would require going deeply into the morphophonology (and especially into the question of increments (*cāriyai*)).

[37] It should be added that characterizing an item as "uninflected" does not necessarily mean that it can have only one form, because the choice between variant forms can be dependant on phonological conditions, as seems to be the case for an item like *taṭam/taṭavu*.

strict separation between what belongs to U-syntax and what belongs to M-syntax is that in some poems, and especially in long poems (but not exclusively) some element which clearly should not be considered as belonging to a U-component seems to be related to an element which belongs to a U-component but which is not its head. One such example is the following:

..... entai^{N} tanta$^{V\text{-}PE2}$ [(((koḻu^{A0} : mīṉ^{N}) - uṇaṅkal^{N}) -paṭu^{V0}) : puḷ^{N}] ōppi$^{V\text{-}VE1}$
..... our_father^{N} give$^{V\text{-}PE2}$ [(((fat^{A0} : fish^{N}) – drying_pieces^{N}) -befall^{V0}) : bird^{N}] chase$^{V\text{-}VE1}$

"chasing the birds, that befall on the pieces [left in the open] for drying, of the fat fish, that our father brought ..." (AN 20, 1-2)

The problem, if we want to consider [(((koḻu^{A0} : mīṉ^{N}) - uṇaṅkal^{N}) - paṭu^{V0}): puḷ^{N}] as a 4th-degree U-expression, is that what "our father brought" is certainly not *puḷ* ("the birds"), and that it is not the *uṇaṅkal* either, but that it is most probably *koḻu mīṉ* (the "fat fish"). But that makes an element which is apparently deeply seated inside a U-expression syntactically accessible to an element which is clearly outside it, and some explanation has to be proposed for that. I could tentatively suggest two (which are not necessarily exclusive of each other):

- a metrical one: poems are divided into lines (*aṭi*) and our would-be U-expression sits on one line whereas *entai tanta* sits on the former line.
- a chronological one: our poem belongs to a later period, where the duality between the two syntaxes was becoming blurred.

These two cases cannot of course be solved without a much more thorough exploration of a corpus which contains (limiting ourselves to KT, NA and AN) almost 14000 lines, but the questions have to be kept in mind.

Conclusion and open questions

We have now reached a stage where it is necessary to characterize in a general perspective what has been attempted here. We have in front of us a corpus of poetical texts, composed in a language which does not have now, and perhaps never had, native speakers, although those who composed these (often complex) texts had a mother tongue which they designated by the same word as the language of these texts : *tamiḻ* "Tamil". We also have access to some grammatical treatises where a distinction is made between *vaḻakku* "(ordinary) usage" and *ceyyuḷ* "poetry", although many consider that what *vaḻakku* refers to is not completely clear. Moreover, as was already stated at the beginning, very little is known with certitude regarding the dates when the poems were composed and regarding the date when they were collected into anthologies. In this context, the distinction I have made between U-syntax and M-syntax is a hypothesis, waiting for confirmation or for falsification. But that hypothesis has the advantage of being rooted in a traditional CTamil grammarians' conception, which is, given the circumstances, probably the closest we can get to a native speaker's intuition.

Among the features that have been examined here, the most mysterious one is probably the use of the V^0 elements (or plain verbal roots) in the verbal compounds (extended or not). The striking fact is that it had a massive presence in CTamil texts (as attested by our statistics) but that it is not present in modern Tamil, and is not seen in medieval Tamil prose either, but seems to be a linguistic element specially cultivated in poetry. That being the case, what seems strange from a descriptive linguist's point of view is the contention of traditional CTamil grammatical commentators that $\{V^0N\}$ constructions are equivalent both to $\{V^{PE1}N\}$ and to $\{V^{PE2}N\}$. Their standard example is *kol-yāṉai* "murderous elephant", which they declare as being equivalent both to *kollum yāṉai* "elephant which kills" and to *koṉṟa yāṉai* "elephant which killed", where *kol*, *kollum* and *koṉṟa* are respectively the V^0, V^{PE1} and V^{PE2} of the verb *kollutal*. What seems strange in the equivalence statement[38] is that it concerns forms which have a massive presence, both in terms of number of occurrences and of vocabulary richness. A possible explanation is that this equivalence statement implicitly recognizes the duality between the marked syntax and the unmarked syntax. If these two realms are considered as not overlapping,[39] then the equivalence statement takes on a different signification, that of a correspondence between the dual components.

Every study brings with itself the after-thought realization of what could have made it more complete and what could be a future

[38] A possible explanation might be that they were looking for (far-fetched) explanations of the cryptic *Tolkāppiyam* statement concerning the V^0N : *viṉaiyiṉ tokuti kālattu iyalum* (TC409i).

[39] Otherwise, if we see U-syntax and M-syntax as one single system, we have a 3 term opposition between V0 (generic /descriptive), PE1 (imperfective) and PE2 (perfective).

continuation. In the case of the present study, if we consider its emphasis on the examination of V^0N constructions, it must be admitted that a necessary complement would be the study of V^0V^{Aux} constructions in the same corpora.[40] This could even throw some light on our understanding of some V^0N examples, when N is verbal noun.[41] And this brings us back to the consideration of "linguistic plausibility" which was implicit in my statement of "Limitation 4" at the beginning of this study. Is the language of poetry a language? How must linguists handle it? Is the intensive use of V^0 forms an innovation by Tamil poets? Or is it an archaic trait, that preserves a feature that was once more widespread[42]? Can poets "invent" a new language? In which condition and under which influence? Drawing on which resources? An answer to these questions cannot be reached here but they have to be asked, nevertheless.

Bibliographical references

Britto, Francis, 1986, *Diglossia: A study of the theory with application to Tamil.* Washington, D. C. : Georgetown University Press.

Chevillard, Jean-Luc, 1994, "L'adjectif dans la tradition tamoule", in B. Colombat (Ed.), *L'Adjectif: Perspectives Historique et Typologique, Histoire Epistémologie Langage, tome 14, fasc. I,* Presses Universitaires de Vincennes, St Denis.

______, 1996, *Le Commentaire de Cēṉāvaraiyar sur le Collatikāram du Tolkāppiyam,* Publication 84.1 de l'Institut Français de Pondichéry.

______ 2004, "Ideophones in Tamil: a historical perspective on the X-eṉal expressives (*olikkuṟippu āṟṟuppaṭai*)" (pp. 407-433), in Chevillard and Wilden, *South Indian horizons: felicitation volume for François Gros on the occasion of his 70th birthday.* Publications du département d'indologie 94, IFP, EFEO, 2004

Coulson, Michael, 1989, *A critical edition of the Mālatīmādhava,* Originally presented as the editor's thesis (doctoral–Oxford)., revised by Roderick Sinclair, Oxford University Press, Delhi Bombay Calcutta Madras.

Krishnamurti, Bh. (Ed.), Colin P. Masica, and Anjani K. Sinha (assoc. Ed.), 1986, *South Asian Languages: structure, convergence and diglossia,* Motilal Banarsidass.

Lehmann, Thomas, 1994, *Grammatik des Alttamil, unter besonderer Berücksichtigung des Caṅkam-Texte des Dichters Kapilar,* Franz Steiner Verlag, Stuttgart.

Renou, Louis, 1956, "Sur l'évolution des composés nominaux en Sanskrit", *Bulletin de la Société de Linguistique 52,* pp. 96-116, Paris [reprinted in pp. 242-262 of *Louis Renou, Choix d'études indiennes,* EFEO, réimpr. N°9, Balbir N. & Pinault G.-J. (ed.), 1997, Paris.

---

[40] The most visible examples are probably those where V^{Aux} is *tarutal* "give", often found with movement verbs (*eḻu-taru, iḻi-taru,* etc.) which I tend to see as being oriented towards the speaker. Another example is the case where V^{Aux} is *takutal* "to be fit", as in *kāṇ*^{V0} *taku*^{V0} *vaṉappu*^{N} (see^{V0} be_fit^{V0} beauty^{N}) "beauty which deserves to be seen/admired") (AN 220-7).

[41] The example *[tuṇai puṇar uvakai]-y-ar* "those who rejoice in uniting with companions" (AN 30-3), already discussed, might then be seen as based in fact on a serial verb construction, combining *puṇartal* "to unite" and *uvattal* "to rejoice".

[42] And, of course, what is the situation in other Dravidian languages?

Steever, Sanford B., *The serial verb formation in the Dravidian Languages*, Motilal Banarsidass, 1988.

Subramanya Ayyar, V. M., 1975, *Akanāṉūṟu, part I, kaḷiṟṟiyāṉai nirai (1-120), part II, maṇimiṭai pavaḷam (121-300), part III, nittilakkōvai (301-400)*, translated into English by –, Institut Français d'Indologie, Pondichéry, 3 volumes, [unpublished]

Wilden, Eva, 2002, "Towards an Internal Chronology of Old Tamil Caṅkam Literature Or How to Trace the Laws of a Poetic Universe", *Wiener Zeitschrift Für die Kunde Südasiens, XLVI* (pp. 105-133).

______ 2002, Glossary and Statistics of the Kuṟuntokai, Habilitation Thesis, University of Hamburg.

______, forthcoming, Critical edition and translation of NA.

HIERARCHICAL STRUCTURE AND LINEAR ORDER: CORRELATIVE CLAUSES IN HINDI-URDU

ALICE DAVISON

Complex sentences in a language consist of two or more sentences. If they are not in a relation of coordination (or parataxis without an overt coordinating conjunction), then the clauses are in some asymmetric relation of dependency. One clause may be semantically, and also syntactically, dependent on a 'main' or 'matrix' clause. The relative clause construction is an example of a semantically dependent clause, as it serves as a modifier of a constituent in another clause.

The semantic dependency is marked in some way, for example by a special prefix (e.g. 'such that') (1a)[1]. The semantic paraphrase in (1b) has coordinate structure, losing this marker of subordination. The second clause restricts the reference of the common noun *people* in the first clause.

1) a. *People(i) such that they(i) like films tend to have mobile phones.*
   b. *People(x): x tend to have mobile phones & (x) like films*
   c. *People(i) [who(i) like films] tend to have mobile phones.*
   d. *[Which people(i) like films], they(i) tend to have mobile phones.*

The use and interpretation of relative clauses, therefore, crucially depends on a link between the two clauses, the identity of reference between some NP in the relative clause and the NP in the other clause whose reference it restricts. The actually syntactic expression of this coreference and semantic dependency may be internal adjunction of the relative clause to NP, as in (1c), or as a collocation of two separate clauses, as in (1d).

The relation of coreference and semantic dependency is usually

[1] The expression *'such that'* while not usual in colloquial language, is commonly used as a paraphrase of a restrictive relative clause. The expression itself is not a syntactic relative clause. It may be closest in meaning to Hindi *aisaa, jaisaa* 0 'of that kind, of which kind'.

marked overtly in a finite relative clause by a special prefix or pronoun/determiner (*such that, who, which, that*). Most modern Indo-European languages of Europe have lost the Indo-European relative pronoun/determiner series, in favor of an adapted interrogative (e.g. *who, which*) or demonstrative (e.g. *that*). Most of the modern Indo-Aryan languages are distinguished by the fact that nearly all have retained the Old IA tripartite division of pronoun/determiners into relative, interrogative and demonstrative series:

2) a. [Sanskrit] yas 'which (relative)' b. kas 'who?' c. sas d. eṣas

b. [Hindi/Urdu] jo kaun yah/wo.

The IA languages with these inventories of three series therefore have one more way of distinguishing a finite relative clause than is found in European IE languages. Either the determiner indicates semantic differentiation and subordination, or there is some way of distinguishing syntactically subordinate finite clauses from main clauses. South Asian languages which have lost the *yas* relative either adopt non-finite participial relatives (Sinhala; Gair and Paolillo 1998) or adapt an interrogative for the relative marker, as in Konkani (Nadkarni 1970).

Indic relative clauses formed with the distinctive relative demonstrative /pronoun need not have the same kind of syntactic structuring found in languages without this distinctive marking. In this paper, I compare examples from Sanskrit, particularly Vedic Sanskrit, and Hindi/Urdu, representing OIA and NIA languages. I will focus on the formal properties of the relative constructions in these languages, without being concerned about exactly how the formal similarities or dissimilarities have arisen through historical evolution (syntactic/morphological change, convergence or whatever is responsible). I contrast these formal similarities among correlative constructions within Indo-Aryan to the headed relative construction found in many other languages, including English and Japanese.

I will argue that (Vedic) Sanskrit has minimal use of syntactic subordination, and that the relative determiners marking relative clauses introduce both coindexation and semantic subordination, so that the relative-marked clause is interpreted as a modifier of a coreferent constituent in the non-relative clause.[2] Though relative clause structures in Vedic show a very large variety of construction types (Hettrich 1988),

---

[2] Josef Bayer has brought my attention to Hermann 1895, which makes the point that early Indo-European used relative markers for semantic anaphora, but had no distinctive marking of subordinate clauses.

I will argue that Hock (1989) is correct in proposing a 'coordinate' or paratactic relation between the relative and correlative clauses. This relation treats the two clauses as syntactic equals, neither is syntactically subordinate to the other. There is greater freedom in combination in Sanskrit than is found in a modern language such as Hindi/Urdu. The relative clause in HU forms a restricted domain, allowing only relative operators and pronominal coindexation. The restrictions on the relative clause do not carry over to the correlative, suggesting that Hindi/Urdu imposes a hierarchical ordering on relative and other subordinate clauses. Sanskrit seems not to impose consistent left to right ordering for syntactic (as opposed to discourse) reasons. While the modern IA languages show some apparent symmetric relations among clauses, in actual fact subordinate clauses on the left are differentiated from subordinate clauses on the right of the combination of two (or more) clauses. Both kinds of adjunction are examples of syntactic subordination, and what differentiates clauses by position is a combination of pragmatic discourse factors and the properties of determiners/pronouns.

A question which runs through this discussion (but is not addressed in detail here) is whether the correlative construction is fundamentally a paratactic or adjunction-type structure, or whether the correlatives are fundamentally headed relative constructions, and the correlative is the surface manifestation of a headed construction derived by movement. In other words, should we prefer a very abstract analysis based on a headed structure which seldom occurs as such, or should we take the evidence of other Indic languages to be justification for a base-generated correlative structure, which undergoes a process of interpretation linking the relative marked clause to a phrase within the main or correlative clause? I will argue for the latter position, suggesting that the very loosely paratactic structure of Old Indic has acquired more syntactic structuring in modern Indic, so that there are both hierarchical and left-right asymmetries not found in Old Indic.

A. Vedic Sanskrit

The evidence for Old Indic presented here comes from Vedic Sanskrit, primarily from examples cited and discussed in Hettrich 1988, Etter 1985, Hock 1989. Before turning to relative clauses, I want to outline the features of interrogative and subordinate complement clauses. Yes/no questions in Sanskrit are marked by *kim* or some other interrogative in initial position, rather like Hindi/Urdu *kyaa* 'what':[3]

---

[3] The modern Indic languages differ as to whether the yes/no question marker is normally initial or final. Hindi/Urdu, Panjabi, Kashmiri have an initial yes/no marker. Marathi,

3) Yes/no questions:

a. [Sanskrit] *kím* u śréṣṭhah kím yáviṣṭho na ā́jagan
Q best Q youngest 1pl-dat come-aor 3s

'Has the best, has the youngest come to us?' (Etter 1985: 55)

b. [Hindi/Urdu] *kyaa wo kal aa-egaa?*
Q 3s tomorrow come-future-3ms

'Will he come tomorrow?'

Subordinate interrogative clauses in Sanskrit are not marked with any special marker of subordination, except for the quotative *iti* (4a):

4) a. [Sanskrit] sabhā́m eti kitaváḥ pṛcchámāno
company go-pr-3s gambler-nom ask-part-pr-middle

jeṣyā́m **iti** tanvā̀ śū́śujānaḥ
conquer-fut-1s-**quote** thạt-loc swell-perf-prt-middle

'In the company comes the gambler asking, "Will I win?" where he spreads himself.' (Etter 1985: 119)

b. [Hindi/Urdu] *unhõ-ne ham-se puuch-aa [ki kyaa wo kal aa-egaa]*
we-from ask-pf 3pl-erg that Q 3s tomorrow come-fut.

'They asked us whether/if he will come tomorrow.'

Hindi/Urdu marks an embedded yes/no question (optionally) with a marker of subordination *ki* and the yes/no question marker *kyaa*. In the

---

Gujarati and Sindhi in the west and Bangla, Assamese, Oriya and Nepali in the east place the Q clitic in final and non initial position. The examples in (i)-(iv) are from Bangla (Dasgupta to appear).

i. *ajke briSTi poRbe(-)**ki**?*
today rain will-fall(-)Q 'Will it rain today?'

ii. *ajke briSTi(-)**ki** poRbe?*
today rain(-)Q will-fall

iii. *ajke(-)**ki** briSTi poRbe?*
today(-)Q rain will-fall

iv. ***ki** ajke briSTi poRbe?*
Q today rain will-fall

Sanskrit example (4a) the main verb 'ask' selects for a clause object which is a (yes/no) question, perhaps obviating the need for the special syntactic marking of subordination which is available in the modern languages.

Other kinds of questions mark a specific constituent to be questioned, using one of the 'k' series of interrogative pronoun/determiners (5a,b), here *kathā* 'why' and *kas* 'who'. The whole sentence is thereby marked as a question.

5) a.	**kathā**	**grā́maṃ**	**ná**	**pṛcchasi?**
	why	village-acc	not	ask-pr-2s

'Why do you not ask about the village?' (Etter 1985: 120)

b.	**kás**	tád	veda	[yád	ádbhutam]?
	who-nom	that-acc	know-pf 3s	rel	miraculous

'Who knows that thing which is miraculous/who knows [what is miraculous]?' (Etter 1985: 196)

If such a question clause is the semantic object of a verb, however, it is phrased in Vedic as a correlative construction, with a relative determiner/pronoun corresponding to what would be an interrogative in the modern languages (6). Matrix and subordinate questions differ in form in Vedic:[4]

6) [Sanskrit]

a.	vidmā́	**tám** útsam	**yáta**	ājagántha
	know-pr-1pl	that spring-acc	rel-whence	come-pf-2s

'We know that spring from which you have come.=We know from which spring you have come.' (Hettrich 1988: 523)

b.	ná	ví jānāmi	**yád**	ivedám	ásmi
	not	know-pr-1s	rel-acc	like-that	be-pres-1s

'I don't know what I am, as it were.' (Hettrich 1988: 519)

[4] Probal Dasgupta reminds me that this method of expressing 'embedded' questions is also found in Ancient Greek. (Dasgupta, p.c.)

7) [Hindi/Urdu]

ham (yah)	*jaan-te*	*hai~ [ki **kaun/*jo***	*aa-e~ge]*
we this	know-impf	are that who?/*rel	come-fut.

'We know [who will come].'

The modern languages clearly distinguish subordinate constructions from matrix clauses, and express questions with the same interrogative words whether the clause is a matrix clause or the complement of a main verb. The formal difference between relative and interrogative clauses which is so clearly marked by the use of the 'y' relative or 'k' interrogative series is obscured in English, for example, because in both contexts an interrogative is used. In the rest of this section, we ask whether there is evidence from the older stage of Indic for syntactic subordination.

The correlative construction in Sanskrit consists of a clause marked by some member of the 'y' series, linked with another clause. This clause contains a phrase which is modified by the relative clause. The order is not fixed—the relative clause may be to the left or the right of the linked correlative clause.

8) [Sanskrit]

a. [Left relative]

[padáṃ	**yád**	víṣṇor	upamáṃ	nidhā́yi]
footstep-acc	rel-acc	Vishnu-gen	highest	put-down-aor-psv-3s

téna	pāsi	gúhyaṃ	nā́ma	gónām
this-inst	protect-pr-2s	secret	name	cows-gen

'You protect the secret name of the cows with the footstep of Visnu which is left in the highest.' (Hettrich 1988: 540)

b. [Right relative]

idáṃ	dyāvāpṛthivī	satyám	astu
that	heaven-earth	truth	be-3pl imper

[pítar	mā́tar	**yád**	ihópabruvé	vām]
Father	Mother	rel	here ask-pr-middle-1s	you-pl-acc

'Let this be truth O heaven and earth, *which* I ask you here, Mother and

Father.' (Hettrich 1988: 571)

9) [Headed relative (?)]

a.	ná	mṛ́ṣā	[śrāntáṃ	[**yád**	ávanti	devā́ḥ]]
	not	useless	pain	rel	favor-pr-3pl	gods

'The [pain [**which** the gods favor __]] is not useless.' (Hettrich 1988: 541)

Hettrich includes a number of examples such as (9), in which the relative pronoun immediately follows the head N. It's not clear that this is the only possible construal.[5] For example, this sentence can be parsed as a correlative construction simply lacking a demonstrative in the correlative clause:

b.	ná	mṛṣā	śrāntaṃ	[yád	ávanti	devā́ḥ]
	not	useless	pain	rel	favor-pr-3pl	gods

'The [pain [**which** the gods favor __]] is not useless.'

The head N is not fixed as an obligatory part just of the relative clause. It is able to occur in the relative clause (10a), the correlative clause (10b) or both (10c):

10) a. [In the relative clause]

[padáṃ	**yád**	víṣṇor	upamáṃ	nidhā́yi]
footstep-acc	rel-acc	Vishnu-gen	highest	put-down-aor-psv-3s

téna	pāsi	gúhyam	nā́ma	gónām
this-inst	protect-pr-2s	secret	name	cows-gen

'You protect the secret name of the cows with the footstep of Visnu which is left in the highest.' (Hettrich 1988: 540)

b. [In the correlative, main clause]

[**yán**	mányase	váreṇyam]
rel-acc	think-pr-middle 2s	desirable

[5] I am indebted to H. Hock for pointing this out. It may be that there is no unambiguous evidence for head relative clauses in Sanskrit.

índra	dyukṣáṃ	tád	á	bhara
Indra-voc	heavenly	that		bring-2s-imper

'Bring us the heavenly (gift) O Indra which you consider excellent.' (Hettrich 1988: 541)

c. [In both clauses]

[yá́ ápo	divyá́	utá vā	srávanti]
rel waters	divine	prt or	flow-pres-3pl

tá́	ápo	devī́r	ihá	mā́m	avantu
those	waters	divine	here	1s-acc	serve-imper-3pl

'Those divine waters should serve me which flow.' (Hettrich 1988: 533)

In sum, Vedic Sanskrit uses the 'y' relative series freely to coindex constituents shared by two clauses, giving a restrictive semantic interpretation to the relative-marked clause. This coindexing takes on the function of marking the semantic complement of verbs taking interrogative complements, such as 'ask' and 'know', which do not have semantic objects marked with the 'k' interrogative series. Complement clauses can also be marked with the quotative suffix *iti*

B. The syntactic relation between the relative and correlative clause in Sanskrit

In a very interesting and thoughtful paper on the correlatives in Old Indic, Hock (1989) raises some very important questions about the syntactic relations between the relative and correlative clauses in this construction. He gives a number of arguments for a simple linking of two clauses, in a paratactic or coordinate structure without a conjunction:

11) Parataxis or coordination, not asymmetric adjunction? (Hock 1989)

S

S1	S2
... yat ...	... tat ...
... tat ...	... yat ...

This structure predicts that the two linked clauses are of equal status, and that what may occur in one may occur in the other, regardless of whether it is marked as a relative (*yat*) or not. One of the most compelling pieces of evidence for these predictions is the sentence in (12):

12) Sanskrit:

[yát	kim	ákaraṃ]	**[tásmád**	idám	ápād(i)
rel	what	do-aor-1s	that-abl	this	befall-aor-3s

'*What did for which reason I did __], for that reason this befell'. (difficult to render into grammatical English-Hock suggests 'Because I have done what? therefore this has happened.') (Hock 1986: 7)[6]

Though quite a rare example, we may take it as a sentence which was grammatical in (early) Sanskrit. What is unusual is the presence of a question word *kim* within the relative clause, a combination which we will see is highly ungrammatical in the modern IA languages. Of course, a question word is quite grammatical in the correlative clause (13):

13)	*kás*	**tád**	veda	**[yád**	ádbhutam]?
	who-nom	that-acc	know-pf 3s	rel	miraculous

'Who knows what thing is miraculous/that thing which is miraculous?' (Etter 1985: 196)

Hock proposes structure which is symmetric; neither clause is subordinate to the other. This construction is a bit surprising in the sentences which get a subordinate question interpretation (6a,b), but it is consonant with the other evidence for no syntactic differentiation of the relative clause. In (6) one may attribute the subordinate semantic interpretation to the lexical properties of the verb *pṛcch* 'ask', which gives the right interpretation in spite of the coordinate syntactic character of the sentence.

In addition, multiple combinations of clauses are possible (see Hock 1989 for additional examples), including some which are comparable to possibilities in the modern IA languages, and others which are not. In (14) there are two relative-correlative links in a three-clause sequence [I-III]:

14)	[I]	**yo(i)**	vai	śreyasaḥ	pariveṣaṇam	avavadati
		rel-nom	emph	better-gen	food-acc	deprecates
	[II]	**yayā (k)**	vai sa(j)	**tam(i)**	ārtyā	kāmayate
		rel-inst	emph he	him	affliction-inst	afflicts

[6] An alternative translation, 'Has this happened to me because I did that?' (F. Smith p.c.) still places the question marker *kim* inside a relative clause, which would be impossible in HU.

[III]	**tayā (k)**	enaṃ (i)	ninayati
	that-inst that-acc	he	wants to afflict

'Who(i) deprecates the food of his(i) better(j), he(i) is afflicted by him(j) with whatever afflictions (k) he (j) wants to afflict him(i) with.' (Hock 1989: 108)

Schematically, the two links are as follows:

15) a. [I] yo(i) [II] tam(i)

b. [II] yayā (k) [III] tayā (k)

The semantic dependency marked in clause [I] is met by the pronoun in clause [II], while the relative dependency introduced in clause [II] is met by the pronoun in clause [III]. As we will see, Hindi/Urdu allows these local dependencies in iterating clauses. Vedic Sanskrit also allows dependencies which are not exactly local, and cut across one entire finite clause (16):

16)	[I]	oṣati ha	vai **sa(i)**	tam(j)
		burns prtl	prtl he	him
	[II]	*yo*(j)	'smāt pūrvo bubhūṣati	
		rel-nom	before desid-be	
	[III]	ya*(i)*	evaṃ	veda
		rel	thus	knows

'He who knows thus burns him who wants to be before him.' (Hock 1989: 108)

17) a. [I] sa(i) [III] ya(i)

b. [I] tam(j) [II] yo(j)

The dependency in (17a) between clause [I] and clause [III] is a non-local dependency, contrasting with the local dependency (17b) between clause [I] and clause [II].

The evidence from Sanskrit for the symmetric syntactic relation in (11) is summarized in (18):

18) a. A question word is possible in the relative as well as the correlative clause.
    b. The N head may be expressed in either the relative or the correlative (Hettrich 1988)
    c. 'Embedded questions' use a relative pronoun to link the clause to a demonstrative in the correlative clause- there is -no specialized form marking of subordination.
    d. Relative-correlative dependencies need not be strictly local, between adjacent clauses.

So I will conclude that early Sanskrit offers no unambiguous evidence for differentiating the relative clause as a clause subordinate to the main clause, or combined with a head N. The modern languages, however, offer very strong evidence for asymmetry, both hierarchically and in terms of linear order.

C. Three types of relative clauses with relative pronouns in Hindi/Urdu

In this section we now turn to the focus of the paper, the relative clause constructions in Hindi/Urdu. Unlike Sanskrit, there is unambiguous evidence for a headed relative clause structure in (19a-c). This structure is required for the non-restrictive relative interpretation, otherwise it is rather limited in use.[7] In fact it may not be as productive across all the relative pronoun possibilities as the corresponding structure is in English. The exception would be relative clauses adjoined to proper names, which have a non-restrictive interpretation (19d).

19) a. [*NP* [jo x]] -NP adjoined finite relative

b.

[*ek*	*aur*	*baccaa*	[jo *us-se*	*baRaa*	*thaa]*	*ek*
one	and	boy	rel 3s-than	big	was	one

bachiyaa-ko	*dhakel-kar*	*daayare-se*
calf-f-dat	push-prt	ring-from

---

[7] The structure in (12) often is used in a kind of adjoined topic construction, with a pronoun in the main sentence:

i) *[wo*	*kitaab*	*[jo*	*kaafii*	*rocak*	*hai]] [wo*	*kho*	*ga-ii]*
that	book	rel	rather	interesting	is 3s-nom	be-lost	go-pf

'The book [*which* is rather interesting], **it** got lost.'

duur	*hataa-ne-kii*	*ceSTaa kar*	*rahaa*	*thaa.*
far	remove-inf-gen	attempt do	prog	was

'Another boy who was older than him was trying to remove the calf from the ring by pushing (it).' (Rakesh 1961: 89)

c.	*ek ciiz*(i)	[*jis-se*	*man kii*	*uljhan*	*aur*	*baRh-ne*
	one thing	rel-by	mind-gen	anxiety	and	increase-inf
	lag-ii]	*wo*(i)	*macchlii-kaa*		*gandh hai.*	
	begin-pf	that	fish-gen		smell is	

'One thing [because of which (my) anxiety of mind began to increase] it's the smell of fish.' (Rakesh 1961: 20)

d.	*bhopaal*	*sTeshan-par*	*meraa*	*mitr*	*avinaash*
	Bhopal	station-on	my	friend	Avinash

[jo *wahaa˜*	*nikal-ne*	*waale*
who there	come-out-inf-part.	

hindii	*dainik-kaa*	*sampaadan*	*kar-taa thaa]*	*mujh-see*
Hindi	daily-gen	editing	do-impf was	me-with

mil-ne-ke liye	*aa-yaa*	*thaa.*
met-inf-for	come-pf	was

'At Bhopal station my friend Avinash [who edited a Hindi daily which appeared from there] came to meet me.' (Rakesh 1961: 10)

In addition to NP adjoined relative clauses, there are relative clauses are adjoined either to the left or the right of the main clause (20)-(21)[8]:

---

[8] Constructions of this type are found in most of the Indic languages, except for those at the periphery of the Indic area. Sinhala is a notable exception to the Indic pattern (15). It has only a head-final participial relative construction. Even a biclausal structural like (16) fails to have a correlative interpretation. Sinhala has not only lost the 'y/j' series of relative pronouns, but it diverges from Malayalam, whose syntax it strongly resembles, in not having a correlative construction based on the interrogative (17).

15) [Sinhala] — The 'ya' series of specifically relative pronouns is lost; no correlatives.

[[*siri gunəpaalaTə* ____	*dunnə] poTə*
Siri Gunapala-dat	give-past book

'The book [which [Siri gave ___ to Gunapala] (Gair and Paolillo 1997: 54.)

20) Left adjoined to main clause

a. [[jo N . x .] *wo (N)*] Sentence-initial relative clause

b. [*isliye kaakaajii* [PRO *pii-ne -ke baad*] *biiRii-ke* **jo**
this-for Uncle drink-inf-gen after biri-gen

"Thuu˜Th" *phe˜k de-te,*]
which stumps throw give-impf

[**unhe˜** *curaa-naa shuruu ki-yaa*]
3pl steal-inf beginning do-pf

'Therefore (we) began to steal the "butts" [**which** Uncle threw away after smoking them].' (Gandhi 1969: 21)

21) Right-adjoined to main clause

a. [wo *N* [jo x]] Sentence-final relative clause

b. *[unho˜-ne apne irdgird* **aìsaa pardaa** *khii˜c li-yaa]*
3pl- -erg self all-around such curtain draw take-pf

[jis-ke *piiche ve apne dard chipaa sak-e˜*]
rel-gen behind 3pl self's pains hide be able-cont

---

16) [Sinhala [*mee* ***kawru*** *hari narəkə kenek api atərəpilisindila tiyenəwa*].
this who etc bad person us among conceive-prt exist

[***eekə*** *nisaa tamay mee apiTə okkomə karərə*]
that-one because indeed that us-dat all trouble

a. 'Some bad person or other has been conceived among us. That's the reason we have all this trouble.' (Gair and Paolillo 1997: 59)

b. NOT 'We have all this trouble because of some bad persion who has been conceived among us.' (James Gair, p.c.)

17) [Malayalam]
[*enn-e* ***aarə*** *nuLLi *0/-oo*] **awan** *duSTam aaNə*
me-acc who pinched -or he wicked man is

'The person who pinched me is wicked.' (Jayaseelan 2001)

Though the Malayalam correlative (17) might offer a model for a correlative construction for Sinhala, even a structurally similar sentence (16) cannot have a relative interpretation. Shina speakers can produce a correlative structure on the model of *jo* clauses in Urdu, but the Shina version uses an interrogative, like the Dravidian structure. (Peter Hook, p.c.)

'She drew *a curtain* completely around herself [**behind which** she could conceal her pains].' (Jayekar 1992)

The NP-adjoined finite relatives in (19) are clearly in a subordinate relation to the main clause, as they may be wholly contained within the main clause (19b-d). The more usual relative clauses are the clauses adjoined to the left (20) or right (21) of the correlative clause. In the next section I will give arguments for the syntactic subordination of the relative clause. The relative clause forms a restricted domain, prohibiting various relations which are permitted for the correlative clause. Since Sanskrit does not seem to restrict relative clauses in these ways, the syntax of the HU relative must be responsible, rather than the semantics of the relative marker, which specifies semantic subordination. In both languages, the relative clause acts as a restrictive modifier on a constituent of the main clause, and so it is semantically subordinate to the main clause.

D. Arguments for asymmetry of adjunction in Hindi/Urdu

From the evidence, the modern IA languages introduce a hierarchical asymmetry in the syntax, not a property of the paratactic structure in (11). In this next section, I will give two arguments for regarding the relative clause as syntactically subordinate. The subordination relation is expressed as representing the relative clause as a CP adjunct to IP in (22):

22) a. Left relative b. Right relative

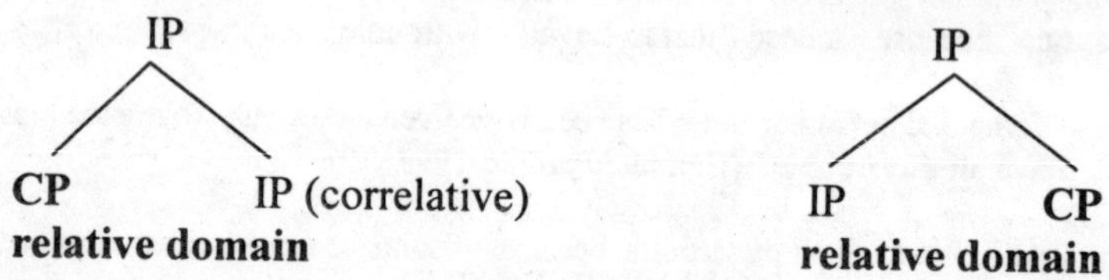

I assume that IP (Inflectional phrase) stands for a tensed clause, omitting any markers it might have for subordination or illocutionary force. These are associated with the CP (Complementizer phrase), which stands for the tensed clause IP PLUS markers of subordination and illocutionary force. It is where the semantic scope of questions and relative phrases is syntactically represented.[9]

[9] Though IP and CP are represented as types of phrases, they actually represent clauses, either independent sentences or sentences in combination with other sentences. The head of IP is the clause tense, and the head of CP is the marker of subordination or clause type

There is very robust evidence in the modern language for differentiating between the relative and the correlative, unlike what seems to be the case of Sanskrit. Only main clauses can be marked as questions, not relative clauses. Relative clauses, whether on the left or right, reject internal question phrases (22a)-(23a):

22) [Left relative] (No question within the scope of a relative **jo**)

a. **[jo kitaab* **kis-ne** *likh-ii hai]* **wo** *aap-ko sab-se acchii lag-ii/?*
rel book who-erg write-pf is 3s you-dat all-from good strike-pf

*Who did you like best the book [that ____ wrote___]?

b. [**jo kitaab** *us-ne likh-ii hai*] **wo** *kis-ko sab-se acchii lag-ii?*
rel book 3s-erg write-pf is 3s who-dat all-from good strike-pf
(Question in correlative)

'Who likes best the book [**that** he/she wrote___]?'

23) [Right relative] (No question word allowed within the scope of a relative **jo**)

a. ***wo kitaab** *aap-ko acchii lag-ii* [**jo** kis-ne *likh-ii hai*]?
that book you-dat good strike-pf rel who-erg write-pf is

**Who* did you like the book [that ____ wrote___] ?

b. **wo kitaab** *kis-ko acchii lag-ii* [**jo** *us-ne likh-ii hai*]?
that book who-dat good strike-pf rel 3s-erg write-pf is
(Question in the correlative)

'*Who* liked the book [**that** he/she wrote___]?'

On the other hand, the correlative clause may have an interrogative in it with semantic scope over the whole complex sentence (22b)-(23b).

We summarize the differences of good and bad results in (24), using left relatives as the example:

(complment clause, relative or interrogative clause, etc.). So they are both phrases and sentences, allowing sentences to be represented in the same way as internal constituents of clauses.

24) a. Left relative—bad result

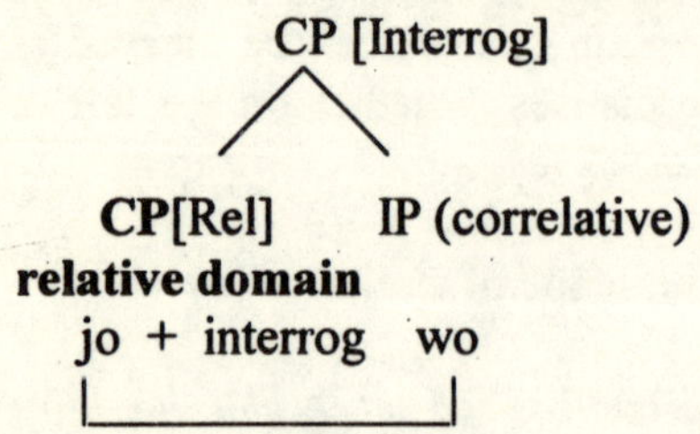

b. Left relative—good result

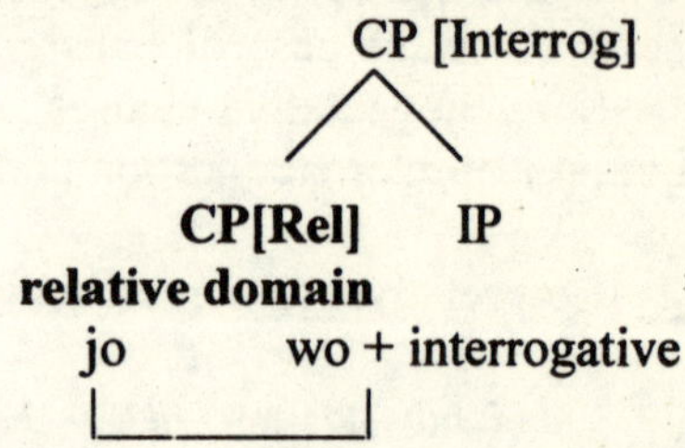

The relative pronoun/determiner defines a domain which is opaque to questions, whether they have scope over the relative domain alone, or include the main clause as well. This means that a question phrase within the relative clause is always ungrammatical. I take this fact to be evidence for syntactic as well as semantic subordination of relative clauses in the modern IA languages.

In this next section, we see another type of evidence for distinguishing relative clauses from ordinary clauses. Ordinary clauses allow pronouns to have antecedents either within the same clause or in adjacent clauses, perhaps some distance away. Relative pronouns/determiners must be coindexed with a pronoun in exactly the next clause, the IP to which the relative CP is adjoined. The coindexed pronoun cannot be two or more clauses away. This condition was noted independently for other Indic languages, Konkani (Nadkarni 1980) and for Bangla in, Dasgupta 1980. The condition, which Dasgupta named *the Simplexity constraint,* is discussed in the final sections of this paper. See also discussion in Hock 1989.

The following examples are from McCawley 1993, showing the iteration of relative clauses to the left. A relative clause first establishes an antecedent for a pronoun in the next clauses (italicized phrases), but that clause also introduces another relative phrase, also coindexed with a pronoun (phrases in bold type):

25) [I] [jo aadmii*(i)* *caay pii* *rahaa hai*]
which man tea drink prog is

[II] [*mai˜* **jis makaan(j)** -me˜ <u>us-ke liye</u>*(i)* *kaam kar rahaa huu˜*]
I which house-in 3s-for work do prog am

[III] [*raam pichle saal* **wahaa˜ (j)** *rah-taa thaa*]
Ram last year there stay-impf was

'The man who is drinking tea, I'm doing work for him in the house [where Ram was living last year; Ram was living in the house where I am doing work for the man who is drinking tea.' (McCawley 2004: 307)

This construction is somewhat difficult for speakers to process, but it is well-formed provided that each relative phrase corresponds to a coindexed pronoun in the adjacent clause. Using the same schematic summary which described Sanskrit iterating clauses, (25) has the dependency relations in (26)

26) a. [I] [*jo aadmii*(i)] [II] [*us-ke liye*(i)]

b. [II] [*jis makaan*(j) [III] [*wahaa˜* (j)]

An example of the violation of the Simplexity constraint is shown in (27). Here the italicized *jo aadmii* in [I] corresponds to a pronoun two clauses away in [III], as shown the schematic summary in (28):

27) *[I] [jo aadmii*(i)* *caay pii rahaa hai*]
rel man tea drink prog is

[II] [**jis makaan-me˜** (j*)* *mai˜ ab rah-taa huu˜*]
which house-in I now stay-impf am

[III] [wo*(i)* *pichlee saal* **wahaa˜ (j)** *rah-taa thaa*]
3s last year there stay-impf was

'The man who is drinking tea, he lived last year in the house where I am now.' (McCawley 2004: 307)

28) a. *[I] [jo aadmii(i)] [III] [wo(i)]

b. [II] jis makaan-me˜(j)] [III] wahaa˜(j)]

The ungrammaticality of (27) stems from the non-local coindexing dependency in (28a), crossing over clause [II]. This dependency was however found in Sanskrit in (16)-(17), where it is apparently grammatical. Hindi/Urdu allows iteration of relative clauses, like Sanskrit, but HU has added a syntactic condition which says that the semantic dependency introduced by the relative pronoun must be met in a syntactically adjacent clause. This relation of syntactic adjacency follows from adjunction of the (subordinate) relative clause rather than parataxis of clauses of equal status.

The lexical/syntactic constraint on relatives is shown schematically in (29) A relative **jo** has to be coindexed with *wo* SOMEWHERE in the adjacent clause, defined by the adjunction relation. This condition (Dasgupta's 1980 Simplexity condition) applies to both left and right relatives.

29) CP

CP[Rel] IP
Jo **wo** [wo can be in a subordinate clause within IP]

I conclude that Hindi/Urdu as a representative of a modern Indic language shows clear evidence for syntactically differentiating relative clauses from the associated correlative clause. There are reasons to represent relative clauses as in an adjoined relation. The requirements on relative clauses are translated into a hierarchical structuring which is asymmetrical for relative and main clauses. By contrast, the Sanskrit evidence supports a loose and syntactically symmetric association of clauses, as proposed by Hock 1989. The burden of a relative interpretation is borne by the lexical features of the relative pronouns. The Sanskrit relative construction carries over to reported questions (4a,b). The subordination of the reported question is expressed lexically by the verb of asking, rather than syntactically marked by a complementizer.

E. Īs Hindi a linearly symmetric language?

In the previous section, we reviewed evidence from HU (and similar languages) for hierarchical asymmetry. I propose that the syntactic relation is an adjunction relation, as in (29), between relative and correlative clauses, rather than parataxis, as in (11). The evidence for asymmetry applies to both left relatives and right relatives. The next question is whether there is linear symmetry between relative and other clauses. That is, do relative clauses adjoin freely to either the left or right of the host or matrix clause, with no difference of status or properties? I will propose that there are some clear differences (as others like Dayal 1996, Dwivedi 1993 have also proposed). I will relate these differences to discourse factors, rather than to differences of syntactic derivation.

At first glance it seems that HU has symmetric possibilities for relative, conditional and complement clauses. Full relative clauses can precede or follow the main clause, as we have seen above. In addition to NP-adjoined clauses on the right, as in (19), HU has a relative modifier to the left of NP:

30) a. [_______ *ghaas-par* *khel-te hu-e/ *khel rahe hai~] laRke*
grass-on play-impf be-pf/play prog are boys

'The boys [who are playing on the grass].' (Subbarao 1984: 19)

b. [______ *nau baje* *dauR-ne]* *waale log*
9o'clock run-inf nom. People

'The people [who run at 9 o'clock].' (Subbarao 1984: 19)

But these left-adjoined modifiers have only non-finite inflection, and they are restricted in that the head NP may be coindexed only with the subject of the modifying clause (or the direct object of perfective participles).

Complement clauses may precede or follow the verb of which they are the object, sometimes with a difference of meaning in (31a,b). There is some differentiation required by position. The complement clauses which are in object position before the verb must be non-finite. In this position finite clauses are not permitted (31c).

31) a. *madhuu-ne* [PRO *baahar jaa-ne]* *-se* *inkaar ki-yaa*
Madhu-erg outside go-inf -from denial do-pf

'Madhu refused [PRO to go outside].' (Subbarao 1984: 36)

b. *madhuu-ne* *(is-se(i))* *inkaar ki-yaa [ki* *wo* *baahar* *ga-ii](i)*
Madhu-erg this-from denial do-pf that 3s outside go-pf

'Madhu denied [that she went outside].'

c. **madhuu-ne* *(is-se)* *[ki wo* *baahar* *ga-ii] inkaar ki-yaa*
Madhu-erg this-from that 3s outside go-pf denial do-pf

'Madhu refused / denied [that she went outside].'

Finite clauses may be adjoined to the left (32), and coindexed with *yah* 'this' or *aisaa* 'such', but the complementizer *ki* 'that' is ungrammatical. See also examples and discussion in Subbarao 1984.

32) [(**ki) duniyaa˜* *-me˜* *biiRii-kaa* *itnaa* *zabardast* *shauk*
world -in biri-gen so-much powerful enthusiasm

kyo˜ *hai*](i)
why is

ise(i) *mai˜* *kabhii* *samajh* *nahii˜* *sak-taa* *huu˜*
3s-prox-dat I sometime understand not be-able-impf am

'[Why there is in the world such powerful enthusiasm for biris], (this) I cannot understand.' (Gandhi 1969: 21)

The grammar of Hindi/Urdu places a grammatical requirement on complement clauses in complement position: they must be non-finite. Finite clauses may be adjoined to the right, coindexed with an internal complement (e.g. *is-se* 'this from' in (31)). Less commonly they may be adjoined to the left, but without the possibility of the complementizer *ki*. Finite clauses are different from non-finite clauses in other ways. Finite clauses form a domain for questions, as in the sentence in (32): the subordinate clause forms a 'why' question. Non-finite clauses do not form a domain for a question, and instead, the question interpretation must include the main clause:

33) a. *wo* [PRO *kahaa˜* *jaa-ne]-kii* *soc* *rahaa hai?*
3s where go-inf-gen-f think prog is

'**Where** is he thinking of [PRO going ___]? ['where?' > 'think']
NOT 'He is thinking about [**where** to go].'

b. *wo* *soc rahaa hai [ki* *tumhe~* [PRO *kahaa˜* *jaa-naa]* *caahiye*]
3s think prog is that you-dat where go-inf ought

'He is thinking about [**where** you should go___] '['think' > 'where?'][10]

[10] Bangla differentiates between finite clauses in complement position, and adjoined to the left and right (Dasgupta 1980, 1995, Bayer 1996), with differences of opacity to wide wh- question scope. *je* marked clauses on the right are opaque, *bole* -marked finite clauses and bare clause to the left are transparent.
[Bangla]

i). *chele-Ta* *e* ***kOtha*** *jan-e* *[je /*O* *baba* *aSbe*]
boy cl this matter know-3 that father come-fut3

'The boy knows [that his father will come]' Bayer 1996: 257 (**je** is obligatory)

ii). [[*or baba aSbe]* ***bole]*** *chele-Ta (*e koTha) Suneche*
his father come-fut3 quot boy-cl this matter hear-pts3

'The boy has heard [that his father will come]' Bayer 1996: 255

iii) *ora [[* ***ke*** *aSbe]* ***bole]*** *Sune-che* (?) (Quotative clauses are optionally transparent)
they who come-FUT3 quot hear-PTS3

i. 'They have heard [*who* will come].' (Opaque reading) [Stress on matrix V *Suneche*]

ii. '*Who* have they heard [___will come]?' (Transparent reading [Stress on *ke* 'who' Bayer 1996, Dasgupta 1980.

NOT '**Where** is he thinking [that you should go ___]?'

As this example shows, a finite clause is an opaque domain for interrogative scope; all other things being equal, an interrogative phrase has scope only over its immediately containing finite clause, not over a higher clause. For exceptions, variations on questions which allow wide scope meanings for questions, see Davison 1988, Dayal 1996. Non-finite clauses are transparent, and a wh-phrase must have scope over the next superordinate finite clause. The opacity of all finite clauses is a much stronger condition on interpretation in Hindi/Urdu than in languages like English. The restrictions on finite clauses in HU consist in part of the opacity induced by finite tense/aspect/agreement morphology, and in part by the adjunction relation, which marks a finite clause as syntactically subordinate.

In this section, I have considered subordinate clauses which have a complement interpretation, not a modifier interpretation as relative clauses. In principle, subordinate clauses have some freedom of occurring to the left or right, but Hindi/Urdu imposes strict conditions, differentiating between clauses in complement position, which are non-finite and wh-transparent, and clauses adjoined to the left or right, which must be finite and wh-opaque. Finite clauses to the left lack the complementizer *ki* 'that' which is possible for finite clauses on the right of the main clause.

F. Linear order and the asymmetries in Hindi/Urdu relative clauses

In earlier sections it has been shown that Hindi/Urdu makes syntactic distinctions between subordinate and matrix clauses to a degree apparently not found in early Sanskrit, which concatenates clauses paratactically (Hock 1989). Both Hindi/Urdu and Sanskrit make semantic distinctions between main and dependent clauses, by virtue of the relative pronoun/determiners, but Sanskrit does not make syntactic hierarchical distinctions. The hierarchical distinction of main/subordinate clause has consequences for limits on possible interpretations of complex sentences, and the question and relative operators within them. The result is that Sanskrit allows clause combinations and interpretations which are ungrammatical in the modern Indic languages.

In this section, I consider questions of linear order. I will assume that in Hindi/Urdu, subordinate finite clauses are represented as adjuncts rather than coordinated or paratactically conjoined clauses. But nothing about the adjunction relation itself determines whether the adjunction is to the left or the right. In principle, a finite subordinate clause can be adjoined in either position, but it was shown in the last section on complement clauses that in actual fact, there are always some differences in form and interpretation between left and right adjuncts. This difference is quite general in modern Indic languages. The difference between left and right adjuncts most clearly shown in languages such as Bangla and Marathi, which use the quotative suffix on complements to the left, and a prefix of subordination for right adjoined complements (though the entire range of adjoined clauses shows somewhat more variety that this summary would suggest (Bayer 1996, 2001, Masica 2000).

The correlative construction crucially involves (at least) two critical relations: (1) a coindexing relation between the phrase in the matrix clause which is restrictively modified by the relative clause, and the *jo* phrase in the relative clause itself, and (2) an ordering relation; the relative clause precedes, follows or is internal to the main clause. The first relation is a syntactic/semantic relation. The second reflects discourse pragmatic relations, in effect independently of the syntactic construction linking the two clauses, in addition to the coindexing/modification requirement.

The first discourse effect is the 'partitive effect' discussed by Srivastav Dayal 1991, Dayal 1996. An argument for deriving left relatives differently from right relatives is that left relatives are subject to a restriction on coindexing while right relatives are not. Hock 1989 points out that this partitive requirement applies to discourse sequences in general. If there is an anaphoric relation between a plural antecedent preceding a singular NP, a partitive phrase is required referring to the plural antecedent. The partitive phrase may not be omitted. But this is not a special feature of left relatives, but of linear sequences in general.

34) a. (i)	*shimlaa-me˜*	*mere*	***kaii***	***sahayogii***	*dakSiN*	*bhaarat-ke*	*the*
	Simla-in	my	few	associate	southern	India-gen	were

(ii)	**un-me˜-se**	**ek**-*ne*	*kah-aa thaa*	*[ki rah-ne-ke liye*
	3pl-in-from	one -erg	say-pf was	that stay-inf-for
	kanaanor	*bahut*	*acchii*	*jagah* *hai*
	Kananor	very	good	place is

'(i) In Simla *a few of my associates(i)* were from South India. (ii) One **of them(i)** said that Kananor is a very good place to stay.' (Rakesh 1961: 10)

35) a.	**ve**	**laRke**	*bahut*	*caalaak hai˜,*	**un-me˜-se** /*0
	those	boys	very	clever are	3pl-in-from

har ek	*meraa*	*chaatr*	*hai*
each one	my	student	is

'Those boys are very clever, *each one of them* is my student.'

In addition to the cardinal numbers, the quantifiers which require the partitive are basically singular (*har ek, pratyek* 'each'; *kaun* 'who'), and mostly belong to the class of *weak* quantifier, whose interpretation is affected by the contents of the discourse universe.

Left relatives serve as a (discourse) context specifying a reference set.

Correlatives are also subject to the partitive requirement for linked a weak quantifier with a plural antecedent, including relatives on the right.

36) *old goaa-me˜*	*kaii*	*baRe baRe*	*girajaaghar(i)*	*hai~,*
Old Goa-in	several	big -big	churchbuilding	are

jin(i)-me~-se	**ek me˜**
rel -in-from	one-in

.... *seNT*	*fraaNsis-ke*	*shariir-kaa*	*pradarshan*	*ho*	*rahaa*	*thaa.*
saint	Francis-gen	body-gen	exhibition	be	prog	was

'In Old Goa there were several huge churches, in one of which the exhibition of the body of St. Francis was going on.' (Rakesh 1961: 36)

So the partitive relation summed up as:

37) [plural reference set] (i) — [[plural pronoun(i) -from] weak quantifier]

It is independent of the syntactic relation between the two clauses. It holds for both sequences of sentences in discourse, and relative-correlative clause linked in a syntactic adjunction relation.

G. Topic and focus

Besides the partitive relation just discussed, discourse relations include *topic* and *focus,* which no doubt are factors which apply in Sanskrit as well, but which are not so clear because of the immense temporal distance between the older Vedic language and the present day.

The left correlative has the properties of a topic, with presupposed meaning and a default definite interpretation (38)-(39)

38) Definite interpretation

isliye	*kaakaajii*	*[pii-ne -ke baad]*	*biiRii-ke*
this-for	Uncle	drink-inf-gen after	biri-gen

jo	**"Thuu~Th"**	*phe~k*	*de-te,*
rel	stumps	throw	give-impf

unhe~	*curaa-naa*	*shuruu*	*ki-yaa*
3pl	steal-inf	beginning	do-pf

'Therefore (we) began to steal the "butts" [**which** Uncle threw away __ after smoking (them).' (Gandhi 1969: 21)

39) Definite interpretation

jis hoTal(i) *-me~*	*mai~*	*khaanaa*	*khaa-ne*	*jaa-taa*	*thaa,* **usii**
rel restaurant-in	I	food	eat-inf-obl	go-impf	was-that-emph

hoTal(i)-me~	*khaanaa*	*khaa-ne*	*dhayanmay*	*naam -kaa*	*ek*	*yuvak*
restaurant-in	food	eat-inf	Dhayanmay	name -gen	one	youngman

bhii	*aa-yaa*	*kar-taa thaa*
also	come-pf	do-impf was

'A young man named Dhayanmay was in the habit of coming to eat in *the same restaurant* where I also went to eat.' (Rakesh 1961: 79)

The definite interpretation may be cancelled in favor of a generic, non-specific interpretation.

40) Generic, non-specific indefinite

[jo(i)	*akelaa*	*safar*	*kar*	*rahaa hai,*	**us(i)***-kaa*	*udaas ho*
rel	alone	travel	do	prog is	3s-gen	depressed be rise-inf

uTh-naa to	*aur*	*bhii*	*swabhaavik*	*hai*
emph	and	also	natural	is

'*Whoever* is travelling alone, [his becoming depressed] is all the more natural.' [For a person who is travelling alone to become depressed] is all the more natural. (Rakesh 1961: 40)

41)

jo	**koii/bhii**	*pariikSaa*	*baiTh-egaa,*	**us-ko/unko**
rel	some/even	exam	sit-fut.	3s/3pl-dat

acchaa *nambar* *mil-egaa*
good grade receive-fut

'*Whoever* takes the exam will get a good grade.'

The relative-correlative order is the unmarked order for correlatives with a definite interpretation. In 'marked' cases, the *jo* clause can follow the main clause, still with a definite interpretation forced by the preceding antecedent, which has a demonstrative:

42) a. **[jo aurat** *darwaaze-ke paas khaRii hai***], us-ko** *mai˜* *jaan-tii*
rel woman door -gen near standing is 3s-dat I know-impf

huu˜.
Am

'I know [*the woman* [who is standing near the door]].' (Gambhir 1981: 186)

b. **us aurat -ko** *mai˜* *jaan-tii* *huu˜* **[jo** *darwaaze-ke paas*
that woman-dat I know-impf am rel door -gen near

khaRii hai]
standing is

'I know [*the woman* [who is standing near the door]].' (Gambhir 1981: 186)

The leftward position of a constituent tends to induce a topic interpretation, reinforced by *jo* in several uses, the relative and a topic marking function. In the latter case, the *jo* marker follows the topicalized element (here I am conflating Gambhir's 'reason' and 'thematic' uses, 1981: 166-175). The topicalized entity may be a proper name (43b), a typical shared discourse referent, or if it is an indefinite common noun, it can be introduced by context. (43c)

43) a. *niiraa* **jo** **bimaar** *thii, mai˜* **isliye** *nahii˜* *aa-yii* ['Reason' jo]
Nira rel sick was I this-for not come-pf

'*Because Nira* was *sick*, I did not come; as for Niraa she was *sick*, *therefore* I didn't come.' (Gambhir 1981: 166)

b. *maleriyaa* **jo** **hai** **wo** *barsaatii* *mausam-me˜* *phail-taa* *hai*
malaria rel is 3s rainy season -in spread-impf is
[Thematic jo]

'As for malaria, it spreads in the rainy season.' (Ibid)

c. I have three exams: [Context]

pahlaa	**jo**	**hai**	**wo**	*das*	*maarc-ko hai...*	[Thematic jo]
first	rel	is	3s	10	March-dat is	

'As for the first, it is on March 10.' (Gambhir 1981: 173)

Interestingly, the thematic *jo hai wo* construction never allows a reverse order of relation following the main clause (Gambhir 1981: 169). This fact suggests that the topic marker *jo* is most compatible with proper names and pronouns, which by definition are part of the discourse context, and forces a topic interpretation. In Rizzi's account of the phrases in the Left Periphery (1998), relative operators and markers of subordination are in the outermost, leftmost (FORCE) position, and serve the general function of relating a subordinate clause to a higher syntactic or discourse context; a Topic position is adjacent and to the right of the Force head. These head positions could be fused, drawing a phrase with these properties to the Specifier position.

Correlatives on the right, however, typically get a focus or 'new information' interpretation. They are quite often found in sentences which introduce or mention a specific indefinite DP.

44) Specific indefinite interpretation of a right relative

a.

aur	*ham dono˜-ke*	*biic-me˜*	**relve kaa**	**borD** *lag-aa thaa,*
and	we both gen	between-in	railway-gen	board fix-pf was

jis(i)-par	*likh-aa thaa—*
rel-on	write-pf was

'madad	*caahiye?'*
help	needed

'And between us two *a railway board(i)* was fixed, *on which*(i) was written, "Do you need help?"'

b.

borD-ke	*niice* **sahaayak-kii**	**kuursii(i)**	*rakh- ii thii,*
board-gen	below assistance-gen	chair	place-pf was on

jis(i)-par	*us*	*samay*	*koii*	*nahii˜*	*thaa.*
Which	that	time	some	not	was

'Below the board *there was a chair for assistance(i), on which* (i) at that time no one was sitting.' (Rakesh 1961: 25)

45) Non-specific indefinite interpretation, right relative

na	*jaan-e*	*us*	*insaan-kii*	*zindagii-me˜*	*kahaa˜*	**kaun-saa**
not	know-cont.	that	man-gen	life-in	where	what-kind

zakhm*(i)*	*thaa*
wound	was

jo(i)	*merii*	*zaraa-sii*	*asaavdhaanii-se*	*chil*	*ga-yaa*	*thaa.*
rel	my	rather	carelessness -with	be-scraped	go-pf	was

'One couldn't know *what sort of wound* there was where in this man's life, which was scraped by my carelessness.' (Rakesh 1961: 27)

Both topic clauses and focus clauses are possible within the same sentence:

(46) Both left and right relatives

jidhar(i)	*mai˜*	*baiTh-aa*	*thaa,*	*udhar(i)*	*niice*
rel-where	I	sit-pf	was	there	below

ek	**ghaaTii(j)**	*thii* [**jis(j)-me˜**	*ghane naariyaal*	*ug-e*	*hu-e*	*the.*]
one	valley	was rel-in	thick coconut trees	sprout-pf	be-pf	were

'Below *the side* of the train where I was sitting, there was *a mountain pass in which* coconut trees were growing thickly.' (Rakesh 1961: 31)

The location where the author was sitting is part of the overall discourse context, while the *mountain pass* is introduced as a specific indefinite followed by asserted/focused information. This construction occurs in subordinate as well as main clauses:

47)

is	*biic*	*sun-aa [ki* **ek prakaar**	**-kaa paudhaa**
this	among	hear-pf that one kind	gen plant

hai (us-kaa	*naam*	*mai˜*	*to*	*bhuul*	*ga-yaa huu˜),*
is 3s-gen	name	I	topic	forget	go-pf am

jis	*-ke*	*DaNThal*	*biiRii –kii*	*tarah*	*jal-te*
which	-gen	stems	biri-gen	manner	burn-impf

hai˜	*aur*	*phuu˜k-e*	*jaa*	*sak-te*	*hai˜*
are	and	puff-pf	go	be-able-impf	are

'Meanwhile, we heard that there is *a plant of some sort* (I forget its name) **whose** stems burn like a biri, and can be smoked.' (Gandhi 1969: 21).

Dwivedi (1994) shows that left relatives freely allow syntactic extraction, while right relatives resist extraction. This property would be explained if right relatives are focused, forming boundary of the focus domain which may not intervene in a NP ....pronoun chain. Note that the coordinate relative clause is part of a subordinate *ki* clause, so that contra Dwivedi, it can't be regarded as part of a totally separate 'afterthought' sentence. Of course afterthoughts *can* be expressed with this construction, but not all the properties of right relatives are explained as afterthoughts. Rather, I think Gambhir 1981 is closer to the mark saying that topic extraction depends on the extracted constituent forming a topic for the whole structure, and since clauses are the right are focused rather than topicalized, they make very poor candidates for being a sentence topic.

F. Relative clause derivation

What I have proposed here is a minimal account of the properties of *jo* in the modern language, in this case in Hindi/Urdu. It combines some general discourse properties of left vs right position, overlaid on an adjunction construction (29) which places a syntactic relative adjunct CP either to the left or right of the main IP clause, in a larger construction which has the label of CP, allowing for its own illocutionary force. The relative clause CPs are marked by *jo* etc. as modifier clauses. The 'main' CP may be marked as a question or command (or statement).

In all three constructions, the relative determiner/pronoun **jo** links a property clause with a NP, in the matrix clause via a shared constituent, which may be adjacent to the relative clause or may not. The differences of definiteness interpretation follow from the combination of an underspecified relative marker **jo** with other information, such as particles, other determiners, and linear order, which reflects information available at a given point in the interpretation process.

I propose that the differences are not best explained as different translations of **jo**, nor in different syntactic relations derived by syntactic movement from a Head +Relative structure like (19). Rather, *jo* is the same in all contexts, but underspecified for definiteness. The differences between left and right clauses follow from the left-right order of the two clauses in the construction, and the information which is available in a left-right sequence of steps in constructing an interpretation (as suggested by Kempson et al 2001).

There are many similarities between early Sanskrit and modern Indic relative clauses. The relative operator expressed as *yas/jo* introduces an indefinite referent, which can or must be linked to a corresponding referent in another clause. The interpretation may be strengthened to a definite interpretation (uniqueness in the context) if the relative clause is in left or topic position (at least in the modern language) as in (38)-(39), or if there is a specific antecedent for a right relative (42b). It may also be given a specific indefinite interpretation, as in (44), with a specific indefinite antecedent with *aisaa* 'such' *koii* 'some' 21). The definite interpretation can be cancelled with an indefinite marker *koii* 'some; or indefinite focus particle *bhii* 'also/even'. Nothing otherwise forces a left or right position in this account.

H. Conditions on relative clause construal

What differentiates the early language from the modern languages is a syntactic relation, and a syntactic requirement. The syntactic relation is syntactic subordination in the modern languages. Nothing requires syntactic subordination in Sanskrit, allowing for the many instances of sentences in Sanskrit which would be ungrammatical in the modern languages. The modern languages freely allow adjunction to NP, forming NP-headed relative clauses, as well as left or right adjuncts.

The syntactic requirement is Dasgupta's 'Simplexity' account, which says that the relative must be linked with a referent it modifies, and this referent must be in the nearest major constituent, namely somewhere in the IP or NP to which the relative is adjoined. (in the structures (29) and (19)). The Sanskrit sentences cited above are all violations of Simplexity. This requirement is absent from Sanskrit (and other early IE languages); it is possible to introduce a relative clause marked with the relative determiner *yas* which corresponds to no corresponding coreferent.

Finite clauses in Indic languages seem to form autonomous domains which resist movement into them. They also resist construal relations like agreement which cross finite clause boundaries (cf. Gambhir 1981). Relative clauses in both Sanskrit and Hindi/Urdu are subject to a condition on local interpretation, which says that the relative operator within a tensed clause has scope over its own clause only. I represent a relative clause with the syntactic schema (48)a. Its semantic representation is shown schematically as (48)b:

48) a. Syntax $[_{CP}$ $[_{IP}$ yas/jo V-finite]]

b. Semantics $[_{CP}$ REL(i) $[_{IP}$ (i) V-finite]]

c. Ill-formed $[_{CP}$ REL(i) $[_{IP}$ V-finite $[_{CP}$ $[_{IP}$ (i) V-finite]]

The construal relation of the relative operator and a syntactic position may not cross more than one IP (48c). (Or in other words, there is no cyclic, CP to CP wh movement).

There are another requirement on relative clause: they must also be construed with the syntactic phrase they modify. This construal relation is always subject to Simplexity in Hindi/Urdu, but not (necessarily) in Sanskrit. The difference lies in the difference between the paratactic structure in Sanskrit (49) with the requirement of adjunction in Hindi/Urdu (50):

49) [Sanskrit]

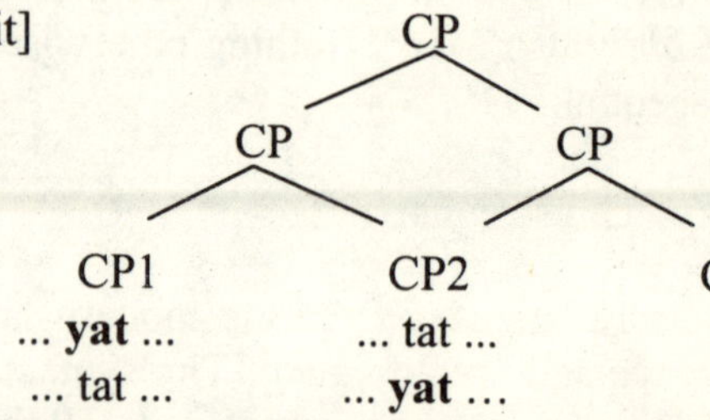

50) a. Left relative b. Right relative [Hindi/Urdu]

In Sanskrit, the relative in CP1 (construed as in (549) is linked with *tat* in CP2, the normal case, or as we have seen earlier, somewhat exceptionally it can be linked with *tat* in CP3.

Such cases of linking a relative and a correlative across another complete clause CP3, skipping CP2, are ungrammatical in the modern languages. They are ruled out by the Simplexity condition (51): 51) Simplexity: a relative CP must modify a phrase in adjoined IP but not outside/above the its local adjunction structure labeled IP.

The relative may modify anything *within* IP, or dominated by IP in subordinate clauses, but it may not modify anything in a third clause outside of the adjunction structure—what is shown in (49) for example.

It is somewhat mysterious exactly how the modification relation is established in Sanskrit. In some ways the results are exactly what is required in Hindi/Urdu, if a relative in CP1 is construed as a modifier of a phrase in CP2 (or vice-versa). But there is some freedom to look further into CP3.

There are other anomalies as well a relative need not modify anything. Kiparsky (1989) cites sentences from Sanskrit and other early IE languages in which a relative pronoun is used without a corresponding pronoun or other constituent in the correlative clause. The relative pronoun in such cases gets a non-specific indefinite interpretation, and the whole clause is conditional. This sentence would also violate the Simplexity condition, because the relative clause does not modify any constituent within IP, though it might be said to modify IP itself as an adverbial clause.

52) yásyānakṣā duhitā jātv āsa, kás tām
whose blind daughter birth-loc is who-nom that

vidhām abhí manyāte andhām
know-prt prcl desire-pr-mid-3s blind-fs-acc

'Whose (= if someone's) daughter is eyeless from birth, who would, knowing it, desire the blind one?' RV 10.27.11 (Kiparsky 1994)

I. Deriving relative clauses

The coreference which is restricted by Simplexity is required by the relative determiner/pronoun itself, but it is also required by the determiner/pronoun in the matrix clause. This is normally one of the *wo* 'that' series of distal demonstratives, used anaphorically with a discourse antecedent. It would be exceptional to use one of the *yah* 'this' series, reserved for referents in the presence of the speaker. So the question is, does the relative coindexing originate as anaphora in discourse, as suggested by *wo* 'that' or as bound variable required by the relative operator *jo*? Or are there features of both which must be reconciled by the grammar?

Most previous analyses have given greater weight to the bound-variable properties of *jo*, basing the syntactic derivation of correlatives on the head relative structure by means of movement rules (Dayal 1996, Dwivedi 1994 and others). McCawley (1993) proposed instead that the correlative adjunction structure should be the basic structure, deriving 'semantic subordination' of the modifier clause by coindexation of the relative clause with the modified phrase. The idea of 'semantic subordination' does not necessarily depend on a specific relation of syntactic subordination (such as the NP-[relative clause] head relative structure). Early Sanskrit (5)-(6) used paratactic relative clauses as what would be marked in the modern languages as interrogative complements. Bhatt 2003 proposes both kinds of derivation.

The approach proposed here offers some opportunities for discourse factors to be involved in the interpretation as well as the semantic requirements of *jo*. Discourse factors are sensitive to the linear order of constituents (as well as syntactic subordination). I have mentioned four factors which serve to differentiate correlative clauses on the left from those on the right. Together with some of McCawley's observations, they suggest that the syntactic/semantic properties of correlative constructions derive from a combination of (i) the adjunction relation, (ii) the semantic requirements of *jo*, (iii) the opacity of finite clauses and (iv) the linear order of the clauses determined by discourse factors topic and focus.

The derivational history of relatives in Hindi/Urdu by this account is relatively simple. I will assume, following McCawley 1993, that relative adjuncts are base-generated in their surface position. They are then interpreted by the semantics of the relative operator, which must link the relative clause to a coreferent in the domain permitted by Simplexity, with the exact strength of the reference determined by the pragmatic features of the relative clause, its position and modifiers, and by any determiners or quantifiers on the coreferent.

I do not assume that right relatives are necessarily extraposed NP head relatives, not that left relatives *jo N* are left-ward moved from the coreferent in the correlative clause, leaving behind a gap or resumptive pronoun (contra Dayal 1989, 1996). The extraction analysis won't work for the simplexity violations in Sanskrit, such as (52). Since there is no head for the relative clause in the other clause in (52), relative clauses in early Sanskrit cannot, as Kiparsky 1989 notes, be extracted from the main clause. Likewise, the extraction analysis does not explain the many possible instances of relative clauses of the form *jo N...wo N,* such as (53).

53) ... *mujhe* *yah* *lag-taa* *to* *hai [ki* *bas yaa* *Tren- me˜*
I-dat this seem-impf topic is that bus or train-in rel

jis khiRkii-*ke* *paas*
window-gen near

mai˜ *baiTh-taa* *huu˜,* *dhuup* **usii** **khiRkii** -*se*
I sit-impf am sunlight that-emph window-through

ho-kar *aa-tii hai.*
be-prt come-impf is

'It seems to me that in the bus or train, the sunshine comes in through the very same window near which I am sitting.' (Mohan Rakesh p. 13)

Conclusion

In this paper, I have compared the finite relative constructions in early Sanskrit and Hindi/Urdu as a modern Indic language. Both languages preserve the distinction between relative and interrogative determiner/pronouns. Relative clauses is Sanskrit combine with other finite clauses in a paratactic relation, as argued by Hock 1989. As Etter 1985 and Hettrich 1988 have shown, While there are embedded yes/no questions with the quotative its from earliest times in Sanskrit, the language does not mark syntactically embedded interrogative clauses with interrogative forms. Instead, the interrogative complement is expressed as a paratactic relative construction which construes the embedded clause as a modifer of the constituent in the main clause. The paratactic relation permits many more possibilities for interrogative scope not allowed in the modern languages. Many combinations which are ungrammatical in Hindi/Urdu are possible in Sanskrit.

The relative clauses in Hindi/Urdu preserve much of the syntactic properties of the older construction, but with a sharper differentiation of relative and correlative clauses. The relative clause is adjoined to a main clause, and forms a closed syntactic domain (cf. Speas 1991). The syntactic subordination relation is subject to Dasgupta's Simplexity condition, which says that the relative must modify a phrase somewhere in the main clause. This differentiation between main and adjoined finite relative clauses corresponds to other difference between finite complement clauses. Relative clauses occur both before and after the main clauses. Left and right relative clauses have many differences (Dayal 1996), but the differences don't motivate sharply different syntactic derivations. Rather they motivate a process of semantic interpretation of the structures as they appear in the surface (as suggested by McCawley 1993). There is abundant evidence that relative clauses have topic properties on the left, and focus properties on the right. The relative in itself is therefore underspecified for definite reference. The differences among the generic, non-specific interpretation, the specific indefinite interpretation and definiteness is, in this account, calculated from the position of the relative clause, the combinations of determiners in the relation, and the properties of the coindexed phrase in the main clause.

It is also possible that the differences of left and right relative clauses follows from a single, underspecified interpretation of *jo* which gets interpreted using the information available in the sentence and context as the sentence is processed from left to right (Kempson et al. 2000).

Acknowledgments

An earlier version of this paper was presented at the ICOSAL-5 conference at Moscow State University, Institute for African and Asian Studies, July 5-9, 2003. I am grateful to the organizers, especially Lyudmila Khokhlova and Boris Zakharin, for the immense amount of encouragement and practical help which they gave to the participants and which made the conference a success. I am grateful also to the University of Iowa for an International Travel grant to attend the conference. The bibliographic resources if the University of Konstanz library were of crucial help in preparing the conference paper. The writing of this version of the paper was done when I was a fellow of the Obermann Institute for Advanced Study, University of Iowa in 2003-4, and I thank the Institute and its director Jay Semel for their thoughtful support of my research. I am very grateful to Colin P. Masica and Hans Hock for detailed comments and corrections on this written version.

Many thanks also to the conference participants for their comments, especially Probal Dasgupta, Colin P. Masica, Hans H. Hock and Peter Hook.

References

Bayer, Josef (1996) *Directionality and logical form.* Dordrecht: Kluwer Academic Publications.

____ (2001) Two grammars in one: sentential complements and complementizers in Bengali and other South Asian languages. In P. Bhaskararao and K. V. Subbarao (eds.) *Yearbook of South Asian languages.* New Delhi: Sage Publications.

Bhatt, Rajesh (2003) Locality in correlatives. *Natural language and linguistic theory* 21: 485-541.

Dasgupta, Probal (1980) *Question and relative and complement clauses in a Bangla grammar.* New York University unpublished dissertation.

____ (to appear) The ubiquitous complementizer. Festschrift for K. A. Jayaseelan.

Davison, Alice (1988) Operator binding, gaps and pronouns. *Linguistics* 26: 181-214.

Dayal, Veneeta (1996). *Locality in Wh- quantification.* Kluwer Academic Publishers.

Dwivedi, Veena (1994) *Syntactic dependencies and relative phrases in Hindi.* U. of Massachusetts unpublished dissertation.

Etter, Annemarie (1985) *Die Fragesätze im Rgveda.* Berlin: Walter de Gruyter.

Gair, James and John Paolillo (1998) *Sinhala.* LINCOM Europa.

Gambhir, Vijay (1981) *Syntactic restrictions and discourse functions of word order in standard Hindi.* University of Pennsylvania unpublished dissertation.

Gandhi, Mohandas K (1969) *aatmakathaa (Autobiography).* Ahmedabad: nawajiivan prakashan mandir. (Hindi translation)

Hermann, Eduard (1895) *Gab es im Indogermanischen Nebensätze*? Dissertation, University of Jena.

Hettrich, Heinrich (1988) *Untersuchungen zur Hypotaxe im Vedischen.* Berlin:de Gruyter.

Hock, Hans H. (1989) Conjoined we stand: theoretical implications of Sanskrit relative structures. *Studies in the Linguistic Sciences* 19.1, 93-126.

Jayakar, Pupul (1992) *Indira Gandhi.* New Delhi, Viking/Penguin. Hindi excerpt in Hindi edition of *India Today*, 15 October 1992, 4-59.

Jayaseelan, K. A. (2001) Questions and question-word-incorporating quantifiers in Malayalam. *Syntax* 4: 263-93.

Kempson, Ruth, Dov Gabbay and W Meyer-Viol (2001) *Dynamic syntax.* Oxford: Blackwell.

Kiparsky, Paul (1994) Indo-European origins of Germanic syntax. In Adrian Battye and Ian Roberts (eds.) *Clause structure and language change.* Oxford: Oxford University Press.

Masica, Colin P. (2000) Alternating embedding strategies in Gujarati. In P. J. Mistry and Bhyarati Modi (eds.) *Vidyopaasanaa: Studies in honour of H. C. Bhayani.* Mumbai and Ahmedabad: Image Publications Pvt. Ltd.

McCawley, James (2004) Remarks on adnominal, adsentential and extraposed relative clauses in Hindi. In Veneeta Dayal and Anoop Mahajan (eds.) *Clause structures in South Asian languages*. Dordrecht: Kluwer Academic Publishers.

Nadkarni, M. V. (1970) *NP embedded structures in Kannada and Konkani.* UCLA unpublished dissertation.

Rakesh, Mohan (1961) *aakhirii caTTaan-tak.* Delhi: Raajkamal prakaashan private limited.

Rizzi, Luigi (1997) On the fine structure of the left periphery. In L. Haegeman, ed. *Elements of grammar*. Dordrecht: Kluwer Academic Publishers, 281-337.

Speas, Margaret (1991) Generalized transformations and the D- structure position of adjuncts. In Susan D. Rothstein (ed) *Syntax and semantics 25, Perspectives on Phrase structure.*

Srivastav (Dayal), Veneeta (1991) The syntax and semantics of correlatives. *Natural language and linguistic theory* 9, 637-686.

Subbarao, K. V. (1984) *Complementation in Hindi syntax.* Delhi: Academic Publications.

POSTVERBAL SUBJECTS IN TELUGU AND OTHER LANGUAGES

COLIN P. MASICA

1. Introduction: the background of this paper

At the XX South Asian Languages Analysis Roundtable Conference held in Iowa City in late June 2002, I presented a paper, "Possible Functions of an Alternative Word Order in Telugu: V(erb)-S(ubject)", reporting my findings after I had decided to explore a phenomenon that had struck my attention, namely, that violation of the "canonical" SOV (Verb-final) word order, particularly with regard to the position of the Subject, is quite common in some Telugu texts. In one striking case, it turned out to affect a clear majority of sentences. I also discovered that such violations were much less common in Hindi texts, and that the violations were moreover confined to a different discourse context – dialogue, typically affectively marked. The Telugu examples, by contrast, were mainly in affectively <u>un</u>marked narrative (although there were a few examples of the Hindi kind also, i.e. in dialogue passages).

I noted then that the effect of this postverbal placement in both Telugu and Hindi seemed to be "de-emphasis", with an affect, if any, of "casualness"– except in the case of a small subset of sentences where the effect was the precise opposite – "emphasis" – and that sentences of the latter type are structurally marked ("clefted") in Telugu. I speculated as to whether a subfunction of the right-displaced non-emphatic Subjects might be "clarification" of who was the actor in a fast-paced narrative (otherwise, if de-emphasis were the only function, why not leave them out altogether?) I rashly speculated further that these statistics might herald a typological shift in word order type – on the ground that the unmarked order (or unmarked anything) in a language is supposed to the most frequent. What happens when it is not?

Let me first put that last error to rest, and affirm that the SOV order in Telugu or Hindi does not seem to be in danger. Not from these phenomena, at any rate. According to Dryer 1995, Greenberg 1966, with whom this dogma originated in his pioneering paper on language universals, is wrong here: the (pragmatically) unmarked word order is not necessarily the most frequent, but is more usefully described as the *default* order – the order that is used "elsewhere, once the situations in which the pragmatically marked orders are used have been characterized." (Although there is indeed much interest in changes in word order typology these days, the focus has been is on changes from SOV and VSO to SVO. Not to OVS!)

That brings us to the substance of this paper. Although merely statistical studies may serve to alert us to the fact that a phenomenon exists that requires explanation, they do not provide such an explanation. I have subsequently been reminded, however, that these questions have been a topic of much discussion and research for a long time, going back to Comrie 1981 and before that, to Prague School ideas concerning Functional Sentence Perspective. More recently, they have been the focus, not only of a number of articles in *Language* and elsewhere, but of a several productive symposia, e.g., on "Word Order in Discourse" held at the University of Wisconsin, Milwaukee in April 1991, and a Parasession of SALA XIV, held at Stanford in 1992, on word order in South Asian languages, resulting in the publication later of collections of very useful papers. There is no need, therefore, to reinvent the wheel, and no excuse for vague speculation about "style". A number of specific proposals have been made regarding functions of and constraints on word order variation. Building on this, clearly what I need to do is test them on my data (an expanded version of my original data) and see what further questions arise.

It is still necessary to do some counting, but instead of overall counts that may involve a confusion of different subgenres, contexts, and circumstances, it will be a more focussed counting, directed by particular questions suggested by all this work.

2. Typologies of postverbal positioning

Of particular relevance is a paper by Herring 1994, "Postverbal position in Tamil", using a somewhat different corpus than I have used, i.e. including oral narratives as well as written stories. Referring to earlier work by Kuno 1978 (on Japanese), Erguvanlı 1984 (on Turkish), Kim and Shin 1992 (on Korean), and Junghare 1985 (on Indo-Aryan), she concludes that postverbal elements in Tamil fall into three distinct categories: "afterthoughts", "backgrounding", and "emphatic focus". (As we shall see later, there may also be a fourth.) Although Herring contrasts this analysis with those of the other authors mentioned, I find that – except for Kuno, for whom everything is subsumed as "afterthought", they have, more or less, come to the same conclusions, albeit with some differences in terminology, e.g., "de-emphasis" for "backgrounding". As, with less theoretical sophistication, had I. (In Turkish, the postverbal "emphatic-focus" type seems to be lacking: emphasis apparently involves only emphatic stress on <u>pre</u>verbal elements, if I interpret Erguvanlı correctly.)

In any case, an "afterthought" is distinguished from all the other types (except by Kuno) typically by a slight pause. It is not part of the intonational contour of the sentence, and not part of the grammatical structure of the sentence, which is complete without it.

Herring distinguishes <u>three concentric postverbal positions</u> occupied by her three functional types: the innermost, occupied by postverbal *emphatic focus*, is part of the *sentence*, or rather, "inside the clause"; the next, occupied by what she calls *antitopics*, is part of the pragmatic *utterance;* the outermost, part of the "extended utterance", contains the *afterthought* material. They are increasingly less tightly bound to the sentence. Moreover, while backgrounded antitopics and emphatic foci can be said to be "moved" to their postverbal positions, afterthoughts do not <u>move</u>, but end up at the end of the utterance, "by default, as a consequence of the linear nature of speech production."

It will be noted that the other studies mentioned by Herring are all of SOV languages, moreover of languages with case systems that mark grammatical functions and make word order available for pragmatic functions. Comparisons with Japanese and Korean are complicated by the fact that these languages have "Topic" – as well as "Subject"-marking particles, and lack verbal agreement. Turkish does not present these problems, and – for whatever reason – it resembles (some) South Asian languages more closely in additional ways not strictly related to SOV typology. Most relevant to our purposes here – which entail the investigation of pragmatic functions – is the fact that (like Hindi-Urdu in particular) Turkish has *definite-object marking* (indicating the previous mention or identifiability of a referent used as the Direct Object of a verb), as well as what is in effect an *indefinite article* – an unstressed form of the word for 'one' *(bir)*, similar to unstressed or truncated forms in South Asian languages (H-U. *ek*, Tel. *oka,* Tam.-Mal. *oru*) – indicating new information.[1] Like Dravidian but unlike Indo-Aryan, in Turkish the Accusative is distinct from the Dative. Again like Dravidian (cf. Krishnamurti & Gwynn 1985: 88), the Accusative is used with +Animate Objects whether definite or not (Erguvanlı 1984: 19 – the example she gives is:)

---

[1] Purely impressionistically, Turkish *bir* seems to be used more extensively than its South Asian counterparts. But this needs a separate investigation. There are some syntactic differences as well: as an Indefinite Article, *bir* comes between adjective and noun – *güzel bir bahçe* 'a beautiful garden'; when used as a numeral, 'one', it precedes the adjective. See Lewis 1967: 54 for more discussion.

1) Tu. *Ben insan-lar-I* *sev-er-im*
I man-Pl-ACC like-Aor-1sg[2]

'I like people/(human beings in general).'

Complicating things further, the Accusative may be used – in both Turkish and Dravidian – with an Object already marked with the Indefinite Article:

2) Tu. *Murat bir kitap oku-yor*
Murat a book read-Pres(3sg)

'Murat is reading a book.' [Erguvanlı 1984: 21]

3) Tu. *Murat bir kitab-I oku-yor*
Murat a book-ACC read-Pres(3sg)

'Murat is reading a (certain) book.' [Erguvanlı 1984: 22]

Perhaps more clearly:

4) Tu. *Her gün bir gazete oku-yor-um*
each day a newspaper read-Pres-1sg

'Every day I read a newspaper.' (= some newspaper)

5) Tu. *Her gün bir gazete-yi oku-yor-um*
each day a newspaper-ACC read-Pres-1sg

'Every day I read a (particular) newspaper.' [Lewis 1967: 248]

6) Te. *waaT-anniTi-loo-ki* prominent-*gaa* *kanipist-unna oka pootu-nu*
them-Obl-all-Obl-in-DAT prominent-ly appear-PrAdjPpl a male-ACC

paTTukun-i, *daani kommu-l-a-ku* *wreelaaDadiisi–w-*
grab-refl CP its(GEN) horn-Pl-Obl-DAT hang-PrAdjPpl

unna muuTa-n-oka-daanni *Shaadoo daggiri- ki* *tiisuku-waccae-Du*
bundle –a certain-ACC Shadow-vicinity-DAT take-come-Past-3Msg

'Grabbing a (certain) male-(goat) that stood out prominently from all the others, he brought a (certain) bundle that had been hanging on its horns to the Shadow.' [Madhu Babu 1992: 29]

---

[2] In glossing the Turkish examples, I am attempting to follow the terminology of Lewis 1967.

Cf. Hindi also:

7) Hi. *baink kaa kaam samaapt kar-ke rohit lauTaa to*
"bank"-GEN work complete do-CP Rohit return-Pfv –Msg then

seTh ke kebin ke baahar ek laRkii ko dekh-kar ThiThak gayaa
Seth-GEN "cabin"-outside a girl-DAT see-CF stop go-Pfv-Msg

'When Rohit returned after finishing his business at the bank, he stopped suddenly on seeing a girl outside the Seth's cabin.' [Nanda 1973]

Erguvanlı calls these *specified indefinites*, in contrast to Objects without case-marking, which are *unspecified indefinites*. They have different privileges of occurrence.

Since questions have been raised – and are raised again in this volume [see the paper by Hans Hock] – concerning the nature of the resemblances between Turkish and South Asian languages[3]– do they represent areal-historical *convergence*, or are they merely coincidences of SOV typology? – it might be worthwhile, before proceeding, to review some conclusions reached by Erguvanlı regarding pragmatic functions of word order in Turkish.

3. Constraints on marked orders

According to Erguvanlı, there are constraints on marked orders (i.e. other than SOV – there is a slight initial difference from the South Asian norm in that the unmarked order is said to be S-DO-IO-V, rather than S-IO-DO-V, but that need not detain us here), best seen in terms of the complex interplay of semantic features of definiteness, animacy, and "referentiality" with the basic functional slots of ***Topic*** (initial position), ***Focus*** (immediate preverbal position), and "***Background***" (postverbal position).

a. **"Non-referential"** NP's have no actual "referent" in the real world to which they refer; they are general, unmarked for number or for definiteness (we might wish to say they are "maximally indefinite" – except that in this light the term "indefinite" should perhaps be reserved

---

[3] Ideally, comparisons should be made on historical grounds with Central Asian Turkic languages rather than with the Turkish of Turkey. But the latter is better studied, and various observers (e.g., the former Ambassador of India to Turkey, the Hon. K. Gajendra Singh [personal communications] have been struck by the similarities of Hindi and Panjabi even to Turkish itself. The principal Turkic languages are very similar. Nevertheless, it would be helpful to have available a comparison of Turkish and Central Asian Turkic.

for newly introduced but potentially real entities), and cannot be relativized or pronominalized. As Objects, they combine with a general verb (e.g., "do") to express a single activity. This category is paralleled in South Asian languages: e.g., H-U. *istemaal karnaa* 'use (Tu. *istimal etmek*), *madad karnaa* 'help' (Tu. *imdad etmek*), cf. also *khaanaa khaanaa* 'eat' (Tu. *yemek yemek*)', etc. (Cf. the non-referential equivalent of an earlier example:

8) *Murat kitab okuyor*
Murat book read-Pres(3sg)

'Murat is book-reading' – i.e. 'Murat is reading'.)

In this function they cannot be moved.

b. ***Topics*** are usually but not necessarily Subjects; they may be another fronted NP (e.g., an Object), which "links the predication with previous discourse or background"; as they represent old and/or known information, they must be definite – unless they are animate, in which case (another complication disturbing the neatness of the picture) – because (according to Erguvanlı) animacy is associated with agenthood and hence "natural" topicality. Indefinite but +animate NP's override this constraint and may also be Topics – although this would seem to contradict the essential notion of "Topic", since they constitute information new to the discourse[4]. But this phenomenon is of course found not only in Turkish, but in English, Hindi, and other languages:

9) *kuhaase me~* *lipTii* *a~dherii raat kaa*
fog-OblM-in whitewash(PfvPplF) dark-F night-GEN-Msg

siinaa ciir-te hue *ek Taiksii*
bosom teari-ImpfAdvPpl a taxi

diinaapur ke *choTe-se* *sTeshan ke paas aa-kar rukii*
Dinapur-GEN-OblM small-OblM-ish-OblM station-near come-CP stop-Pfv-Fsg

'Tearing through the bosom of the dark night whitewashed with fog, a taxi came to the little Dinapur station and stopped.' [Nanda 1973: 7]

Here the Topic/Subject (the taxi) isn't even +Animate, although

[4] As I struggle with these concepts, I realize much thought has long ago been given to them, and collected in such volumes as Li (ed.) 1976, *Subject and topic*. They contain much discussion of Topics in such languages as Chinese and Japanese, translated by English "As for X…., …" – but that is not what is in question here.

perhaps a certain animacy (or agency) gets attributed to it, since it moves and "stops". But this is also the opening line of the novel; opening lines often have special characteristics, designed to capture the attention of the reader, particularly in terms of definiteness marking. E.g., an NP may also be presented as a Topic, and Definite, even though there is no previous discourse context to provide this status – as a kind of conventional teaser, with the implication that "the identification will be provided in due course: read on!". But it is possible that Ex. 9, and even animate-indefinite Subjects, are not really Topics at all, but something else, of which more below.

c. The immediate preverbal ***Focus*** position is privileged for new information, hence for indefinitely-marked NP's. Not only indefinite Objects, but indefinite Subjects as well obligatorily move to this position (unless they are +Animate, as we have seen, in which case the movement is possible but not obligatory). This is accordingly the unmarked position also for *Question words*, which seek new information, as well as for the answers to them. However, a non-referential NP bound to the Verb in a semantic unit has priority of occurrence over even the aforementioned categories, bumping them to the left.

An Object may be definitized, as we have seen, in which case it is no longer bound to the Focal position and may move to another position, including initial (Topic) position, and Oblique NP's and Adverbs may occupy the Focal position. In general, if all NP's in a sentence are definite, there are no restrictions on where they may occur – although departures from SOV order are nevertheless "marked". Similarly, if both S and O are inanimate, there are no restrictions. (Erguvanlı's example is:)

10a,b) *Yol-u bir araba tıka-mıS* ~ *Bir araba yol-u tıka-mıS*
way-ACC a cart block-Infr.Past ~ a cart way-ACC block-Infr.Past

'A cart has blocked the way.' (South Asian examples, anyone?)

d. Finally, the ***"Background"*** or postpredicate position – our real concern here – involves the following constraints and effects – often a "mirror image" or direct opposite of those of the Focal position:

i) There is "discourse presupposition" – recoverability from either the discourse or the wider context (vs. "new information" in the Focal position);
ii) That is, in the case of Subject and Object NP's. However, this is less clear in the case of other elements which may be postposed; Oblique NP's, adverbs, and subordinate clauses;

iii) In any case, the effect is "defocusing" – i.e. the postposed elements are downplayed in importance (vs. the preverbal position as "focus" of the sentence);

iv) The constituents must be *definite;* this of course is a property of discourse presupposition, and overlaps with topicalization, the difference being perhaps that these are even more readily available from the context than regular sentence-initial Topics; they "cannot be indefinite NP's" (vs. indefinite NP's in the Focal position);
This restriction does not imply to Imperatives, which are structurally different from statements;

v) They may not be a question word or a constituent containing a question word; (vs. the Focal position as the unmarked place for these);

vi) They are always unstressed (vs. sentence stress, normally, on the constituent in the Focal position);

vii) There may be <u>multiple</u> postposed constituents – even to the point of leaving the Verb as sentence-initial – so long as they meet the above criteria; (here the mirror-analogy fails, in that there is only one constituent in Focal position)

11) H. *"kab se hai˜ ||* *aap /* *is* *gããv me˜ ?*
when-from are you this-Obl village in

'How long have you been in this village?' (Nanda 1973: 31)

12) Tc. *...uttara disha-ku* face-*cees-t-unna pradesham-loo kanipinc-indi* ||
northern direction-DAT 'face' do(PrAdjPpl) country-inappear-Past-3Fsg

atani-ki / pedda ceTla toopu
him-DAT large tree-pl-Obl grove.

'...in the country facing north there became visible to him [= he saw] a grove of large trees.' [Madhu Babu 1992: 41] [NB: the second postposed constituent violates Constraints (a) + (d) above.]

viii) They are not necessarily deletable without altering the meaning of the sentence; (in contrast with "afterthought" material – uttered after a sentence is already complete – postposed "background" elements are part of the sentence "strategy"). Erguvanlı's examples are:

13) Tu. *Ben sinema-ya git-mem | <u>bir daha sen-le</u>*
I movies-DAT go-Neg-1sg again you-with

'I <u>won't</u> go to the movies <u>with you</u> <u>again'</u> <u>vs</u>.:

14) Tu. *Ben sinema-ya git-mem*
I movies-DAT go-Neg-1sg

'I don't go to the movies'

[The verbal form, just as in Telugu, can be Future or Habitual, depending on the context – here crucially provided by the postposed element.]

In Ex. 11 and especially 12 above, the sentence would make little or no sense without the postposed elements.

To summarize the essence of this somewhat shaky set of principles (shaken partly by my attempt to extend them from Turkish to South Asian languages): the functional slots T(opic), F(ocus), V(erb), and B(ackground) are fixed positions; the grammatical arguments S(ubject), O(bject), Obl(ique Adjunct) and Adv(erb) are placed in or shifted among them in accordance with constraints of definiteness, animacy, and referentiality.

4. Discourse-predictable information: the three strategies

There is one more point made by Erguvanlı that we need to take note of before moving on. She says that Turkish (to which we may hypothetically add, most South Asian languages) has "three strategies" to express "discourse-predictable" information:

a. pronominalization;
b. deletion (i.e. absence of an element, i.e. *zero anaphora* – see section 7 below);
c. postverbal placement.

Topics, by contrast, are "known" but not "predictable".

5. Emphatic focus

Returning now to Herring's formulations, we may note that *emphatic focus* (lacking in Turkish as far as I am aware, but characterized by a special – clefted – construction in Telugu [see Masica 2002] as well as in Sinhala [Herring & Paolillo 1995: 173ff.] is in many respects the polar opposite of defocused "background" material: it is, for example, contrastively stressed. It may be indefinite (new information) – or, if old information, non-predictable, i.e. not redundant. Herring's Tamil examples (involving no special construction) are:

15) Ta. *uTaṉee paartaaL || atilee orutti!*
at-once look-Past-Fsg || that [group]-in-Emph a certain-one-F

'Suddenly one of them [girls playing in the water] looked up!'

16) Ta *itai-k-keeTTaan* || *vituran.*
This-ACC hear-Past-3sgM || Viduran

'Viduran heard this.' [Herring 1994: 139-40]

But are these postposings, albeit non-redundant, really "emphatic"? Herring herself seems to have had second thoughts on this (1995), of which more presently [see Section 10 below, on "Presentationals"].

In any case, these emphatic postposings are much less frequent than the other, "backgrounding" kind (under 10% in Herring's 1994 corpus, which includes much oral material). Of more immediate interest are Herring's insights into the other kind of postposing – the backgrounded or de-emphasized elements. These she divides into two subcategories:

6. De-emphasized elements, type A: adverbials and dependent clauses

In the first type, involving adverbials and dependent clauses, postposing merely "signals lesser importance vs. preverbal constituents". It is nevertheless striking that "rigid" SOV languages like Turkic and Dravidian permit this rather freely in speech, and even in "literary" (as opposed to "expository") writing. Long ago, Arden observed that although the "correct" form is Verb-final, "this is not always observed" in speech, and instead of

17) Ta. *viiTTu-k-ku-p-poo-kir-aay-aa?*
house-Obl-DAT go-Pres-2sg-Q

'Are you going home?'

one will hear:

18) Ta. *poo-kir-aay-aa* *viiTTu-k-ku?*
Go-Pres-2sg-Q house-Obl-DAT [Arden 1942: 178]

Similarly, in Telugu

19) Te. *mundu-ku was-t-unna aDugu-l-a cappuDu aagi-pooyindi||*
front-DAT come-PresAdjPpl steps-pl-Obl sound stop-CP-go-Past-3sgFN ||

haThaattu-gaa
sudden-ly

'The sound of the advancing foosteps stopped suddenly' [Madhu Babu 1993: 47]

20) Te. *"kaalu jaari paDa-pooyaew-aa?" niiTi ancuku*
foot slip-CF fall-Inf-go-Past-2sg-Q water-Obl edge-DAT

parigettukuNTuu wacci,
run-PresAdvPpl come-CP

paiki raawa-Taani-ki ceeti-ni andis-t-uu aDigaeDu ||
up come-VN-DAT hand-Obl-ACC stretch-PresAdvPpl ask-Past-3Msg ||

saanubhuuti ninDina kaNTham-too
sympathy fill-PastAdjPpl voice-INSTR

'"Did your foot slip?" he asked, in a voice full of sympathy, running to the edge of the water and stretching out his hand to pull him up.' [Madhu Babu 1993: 26]

21) Te. *maroosaari paadaanni paiki ettaeDu || inkoo tannu tanna-Taani-ki*
another-time foot-ACC up lift-Past-Msg || another kick (to)-kick-VN-DAT

'He lifted up his foot to deliver another kick.' [Madhu Babu 1993: 17]

22) Te. *andukee neenu aricaenu || "hatyaa idi" ani*
therefore-Emph I shout-Past-1sg || murder this {quot}

'That's why I shouted, 'This is murder!'' [Rao 1967: 110]

23) Te. *ramanarasu-nu wadili weesaeru || nirdoS ani*
Ramanarasu-ACC release-CP toss-Past-3pl || innocent {quot}

'They released Ramanarasu, (declaring) him innocent.' [Rao 1967: 112]

(Some of these, e.g. Ex. 19, may indeed be of "lesser importance", but is this true in every case? The judgment is quite subjective, if not in fact excluded, as in Ex. 22.)

In Hindi-Urdu nominal complement clauses with *ki* already occur postverbally – which is one reason (along with the placement of relative clauses) why it is a "*non*-rigid" SOV language. In Gujarati the two types are in fierce competition. (The *ki*-complementizer construction has been borrowed – from Persian, as also in the Hindi and Gujarati cases – by Turkish itself:

24) Tu. *Emin-im ki Ali sınıf-ın-I geç-ecek-tir*
certain-1sg that Ali class-his-ACC pass-Fur-3sg

'I'm certain that Ali will pass his class'

– which can also be expressed "by a structure that is more consistent with the syntax of the language", e.g.

25) Tu. *Alı-nın sınıf-ın-I geç-ecek-in-den emin-im*
Ali's class-his-ACC pass-Fut-his-ABL certain-1sg

= lit.'I'm certain of Ali's passing his class' [Erguvanlı 1984: 85-86]

To my knowledge no one has suggested demoting Turkish from its "rigid" SOV status because of sentences like (24) – even though relative clauses of the postposed Indo-European type, also using the ubiquitous *ki*, have also taken root [see Lewis 1967: 212].

7. De-emphasized elements, Type B: antitopics (vs. zero-anaphora) in Telugu

What is of even greater interest, however, is Herring's concept and category of *antitopic*, the postverbal positioning of which "signals the transitional discourse-pragmatic status of (typically) NP referents" – that is, of Subjects and Objects (mostly of Subjects), "reintroducing previously active thematic referents (typically) because another referent has taken over as Topic in the interim" [emphasis mine]. (I'm not quite sure what *anti-* in "antitopic" means [cf. *anticausative*, etc.] – that it is not a Topic? That it is the opposite of Topic? That is true only with regard to its placement. Surely, as Herring herself indicates in the context of her argument, it is a Topic, albeit a demoted one – "defocused" isn't the word, since Topics are not in "focus" anyway. Often it is necessary for the clarification of the narrative – a reminder of who is the actor at the moment.

Herring notes that it often (78% of the time in her corpus of written narratives) denotes a switch of Subject/Topic from that of the preceding utterance. Or (in 69% of her cases) that there will be a switch of Topic in the succeeding utterance. Or both (meaning that the "antitopic" functions as Topic only for the course of a single sentence). These two conditions, separately or together, account for 93% of her antitopics. While not universal, this "rule" is "highly systematic in a number of written short stories."

I was naturally tempted to test this idea on my Telugu corpus, where all I had – except for my speculative "insights" which seem to have been correct as far as they went – was an overall body of statistics that seemed to contradict basic SOV typology. Starting with an enlarged (doubled) sample (40pp.) of my central Telugu text, Madhu Babu's action novel *Midnight Plus One* – the narrative portion only (the reported dialogue presents special complications), I found that **95%** of the postverbal

Subject/Topics (220 out of 232) did involve a topic shift from the preceding utterance. Of those which did not, 3 examples involved a topic shift in the succeeding utterance. (This category seems less important in this sub-corpus than in Herring's, with only 28, or 13%, of the utterances involving shift from previous topic also involving shift in subsequent topic. The reintroduced topic continues its reign for a longer stretch of the discourse.)

Looking at it another way, "topic shift" <u>entails</u> postverbal placement of the Subject/Topic in 89% of the cases. The exceptions often involved verbal nouns or other abstract Subjects, Dative Subjects (although these are frequently postposed as well), impersonal expressions, or the postposing of other material.

There were, incidentally, very few postposed Objects. To qualify as "antitopic", presumably the Object would have to be promoted to Topic in the first place.

Pursuing this further, I decided to check what happens when there is no topic-shift vis-à-vis the preceding utterance – when the topic remains the same. Recalling Erguvanlı's "three strategies" [see above, section **4**] for expressing discourse-predictable information, **postverbal positioning** has been pre-empted, as we have just seen, for reintroducing temporarily displaced Topics. That leaves **pronominalization** and **"deletion"** (= zero anaphora). It turns out that pronouns are typically used (in this text) postverbally, in the same topic-shift function as nouns, and that the preferred strategy is zero anaphora: **60%** of the continued-Topic utterances employ zero anaphora. (Or to put it another way, <u>all</u> of the instances of zero anaphora in the narrative involve identity of Topic with the immediately preceding utterance.) That is partly enabled in Telugu by the fact of person-gender-number marking on the Verb, but in the 3rd person there would still be considerable room for confusion as to which of several qualified referents is meant, were it not for this "rule".

Some typical examples of these two phenomena working together in context [Madhu Babu 1993: 33-34]:

25) Te. *tana-raaka-nu gurinci andari-ki TaanTaan-ceey-akunDaa*
his-come-NegPpl-ACC-about so-many-persons-DAT proclaim-without

rahasyangaa-w-uncin-aTl-aytee baagunDee-d-ani talapoos-t-uu,
secret-Adv leave-thatway-if{cmpl} good-would-be-Quot{cmpl} consider- PresAdvPpl

mancam-miida meenu waal-c-ae-Du || SaaDoo
cot-upon body lay-Tr-Past-3Msg | | Shadow

'Considering that it would be better if his coming remained private, without proclaiming it to so many persons, <u>the Shadow</u> laid his body down on the cot.' [new topic – NB previous topic was "the old man" – it is difficult to know where to begin!]

26) Te. *vriddhuDi-kaNTe vayasu-lo pedda-di-gaa agupincaDam-too-baaTu,*
oldman-GEN-than age-in great-Fsg-Adv appear-VN-along-with

oopika-loo-kuuDaa atani-kaNTe adhikuraalee-n-ani
stamina-in-also his-(GEN)-than superior-person-Emph-Quot{cmpl}

niruppincukunna-di || atani bhaarya
demonstrate-Past-Fsg | | his-(GEN) wife

'Along with appearing to be older than the old man, his wife demonstrated that she was superior to him in stamina as well.' [new topic: the wife]

27) Te. *ara-gaNTa-loo annam waNDi, [Ø] waar-iddari-nii loopali-ki*
half-hour-in food cook-CP, [zero = "she"] they-two-ACC-Emph inside-to

pilic-in-di
call-Past-Fsg

'Having cooked food in half an hour, she called the two of them inside.' ['wife'-topic continued]

28) Te. *iNTi madhya-bhaagam-loo baasipeTTu weesu-ku kuurcunn-aa-Du || SaaDoo.*
house-GEN mid-part-in cross-legged sit-Past-Msg | | Shadow

'The Shadow sat down to eat cross-legged in the middle part of the house.' [new topic: the "Shadow" again]

29) Te. *aapyaayam-gaa pilakkaris-t-uu [Ø] aame peTTi-na*
amiable-Adv chat-PresAdvPpl [zero = 'he'] she put-PastAdjPpl

jonna-n-anni purti-gaa aaraginc-ae-Du
–jowar-all complete-Adv consume-Past-Msg

'While chatting amiably, he consumed all the jowar she set (before him)' ["the Shadow" continues as topic]

30) Te. *antakumundu vridduDu icc-ina aaku-l-loo*
previously oldman give-PastAdjPpl leaf-pl-in careful-Adv

jaagrata-gaa daacukunnawaaTi-too
save-PastAdjPpl-3plPN-Obl-INSTR

[Ø] inkoo cutta cuttu-koni maLLi nulaka-mancam
[zero = 'he'] another cigar roll-CP again string-cot upon

miida paDu-kunn-aa-Du
lie-down-Past-Msg

'With the carefully-saved leaves the old man had given him previously, he rolled another cigar, and lay down again on the string cot' ["the Shadow" continues as topic]

With regard to what constitutes identity or difference of Topic, it should be noted that where dialogue is quoted, the reference is to the topic (identical or different) preceding the dialogue.

There are only a few instances of "indirect" topical reference, e.g., Ex 31-32

31) Te. *winirees-ina viSayam jñapti-ki raawaTam-too nalla-gaa*
toss-away-PastAdjPpl thing memory-DAT come-VN-INSTR

kamili-pooyindi | | *atani wadanam.*
black-Adv blacken-go-Past-Fsg he (GEN) face

'With the recollection of what he had tossed away, HIS countenance fell (= "turned black")' [switch of Topic]

32) Te. *tanu eemii ceeya-leeka-poo-t-unnaan-ee anna baadha guNDelni*
self anything do-unable-Pres-1sg-Emph {compl} vexation heart-ACC

piNDi–wes-t-uNDagaa [Ø] marinta-gaa
pinch-Intens.-Pres-'since' [zero = 'he'] even-more-Adv

kaNThanni penci
voice-ACC raise-CP

maaroo-sari tana warandar-nii pilicae-Du
another-time self-GEN 'men' ["those-others"]-ACC call-Past-Msg

'As his cockiness was squeezed out by vexation at the fact that he himself was not able to do anything, HE raised his voice even more and called his men again.'

(Here the perceived connection may be to the Genitive *atani* 'his' in the previous sentence, or perhaps merely to the reflexive *tanu* in the embedded sentence within Ex 32 – except that the Verb in the embedded sentence – *eemii ceeya-leeka-poo-t-unnaan-ee* – is 1st Person, not 3rd

Person: 'that I myself am unable to do anything'. In any case, there is no perceived change of Topic, or perhaps simply no difficulty in understanding who is doing the shouting.)

Generally, however, the identity or non-identity of Topic is quite literal, and the context is immediate. There is nothing like the situation described for Polish by Jacennik and Dryer 1992, where the relationship may be very general (e.g., part to whole, member of class, even family relationship) and the relevant context is extended (an arbitrary limit) to the preceding 20 clauses.

It was noted earlier that quoted dialogue presents some complications. For one thing, Imperatives need to be excluded. They are structurally different in that they usually have no overt Topic, which is "understood" as the addressee. With them have to be classed what Krishnamurti & Gwynn 1985 call the Hortative, "Let's V..." – a subvariety of Imperative in which the Topic – "we" – is also understood and not expressed. These two, along with impersonals in *–aali, aalsindi* ("Obligational") account for nearly 20% of the dialogue utterances in the primary text. More importantly, the discourse context involves not merely what has been said previously, but the extralinguistic circumstances of who is addressing whom, who else is present at the exchange, what can be inferred about the participants' knowledge, and so forth. This affects the use of zero anaphora, found in 28% of the non-Imperative utterances, involving Topic-shift or not. (It is difficult to decide what constitutes Topic-shift, unless it occurs in a succession of utterances by the same speaker. When a different speaker starts talking about himself, or questions or answers a second speaker, do we call that also Topic-shift – or is the Topic a "given"?

33) Te. *"nii-ku maaTa eema-ni iccae-nu bee? nii daggira aayudhaalu kon-T-*
you-DAT word what-ACC give-Past-1sg Expl? Your(GEN)
aan-ani cepp-ae-n-aa?..."
vicinity weapon-pl buy-Fut-1sg-Quot{Cmpl} say-Past-1sg-Q

'What "word" did I give you? Did I say I would buy the weapons you have?' (The dacoit-chieftain is responding to the accusation that he is not a man of his word: the *–nu/-n-aa* [1sg ending] makes it clear that he is talking about himself) [Madhu Babu 1993: 17]

Nevertheless, what Erguvanlı calls the "non-contrastive" (or we might say, semi-redundant) use of postposed pronouns is fairly common in both Turkish and Telugu conversationally and therefore also in written dialogue:

34) Tu. *Anne-m-in çok selam-I var || siz-e*
mother-my-GEN much greeting-her exist || you-DAT

'My mother sends [you] her greetings [lit. "has much greeting for you"] (Obviously, 'to you'.) [Erguvanlı 1984: 58]

35) Te. *"nuww-ewari-w-oo, ikkaDi-ki enduku waccaew-oo*
you-who-{cmpl], here-DAT why come-Past-2sg-{cmpl}

telusu-kookuNDaa khatam ceeya-walasi-wacci-n-anduku caalaa
know-without, end- do-Inf-Oblig.-come-PastAdjPpl-because much

baadhapaDu t-unn-aa-nu || [neenu]"
feel-sorry-Pres-Dur-1sg || I

'Without knowing who you are or why you have come here, I am very sorry that now I have to finish you off' (In the situation, who else would be about to "finish him off?" – clear in any case from the 1st person verb in *–nu.*) [Madhu Babu 1993: 10)]

36) Te. *ikkaDi-ki daggar-loo-nee-w-unna sayyadpuur* ice factory*-loo*
here-DAT vicinity-in-Emph-existing Sayyadpur 'ice factory'-in

pani-ceestuu-w-unTaa-mu || meemu
work-do-PresAdvPpl-Dur-Pres-1pl | | we

'We are working in the Sayyadpur Ice Factory which is right near here.' (The speaker has been asked to identify himself and his companion.) [Madhu Babu: 1993: 45]

Of the postverbal Subjects in the dialogue portions of the primary Telugu text, 67% are pronouns. However, several of these are emphatic, not "backgrounded":

37) Te. *"nii-ku kaawaal-sina manbarii sardaar-ni || neenEE"*
you-DAT want-AdjPpl Manbari Sardar-PN1sg | | I-Emph

'I am the Manbari Sardar you wanted.' [Madhu Babu 1993: 12]

Another common locution is the inversion of Subject and Predicate in Nominal sentences involving 'this/that [is… PredN]'.

38) Te. "Border Guard*-ulu taracu-gaa tirig-ee pradeesham || idi"*
Border Guard-pl often-Adv roam-PresAdjPpl area | | this

'This is an area where the Border Guards often roam'. (This typically involves a change of Topic, and would seem to be "backgrounded" or redundant, not by previous reference but perhaps through a gesture.) [Madhu Babu 1993: 18]

However, it can also be emphatic (= suffix *–ee*):

39) Te. *"aayudhaalu daaci-w-unci-na cooTu || idEE, manbarii saab"*
weapons hide-CP-put-PastAdjPpl place | | this-Emph, Manbari Sahib

'THIS is the place where the weapons are hid, Manbari Sahib.' [Madhu Babu 1993: 18]

Nevertheless, a considerable portion of the dialogue utterances (36%) is in the canonical SOV order – or if we look at V-finality only, and include the Imperative and zero-anaphora utterances, the figure is 65% – as compared with the narrative portion, where the figures are 10% and 22% respectively. (One might ask, with regard to the 10% figure, if 90% of the narrative sentences have the Subject at the end, or omitted, what then is the function of having it in its "proper" place, sentence initial or at least preverbal?)

8. Comparisons with Hindi-Urdu and other Indo-Aryan languages

Turning to Indo-Aryan, and using a larger sample corpus than in my earlier paper, I continue to find a very different situation. In a 50-page sample of Gulshan Nanda's novel *Ajnabii*, I can find only 22 examples of postverbal material – only 10 involving Subjects – almost all of them in dialogue (the remainder in rhetorical asides to the reader), more than half of them in questions[5], and all of them functioning to de-emphasize the constituents involved.

40) H. *"kitnii duur hai˜ || aap kaa ghar?"*
how-much distant is | | you-GEN house

'How far is your house?' [Nanda 1973: 32]

Even when the utterance is emotionally charged, the emphasis (and the stress) is not on the postverbal element:

---

[5]This appears to be in fact the normal form for questions. It was evident, for example, in the Hindi film *"Pakeezaa"* broadcast nationwide in the USA on the Turner Classic Movies TV channel June 19, 2003, which a friend called and alerted me to, saying it had "lots of good Urdu dialogue". Just about every question had the Subject at the end.

41) H. *"golii maaroo || (us iNTarvyuu ko) aur laanat bhejo ||*
bullet strike-Imper. | | that-Obl "interview"-DAT/ACC and curse send-

(us naukarii par)!"
Imper || that-Obl job-on

'Shoot that interview and to hell with that job!" [Nanda 1973: 55]

The system of topic-switch signalling in narrative by postverbal placement of the Subject which Herring found in Tamil and which I have now also found in Telugu <u>is totally absent in all the Hindi literary material</u> I have examined so far (Nanda, Premchand, Mohan Rakesh, Yashpal, Ashk).

In a 50-page Gujarati sample from a detective-action novel (*Be-imaan* 'Dishonest' by Kanu Bhagdev) similar in genre (or so I thought) to the Telugu action novel sampled, it was also not to be found, and there were only 3 examples of postverbal material in the dialogue portions, all of them again in questions:

42) G. *"bol, shu˜ joie che || taare?"*
speak, what wanted is || you-Gen/LOC

"Speak, what do you want?"

9. Other languages

I was hoping to sample literature in Malayalam and Bengali also, because of special features of the systems of pragmatic marking found in these languages (absence of verbal agreement in the former, and definite article-like suffixes in the latter), but couldn't manage it for this paper. There are indications, however, even in learning materials from CIIL[6], of extensive use of word order variation in Malayalam, probably for pragmatic purposes (although the author merely notes [p.19] that "word order is not rigid"). K. V. Subbarao [personal communication] informs me that, despite the lack of personal endings on the verb, *zero anaphora* is widely used in Malayalam – and in Tibeto-Burman languages he has studied which also lack personal endings: "it all depends on <u>context</u>".

Erguvanlı 1984 does not identify topic-switch signalling as a function of postverbal placement of Subject in Turkish, but – although she too samples 50 pages of a literary text [p, 41, fn. 15] along with taped conversational material and "my own native speaker intuition" on variants of single sentences – she was not looking for it [nor was I, until

---

[6]B. Syamala Kumari 1981. *An intensive course in Malayalam.* Mysore: CIIL

Herring drew attention to it]; her focus was only on indefinite NP's "since it is such NP's that are subject to restrictions of word order." Subjects (Topics) are typically definite (almost by definition), unless marked otherwise. Therefore I do not know at this point whether postverbal placement is used for this purpose in Turkish or not.

Ranging further afield, however, we find that word order variation is extensively used for pragmatic purposes in such languages as Russian and Czech[7]. A random inspection of the first page of Boris Pasternak's novel *Doktor Zhivago* turned up the following sentences with postverbal Subjects:

43) R. *Nachalas'* || *strashnaya gonka*
begin-Past-FsgRefl | | awful-Fsg rush

'An awful rush began'

44) R. *Otbarabanil* || *dozhd' kom'yev, kotorymi*
rattle-Past-Msg | | rain clod-GENpl -which-MplINSTR

toroplivo v chetyre lopaty zabrosali mogilu
quickly in 4 shovels fill-Past-pl grave-ACC

'There rattled a rain of clods, by which they quickly with four shovels filled up the grave.' [please forgive my awkward translations!]

45) R. *Na ney vyros* || *kholmik*
on it-Fsg-LOC grew-up-Past-Msg | | mound-dim

'On it a little mound arose.'

46) R. *Na nego vzoshol* || *desyatiletniy mal'chik*
onto it-Msg-LOC mount-Past-Msg | | ten-year-old boy

'A ten-year-old boy got up on it.'

47) R. *K mogile proshol* || *chelovek v chornom*...
to grave-DAT pass-through-Past-Msg | | man in black-Msg-LOC

'A man in black passed through to the grave.'

---

[7] This has reportedly been much studied by linguists of the Prague School, although this work is not presently available to me. There is some reference to it in Comrie 1981, however, pp 68-78. There is a good discussion of some functions, of "inverted word order" in Russian in Borras and Christian, 1957, Ch. VIII, including the pragmatic functions of definite and indefinite, but without the aid of theoretical pragmatics, as yet undeveloped.

Could it be that this phenomenon – right-shifting of Subject/Topic – is a property, not of a particular word-order type (Russian is SVO, not SOV), but of a particular pragmatic type – which have inflections to mark grammatical functions, lack articles to mark pragmatic functions, and therefore can (and must) rely on word order for the latter?

But let us look still further afield. Spanish is a language fully equipped with articles. Yet here also we have no trouble in finding right-shifting of Subjects[8] (although perhaps not as often as in Russian). E.g., from Mariano Azuela's classic novel of the Mexican Revolution, *Los de abajo* 'Those From Below':

48) Sp. *Se oyó* || *un ruido de pesuñas en*
Refl-hear-Past3sg || a(Msg) sound of hooves in

el pedregal cercano…
the rocky ground nearby(Msg)

'A sound of hooves was heard on the nearby rocky ground.'
[Azuela 1958: 7]

49) Sp. *Por la noche regresó* || *la Codorniz con la*
during the night returned-Past3sg | | La Cordoniz with the-Fsg

sotana del cura
cassock of-the-Msg priest

"At night La Codorniz came back with the priest's cassock.'
[Azuela: 1958: 31]

So, are we dealing, then, with a quasi-universal phenomenon – at least in languages where word order does not play a primarily grammatical role?

Even in Chinese, where it allegedly does, it has been shown that it plays a pragmatic role as well. In fact, it has been persuasively argued [Chafe 1976, Li & Thompson 1981, LaPolla 1995], that that is the only role it plays. To take the simplest case, and the one most relevant to the present discussion, a preverbal Subject is definite, while a postverbal Subject is indefinite:

50) Ch. *rén lái le*
person come Pfv

'THE person/persons has/have come' **vs.**

---

[8] Ex. 48-49 are Indefinite, but "backgrounded" definite S are also to be found: *Sonó el teléfono* 'The telephone rang' – maximally defocussed, because what else would ring? Here the definiteness comes from the situation, not from previous discourse reference.

51) Ch. *lái le rén le*
come˜Pfv person Pfv

'SOME person/persons has/have come' [Li & Thompson 1981: 20])

But let us take a closer look. Recall Erguvanlı's stricture that in the SOV language Turkish, postverbal Subjects must be definite. Herring's notion of "antitopic" also implicitly requires definiteness. The postverbal Subjects in Ex. 43-48, and Ex. 51, i.e. in SVO or quasi-SVO languages, are indefinite. Something different is going on there.

(In SVO as well as SOV languages, we find definite NP's in this position due to the widespread[9] – and borrowed? – literary convention of handling quotes: *"X" said John. "Y" said Mary.* Actually, many – 81% – of Herring's examples of switch-reference postposing in written narrative are of this type, "to signal a change of speaker" [Herring 1994: 130]. Only a few of the examples in the Madhu Babu adventure epic are of this type, but it looms larger in some other Telugu literary samples. Although as noted in Masica 2002 it seems not to have caught on in Hindi[10] – where I have yet to find an example – possibly for structural reasons connected to the *-ne* construction, perhaps because of their cross-linguistic provenance such examples should be bracketed or set aside.)

10. Presentational Focus

Unfortunately, we find that a number of the postverbal Subjects in the central Telugu corpus are also in fact indefinite. Although they do signal a change of topic, they also introduce a protagonist or entity previously unknown to the discourse:

52) Te. *oDDu ekkenduku kaastanta kaSTa-paDu-t-uNDa-gaa, atanni*
bank climb-in order to a little struggle-PrAdvPpl-while, he-ACC

cuus-ae-Du || aDavi ancu-na-w-uNDee poda-l-loo meeka-l-ni
see-Past-Msg forest edge-LOC-exist-PrAdjPpl bush-plObl-in

meeppu-koow-aTaani-ki wacc-ina wridduDu okatanu
grazeVN-to goat-pl-ACC come-PastAdjPpl oldman one-person

---

[9] E.g., in Russian, in M. A. Bulgakov's science fiction story *Rokovyie yaitsa* 'The fatal eggs', we have in succession, *okliknul Shchukin , molvil Polaitis, krichal Shchukin, vorchal Shchukin, rasporyadilsya Shchukin, zametil Shchukin, shepnul Shchukin, kriknul Shchukin, kriknul Polaitis,* and *promychal on*. Another writer, M. Zoshchenko, however, avoids this entirely in his story *Kocherga* 'The Poker': *on skazal, direktor diktoval, on ... skazal, sekretar' skazal, on skazal*, etc. Perhaps our Russian colleagues can tell us: does this affect the tone of the stories?

[10] Nor in Gujarati.

'As he was struggling a little in order to climb onto the bank, an old man who had come to graze his goats in the bushes that were on the edge of the forest saw him.' [Madhu Babu 1993: 26]

53) Te. *padi-kSaNaa-l-a taruwaata atan-i dRSTa patham-loo-ki wacc-ae-y* ||
ten-second-pl-Obl after he-GEN vision path-in-to come-Past-3pl-Inan ||

reNDu aakaaraa-lu.
two figure-plM

'After 10 seconds, two figures came into the path of his vision.' [Madhu Babu 1993: 35]

In a subsequent paper (Herring & Paolillo 1995), Herring confronts this problem, and introduces the concept of presentational focus, in the context of a discussion of the view that, because "there are plausible cognitive and functional motivations for placing salient information in sentence-final position: people better retain in short-term memory that which they have heard or read most recently, a tendency which takes on functional significance when the final focused element becomes the topic of subsequent discourse" [Herring & Paolillo 1995: 163], this "universal tendency" may override the strictures of SOV typology.

I think would be going too far, however, to use this to challenge the conventional idea that the Focus position in SOV languages is immediately preverbal, and to argue that this is due to a confusion between Focus and grammatical Object. The Object often is the "new information", hence in Focus. It is only when the new information is a Subject that a problem arises, and demands another functional "slot" to "present" it as such. Very few, if any, "Presentationals" are Objects. (Many of Herring's examples are from oral narratives where the presentation occurs in a truncated sentence, with the verb dropped, therefore becoming utterance-final "by default" – this does not mean they are postverbal; if the missing verb were to be supplied, they would become preverbal, e.g., her Ex. 16, p.185: *atile oru periya cinkam* ... 'Among them, a big lion' [i.e. *iruntatu*, 'there was']. It is unnecessary to rely on this special oral presentational strategy – on which further doubt is cast by the fact that the succeeding utterance also lacks a verb – *cinkatt-ai kaN-taa ellaa ellaa* animals-*ukkum payam*... 'Whenever they saw the lion, all the animals were afraid' [i.e. *payam uNDu* 'fear existed'] to establish the point, as the Telugu examples show.)

Therefore, it seems quite acceptable, for SOV languages, **to posit two Focal slots**, the normal, preverbal one primarily for Objects, and a postverbal one for **presenting new Subjects**, giving a functional scheme of **T (X) F V P/E (anti-T)**.

The situation in SVO languages like Russian is quite different, in that the normal Focal position is already postverbal. It is normally occupied by the Object, but is available, as shown in Ex. 43-47 above, for presenting new Subjects[11] as well. In that case, an Object, if any, is most likely old information and can be front-shifted (topicalized), vacating the slot for the Presentational Subject. (Jacennik and Dryer 1992 suggest another principle may complement this: there is a preference, in SVO languages, for having the two primary NP's on opposite sides of the V: Subjects tend to be right-shifted when the Object is topicalized and left-shifted. This is all quite different from the dynamics of SOV languages.)

Both Erguvanlı and Herring make the point that the word order variants we have been discussing are to be found mainly in literary narrative and in spoken language. In more formal styles – including news reporting – the canonical norms of the language tend to be strictly followed close to 100% of the time. This does not mean, however, that the word order variants in written literature are necessarily reflective of the spoken language. As we have seen, they are often a matter of special stylistic conventions, peculiar to their genre. Often nobody "talks that way" (although, in a literate society, they sometimes begin to: cf. the increasingly common current locution in spoken English, *That being the case...*, or *Having said that...*)

There are differences not only between genres (or registers) but also among authors. Some may choose to employ the available stylistic options (or exercise them in particular contexts) more than others. I had intended to provide you with detailed examples of this, but since I have already done so in my 2002 paper, and this is already overlong, I will confine myself to a closer look at an additional story by P. Sambasiva Rao, followed by a more general summary. In Rao's story (*hatyaa/ aatmahatyaa/*) of 125 sentences, topic-switches are by no means always marked by a postverbal Subject. However, a postverbal Subject does always indicate a topic-switch – except in three cases, two of which involve the beginning and final lines of the story, where often special stylistic devices come into play. In the third, one could argue that the topic was not the Subject (in this case a Dative Subject – a slippery category from this point of view – and in any case, postverbal) but something else, namely the "presentationally focussed" right-shifted subordinate clause (underlined below, marked by the final Complementizer *–ani)*:

[11] Sometimes also of re-introducing old Subjects: cf. Spanish example (49).

54) Te. *taruvaata telisindi | prakaash raawu-ku, raama-narasuku*
afterward find-out-Past-sg-Inan | Prakash Rao-DAT, Ramanarasu-DAT

caalaa sambandhaa-lu
many marriage-offer-pl

wacci veLLi pooy-aey-ani
come-CP-go away-CP go{Intens.)-3pl-Inan-{cmpl}

'Later Prakash Rao came to know that that Rama Narasu had already had many marriage offers.' [Rao 1967: 111]

Therefore, in the immediately following sentence "Prakash Rao" could be understood as a different, reintroduced topic:

55) Te. *modaTa biida meenarikam wadd-anukoni kotta sambandhamu*
at first poor cross-cousin-marriage not-wanted say-CP, new alliance

manchid-eedaynaa celleli-ki kuduruddaam-ani aneeka prayatnaa-lu ceesi,
good-any younger-sister-DAT arrange-Hort-{cmpl} many attempt-pl make-CP

ciwaraku diinini nishcayincaeDu || prakash raawu [ibid.]
ultimately this-ACC decide-Past-Msg || Prakash Rao

"After having first rejected a marriage alliance with a poor cross-cousin, and after making numerous attempts to arrange a better [= extra-familial] marital alliance for his sister, Prakash Rao had ultimately decided on this one."[12] [ibid.]

For the remaining Telugu corpus (not analyzed in this paper), we may say that (in contrast with Hindi) marked word orders, though not as dominant as in Madhu Babu's writing, are nevertheless found more in the narrative portions than in the dialogues, and that zero anaphora marks "continued Topic".

11. Conclusion

A number of languages of different types and genetic stocks, sometimes loosely labeled "free word order" languages, show considerable "variation" in word order because, first of all, they have agreement and

[12] The translation of these sentences in the conference version of my paper was incorrect, due in part to the multiple anaphoric references which were unclear to me because of my insensitivity to the cultural context. I thank K. V. Subbarao and S. P. Vasireddi for setting me straight. [E.g., /sambandham/ means 'marriage offer', not 'marriage'; the word /kotta/ 'new' implies 'outside the family' here.] The syntactic point remains the same.

case-marking devices that make their argument structure clear regardless. In most cases they may still be said to have a "basic" or "unmarked" order (which may or may not be the most frequent), from which the others are marked deviations. While some of this word order variation is partly no doubt a matter of stylistic option in all the languages exemplifying it which are discussed in this paper ("emphasis" may be subsumed under stylistic options), in some of them at least it also enters the realm of pragmatic structure, and seems to be rule-governed and highly systematic – another set of rules, superimposed on the basic word order patterns of the language. Word order "variants" become a **discourse-marking device**. Although some universals of linear information-processing may be relevant, both the stylistic options and the discourse-marking devices are clearly not the same for all languages with word order variation, but are different for different basic word order types (and subtypes), depending especially on the canonical positions of the Verb and of the utterance Focus – but also apparently on other factors which are not as yet clear, e.g. in Telugu and Tamil vs. Hindi and Gujarati.

Moreover, although some discourse-marking devices (e.g. definite object marking) are shared by the Indo-Aryan languages of northern South Asia and Turkic languages, perhaps because of areal and historical factors, when it comes to word order variants, stylistic or pragmatic, there appears to be as much or more in common between the "rigidly" SOV Dravidian and Turkic languages, possibly because of deep typological factors. It is not yet clear whether this includes topic-shift marking, although right-shifted Subjects – when they are not Presentationals! – and Objects are in both cases both "known" and "de-emphasized" information.

In general, however, word order variation would seem to be a fruitful area in which to explore discourse-marking structure.

References

Arden, A. H. 1942. *A progressive grammar of common Tamil.* 5th edition, revised by A. C. Clayton. Madras: Christian Literature Society for India.

Azuela, Mariano. 1958. *Los de abajo.* Mexico City: Fondo de Cultura Económica.

Bhagdev, Kanu. 1991. *Be-imaan.* Rajkot (Saurashtra, Gujarat): Navayug Pustak Bhandar.

Borras., F. M., and R. F. Christian. 1957. *Russian syntax.* Oxford: Clarendon Press.

Butt, Miriam, Tracy Holloway King, and Gillian Ramchand. 1994. *Theoretical perspectives on word order in South Asian languages.* Stanford (CA); Center for the Study of Language and Information. (CSLI Lecture Notes, No. 60).

Chafe, Wallace L. 1976. Givenness, contrastiveness, definiteness, subjects, topics, and point of view. In: Li (ed.) 1976: 27-55.

Comrie, Bernard. 1981. *Language universals and linguistic typology.* Chicago: University of Chicago Press.

Downing, Pamela, and Michael Noonan, eds. 1995. *Word order in discourse.* Amsterdam & Philadelphia: John Benjamins.

Dryer, Matthew S. 1995. Frequency and pragmatically unmarked word order. In Downing and Noonan, eds. pp. 105-136.

Erguvanlı, Eser Emine. 1984. *The function of word order in Turkish grammar.* Berkeley, University of California Press. (University of California Publications in Linguistics, Vol. 106).

Greenberg, Joseph. 1966. *Language Universals (with special reference to feature hierarchies).* The Hague: Mouton.

Herring, Susan C. 1994. Postverbal position in Tamil. In; Butt, King, and Ramchand, eds., pp. 110-152.

Herring, Susan C., and John C. Paolillo. 1995. Focus position in SOV languages. In: Downing and Noonan, eds. Pp. 163-198.

Jacennik, Barbara, and Matthew S. Dryer. 1992. Verb-Subject order in Polish. In: Payne (ed.). pp: 210-241.

Krishnamurti, Bh., and J. P. L. Gwynn. 1985. *A grammar of modern Telugu.* Delhi-Bombay-Madras: Oxford University Press.

LaPolla, Randy J. 1995. Pragmatic relations and word order in Chinese. In Downing & Noonan (eds.): 297-329.

Lewis, G. L. 1967. *Turkish grammar.* Oxford University Press.

Li, Charles N. (ed.) 1976. *Subject and topic.* New York: Academic Press.

Li, Charles N., and Sandra A. Thompson. 1981. *Mandarin Chinese: a functional reference grammar.* Berkeley: University of California Press.

Madhu Babu, 1992. *MiDnaiT-plas-wan* (2 vol.). Vijayawada: Madhubabu Publications.

Masica, Colin P. 2002. Possible functions of an alternative word order in Telugu: VS. (Paper presented at SALA XX, Iowa City, IA, June 21-23, 2002.)

Matson, Dan M., and G. N. Reddy. 1967. *Graded readings in modern literary Telugu.* University of Wisconsin.

Nanda, Gulshan. 1973 (8th ed.) *Ajnabii.* Dilli: Ashok Pocket Books.

Pasternak, Boris. 1957/58. *Doktor Zhivago.* Ann Arbor: University of Michigan Press, by arrangement with Giangiacomo Feltrinelli Editore, Milano, Italy.

Payne, Doris L. (ed.) 1992. *Pragmatics of word order flexibility.* Amsterdam & Philadelphia: John Benjamins

Rao, Potukuci Sambasiva. 1967. Hatyaa? Aatmahatyaa? In: Reddy and Matson, eds. pp. 109-116.

Abbreviations

1 – First Person
2 – Second Person
3 – Third Person
ABL – Ablative
ACC – Accusative
Adj – adjectival
Adv – adverbial
Aor – Aorist [Turkish tense]
Ch. – Chinese
cmpl – complementizer
CP – conjunctive participle
DAT – Dative
Dur – Durative (Te. verb form)
Emph – emphatic
Expl – expletive
F – feminine
Fut – Future
GEN – Genitive
Guj. – Gujarati
H. – Hindi-Urdu
Hort – Hortative
Imp – Imperative
Tu. – Turkish
VN – verbal noun
Impfv - imperfective
Inan - inanimate
Infr – inferential
INSTR – Instrumental
LOC - Locative
M – masculine
N – neuter
Neg – negative (inflection)
Obl – Oblique
Pfv – perfective
pl – plural
PN – pronominal ending (Te.)
Ppl – participle
Pr(es) – Present
Q – question markeri
Quot – quotative
R. – Russian
Refl – reflexive (R. verb form)
sg – singular
Sp. – Spanish
Ta. – Tamil
Te. – Telugu

LANGUAGES WITHOUT NOUNS AND VERBS? AN ALTERNATIVE TO LEXICAL CLASSES IN KHARIA

JOHN PETERSON[1]

1. Introduction

The Munda languages are well-known for the fact that the noun-verb distinction, if one exists at all in these languages, is very weak. For example, most previous studies on the North Munda languages Santali, Mundari and Ho (Bodding (1929), Hoffman (1903) and Deeney (1975), respectively) argue that any lexeme in these languages can fill a function similar to that filled by nouns and verbs in English, while in one recent study on Santali (Neukom, 2001) it is argued that although Santali does possess some verbs, i.e., elements which may never combine with demonstratives or function as arguments, it otherwise merely possesses "one major word class, subsuming what corresponds to noun and verb in other languages." (Neukom, 2001: 20)

In the following pages I discuss this topic for Kharia (South Munda). I will argue that, while an analysis of Kharia into the usual parts-of-speech may often seem possible, at least if one assumes that all lexemes are "precategorial", assuming the presence of nouns, verbs and adjectives nevertheless causes more difficulties than doing away with them altogether and simply assuming two classes in the lexicon: open (lexical morphemes) and closed (grammatical morphemes). As it turns out, although it is possible to divide the closed class into further subclasses (postpositions, numeral classifiers, etc.), we shall see that this is not

---

[1] Data for this study were collected during four research trips to Jharkhand over the past four years, amounting to approximately six months altogether. I would like to thank the German Research Council (DFG) for generous grants which made two of these trips possible.

Previous versions of the present study were presented at the European Association of South Asian Studies Conference in Lund, July 2004, and at the European Meeting on Munda Languages, Leipzig, October 2004. I would like to thank the participants of these meetings for their comments and suggestions. Thanks also to Graham Katz for his comments on an earlier version of this study. Needless to say, I alone am responsible for any errors which may have found their way into the text.

possible for the open class.

The argumentation in the present paper is predominantly structural although semantic aspects are also considered to some extent. The reason for this emphasis on structure is the following: "Noun" and "verb" are *grammatical categories*. Like other grammatical categories, e.g. grammatical gender or tense, although they of course are related to extralinguistic phenomena, they do not show a one-to-one correspondence to these.

To take one well-known example, German has three grammatical genders, MASCULINE, FEMININE and NEUTER and one could conceivably argue that there are three "natural" genders as well, namely MALE, FEMALE and INANIMATE, with which they are related. Often the two do in fact coincide: *der Mann* 'the man' (MASCULINE), *die Frau* 'the woman' (FEMININE) and *das Boot* 'the boat' (NEUTER), but more often than not there is no correspondence: *der Tisch* 'the table' (MASCULINE), *die Tür* 'the door' (FEMININE), *das Mädchen* 'the girl' (NEUTER). Similar examples for the relationship between tense and time could also easily be cited.

Discrepancies of this type with respect to parts-of-speech are even more notorious, as well-known examples such as *scandal* show: Although *scandal* is a noun and does not derive from a verb, it denotes an event and not a "person, place or thing". Similarly, an *election* is not a "thing" by any stretch of the imagination, although it is a noun: It of course derives from the presumably verbal lexeme *elect* and the nominalizing derivational morpheme *-tion*, but it is not always this easy to decide what the "underlying" part-of-speech of a particular lexeme is. In a number of cases, e.g. *hope* (n./v.), *fear* (n./v.), etc., whether we assume that these are basically nouns or verbs, we will have to make a largely arbitrary decision and will also have to assume zero-derivation to get the "derived" form.

Nevertheless, although many lexemes such as *hope* and *fear* can serve both as predicates and complements, we must still assume the presence of parts-of-speech for English, as ungrammatical forms such as **I televisioned*, **you cassetted* or **the tree's grow* show. Hence when dealing with grammatical categories, semantics must of course be taken into consideration but they will necessarily play a secondary role with respect to structural considerations.

It is common knowledge that grammatical categories of any type must be defined in each language on that particular language's own terms. Thus we cannot rely on the presence of case-marking to show that there is or is not a category "noun" in English (as we can e.g. in Sanskrit) any more than we can use the absence of verbal inflexion to argue that the class of "verbs" does not exist in an isolating language. Here, other means – including semantics and distributional properties – will have to be found.

The case in Kharia is, fortunately, much more straightforward than in English, as the language possesses a rich morphological system for marking TAM, case and person/number/honorific status, one which allows us to immediately identify the function of a clause-level entity as either a predicate or a complement. What makes the issue in Kharia so interesting, and so complex, is that any well-formed phrase, not just a word, can be used as both a predicate and as a complement without any overt "nominalizing" or "verbalizing" derivation or light verb, and forms corresponding to the English **I those three televisioned* are possible in Kharia, although highly humorous, as their meaning would be 'I became those three televisions.' Nevertheless, utterances of this type are both possible and, what is even more striking, completely predictable with respect to their semantics.

The study is structured as follows: Section 2 provides a very basic introduction to Kharia. Section 3 presents data on "nouns" and "verbs" in Kharia, showing that there is much more at issue here than mere "precategoriality". In section 4 I present an alternative to nouns and verbs in Kharia, discussing both complements (4.1) and predicates (4.2) in some detail to show that they differ only with respect to their "functional heads", i.e., the grammatical information at the end of the phrase. In section 5 I begin with a brief discussion of attribution. Here I show that there is in fact no need to assume a class of adjectives, but to do this we must discuss in some detail two forms which could be considered adjectives, namely "participles" (5.1) and "derived nominals" (5.2). In section 5.3 I make use of the discussion in Anderson & Zide (2002) to show that Kharia has a purely phonological constraint requiring (potentially) free-standing forms to contain at least two syllables which, due to the structure of the language, only applies to complements of predicates. Finally, section 6 summarizes the results and discusses their further implications.

2. Typological characteristics of Kharia

Kharia belongs to the southern branch of the Munda family, which forms the western-most branch of the Austro-Asiatic phylum. It is the second largest member of the southern branch, after Sora, and is spoken predominantly in southwest Jharkhand, eastern Chattisgarh and northwestern Orissa, where it is in close contact with the Indo-Aryan languages Hindi, Sadani and Oriya, the Dravidian language Kurukh (or Oraon) and the North-Munda language Mundari, among others.

According to the Internet version of the Ethnologue[2] a total of 278,500 people spoke Kharia in 1994.

Kharia is a predominantly agglutinating SOV language. It is mostly suffixing / enclitic, although it has one infix, the "nominalizer" *-nV-*, to which we will return in section 5, and one prefix/infix, the causative morpheme //OB//, whose form and status as a pre- or infix depends primarily on the structure of the lexical base.

Kharia has three grammatical numbers, both on complements and predicates: Singular (unmarked), dual (marked by *-kiyar*) and plural (marked by *-ki* with complements and either *-ki* or *-may* with predicates).

lebu (= *lebu-Ø*) 'man' *lebu-kiyar* 'two men' *lebu-ki* 'men'
colta-Ø 's/he goes' *colta-kiyar* 'they two go' *colta-ki/colṭa-may* 'they (P) go'

There are three morphological cases in Kharia:

Direct (zero marking) - the case of subjects, non-definite countable objects, and non-countable objects;
Oblique (marked by *-te*) - marks definite countable objects, "indirect objects" and adverbials.
Genitive (marked by *-(y)aʔ*) - the "adnominal" case, through which one potential complement becomes an attribute in a larger complement.

Finally, with the exception of the present perfect and the optative, neither of which marks for voice, all fully finite predicates in Kharia are obligatorily marked for both TAM/voice and PERS/NUM/HON. The markers of these categories are presented in Tables 1 and 2.

Table 1: TAM/basic voice markers in Kharia

	Active	**Middle**
Past (PT) (aspectually neutral)	*-oʔ*	*-ki*
Nonpast General Imperfective (NPT)	*-te*	*-ta*
Nonpast Progressive (PROG)	*-teʔjD*	*-taʔjD*
Irrealis (IRR)	*-e*	*-na*

Table 2: Person/Number/Honorific status markers in Kharia

	Singular	**Dual (/HON)**		**Plural**	
		Inclusive	**Exclusive**	**Inclusive**	**Exclusive**
1	*-iñ*	*-nang*	*-jar*	*-ning*	*-le*
2	*-em*	*-bar*		*-pe*	
3	*-Ø*	*-kiyar*		*-ki / -may*	

[2] http://www.ethnologue.com/show_language.asp?code=KHR (November, 2004)

3. "Funny verbs"

At first glance, most Kharia predicates and their complements appear to be quite typical verbs and nouns, respectively. Here a simple example of each in which it seems clear enough that we are dealing with a verb (1a) and a noun (1b), respectively.

(1) a. *muʔ-ki-may*
emerge-M.PT-3P

'they emerged'

b. *konselDuʔ-Dom-ki-te*
woman-3POSS-P-OBL

'their wives (as object)'

However, the situation in Kharia is not as simple as that. Typical of Kharia, and of probably all other Munda languages as well, is what at first sight appears to be a case of so-called "precategoriality", i.e., that lexemes are neither inherently nouns nor verbs but can function as both. For example, any lexeme in Kharia can function both as a predicate as well as the complement of a predicate. Consider the two sentences in (2) which at least for some speakers of Kharia are both perfectly grammatical utterances:

(2) a.

lebu	*Del-ki-Ø.*
man	come-M.PT-S

'The / a man came.'

b.

bhagwan	*lebu-ki-Ø*	*ro*	*Del-ki-Ø.*
God	man-M.PT-S	and	come-M.PT-S

'God became man [= Jesus] and came [to earth].'
[(2b) adapted from Malhotra, 1982: 136]

Although all speakers insisted that the (2b) would sound more natural if the first predicate were replaced by *lebu hoy-ki*, literally 'became (*hoyki*) man (*lebu*)', a small group nevertheless accepted it as grammatical. Interestingly, although this group was only a small fraction (5 people) of the many Kharia speakers I worked with, they all had the following in common:

- They all came from the same region, namely the immediate vicinity of the city of Simdega in Simdega district in the southwestern-most part of Jharkhand. All speakers from elsewhere who I questioned rejected such forms.
- They were all between the ages of 19 and 32, whereas older speakers rejected (2b) as ungrammatical without further consideration.
- They were also accustomed to reading Kharia: Three members of this group were studying Kharia at the university and were thus accustomed to reading Kharia literature while the other two had composed literature of their own (short stories and song texts). It may be that it was the fact that these five speakers were accustomed to reflecting on their native language, coupled with the Simdega dialect, which is responsible for this variation.

As the exact criteria which contributed to speakers' intuitions on acceptability – especially in an interview situation – need to be studied further, I will restrict myself in the following pages to the responses of those Kharia speakers who accepted examples such as (2b) as grammatical and all examples in the present study are from this group, unless otherwise noted.

Similar to example (2b), "pronouns" can also be used in predicative function, as the following ellicited example shows:[3]

(in a play about me and you, in which both of us will be taking part):

(3)	*"naTak-te*	*iñ=ga*	*ho-kaR-na-iñ*	*ro*	*am=ga*	*iñ-na-m."*
	play-OBL	1S=FOC	3-S.HUM-M.IRR-1S	and	2S=FOC	1S-M.IRR-2S

"umbo?.	*am-na*	*um-iñ*
no	2S-INF	NEG-1S

pal-te.	*DirekTar*	*seng=ga?*	*iñ-te*	*ho-kaR-o?-Ø.*
be.able-A.NPT	director	early=FOC	1S-OBL	3-S.HUM-A.PT-S

am=ga	*am-na-m."*
2S=FOC	2S-M.IRR-2S

""In the play I will be him and you will be me." "No. I can't be you. The director already made me him. You will be you.""

However, there is much more to this issue than mere precategoriality.

---

[3] All examples for which no source is given are from my own interviews. Examples given with a source of the type [BB, 1: 52] refer to texts I have collected with native speakers and will be published in Peterson (in progress).

For example, "nouns" and "pronouns" marked for the genitive can also function as predicates:

(4) a. *ayo-yaʔ* *keciya*
mother-GEN money

'mother's money'

b. *ayo-yaʔ-y-oˀj.*[4]
mother-GEN-*y*-A.PT.1S

'[I] made [it] mother's.'

c. *ayo-yaʔ-ki-Ø.*
mother-GEN-M.PT-3

'[It] became mother's.'

(5) a. *iñ* *ho-kaR-te* *iñ-aʔ-y-oˀj.*
1S 3-S.HUM-OBL 1S-GEN-*y*-A.PT.1S

'I adopted him/her (i.e., I made him/her mine).'

b. *am* *ho-kaR-te* *am-aʔ-y-oˀb.*
2S 3-S.HUM-OBL 2S-GEN-*y*-A.PT.2S

'You adopted him/her.'

Examples (4) and (5) strongly suggest that any analysis of these predicates as "verbs", i.e., as a lexical category, is dubious, as we would have a "verb" consisting of a case-marked "noun". As we shall presently see, however, this is by no means the only problem with such an analysis.

In fact, what appear to be entire "NPs" can also function as predicates. For example, a "noun" with a quantifier as in (6)[5] or a demonstrative (7) can also function as a predicate. Again, if we claim these are verbs, it is not immediately obvious what the structure of this verb could be in (5b) and (6b).

---

[4] *-y-* is a non-phonemic glide inserted in certain phonological environments. Its presence has no implications for our discussion. Note also that the genitive suffix, given as *-(y)aʔ* is also, historically speaking, the glide *-y-* plus the older genitive suffix *-aʔ*, which has now more-or-less been generalized in Kharia into *-yaʔ*.

[5] Numeral specifiers in Kharia often appear together with one of a small number of classifiers, such as *Tho* 'CL', although this is not obligatory.

(6) a.

ubar	*rochoˀb-te*	*col-ki-ñ.*
2	side-OBL	go-M.PT-1S

b.

ubar	*rochoˀb-ki-ñ.*
2	side-M.PT-1S

'I moved to both sides (i.e., this way and then that).'

(7) a.

ho	*rochoˀb-te*	*col-ki-ñ.*
that	side-OBL	go-M.PT-1S

b.

ho	*rochoˀb-ki-ñ.*
that	side-M.PT-1S

'I moved to that side.'

"NPs" containing a genitive attribute can also be used predicatively, as in (8) or (9), which would also seem to indicate that the head of the "verb" is actually the head of a noun phrase. Working with "nouns" and "verbs" here thus brings a number of complications with it which cannot easily be accounted for.

(8)

hoDom	*dinu=jo*	*kongher-te*	*dhoʔ-na-yaʔ*	*kornis-oʔ-Ø*
other	day=ADD	boy-OBL	grab-INF-GEN	attempt-A.PT-S
muda	*um-Ø*	*pal-oʔ.*		
but	NEG-S	be.able-A.PT		

'The next day as well [the witch] tried to grab the boy but could not.' [BB, 1: 52]

(9)

bharat-yaʔ	*lebu-ki*	*bides-aʔ*	*lebu-ki-yaʔ*	*ruprang-ki-may.*
India-GEN	person-P	abroad-GEN	person-P-GEN	appearance-M.PT-3P

'The Indians took on the appearance of foreigners (e.g. by living abroad so long).'

In my opinion, these examples clearly show that we cannot simply speak of nouns and verbs here, at least not in the sense of lexical categories. If these categories do exist in Kharia, they will have to be phrasal in nature.

With some "nominal" predicates with a genitive-case modifier it is possible to analyze these as omitting a postposition which requires the genitive, as in (10). This could then be understood as a kind of obligatory but oblique "object" which is usually marked by a postposition:

(10) *ho-kaR iñ-aʔ (thong / ghaʔD) madet-y-oʔ-Ø.*
3-S.HUM 1S-GEN for for help-*y*-A.PT-S

'S/he helped me.'

However, this is not always possible, and the inclusion of a postposition requiring the genitive is in fact often ungrammatical, as (11) shows:

(11) *iñ hokaR-aʔ (*thong / *ghaʔD) main-oʔj.*
1S 3-S.HUM-GEN for for honor-A.PT.1S

'I honored him/her.'

Rather, although this is still somewhat tentative, the use of the genitive in these predicates appears to be restricted to those cases where we are dealing with "abstract entities" such as *help*, *honor*, etc. which actually refer to an action, not a physical entity and which are loanwords from Indo-Aryan, especially if these are used in the donor language as nouns in light-verb constructions, such as *madaït karek* 'help', literally, 'do help' in Sadani, in which the lexical part of the predicate is a nominal and is accompanied by a "light verb" such as *karek* 'do', *hovek* 'be(come)', etc. More research is necessary on this topic before anything definitive can be said. At any rate, the fact that a postposition cannot always be used in these expressions, as in (11), clearly rules out treating them as deriving from postpositional phrases.

It seems best to me, especially in light of the examples given above, to merely treat them as genitive attributes in a phrase which both semantically and structurally is reminiscent of a nominal phrase in English, but which is clearly not an NP in Kharia. This of course leaves us with the problem of explaining this structure, and I return to this topic in section 4. At any rate, it should be clear by now that "parts-of-speech" in Kharia cannot be relegated to the lexicon and will have to be explained at the phrasal level.

The only real restriction to this type of flexibility is semantic compatibility. For example, *Tebul* 'table' can theoretically be used not only as the complement of a predicate with the meaning 'table' (n.) but also in the middle voice with the meaning 'become a table' or in the active voice with the meaning 'turn (s.th./s.o.) into a table'. Of course, as things seldom become tables this is virtually never found in actual conversations and was only accepted by speakers in the context of fairy tales. Crucially, however, once a proper context had been found it was accepted in predicative function. Similarly, Bodding comments on this topic for Santali:

> "The use of a word may restrict its application to a certain class; in this way a word may become practically a noun or an adjective, &c., according to our terminology. It should not, however, be forgotten that this is the result of the general employment of the word. The nature of a Santal word, as here described, is never lost. The possibility of a manifold use is always there." (Bodding, 1929: 6)

Finally, the following regularities with respect to the predicative use of lexemes and lexical phrases which refer, or can refer, to material entities should be noted:

- This is a *fully productive process*. That is, what we observe here is not a sporadic but interesting use of "nouns as verbs", which could conceivably occur in any language. Rather *any* lexeme, pro-form or "NP" can occur as a predicate.
- Closely connected to this is the issue of *predictability*. The meaning of the predicative use of these typical "NPs" is not idiosyncratic. Any predicate which can denote a material entity *X* means 'become X' in the middle voice and 'make (s.th.) X' in the active voice; any "NP" denoting a location or direction *X* means 'go to X' in the middle voice and 'move (s.th.) to X' in the active. Similarly, a genitive-case "noun" means 'become X's' in the middle voice and 'make (s.th.) X's' in the active voice.[6] The fact that the semantics of the predicative/non-predicative use are not idiosyncratic but fully predictable also suggests that this phenomenon cannot simply be relegated to the lexicon. This is a very different situation than we find e.g. in English, where many, if not most, nominal roots may also be used predicatively, although the meaning of the predicative form is often highly idiosyncratic, such as to *table (a proposal)* or *chair (a meeting)* (examples from Graham Katz, p.c.).
- Finally, as the English translations suggest, these predicates are *dynamic predicates*. They may allow for a stative interpretation, as with the predicative use of *bimar* 'sick' in the following (non-elicited) example.

---

[6] As we shall see below in section 5.1, the same is also true in the other direction when lexemes denoting actions and changes of state are used as complements of a predicate. Here as well the meanings of these forms are completely predictable.

For further functions of the active and middle, cf. Peterson (in press).

(12) *bimar-ta$^{?}$jD-iñ*
sick-M.PROG-1S

'I am/am feeling/am getting sick.'

Nevertheless, they *always* also allow for a dynamic interpretation, which is in fact the unmarked interpretation. To denote a purely stative situation, the free-standing form (see 5.1 below) plus the copula must be used. The corresponding stative form of (12) would be (13), which cannot have a dynamic interpretation.

(13) *bimar* *ai$^{?}$jD-iñ.*
sick NPT.COP-1S

'I am sick.'

We will return to this issue below in section 5, after having shown the structure of complements and predicates in more detail.

4. Lexical and functional heads: an alternative to "noun" and "verb"

Having claimed, and hopefully also successfully shown, that assuming the presence of nouns and verbs in Kharia leads to a number of problems, I present in this section an alternative in which I argue that predicates and their complements are structurally very similar: Both consist of two parts, a lexical head, which need not be a single word but may also contain attributes and one or more specifiers, as well as a functional head. It is the functional head which differentiates between predicates and their complements, and it is only the functional head which differs for the two types. I begin in 4.1 with a discussion of complements of predicates and proceed to show in 4.2 that the same basic structure holds for predicates as well.

4.1 The complement of a predicate

With the term "complement" I refer here both to the arguments of a predicate, i.e., those elements which are required by the predicate, as well as adjuncts, i.e., those elements (excluding postpositional phrases) whose presence is not required by the predicate but which only present further information on location, manner, time, etc.

Complements of a predicate have the following basic form:

LEXHEAD(-NUM)(-CASE)

"LEXHEAD", the lexical head, can be any type of lexical form. It can consist of a simple lexical form, or this basic lexical form may be modified by a (genitive, quantifying or demonstrative) specifier, or by another lexeme. The only condition is that there be some kind of LEXHEAD.

It is not necessary that the semantic head be explicitly mentioned if its identity is sufficiently clear from the context, as long as some other part of the LEXHEAD is present. In this case, the markers for number and case simply attach to the right-most element of the LEXHEAD, regardless of its status. In (14) the semantic head is not overtly mentioned. If it were mentioned, it would be *lebu* 'person' but, as this is clear from the context, it may be omitted. That is, markers for number and case attach to the lexical head at the phrase-level, not at the word-level.[7]

(14) *munuʔsing* *rochob-aʔ-ki*
west side-GEN-P

'the westerners' (i.e., '[people] of the west')

As number and case markers, i.e., the functional head, can attach to any element provided that it is the final element of the lexical head, it is clear that these markers are not suffixes. However, they are more tightly attached to the element preceding them than, for example, the enclitic topic marker =*ga*: The enclitic marker may attach to any word or phrase and may appear more than once within the lexical head. As we shall see in 4.2, it can also appear in both the lexical head as well as within the functional head of the predicate and thus has a very different, much freer distribution than number and case markers. I will therefore treat number and case markers as suffixes, separated from their host by the hyphen "-", although it is important to remember that their status is actually somewhere in between that of suffixes and enclitics. This structure can be summarized schematically as in Diagram 1, followed by an example in Diagram 2. Solid lines in the diagram indicate obligatory components, such as the lexical and functional heads, whereas the dotted line (and the name in parentheses) indicates that these terms are not obligatory. If there is no overt functional head, the values "singular" and "direct case", both unmarked or "zero-marked", are assigned by default, as in the second

[7] Note that there are also markers of inalienable possession which directly follow the last element of the lexical base but precede number and case markers: *aba-Dom* 'father-3POSS' 'his/her father', *beʔT-Dom-ki-te* 'son-3POSS-P-OBL' 'their sons (as object)'. At the moment I do not have enough data to decide whether these should be considered part of the lexical head or part of the functional head. On the other hand, case and number markers clearly belong to the functional head (see below, (15) and (16)).

example in Diagram 2.

The Kleene star on the lexical base (*) indicates that any number of lexical bases is allowed, including zero: There can be none, as in (14), or more than one, when the lexical head is modified by a lexical attribute (i.e., "adjective", see section 5). Finally, the sign "+" indicates that any number of occurrences of the lexical head is possible, as long as there is at least one. This allows structures corresponding to the English noun phrase <u>*those three green chairs of mine*</u> *and* <u>*these six brown tables of yours*</u>, which in the present analysis has two LEXHEADs, underlined in this example. GEN-PART and GEN-POSS refer to partitive and possessive genitives, respectfully. Finally, "⇐" denotes the enclitic/suffixal status of the functional head.

Incidentally, in this scheme the SPECifier *cannot* be considered a functional head, as the lexical head would then contain a functional head which is inherently associated with the complement of a predicate. It is the *functional head to the right* which signals the status of the phrase as either a predicate or a complement, and as we shall see in the next section, SPEC can appear in both predicates and complements. In other words, in this analysis I am forced to reject the notion of a DP for Kharia. Instead, the specifier has a purely semantic/pragmatic function, that of (deictic / anaphoric / cataphoric) reference.[8]

Diagram 1: The maximal possible complement structure (simplified) in Kharia[9]

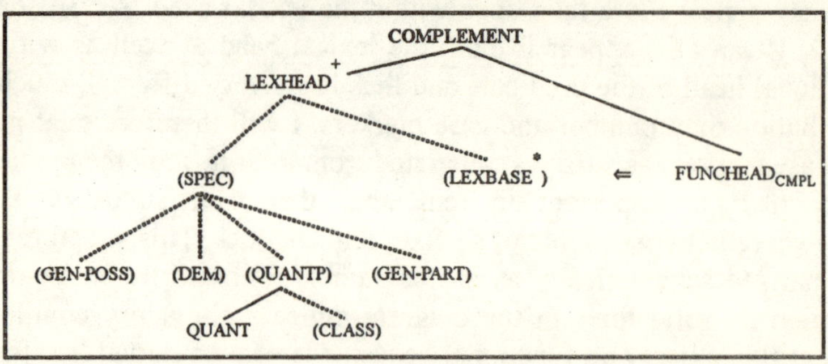

---

[8] One could perhaps argue that it is a special type of adjunct, as it is not obligatory. The problem with this analysis is of course that SPEC is not an adjunct in the usual sense of the word – although various "specifiers" in the broadest sense of the term may co-occur, the number and type of specifiers is strongly restricted. This topic will be dealt with in a later study.

[9] Actually, this structure has been slightly simplified here and does not take predicative attribution (or "relative clauses") into consideration. This is only for the sake of brevity and the inclusion of predicative attribution, before the (SPEC) position, would not significantly alter the diagram or analysis. For examples of predicative attribution, see Peterson (in press).

Diagram 2: Examples for the structure of complements

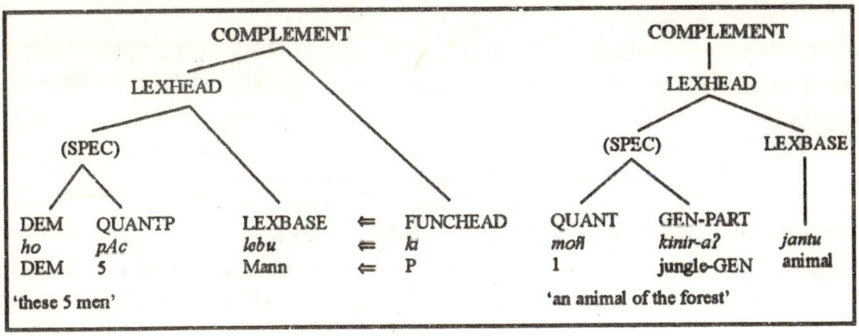

Finally, number and case markers belong to the functional head, not to the lexical head, otherwise they would be of no hindrance in forming predicates such as the following:

(15) *<u>*sahar-te*</u>*-ki-ñ.*
city-OBL-M.PT-1S

'I went to the city.'

(16) *<u>*ubar*</u> <u>*rochoʔb-kiyar*</u>*-ki-ñ.*
2 side-D-M.PT-1S

'I moved to both sides.' (cf. (6))

Recall from the discussion above (examples (4) and (5)) that lexical bases marked for the genitive may be used predicatively, although, as (15) shows, the same is not true of the oblique case. The reason for the different treatment of the two morphologically marked cases appears to be straight-forward: The oblique marker *-te* marks an entire complement, which plays a role – either as argument or adjunct – at the clause level. The genitive-marked phrase on the other hand occurs WITHIN the lexical head – it is not relevant at the clause level but is comparable to any other attribute in this respect, such as the so-called "adjectives" (see section 5), all of which can also serve as predicates. Similar comments then hold for number marking: An element marked for number is automatically marked as an element at the clause level and cannot be part of a lexical base.[10]

[10] Incidentally, this provides further evidence for considering the genitive-marked elements in examples (8) – (11) part of the predicate, and not "genitive objects". If they were clause-level arguments, then the genitive would be a clause-level marker and one would not expect a genitive-marked phrase to be able to serve as the lexical base of a predicate, although (4) and (5) clearly demonstrate that it can.

4.2 The predicate

The structure of a predicate can similarly be portrayed as consisting of a lexical head and markers for predication (= functional head). The basic formula is:

LEXHEAD **(V2)(-PERF)-TAM/VOICE-PERS/NUM/HON**

Here as well "LEXHEAD" can be any type of lexical form. Again the only condition is that there be some kind of LEXHEAD. Also, as with the complements, the functional markers attach to the base at the phrase-level, not at the word-level, but there is a slight difference here.

"V2", often referred to as "explicator verb", denotes markers for categories such as the passive, benefactive, continuative, sequential converbs ("conjunctive participles"), etc., which may stand between the lexical head and the other functional markers, beginning with the perfect. Some of these, such as the anticipatory telic marker *Doʔ D*, which denotes telicity and that something else happened immediately after the event it marks, are homophonous with lexical forms, in this case *Doʔ D* 'take'. However, unlike in most other South Asian languages, the large majority of these markers are not (or are no longer) homophonous with any lexical elements.[11]

V2s may all be considered (grammatical) words since they have their own accent and may be separated from the stem and from each other by enclitic markers such as *=ga* 'FOC', as (17) shows. This is not true of the markers to the right of the V2, beginning with the perfect marker *-siʔ(D)* (cf. example (18).

(17)	*Doko=ga*	*goʔ D-ki-Ø.*
	sit.down=FOC	C:TEL-M.PT-S

'S/he sat down.'

(18)	**Doko*	*goʔ D=ga*	*ki-Ø / *Doko = ga*	*ki-Ø / *Doko = ga*	*siʔ-Ø*
	sit.down	C:TEL=FOC	M.PT-S sit.down=FOC	M.PT-S sit.down=FOC	PERF-S

The markers for the remaining grammatical categories, beginning with the perfect marker, have a status somewhere between that of enclitics and suffixes, similar to that of number and case in complements (see section 4.1). The schematic structure of the predicate given in

[11] An example of a V2 which is no longer homophonous with a lexical form but which may be assumed to have once been used as a lexical base is the ambulative V2 *san*. E.g., the root *sanggoʔ D* 'walk' is obviously connected to this V2 and originally derives from an earlier root **san* 'go' (cf. Santali *sɛn* 'go') and the culminatory telic marker *goʔ D*.

Diagram 3 thus has the exact same structure as the complement of a predicate, given above in Diagram 1, with the exception of course of the type of functional head. Diagram 4 provides two examples of this structure.

Having shown that a division of the lexicon into "nouns" and "verbs" is problematic in Kharia and suggested an alternative, I will now take a look at attribution and its expression in Kharia, restricting myself for the sake of brevity to attributes of complements, although the same comments also apply to attributes of predicates and of clauses. I will show that, at least from a purely structural point of view, there is in fact no need for a class of "adjectives" in Kharia.

Diagram 3: The maximal possible predicate structure (simplified) in Kharia

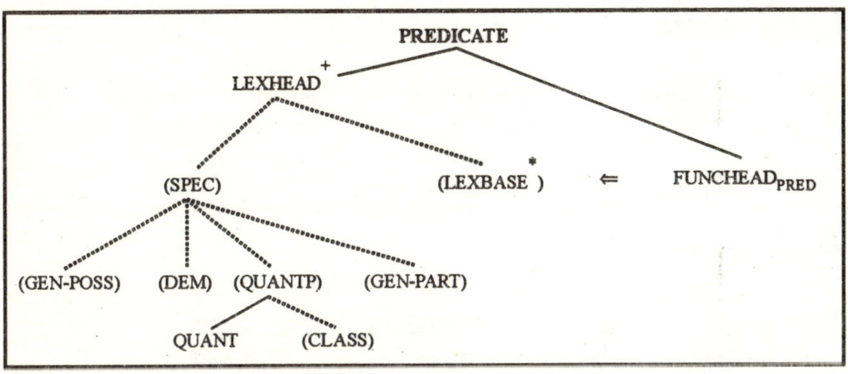

Diagram 4: Examples for the structure of predicates

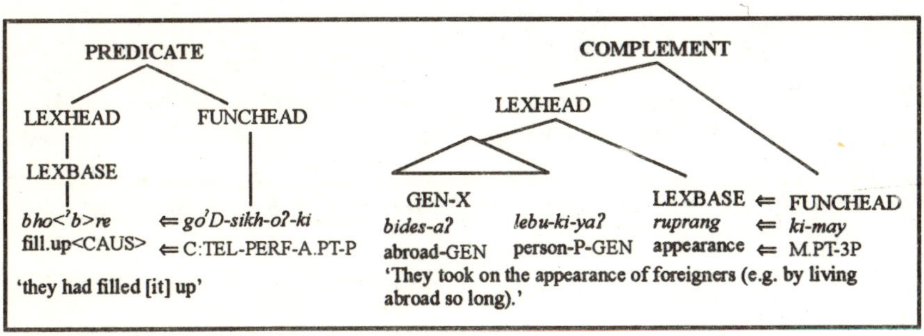

5. Attributes and (potentially) free-standing lexemes

If one uses only morphosyntactic criteria as a guide to determining parts-of-speech, then there is no evidence for a separate class of adjectives in Kharia. Instead, "nouns", finite predicates, as well as "participles" and "nominalized" forms, are found in attributive function.

"Nouns"

(19)	*manus*	*jati*	'humanity'	*iskul*	*koʔghel*
	man	caste		school	vicinity
	Daʔ	*piyas*	'thirst'	'the vicinity of the school'	
	water	hunger			

Finite predicate

(20)	*iñ*	*yo-y-oˀj*	***lebu-ki***	*iñ-aʔ*	*hoTel-te*	*aw-ta-ki.*
	1S	see-y-A.PT.1S	person-P	1S-GEN	hotel-OBL	live-M.NPT-P

'**The people** *I saw* live in my hotel.'

"Participles"[12]

(21)	*iñ-aʔ*	*likha*	***phonTen-te***	*kuy-oˀj.*
	1S-GEN	write	pen-OBL	find-A.PT.1S

'I found **the pen** *I had written with*.'

"Nominalized" Forms

(22)	*khaRiya-ki*	*ber-aʔ*	*ji<ni>b*	***peʔ=jo***	*umay*	*ñoʔ-na*	*laʔ-ki, …*
	Kharia-P	who-GEN	touch-<NML>	rice=ADD	NEG.3P	eat-INF	IPFV-M.PT

'The Kharia did not use to eat **rice** *which had been touched by anyone*, …'

[adapted from Pinnow, 1965: 122]

[12] There are other forms which seem to be participles in Kharia, marked by *-l*. This suffix is only found with predicates ending in *-a(y)*, all of which have been borrowed from Sadani, e.g. *likha-l* 'written' from *likha* 'write'. This form is not accepted by all speakers and it is clear that it has been borrowed – along with the lexeme – directly from Sadani. In the following I will not deal with this marginal form but concentrate on the other forms which are acceptable to, and used by, all speakers.

Let us now take a closer look at the "participles" and "nominalized" forms, as the issue of "nouns" and "verbs" has already been dealt with. In the following I will show that these two forms are merely free-standing forms, which in Kharia are subject to the bisyllabic constraint.

5.1 (Potentially) Free-standing lexemes

Every finite predicate in Kharia has a potentially free-standing form which lacks all TAM and person marking, although it may contain valency-related marking (such as passive, causative, etc.). It may govern an object, which then takes the same marking it would have with a finite predicate, but what corresponds to the subject of the finite predicate appears in the genitive. The free-standing form may also mark for case and number.

It is formed as follows: Polysyllabic stems (= root and derivational markers) undergo no changes, while monosyllabic stems are reduplicated. Thus this type of reduplication is purely phonologically motivated. Some examples can be found in Table 3. As already noted, this form can be followed by case and number markers (including "zero-marking") and functions as the complement of a predicate. The "subject" is then a genitive attribute, as in (23).

Table 3: Examples of simple roots and free-standing forms in Kharia

Simple root	(Potentially) Free-standing form
absiˀb 'begin'	*absiˀb*
aw 'stay; COP'	*aw-aw*
borol 'live'	*borol*
bu̯ʔ 'beat (a drum)'	*buʔ-buʔ*
likha 'write'	*likha* (cf. example (21))
ruʔ 'open'	*ruʔ-ruʔ*
ter 'give'	*ter-ter*
yo 'see'	*yo-yo*

(23) *enem* *raja ro rani-kiyar-aʔ aw-aw-te* *khaRiya-ki*
without king and queen-D-GEN COP-RDP-OBL Kharia-P

kaTiˀj=ko *Dher=ga* *akbakay-ki-may.*
somewhat=CNTR very=FOC be.in.a.flurry-M.PT-3P

'Without there being a king and queen, the Kharia panicked.'
[MT, 1: 104]

As we have seen above, any form which can function as a complement can also be used predicatively, thus like any complement in Kharia, the "free-standing" form can also serve as the lexical base of a predicate and is thus only *potentially* free-standing. When used predicatively, only the middle voice is found, never the active and the meaning is that of a habitual action (NOT iterative!) which is conducted for an almost indefinite period:

(24) *iñ* *Daʔ* *biTh-oʔj.* (UNMARKED)
1S water pour.out-A.PT.1S

'I poured the water out.'[13]

(25) *iñ* *Daʔ* *biʔD-biʔD-ki-ñ*
1S water pour.out-RDP-M.PT-1S (MARKED)

'I poured the water out over and over.'

Example (25) has more or less the meaning 'I poured it out over and over, for years and years (e.g. that was my job)', almost as if one were to say in English 'I was a water-pourer.' The difference seems to be only that the English form is stative, whereas the Kharia form is not.[14]

The free-standing form is also used attributively. In fact, from a purely morphosyntactic point of view, it is best to consider "adjectives" in Kharia to be nothing more than free-standing forms:

Table 4: Free-standing forms and "adjectives"

Simple (bound) root	Free-standing form	"Adjective + noun"
konon '(become) small'	*konon*	*konon bhai* 'little brother'
maha '(become) big'	*maha*	*maha daru* 'big tree'
ruʔ '(become) open'	*ruʔ-ruʔ*	*ruʔ-ruʔ kaʔbTo* 'open door'
rusung '(become) red'	*rusung*	*rusung oʔ* 'red house'

This is even true of "basic adjectives" such as *sang-sang* 'yellow', which has however now been largely replaced by the Sadani loan word

---

[13] All root-final plosives are regularly devoiced and aspirated before the active past suffix *-oʔ*, thus the root-final *D* in *biʔD* regularly becomes *Th* in the active past.
[14] Although the Kharia construction obviously exploits the fact that the free-standing form is usually a stative form (see below, examples (30) and (31) to denote habituality.

piyar, although it is still commonly used with the meaning 'turmeric'. For example, it is still found in Floor et al. (1934: 112), given with the meaning 'turmuric [sic!], yellow'.

Table 5: *sang-sang* 'yellow; turmeric'

Root	Free-standing form	"Adjective"
sang '(become) yellow'	*sang-sang*	*sang-sang* 'yellow; turmeric'

This bisyllabicity is typical of ALL lexemes used attributively, with the exception of a few high-frequency loan words from Sadani, e.g. *bes* '(become) good', *khus* '(become) happy' or *lil* '(become) blue'. In fact, it is true of *complements* in general and there is no reason, other than the English translation, for differentiating between attributive forms and complements. In other words, every free-standing form may be used attributively (cf. example (19)), and can also be the only lexical base, to which number and case markers attach. This is shown in the following example.

(26) *aning* *na* *tar-e-ning* *na* *tar-tar-te* *yo-ye-ning.*
1P.INCL NEG kill-A.IRR-1P.INCL NEG kill-RDP-OBL see-A.IRR-1P.INCL

ina *laRe-na-ning?*
why fight-M.IRR-1P.INCL

'We should neither kill nor should we watch killing. Why should we fight?' [MS, 1: 210]

Here, the lexeme *tar* 'kill', which refers to an action and is used predicatively in (26) (*tarening* 'we should kill'), is also found in the same sentence used as a complement, 'the act of killing', which is the object of the predicate *yoyening* 'we should watch'.

This is the reason that in Diagrams 1 and 3 above we find the lexical base given as "(LEXBASE*)" with the Kleene star – the only difference between the semantic head and any other lexemes is that the semantic head is of course more basic, semantically speaking, than the other lexemes, which serve to modify it. But from a morphosyntactic point of view, these are simply juxtaposed words. Whether or not these refer to actions (e.g. 'go'), changes of state (e.g. 'become red') or physical entities (e.g. 'table') is unimportant and all free-standing forms can function both as the lexical head of a complement or as a modifier of such a head.

Potentially free-standing forms have no inherent orientation with respect to subject, object, instrument, locative, etc., nor with respect to tense, as shown in (27) – (29). Recall that *iñ-aʔ* in (27) and (28) appears in the genitive as it is the "subject" of the free-standing form, not because of what would appear to be the head nominal (*lebu* and *kuñji*, respectively). The structure of (27) – (30) is thus parallel to that of (23).

(27)

iñ-aʔ	*yo-yo*	**lebu**
1S-GEN	see-RDP	person

'**the person** I saw / see / will see'

(28)

iñ-aʔ	*dura-te*	*ruʔ-ruʔ*	**kuñji**
1S-GEN	door-OBL	open-RDP	key

'**the key** I opened/open/will open the door with'

(29)

iñ-te	*yo-yo*	**lebu**
1S-OBL	see-RDP	person

'**the person** who saw / sees / will see me'

This lack of temporal or other orientation is of course to be expected if one recalls that these forms are not participles but rather potential complements in attributive function. Their meaning, which is entirely predictable and depends on the underlying *Aktionsart*, is that of '(having become) X' with changes of state, e.g. *rusung* '(having become) red', *maha* '(having become) big' or 'the act of X-ing' with actions, such as *yo-yo* 'the act of seeing', *ruʔ-ruʔ* 'the act of opening', etc. It seems that this form is preferred in Kharia when the action referred to is either already known or the speaker believes that the hearer will treat it as known information,[15] although this remains to be studied in detail. When it is new information, it appears that the fully finite form, shown in (20), is used.

The free-standing form, when used predicatively with the copula, is also the only means of denoting a purely stative predicate in Kharia. In the nonpast there are two copulas. The use of the copula *heke* denotes an inherent property, while the use of *aiˀj* denotes a non-inherent property, such as location.

(30)

lekin	*khaRiya*	*lang*	*iswar-aʔ*	*ter-ter*	*heke-Ø*.
but	Kharia	language	Lord-GEN	give-RDP	NPT.COP-S

[15] E.g., what Lambrecht (1994) refers to as "accommodated" information.

'But the Kharia language <u>is a gift of the Lord</u> (= <u>is a Lord's given</u>).' [MS, 1: 267]

(31)

Dera	*<u>kui-kui</u>*	*<u>ai$^{?}$j-Ø</u>.*
abode	find-RDP	NPT.COP-S

'A place to live <u>has been (= is) found</u> (i.e., we have found an apartment).'

Finally, although comparatives and superlatives are usually considered a sure indication of "adjective-hood", in Kharia the same construction may be used with what corresponds to both adjectives and nouns in English, provided that the concept in question is scalar. For example, comparatives and superlatives in Kharia have the typical South Asian SMA-structure (Standard-Marker-Attribute) and are formed by placing the standard first, followed by an ablative postposition, either *se* or *tay* 'from', with the scalar word following this. The only difference between the two is that the standard in the superlative construction is virtually always *sou$^{?}$b* 'all'. Consider the following two examples:

(32)

simRa	***<u>sou$^{?}$b</u>***	***<u>se</u>***	***<u>maha</u>***	***<u>be$^{?}$T-Dom</u>***
Simra	all	ABL	big	son-3POSS

'Simra, **<u>the eldest brother</u>**' [AK, 1: 71]

(33)

<u>sou$^{?}$b</u>	***<u>se</u>***	***<u>suru-te</u>***	*ponmesor*	*ap*	*aw-ki-Ø.*
all	ABL	beginning-OBL	God	Father	COP-M.PT-S

'**<u>In the very beginning</u>** there was God the Father.'

5.2 The "nominalizer" *-nV-*

There is also an older infixing process which is no longer productive but which is found with ca. 50 different lexemes. Here, the infix *-nV-* is inserted into the root, where *-V-* has the same quality as the vowel preceding *-n-*. Table 6 gives a few examples. Note that the resulting semantics are not entirely predictable in the "nominalized" form, unlike the free-standing form discussed above.

Table 6: Examples of simple roots and "nominalized" forms

Simple root	"Nominalized" form
bel 'spread out (a mat or bedspread)'	*be<ne>l* 'bedding'
bui 'raise (an animal)'	*bu<nu>i* 'pig'
Deˀj 'chop'	*De<ne>ˀj* '(large) hatchet'
jiˀb 'touch' (v.)	*ji<ni>ˀb* 'touch (n.), touching'
peˀD 'blow (a pipe)'	*pe<Ne> ˀD* 'large fife or flute'
sel 'pray'	*se<ne>l* 'prayer; pray'
uʔphe 'three'	*u<nu>ʔphe* 'three each'

This affix, which is found in many Austro-Asiatic languages, might be considered a nominalizer, although forms such as *uʔphe* / *u<nu>ʔphe* 'three / three each' call this into question. Also, in some cases, such as *sel*, the infixed form *se<ne>l* has now virtually replaced the non-infixed form in both functions, although *sel* is still found in the texts in Pinnow (1965). Speakers I questioned rejected it, however, even in predicative function. Finally, as (22) shows, the infixed form may also be used attributively.

5.3 Bimoraicity, bisyllabicity and free-standing forms

In their recent study Anderson & Zide (2002) present evidence from a large number of Austro-Asiatic languages, both Munda and non-Munda, which strongly suggests that Proto-Munda, and probably Proto-Austro-Asiatic, had what they refer to as the "Bimoraic Constraint" which required nouns to contain at least two morae. They write: "A minimally bimoraic shape appears to have been obligatory for free-forms of nouns [as opposed to compound forms, JP] in Proto-Munda and many of its daughter languages, which necessitated (and in Gtaʔ continues to necessitate) the combining of the root element with some derivational process (in particular, prefixation, infixation, reduplication, compounding, or suffixation." (Anderson & Zide, 2002: 55). In their definition, a mora is linked to any one of the following: 1. any vocalic nucleus, 2. a consonant in word-initial position before another consonant, and 3. a post-vocalic [ʔ] in final position (in some languages).

The data they list in tables (3) and (4) of their study (Anderson & Zide, 2002: 57f.) clearly indicate that Kharia also had this bimoraic constraint for free-standing "nouns" and that at least the following three means were employed to make a monomoraic form bimoraic: 1. The glottal stop, cf. Kharia *tiʔ* 'hand' with Juang *iti*, Gtaʔ *titi*, etc. (but also Santali *ti*); 2. reduplication, cf. Kharia *sang-sang* 'turmeric' vs. Gutob *sasang*, Gtaʔ *ssia*, and 3. the infix *-n-* (here referred to as *-nV-*, see section 5.2).[16] Thus, assuming a syllable with the structure CV by way of example, deriving a bimoraic structure in Kharia results in one of the following structures: 1. CVʔ, 2. CV-CV, 3. CV-*n*-V.

Finally, and quite importantly, the authors note that each language subject to the bimoraic constraint may have generalized a particular derivational element in order to fulfill the bimoraic constraint (Anderson & Zide, 2002: 56). As have seen, in Kharia reduplication has become virtually the only means of deriving free-standing forms, although there are clear traces of other strategies, most notably the -*nV*-infix.

Although I agree entirely with Anderson & Zide's hypothesis that a bimoraic constraint held in Proto-Munda, I believe a slight change has taken place in Kharia so that the bimoraic constraint is not descriptively adequate for the modern language. Kharia strongly disfavors monosyllabic words, and I believe that reduplication and infixing, two of the language-specific strategies Anderson & Zide (2002) refer to, are derivational strategies predominantly used to avoid monosyllabic words. Thus, the *bimoraic* constraint on free-standing forms in Proto-Munda, and undoubtedly also in Proto-Kharia, has given way to a *bisyllabic* constraint on free-standing forms in modern Kharia. The difference between the two in Kharia is only noticeable in one form: Syllables with the form CVʔ are monosyllabic but bimoraic. Thus, in earlier stages of Kharia a bimoraic syllable like *ruʔ* 'open' would have counted as a free-standing form but in the modern language it must be "strengthened", i.e., it must be made bisyllabic, preferably through reduplication, e.g., *ruʔ-ruʔ* 'the act of opening'.

Due to the structure of the language, this constraint applies only to complements of predicates in Kharia: As the markers which signal complements (number and case) may both be lacking (or "zero morphemes"), a monosyllabic word could result, which should be avoided. This is never possible with a finite predicate, which is always overtly marked for at least one grammatical category (cf. again Tables 1 and 2) and, with that, is always at least bisyllabic. As such, there is no need to "strengthen" predicates by adding a second syllable, whether through reduplication or, in the older language, through the infix -*nV*-.

As a simple example, consider the following:

---

16 Another means referred to by the authors is the "potentially non-random patterning in Kharia of the prefix *kon-* in words referring to small animals or words roughly falling into a category of 'diminutive' or 'affectionate'; ..." (Anderson & Zide, 2002: 56). However I believe that – as the authors' quote implies – the use of *kon-* was restricted to cases referring to a small entity. As such, although it *could* fulfill the bimoraic constraint, as it effectively creates a second syllable and thereby adds one mora to the base, it was not primarily motivated by this constraint but rather simply compatible with it. See also the derivation of *konDeʔj* 'hatchet' below.

De^{ʔ}j 'chop',	**kon* '(become) small',	*konDe^{ʔ}j* 'small hatchet'
De<ne>^{ʔ}j '(large) hatchet'	*ko<no>n* '(become) small'	

**kon*, no longer productive, is found in a number of old compounds: *kongher* 'young man', *konrakhiya* 'teenage-boy', *konsel* 'young woman', *konDuʔ* 'child', etc. However, when it is not part of a compound, i.e., when it is a separate word, **kon* had to be "strengthened" by adding a syllable, in this case through the *-nV-* infix, yielding the free form *ko<no>n*, which in the modern language has now completely ousted **kon* in predicative and attributive function.[17]

This is shown most clearly in a comparison of the two words for 'hatchet': When speaking of a small hatchet, **kon* was part of a compound with the root *De^{ʔ}j*, yielding a two-syllable word, *kon-De^{ʔ}j*, literally 'small-chop', which did not need to be strengthened. However, when not speaking about a small hatchet but rather a normal-sized or large hatchet, **kon* was obviously not included in the word formation, resulting in the monosyllabic **De^{ʔ}j*, which was thus strengthened to *De<ne>^{ʔ}j* through the *-nV-* infix. The modern language clearly prefers reduplication, but both strategies result in bisyllabic words. However, reduplication in the modern language has a somewhat different function than the *-nV*-infix appears to have had. Note that while the *-nV*-infix derives free-standing forms whose semantics are largely unpredictable (cf. once again Table 6), reduplication is *entirely* predictable, e.g. *ter* 'give', *ter-ter* '(the act of) giving' vs. *te<ne>r* 'generosity, grace; gift'. Thus it could well be that Proto-Kharia had both nouns and verbs with overt derivational morphology to derive one set from the other, predominantly through *-nV*-infixation, yielding semantically unpredictable forms, whereas in the modern language reduplication is a purely phonemic filter, ensuring the bisyllabicity of free-standing forms, and is absolutely productive and predictable.

There are of course exceptions to the rule of bisyllabicity:

lang 'tongue' *moʔ* 'smoke' *mo^{ʔ}D* 'eye' *seʔ* 'louse' *tiʔ* 'hand'

---

[17] As the following shows, *konon* has now spread to predicative functions: After hitting my head several times in Simdega on low doors while entering cars, buses or people's homes, a friend of mine began saying to me jokingly, before we were to enter a house:

konon-na-bar!	'Become small! / Make yourself small!'
become.small-M.IRR-2HON	

As *konon* is undoubtedly much more common in attributive function than in predicative function, it is easy to imagine that the free-standing form, used in attribution, has generalized to the predicative function as well, especially since the infix *-nV-* is no longer productive.

However these exceptions are exceedingly few in number and, incidentally, very common words, which in any language tend to be somewhat irregular. Also, as markers for inalienable possession may have been more common in the older language than in modern Kharia (cf. Malhotra, 1982: 101, 356), it may well be that at least those monosyllabic complements which refer to body parts once obligatorily appeared with a marker of inalienable possession. Hence, there would have been no need to "strengthen" these forms through infixation or reduplication. This topic requires further study.[18]

6. Summary and conclusions

For the language of those speakers who accept sentences of the type in examples (2) – (11) as grammatical, assuming the presence of parts-of-speech as lexical classes in Kharia causes a number of analytic difficulties which do not lend themselves to any easy solution.

I conclude that the lexicon consists merely of two classes, open and closed. The open class consists of lexical morphemes, roughly those morphemes referring to entities and events in "the real world", whereas the closed class consists merely of grammatical morphemes. Interestingly, within the closed group we do find a further differentiation into parts-of-speech: Demonstratives, classifiers, postpositions, V2s, etc., but no similar division can be shown for the open class.

Some members of the closed class, such as the demonstratives, combine in a regular way with lexical morphemes to form a functionally underspecified LEXICAL HEAD. Whether this functions as a predicate or as the complement of a predicate in a particular clause is indicated by the markers to the right of the phrase, which I term the FUNCTIONAL HEAD. It is this functional head which signals the function of the phrase in the clause and which attaches to the final element of the lexical head, regardless of its status. This is shown schematically in Diagram 5.

With respect to semantics, it is important to note that there is a distinct preference for physical entities to be used as complements of a predicate and less seldom as a predicate, unless they combine with a copula (with either the meaning 'be' or 'become') or some other "light verb", such as *karay* 'do', in imitation of the Indo-Aryan construction. This was, in fact, the criterion that distinguished the small group of speakers I worked with who accepted predicates such as those found above in section 3 from those who did not. But even those speakers who accepted sentences such as (2b) were quick to add that, while not wrong,

[18] Interestingly, most of the irregular forms given here are bimoraic, although they are not bisyllabic.

the predictive use of such lexemes is not common. In other words, they also had a certain aversion to lexemes which can refer to physical entities being used as predicates, although they did accept them as grammatical. On the other hand, there is no similar restriction for lexemes denoting an action from being used as complements, provided that they are bisyllabic.

Diagram 5: Common maximal structure (simplified) of complements and predicates in Kharia

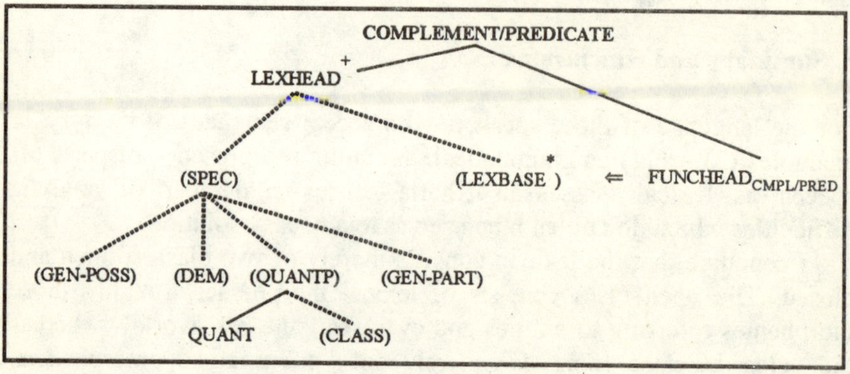

This asymmetry is hardly surprising when one considers the meaning of predicates based on lexemes which refer to physical entities: 'become X'. In the real world, things don't tend to 'become a table' or 'become a television', hence predicates of this type, although in theory possible, were often rejected without further consideration, but when placed in the context of fairy tales they were accepted. This is clearly connected to convention: For events which commonly take place, there is no question of the acceptability of a particular lexeme as a predicate, but for events which are only theoretically possible – or even impossible – it comes as no surprise that speakers were reluctant to accept such examples, just as most speakers of English would probably reject sentences such as *I became those three tables*, which is "grammatical", although it is at best highly unusual.

In sum, NOUNS and VERBS, like TENSE and GRAMMATICAL GENDER, are grammatical categories based, more-or-less loosely, on the semantic categories of REFERENCE, PREDICATION, TIME and NATURAL GENDER, respectively. Just as not all languages have tense or grammatical gender, there is no logical reason that all languages should have nouns and verbs. Of course, just as any language can refer to time and natural gender even if it does not have tense or grammatical gender, so too can every language express reference and predication even if it does not have nouns and verbs, and I believe Kharia is such a language.

However, it should also be stressed here that Kharia nonetheless has two *grammatical categories*, predicates and their complements, which are (loosely) based on predication and reference, but there are at least two crucial differences between these and nouns and verbs, at least as these terms are usually employed:

- These categories in Kharia (i.e., predicates and complements) are not LEXICAL categories but are clearly PHRASAL in nature.
- These phrases are not endocentric, hence we are not dealing merely with NPs and "verbal phrases" in Kharia. In other words, this is not just a discussion of nouns and verbs "moved up" one syntactic notch from the word level to the phrase level.
- For example, calling the predicate e.g. in (6b) a verbal phrase overlooks the fact that its semantic head, *rochoˀb* 'side', is hardly a likely candidate for a verb, as it is preceded by a demonstrative specifier. In the analysis here, *rochoˀb* is simply the last element of the lexical head and *ho* 'that' its specifier. *ho*, as a member of the closed class, belongs to a lexical subclass (demonstrative), but *rochoˀb*, as a member of the open class, does not.

Before concluding, I would like to briefly turn to the discussion in Bhat (1997) and how the Kharia data fit in. Briefly summarized, Bhat notes that, as languages show a great deal of variation with respect to how strongly nominal and verbal classes differ from one another and as to how rigid this distinction is, it seems best to not ask *whether* nouns and verbs exist in a particular language but rather *to what extent* that language differs from his idealized language, one which does not make any distinction between nouns and verbs.

In such an ideal language, reference is expressed through person-number-gender markers on the predicate and the "argument-like structures that occur in the sentence would only have the function of modifying either the nuclear part of the predicate or the elements which occur with it, such as the personal affixes, and also the affixes that denote time, place, manner, etc." (Bhat, 1997: 232). In other words, in this construct overtly expressed complements only serve to further modify the elements marked on the predicate.

This approach has one major advantage, namely that there is no longer any need to find a language in which there are no signs of nouns and verbs, but rather the question should merely be to what extent the language in question differs from this ideal. "That is, the usually raised question as to whether there can be any language that does not make any distinction between nouns and verbs becomes irrelevant. Further, the discovery of additional differentiating characteristics (between nouns and verbs) in any given language would not make it necessary to discard the original assumption; it would only make it necessary to reassign that language to a less closer position" (Bhat, 1997: 247).

As intuitively appealing as Bhat's suggestion is, if I understand it correctly, Kharia does not seem to fit well into this scheme. Unlike the North Munda languages Bhat deals with in his study which mark for subject, object and a few other clausal constituents, Kharia marks only the subject on the predicate: There is no marking for objects or any other entities, although Kharia does have predicates which require an object, i.e., an obligatory complement which is marked as either direct case or oblique, depending on its semantics. Hence it is difficult to argue that these overtly expressed complements only modify these elements, as Bhat's construct requires. This would mean that Kharia is quite far removed from Bhat's idealized language, which seems counter-intuitive since in Kharia any lexical morpheme can indeed be (part of) the lexical head of a predicate or complement, which is, after all, the main characteristic of the languages Bhat is describing. Perhaps Bhat's idealized language in which there are no signs of nouns and verbs should be retained as a theoretical construct, but if so it is not entirely clear how this can be defined. Considering all complements of the predicate to be adjuncts may work in some languages with a weak or non-existent noun/verb distinction, but certainly not in all. Clearly, more research on languages like Kharia and other Munda languages is necessary.

Bibliography

Anderson, Gregory D. S. and Norman H. Zide. 2002. "Issues in Proto-Munda and Proto-Austroasiatic nominal derivation: the bimoraic constraint." Marlys A. Macken (ed.), *Papers from the 10th annual meeting of the Southeast Asian Linguistics Society.* Tempe, AZ: Arizona State University, South East Asian Studies Program. (Monograph Series Press) 55-74.

Bhat, D. N. S. 1997. "Noun-verb distinction in Munda languages." Anvita Abbi (ed.), *Languages of tribal and indigenous peoples of India. The ethnic space.* Delhi: Motilal Banarsidass. 227-51.

Bodding, Revd. P.O. 1929. *Materials for a Santali grammar. II. Mostly morphological.* Dumka: Santal Mission of the Northern Churches.

Deeney, J. 1975. *Ho grammar and vocabulary.* Chaibasa: Xavier Ho Publications, St. Xavier's High School.

Floor, H., S. J., V. Gheysens, S. J. and G. Druart, S. J. 1934. *Tea Districts Labour Association. Dictionary of the Kharia language.* Calcutta: Begg, Dunlop & Co., Ltd.

Hoffmann, Revd. J., S. J. 1903. *Mundari grammar and exercises.* [Reprint: New Delhi: Gyan Publishing House, 2001].

Lambrecht, Knud. 1994. *Information Structure and Sentence Form. Topic, Focus and the Mental Representations of Discourse Referents.* Cambridge: Cambridge University Press (Cambridge Language Surveys).

Malhotra, Veena. 1982. *The Structure of Kharia: A study of linguistic typology and language change.* Unpublished Ph.D. dissertation. New Delhi: Jawaharlal Nehru University.

Neukom, Lukas. 2001. *Santali.* München: Lincom Europa. (Languages of the World / Materials, 323).

Peterson, John. in press. *Kharia.* To appear in: Norman H. Zide and Gregory D. S. Anderson (eds.). *The Munda languages.* Routledge: London et al. (Routledge Language Family Series).

Peterson, John. in progress. *Kharia. Grammar, annotated texts and Kharia-English lexicon.*

Pinnow, Heinz-Jürgen. 1965. *Kharia-Texte (Prosa und Poesie). Unter Mitwirkung von Paulus Kerketta und Junas Kullu.* Wiesbaden: Harrassowitz.

Abbreviations

A - active voice
ADD - additive focus
AKT - marker of *Aktionsart*
BEN - benefactive marker
CAUS - causative marker
CLASS - numeral classifier
CMPL - complement
CNTR - contrastive focus
COP - copula
C:TEL - culminatory telic marker
EXCL - exclusive (1/2, non-singular)
FOC - restrictive focus marker
GEN - genitive marker
GEN-PART - partitive genitive
GEN-POSS - possessive genitive
HON - honorific
HUM – human
INCL - inclusive
INF - infinitive marker
IPFV - imperfective
IRR - irrealis
M - middle voice
NEG - negative morpheme
NML - "nominalizer"
NPT - nonpast marker
NUM - number
OBL - oblique marker
P - plural marker
PASS - passive marker
PERF - perfect marker
PERS - person
PT - past marker
QUANT - quantifying determiner
RDP - reduplication (various functions)
REFL - reflexive marker
S - singular
SEQ - sequential converb
TEL - telicity marker
TAM - tense, aspect, mood
-y- non-phonemic glide found in certain phonological environments

PAST MARKERS IN SANTALI: A TYPOLOGY-ORIENTED APPROACH

DMITRI V. SITCHINAVA

The following study is a part of a broader typological investigation of (quasi) synonymous past- and past-like markers (perfect, pluperfect[1], etc.) in the languages of the world. This way of research is particularly interesting for many non-European languages where synonymous tenses are not often described in necessary detail and are presented under misleading terms due to a Eurocentric grammar framework. On the other hand, it is important to point out the common element in their meaning and possible sources of their synonymy. We use the post-structural approach that acknowledges co-existence of multiple synonymous forms achieved during various types of grammar evolution.

Our aim is to characterize the markers of the past tense in Santali. The language (Eastern India [Bihar, Orissa, and West-Bengal] and Bangladesh, about 5.8 million speakers), belonging to the Kherwari group of Munda languages (a branch of Austro-Asiatic), has many properties of interest in a typological framework[2]. "Despite the high number of speakers, the considerable amount of research tradition and the typologically interesting characteristics, Santali has not found much attention in modern Western linguistics", states Lukas Neukom in the preface to his recent work (Neukom 2001: 3) that is perhaps the best description of the language but "is by no means meant to be the last word on Santali" (ibid.).

The main sources of linguistic information on the language are Santali texts, collected in (SFT 1923-1929), grammars (Skrefsrud 1873, Grierson (ed.) 1906/1967, Bodding 1929/1952, Neukom 2001) and also

[1] Following B. Comrie's style (1976, 1985), we capitalize the language-specific grammar categories (e.g. the English *Perfect*), but do not capitalize the cross-linguistic categories (e.g. the *perfect* in the languages of the world).

[2] It should be noted that the other Munda languages/dialects of the Kherwari group have very similar systems of past markers (Pinnow 1966: 121-128), especially the opposition of Aorist **-ki-* vs. Pluperfect (Non-Resultative) **-le-* which dates back even to the Proto-Munda level (ibid.: 144 ff). As far as the details of a system, and especially semantics, are concerned, our study is based only on the Santali material.

Russian studies by Zograf (1960/1990), Lekomtsev (1968), and Friesen (1982). Some results of our previous work on the topic were published in Sitchinava 2001. Since then we have had to reformulate considerably some assessments of that paper, following further typological investigation and considering the material given in the excellent work (Neukom 2001) that appeared later.

In Santali finite verbal forms, the second suffix position ("secondary affixes" in Pinnow 1966: 100) can be occupied by any of five tense-aspect markers[3]:

(1) the zero marker conditioning specific markers of transitivity (Future and Habitual, or the "Non-Past"),
(2) *-e-* (Durative, or Imperfective; zero with intransitive verbs),
(3) *-ke-* ("Simple Past", or Aorist; *-e-* with intransitive verbs),
(4) *-le-* ("Anterior Past", or Pluperfect)
(5) *-aka(wa)-* (Perfect)[4].

The fifth suffix position (or the position of "particles and auxiliaries", according to Pinnow, ibid.) can be occupied by:

-kan-, the marker of Progressive
and/or *-tahe̱~kan-*, a specific Past marker.

In traditional grammars the combinations of the "position II" markers with "position V" markers are treated as markers of different tenses. Friesen (1982), obviously following the Russian grammar framework, examines separately different markers of "tense" and "aspect" and opposes the "imperfective aspect", marked by *-kan-*, to the "perfective aspect" in which Aorist, Perfect, and Pluperfect are included. Neukom (2001) sees the "position V" markers as additional modifiers to the major tense-aspect-marker categories expressed by the "position II" markers. This approach seems the most adequate.

The Perfect *-aka(wa)-* is a complicated category that has prototypical Perfect semantics of a "situation located prior to the reference time, ... its result is still relevant at the reference time" (Neukom 2001: 83). This

---

[3] The tense reinterpretation of the aspectual markers is considered to be an innovation in the history of the Munda languages: "a plausible way is to reconstruct the general Munda verb system is to assume an aspectual orientation <...> a gradual drift towards tense-orientation can be observed in all languages of the family" (Stassen 1997: 552).

[4] In quoting of Santali examples we use Paul O. Bodding's orthography, used in SFT 1923-1929, Bodding 1929/1952 and his Santal Dictionary (partly available online at http://www3.aa.tufs.ac.jp/~mmine/india/Bodding2k/index.html), with some changes following the transcription guideline used in this volume. The orthography of the other sources is unified following this pattern. In glossing the non-verbal forms and affixes we basically follow the labels used in (Neukom 2001).

"current relevance" or "repercussion" of result does not presuppose its material presence (cf. the discussion of perfects in different languages in Dahl 1985: 129-138; Dahl & Hedin 2000). Two more meanings of perfect, well-known cross-linguistically and present in English Perfect as it is described in McCawley 1971 or Comrie 1976: 56 ff, are also to be found in Santali.

There is the resultative (or 'stative' meaning) denoting a present state resulting from a prior action:

(1)	ado	unre	uni	kuRi-do	ona	taben	khAjARi
	then	then	that.AN	girl-TOP	that.INAN	taben	khajari

	motRa-do-e	dipil-aka-t'-a
	bundle-TOP-SUB.3SG	put_on_head-PF-TR-IND

'At the time the girl was carrying the bundle with taben and khajari (species of rice) on her head.' (ibid.: 84)

There is also the experiential meaning, which "expresses that the situation belongs to the subject's experiences" (ibid.: 85).

In earlier descriptions the *-aka*-Perfect is presented rather as a Resultative[5] denoting a present state, than a real Perfect (cf. Maspero 1952: "pour marquer que le résultat de l'action accomplie est durable"). Skrefsrud (1873: 346) shows the resultative meaning of this Perfect (in comparison with Aorist and Pluperfect, in our terminology) using the Santali translation of the Creed, where *duRup'akanae* 'has sat' means that Jesus has seated himself with Father and is still sitting there. In the other contexts, where the present material result is not additionally underscored (*beret' ruARena* 'arose / has arisen-again'), an Aorist form is used. An even clearer opposition: *tolkedeako* (AOR) 'they have tied him' [context: he cannot run away any more now] vs *-ko tolakadea* ("PF") 'they have tied him' [context: if you do not believe it, then go and see him] (ibid.: 347). Bodding (1929/1952: 86) gives also examples showing that "the Perfect tense is often used where we have the Present: *baDae akat'koañ* I know them (lit. I have learnt to know them)"'. However, he claims that "this is due, not to any peculiarity of the Santal Perfect, but to the peculiar meaning of the Santal base-word". "The predominant meaning" of the form, according to his description, "is an act performed and continuing in its result" (ibid: 85).

This descriptive contradiction, alongside with a misinterpretation,

[5] This label for Santali *-aka*-form (and for the parallel forms in other Munda languages) is proposed by Pinnow (1966: 118) who opposes it to the "non-resultative" *-le-* form. The latter has however, at least in the modern language, more complicated semantics (see below).

always possible, of an early missionary grammar, may be also explained by the significant temporal distance between the description of Skrefsrud and more contemporary language data. In this case the *-aka-* form may have followed the grammaticalisation path from a pure Resultative to a more Perfect-like form. The stative uses of this form have become lexically dependent. This type of diachronic evolution is the most typical for this group of categories (Bybee et al. 1994: 105).

Considering the difficulties of assessing perfect forms as instantiating past or present tense (cf. Comrie 1976: 106 ff: perfect is rather "present plus past"; the problem is the subject of a considerable literature), and the problem of whether the perfect belongs at all to the semantic domain of tense, we exclude the *-aka-* form henceforth from our discussion of past markers.

We will examine, one by one, the three Santali past markers, *-le-*, *-ke-*, and *-tahe~kan-*, in order to show that all the three have semantic properties that cannot be generalized by the "Past" label; they all have additional meanings that can characterize them better than the uses which have been considered primary. We will show that those peculiarities correspond to facts already known cross-linguistically.

1. -LE-: a "non-actual/irreal" marker

1. 1. Temporal uses

The Pluperfect (or the Anterior Past, Skrefsrud 1873: 344, Bodding 1929/1952: 72) marker, *-le-*, has a wide range of meanings that cannot be immediately drawn from the traditional meaning of pluperfect as a taxis grammeme, "past before past" (Comrie 1985). It can be found, indeed, in the following type of context:

(2) jemon- e bolo- got'- le- n- a, temon- ge- kin
as-3SG:SB enter- quickly- *LE*- INTR-IND so- FOC-3DU:SB

kilAp- eset'- got'- ke- d- e- a
close- close- quickly- AOR- TR- 3SG:OB- IND

'The moment he got (lit.: "had got") in, they closed and shut him up.' (Neukom 2001: 80)

The taxis meaning (Bodding 1929/1952: "something was done or happened previous to some other event", Neukom 2001: 80: "a background situation that is located prior to a reference point") is not by any means predominant in the texts; cf. the label of the Aorist II proposed by Yu. K. Lekomtsev (1968) or *Präteritum terminativ* (*negativ*) by H. Vermeer (1969).

The *-le*-Pluperfect marks also a significant temporal distance ("It may be used to describe historic events of long ago", Bodding 1929/1952: 72), combined usually with a "loss of importance" (Skrefsrud 1873: 345). This use of pluperfect as a "general remote past" is also attested in Indo-European languages of India, including Bengali, a neighbor of Santali (Dahl 1985: 147):

(3)	koRa-	jokhe̱c'-	iñ	ñe̱l-	le-	d-	e-	a
	boy-	in.time-	1SG :SB	see-	*LE*-	TR-	3SG:OB-	IND

'I saw (lit. "had seen") him when I was a boy.'

By far the most widespread meaning of the finite *-le*-form is the "cancelled result", i.e. e. the cases where the result of an action is no longer valid: "Or it is used, to describe a past action, the effect of which has been nullified, neutralized, superseded or revoked, formally or by a subsequent action or event" (Bodding 1929/1952: 72). This meaning is perhaps the only possible one for the Pluperfect used beyond the narrative, especially in dialogues (Neukom 2001: 81).

(4)	bAgi-	le-	d-	e-	a-e,	he̱c'-	ruAR-	e-	n-
	leave-	*LE*-	TR-	3SG-	IND-3SG	come-	back-	AOR-	INTR-
	a-	e							
	IND-	3SG							

'She left (lit. "had left") him, (but) came back to him (again).' (Skrefsrud 1873: 344-345)

The 'revoking' action is more frequently attested in an Aorist form, but the Perfect with an emphasis on the present result—with a direct opposition between the fruitless action and the actual result—is also found, as in *Iñren gAi reak' janga de **rAput'-le-n-a**, menkhan **bes-aka-n-a*** (Friesen 1982: 50, Macphail 1964: 76) 'My cow **broke** its leg, but later it **was healed**'

These meanings are well-known for pluperfect (Dahl 1985: 147); the meaning of cancelled result is expressed in the majority of pluperfect-having languages—about three fourths of the languages in Dahl's material, including also Hindi and Punjabi. Both the temporal distance and the cancelled result effect seem to be further specifications (mutually independent) of a more general notion of a non-actual "past temporal frame". Cf. Neukom (2001: 81): "the Pluperfect denotes a completed situation, which can imply that the effect of the situation has been cancelled before the present moment". We will see later that these additional semantic elements are not a unique property of pluperfect as a taxis form.

The Santali Pluperfect (6) is attested also instead of Aorist (5) after a negation. This change is obligatory: "the Simple Past is not used with a negation, when this functions as such" (Bodding 1929/1952: 72); "only the forms with suffixes *-let'/-led', -lid, -len* are used" (Friesen 1982: 50):

(5)	goc'-	e-	n-	a-	e
	die-	AOR-	INTR-	IND-	3SG

'He died.'

(6)	ba-	e	goc'-	le-	n-	a
	not-	3SG	die-	*LE*-	INTR-	IND

'He did not die' (lit. 'He had not died')

This phenomenon, although it is not certainly widespread, is not a unique property of Santali. Neukom (2001: 77) supposes that the Pluperfect is older than the Aorist and that the negative context, which cross-linguistically is "more conservative" according to Givón 1979, tends to keep a more archaic form. However this fact has also synchronic and semantic explanations.

E. Contini-Morava in her treatment of the Swahili negated forms (1989) claims that the negative verbal system in this language has no tense oppositions, but is a part of the modal subsystem. A. Urmanchieva (2003) shows that most languages of Africa have a reduced set of temporal-aspectual forms in the negated verb paradigm compared to the affirmative one. The system of negative in Dabida (a Bantu language, E zone) reveals a striking similarity to the above-described property of the Santali Pluperfect. Indeed, the only Dabida form used for negation of a situation located in the past is that of the Remote Past (although in the affirmative paradigm three separate past tenses are distinguished). This Remote Past form has also the semantics of cancelled result and of past temporal frame separated by a rupture from the moment of speech (Urmanchieva 2003: 469). A similar system is found in Nkore-Kiga (Bantu, J zone; ibid.: 469-470) where the Remote Past is used also as a negative correlate of the Perfect form. Urmanchieva states (ibid: 472) that "there is a tendency to represent the situation described by a negative clause as *weakly connected* with the reality, and also to mark a *rupture* between this situation and the present". This hypothesis applies well also to the Santali material: the Pluperfect which has a function of marking the past temporal frames is used to additionally oppose the negated situation to the present reality.

1.2. Modal uses

The proximity of the negative and the modal semantic zone is also evident in the *-le-* marker, which has a set of modal uses. These uses, for the most part with non-finite and non-Indicative forms, are never labeled as Pluperfect, but nevertheless, as we will show, belong to the typologically-known semantic domain of this category. When the modal *-le*-form used is a finite one, it differs from the Pluperfect by absence of a *-t'-* marker in transitive variant. Bodding (1952: 74) considers this use to be a separate tense, the so-called Anterior, which is described like this; "This tense is used to denote an action or a state that takes place or exists previous to something else. It may be priority in time, a possible previous action or a condition that has to be fulfilled before something else will or can take place".

The most careful treatment of this form is the one by Neukom (2001: 89-93) who labels it the Irrealis form. The irrealis is a well-known cross-linguistically verbal category, firstly attested and perhaps better described in the languages of South-Eastern Asia, especially in the Austronesian languages. Among the typical functions of an irrealis category listed in Mithun (1995) the following uses can be found, according to Neukom, in the Santali Irrealis: Counterfactual/Conditional, Future and Hortatory, and Imperative.

This non-indicative *-le-* yields, usually with a conjunction *khan* 'when', and counter-factual semantics, that is, the unreal hypothesis (protasis) in a conditional clause.

(7) ti alo- e sap'- le-tiñ khan do̱-ñ ñurhA-k-
hand PROH 3SG hold- *LE*-my when then-1SG fall- *KE*-

Ø-ok'-a
FUT-INTR-IND

'If he had not taken hold of my hand, I might have fallen down.' (Bodding 1929/1952: 74).

It is a semantic element that additionally links the two senses of the marker. The counterfactual meaning (both in protasis and apodosis of a conditional clause) is known for pluperfect in different languages of the world, including English (cf. the English translation *had not taken,* in Past Perfect), Armenian, Latin, Persian and others; Dahl (1985: 146) attests it as a "fairly common" secondary use of the pluperfect.

The "future" use of the *-le*-form never occurs with the indicative *-a.*

There are two sub-uses of it: affirmative and negative. The affirmative use expresses "intention or obligation" (Neukom 2001: 92), usually with an idea of a consecutive situation that will take place later in the future:

(8) noa ñindA do̱ ṉeṯeregeñ *tahe̱~añga-* *le-* *n-*
rest- LE-

ge, gapa do̱-ñ ñam *baRay-Ø-* *e-* *a*
INTR- FOC search-FUT- 3SG- IND

'To-night I *shall remain* somewhere here until dawn; then I *shall search* for the calf to-morrow.' ("The Story of a Mahra Man", SFT 1923: 252)

The negative use, with a particular negation *o̱ho̱*, signals a "strong prediction that the situation will not take place" (Neukom 2001: 92):

(9) o̱ho̱- ñ lai-le- a
NEG- 1SG:SB tell-*LE*-IND

'I shall not certainly tell!' (Bodding 1929/1952: 74)

Cf. a neutral negation, *ba,* with a neutral Future/Habitual zero marker in (10):

(10) ba- ñ lai- Ø- a
NEG-1SG :SB tell- FUT- IND

'I will not tell, I am not going to tell.'

This use of a conditional form has a typological parallel in Romance, for example in French, where the Conditional is used for an indignant negation of a future event: *Je le dirais! Jamais* 'I will tell this? Never'.

It seems also that some occurrences of *-le-*, listed by Neukom among the conditional uses of Santali Irrealis, are closer to the future uses of it. The temporal subordinate clauses referring to the Future can be cited as an example:

(11) noko sendra ho̱R- ko paro̱m-calao- le- n- khan
these hunt person 3PL.SB pass- go- *LE*- INTR- when

raRa- ka- ñ- pe
rclease-CPL- 1SG:OB-2PL:SB

'When these hunting people have gone, let me out.' (Neukom 2001: 91)

The semantic of a real hypothesis, referring, together with its consequences, to the future, is a boundary zone between the two meanings of Irrealis:

(12) mit'- Tan eskar na~ha~k'-iñ khadle- le- khan-
one- CL alone now-1SG.SB put_into- LE- if-

do- e ruhed- iñ- a
TOP- 3SG:SB scold- 1SB:OB-IND

'If I put in only one (pint) now, he will scold me.'

An identical *-le-* marker denotes the temporal anteriority in Imperative (Bodding 1929/1952: 75); this form is labeled by Neukom (2001: 147-148) Irrealis Imperative:

(13) jo̱m- le- m, ado̱- lañ calak'-Ø- a
eat- LE- IMP:2SG then- 1PL:INCL go- FUT- IND

'Take your food first, then we shall go.'

It is interesting that this form has also the sense of an immediate fulfillment of an action commanded:

(14) he̱c'- le- n- me!
come- LE- INTR- IMP:2SG

'Come here at once!'

It is possible to compare this property e.g. to Russian, where the Past form can be used colloquially as an impolite form of immediate request: *poshël!* 'go!' lit. 'went!'.

This description of the properties of *-le* shows that its *raison d'être* does not consist just in tense marking. In all its uses — both as a tense-aspect marker and as a marker of an Irrealis or Anterior group of meanings — it expresses, together with the idea of an action localized before the speech/reference point, or even instead of it, also additional meanings, belonging to a certain semantic field. Neukom (2001: 80) generalizes all these uses of *-le-* (Pluperfect, Irrealis and Irrealis Imperative) in the following way: "They signal that the situation marked by *-le-* presupposes a subsequent situation. In case of the Pluperfect *-le-* signals anteriority in the past... in case of the Irrealis *-le-* marks the protasis of a conditional sentence... and in case of the Irrealis Imperative *-le-* indicates that the order is the presupposition for another situation".

It seems however that the common property of these uses can be formulated more precisely: it is characterized by an obligatory rupture, or change, between the situation in question from the actual state of things (or "the subsequent situation" in Neukom's terminology). This rupture may be temporal, it may concern the absence of result or even of the situation itself (the use of *-le-* after negation).

The marking of this semantic field is known cross-linguistically. It can be generalized as a "non-actual" past or "discontinuous past" (the latter proposed in (Plungian, Auwera 2003)). The non-actual past markers are attested in a large number of languages of the world, including Polynesian, West African, and different Creole languages. They all have "an additional negative component" ("past & NOT present") that opposes them to "standard past markers" which do not represent any data concerning the present state (ibid.), and also tend to develop certain additional meanings, including cancelled result and the uses of the irreal semantic set (hypothesis, counter-factuality). In narratives, they also used to give the background information that does not belong to the main story line; this kind of discourse is called by T. Givón (1982) "out-of-sequence". These very meanings, as we have already seen, are common derivations in "standard" European-like Pluperfects, like in Romance, Slavic and German languages.

2. -KE- : A past marker and a mood modifier

A proof of the fact that this semantics is not conditioned exclusively by the Pluperfect use of *-le-* consists in the closely related functions of the *-ke-* marker (*-e-* with intransitives). It has as its basic function the denotatin of narrative Aorist. A perfective interpretation is usual for this category: "the Past never refers to a stative situation with past time reference" (Neukom 2001: 78):

(15) khangeko calao *jarway-en-a*, jome lagat' gaDa aRereko *idi-ke-d-e-a*, ar jomeko *porton-ke-t'-a*; adom hoR do roro ar adom hoR geget'ko *dhurau-e-n-a*, hudiñ-ic do dak' sen menteye *gusAu-e-n-a*

'Thereupon they *came together* and *took* her away to the bank of a river, to eat her there, and *commenced to make ready* for eating her. Some of them *took in hand* to singe her, some of them to cut her to pieces, but the youngest one *slipped away* on the pretext of going towards water.'

It has however some values typical for perfects in other languages ("it is used to denote events which have happened just now or recently; to express actions past which have abiding effects", Skrefsrud 1873: 344):

(16) ado-e met- a- t'- ko-a, caba-ke-
then-3SGtell- IDO:AOR- TR-3 PL-IND, finish-AOR-

d-a- ñ.
TR-IND-1SG

'Then he told (them): I have finished (eating).' ["How the Sabai Grass came into existence", SFT 1923: 298].

There is also an "Accidental Past" (Bodding 1929/1952: 76) with *-ke-n-* instead of *-e-n-* in intransitives, which is, morphologically, a more archaic variant of the Aorist (Pinnow 1966: 120) and, semantically, seems to be a split of the original perfect-like semantics of the *-ke*-form (see also Sitchinava 2001: 109). The perfective past forms, indeed, in most languages, are related diachronically to former perfect (anterior) categories (Bybee et al. 1994: 81–86).

At the same time *-ke-*, occupying the II position and combined with the Future/Habitual non-standard set of markers of transitivity, has the following meanings than can be generalized as modal ones (and are viewed by Bodding and by Neukom as a separate mood, Optative):

(1) polite request ("used to express a prayer in the form of a question", Bodding 1929/1952: 73):

(17) mit' Taka- m em- k- iñ- a?
one rupee- 2SG give- *KE-* 1SG- IND

'Would you give me one rupee?'

This form is also "used in invocations to dead persons and to gods" (Neukom 2001: 86):

(18) ma sarhao-k- ok'- ben ar cando aben
MOD praise-*KE-* INTR- 2DU.SB and Chando you-DU

bhor-a-ben- ma!
bless-IDO-2DU.OB-MOD

'May you be praised, and may Chando (a god) bless you two!'[6]

(2) hypothesis, usually in apodosis of conditional clauses (see above the example (7) that contains an occurrence of the hypothetical *-ke-*). In

[6] In the second verbal form in this example, *-ke-* is missing because it is not used with the indirect object (or Applicative) marker *-a-*.

this latter meaning the tense "retains its optative signification" (Skrefsrud 1873: 351).

This property reveals a similarity to Lezgian (Nakh-Daghestanian) where the combination of an "additional" marker with a future gram yields exactly a hypothetical form (Haspelmath 1993). A similar phenomenon is attested in English and Romance (irreal forms like Eng. *he would go,* Fr. *il irait,* Sp. *iría* are also forms of Future-in-the-Past, both semantically and morphologically).

More generally speaking, the parallelism between the Past markers and the markers of irreal moods (including the sense of a non-categorical wish) is attested in numerous languages of different areas, including Europe (cf. Eng. *would, could, might*), Mesoamerica, and some languages of India, especially Marathi (Steele 1975: 200) — the latter fact is particularly interesting for our study. The semantic primitive that links the two uses of the marker is called by Steele "Dissociative" or "Emphasized past". Suzanne Fleischman (1989) points out that "the concept of temporal distance turns out to be a prominent metaphorical template cross-linguistically for the expression of distance along other axes, both grammatical and pragmatic". Her hypothesis is that in such systems the "irreality value" of a mood form should depend upon the temporal remoteness of the corresponding tense form. It may be argued whether Fleischman's explanation is correct with regard to the European tense systems (see in particular Dahl 1997), but her view of American languages finds a close parallel in Santali.

It is interesting to point out that the Uto-Aztecan "Past-Irreal markers" discussed by Steele act not as "standard" Past markers, but as additional modifiers with specific meanings. A corresponding Classical Nahuatl marker, *-tla:-*, added to a verbal stem signifies a counterfactual meaning ('if he *had been* first to fall in the fire…'), and added to an Imperative marker yields the sense of a "polite request", often addressed to gods (Steele 1975: 207). These properties almost exactly correspond to those of the Santali *-ke,* which however chooses for the latter meaning a Future stem instead of the Imperative. So it is possible to consider the "past-irrealis" markers of this kind to be also related to the domain of "non-actual" or "discontinuous" past.

The problem of the etymological and morphological identity of the *-ke-* and *-le-* markers in their aspectual and modal uses is a difficult issue for comparative Munda studies. H.-J. Pinnow, in his reconstruction of the Proto-Kherwari verb system (1966: 152-154) notes that, during its formation, "the functions of the various aspect affixes in the subjunctive were in part changed and in part became more rigidly determined… The continuing dearth of syntactical studies makes it impossible at this time to understand the principles which guided the distribution of the non-factual (subjunctive) forms, each of whose categories appears coupled with an old aspect". The same question — "just what does it all mean?" — is posed by Steele who also investigated the comparative data. We have seen how the use of a typological framework provides an explanation for the development of modal meaning in at least two Santali aspectual affixes.

3. –TAHE˜KAN- : a universal "retrospectivizer"

A past marker occupying the fifth position, *-tahe̲~kan-*, is yet another marker with non-actual semantics. It is added to an inflected word form before the finishing Indicative marker and, along with the Progressive *-kan-*, it has a certain prosodic autonomy (cf. Maspero 1952: "L'expression du temps, d'origine étrangère et récente dans les parlers kherwârî, n'a pas réussi à faire réellement corps avec le verbe et lui reste en quelque mesure extérieure, tout en constituant avec lui un syntagme"); it is often regarded as an auxiliary verb (e.g. in Bodding 1929/1952: 67 or in Friesen 1982: 41). It combines with four of the five markers of the second position, with the sole exception of the *-ke*-form. With both Durative and Habitual, and also with Progressive, it yields, among others, the sense of "Habitual-Past" (Dahl 1985), or of a usual situation in the past that is no longer valid ("habits or customs in the past", Skrefsrud 1873: 347):

(19)	gAi-	ko-	e	jo̲m-	e-	t'-	ko-	tahe̲~kan-	a
	cow-	PL-	3SG	eat-	DUR-	TR-	3SG-	*TAHEKAN-*	3SG

'He (the leopard) was in habit of eating cows.'

With Durative, it also signifies the unsuccessful attempt, or "conative" sense. In the following example the women were unable to perform the sacrifice:

(20)	kutAm.-	e-	t'-	ko-	tahe̲~kan-	a
	sacrifice-	DUR-	TR-	3PL-	*TAHEKAN-*	IND

'We were trying to sacrifice them (i.e. the cow[7]).' ("The story of some women", SFT 1923: 244)

The three combinations of the markers of Actual Present, Habitual, and Progressive, with *tahe̲~kan*, seem to be altogether synonymous; V. Friesen (1982: 53), who labels them Imperfect forms, analyses the first

[7] "It does not seem that they have more than one cow; the plural is in Santali often used for expressing something indefinite, some one or other, about one only" (SFT 1923: 240)

two combinations as elliptical forms. They result, according to his claim, from the omission of markers *-et'-* and/or *-kan-* in the most complicated form Progressive + *tahe̲~kan*, which he considers to be a primary one. This change is explained by the "tendency for simplifying the verbal forms in the Imperfect, which are relatively superfluous". It seems however that an alternative explanation can be proposed, according to which the semantics of 'inactual' neutralizes the opposition between Durative, Habitual and Progressive.

With Perfect and Pluperfect, *-tahe̲~kan-* shifts the meaning of the forms to the Past: we have "Perfect-in-the-Past" and "Pluperfect-in-the-Past": "Anterior Pluperfect… denotes that something had been done or had happened, but had been neutralized, superseded or revoked in the Past; the Tense is also used to denote a conative or frustrated act in the Past" (Bodding 1929/1952: 73).

The combination of *-le-* and *-tahe̲~kan-* yields also a counterfactual meaning:

(21) am alo- m hech'- le- n khan
you not- 2SG come- *LE-* INTR when

iñ tuñ- le- d- e- tahe̲~kan- a
I shot- *LE-* TR- 3SG- *TAHEKAN-* IND

'If you had not come, I would have shot him.' (Skrefsrud 1873: 349)

The form is not used in all the cases when the situation belongs to the past. "It locates the situation in the past, and also it denotes that the situation does not belong to the narrative chain of sequential events… In contrast to the forms the (bare) Imperfective in narratives refers to the situations that are part of the story line" (Neukom 2001: 95). Indeed, the markers of "the discontinuous past" discussed in Plungian & Auwera 2003 usually are not used for characterizing the main narrative chain of the events and so are often described as "idle", "facultative" tense markers. The *-kan-tahe̲~kan* form attested in the texts occurs for the most part in the opening of the story, accompanied often by the adverbials like *sedae jo̲khe̲~n, sedae jugre̲* 'long ago' or *mit'dhao* 'once'. The marker signals that the whole introduced sequence of events belongs to a past temporal frame. In the following sentences the narrator chooses simple Progressive or Actual Present forms, without the modifier. Cf. the following example with a direct opposition between the two forms of the same verb:

(22) …mit' hoRe tahe~kana; ado cet' dorbar coe *calak'kantahe~kana*;
ado baRge cima senteye *calak'kana…*

("Nothing must be told to Women": SFT 1923: 244)

'…there lived a man. One day he *was going* to some meeting or other; whilst he *was walking* (lit. "he is walking") along towards the boundary of his home-field…'

This context is also favourable from the "Pluperfect-in-the-Past", formed by adding of the *-tahe~kan-* to a *-le-*Pluperfect:

(23) ado mit'dhao, kathae, ac' eskarge hAñhar hanhar oRak'te peRahoRok'e
sen-le-n-tahe~kan-a; ado unre uni hanhartet' buDhidae *daka-utuy-e-t'-a…*
go-*LE*-INTR-*TAHEKAN*-IND boil-curry.prepare-DUR-TR-IND

'One day, they say, he had gone alone to visit his father-in-law and mother-in-law in their home. While there his mother-in-law was (lit. "is") engaged in cooking curry and rice…' ("The stupid Son-in-Law"; Grierson (ed.) 1906/1967: IV: 58, 62)

The "Perfect-in-the-Past" — here in the stative meaning — is also used in a beginning of a narration:

(24) tis jokheñre con`, kathae, pea koRa mit'Tan` jojo dare butAReko *duRup-akan- tahe~kan-a,* ar onkoteye mit'Tan` hor parom akana.

'Once upon a time, it is told, three boys were sitting (lit. *had been sat*) under a fruit-tree, near of a road that was (lit. has gone) there.' (Friesen 1982: 48)

This function is evident in the fragments of discourse less than a whole text; the *tahe~kan*-forms are usual means of introducing a new character or a new situation. This property was independently pointed out by us (Sitchinava 2001: 103) and by Neukom (2001: 96). "The example below follows a paragraph which describes the quarrel of a man and a ghost over a girl… The story continues:

(25)
ado	un	jokhen-ge,	kathae,	toyo-	do	oka-	sen
then	that	time-FOC	they-say	jackal-	TOP	where-	ALL

con`	Atiñ-e	cala-	k'-	kan-	tahe~kan-	a
ever	feed-3SG:SB	go-	INTR-	PROGR-	*TAHEKAN*-	IND

'At that time, people tell, a jackal was on his way somewhere to look for food.' (Neukom 2001: 96)

This use of a non-actual form in the beginning of the story (the so-called "initial point shift" or the "before-sequence" use) is a cross-linguistically known property of these markers. In the Old Russian birchbark letters, beyond the literary Slavonic style, the so-called "Russian Pluperfect" (with the auxiliary *byl*) is usually preferred in the first phrases of narratives (Zalizniak 1995/2004: 175-177). This kind of use of *Plusquamperfectum* is found in the texts by some Latin authors (Mellet 1994: 112; Sitchinava 2003: 44). In Anderson (1979) a "narrative" marker in Aghem (a Bantoid language of Benue-Congo family) is described which is used only "in the first sentence of stories which refer to something which happened at some distant time", while all the following story is rendered in another tense, the so-called "consecutive" (see also Plungian & Auwera 2003).

The morphological technique of adding *-tahe̱~kan-* to an inflected word form with semantic "pastification" of it is labeled by Plungian (2001) as "retrospective shift" (cf. also Koval' and Gnalibouly (1997)'s "retrospective tense" concerning Fula forms). This term was used in our 2001 work as a label for all the modifying uses of *-ke-* and *-le-* and also for *-tahe̱~kan-* which acts only as a modifier. The latter is originally developed from a verb meaning 'was', 'was somewhere', 'stayed', Ger. 'blieb' (Skrefsrud: 347, Bodding 1929/1952: 67, Pinnow 1966: 121, Friesen 1982: 41), which is also typical for the markers of this kind (e.g. *val* in Udmurtian (Finno-Ugrian), *bylo* in Russian, *geven* in Yiddish — all three, literally = 'was').

Conclusions

At least two of the three Past markers of Santali, *le-* and *-tahe~kan-*, do not appear to be "classical" tense-aspect markers: they both have the function of signaling a rupture between the present and the past and certain consequences induced therefrom, connected with the categories of result, temporal distance, and modality. They differ by their set of meanings and by their scope of combination from other markers. While the former, *-le-*, is a basic tense-aspect marker and, save in the case of the Irrealis Imperative, does not as act an additional modifier, the latter, *-tahe~kan-* is a marker which is added to an inflected verbal stem and is never used outside backgrounding contexts. Both types of discontinuous past markers are typologically known (Plungian and Auwera 2003). The *-le-* marker, a diachronically older one, has a more elaborated set of meanings and is more deeply integrated into the system of the Santali verb.

The *-ke-* marker, following the language evidence, seems to be a successor of an old Perfect-like form, but has nevertheless meanings known for a "non-actual" past marker, viz. the expression of polite request and condition. Since it is argued in (Plungian and Auwera 2003) that the discontinuous past markers may grammaticalize in the direction of "regular" past markers, an additional synchronic and comparative Munda study is needed to clarify the semantic history of the Santal *-ke-* Past.

Abbreviations

The discussed markers, *-le-*, *-ke-*, and *-tahe̱~kan-*, are glossed literally. The marker of the Aorist however is glossed AOR, as it has two suppletive allomorphs (*-ke-* with transitives and *-e-* with intransitives).

1,2,3 — 1,2,3 person
ALL — allative
AN — animate
AOR — aorist
CL — classifier
CPL — completive
DU — dual
DUR — durative
FOC — focus
FUT — future
INAN — inanimate
INCL — inclusive
IND — indicative
INTR — intransitive
MOD — modal particle
NEG — negation
OB — object
PL — plural
PROH — prohibitive
SB — subject
SG — singular
TR — transitive

References

Anderson, Stephen C. 1979. Verb structure. In: L. Hyman (ed.). *Aghem grammatical structure*. Los Angeles: USC, 73-136 (SCOPiL 7).

Bodding, Paul O. 1929/1952. *A Santal grammar for the beginners*, Benagaria: Santal Mission of the Northern Churches (1st edition, 1929).

Bybee, Joan L.; Perkins, R.; Pagliuca, W. 1994. *The evolution of grammar: Tense, aspect and modality in the languages of the world*. Chicago: U. of Chicago.

Comrie, Bernard. 1976. *Aspect: an introduction to the study of verbal aspect and related problems*. Cambridge: CUP.

Comrie, Bernard. 1985. *Tense*. Cambridge: CUP.

Contini-Morava, E. 1989. *Discourse pragmatics and semantic categorization. The case of negation and tense-aspect with special reference to Swahili.*

Dahl, Östen. 1985. *Tense and aspect systems*. Oxford: Blackwell.

Dahl, Östen. 1997. The relation between past time reference and counterfactuality: a new look. Athanasiadou, A., Dirven, R. (eds.). *On conditionals again*. Amsterdam: Benjamins, 97-114.

Dahl, Östen, Hedin, Eva. 2000. Current relevance and event relevance. Dahl, Ö. (ed.).

Tense and aspect in the languages of Europe. B., N. Y.: Mouton de Gruyter, 385-402.

Fleischman, Suzanne. 1989. Temporal distance: a basic linguistic metaphor. *Studies in language*, 13.1, 1-50.

Friesen, Vladimir I. 1982. *Glagol v santal'skom yazyke* (Verb in Santali). Unpublished PhD thesis. Moscow: Institute for Oriental Studies, Russian Academy of Sciences.

Givón, Talmy. 1979. *On understanding grammar*. N. Y.: Academic Press.

Givón, Talmy. 1982. Tense-aspect-modality: the Creole prototype and beyond. P. Hopper (ed.). *Tense-aspect: between semantics and pragmatics*. Amsterdam: Benjamins, 114–163.

Grierson, Sir George A. (ed.) 1906 (reprinted 1967). *The linguistic survey of India*. Vol. IV. Delhi-Varanasi-Patna.

Haspelmath, Martin. 1993. *A grammar of Lezgian*. Berlin: MdG.

Koval', Antonina I.; Gnalibouly, B. A. 1997. *Glagol fula v tipologicheskom osveshchenii* (The Fula verb in a typological perspective). Moscow, Russkie slovari.

Lekomtsev, Yuri K. 1968. Nekotorye kharakternye cherty santal'skogo predlozheniya (Some properties of the sentence in Santali). *Yazyki Indii, Pakistana, Nepala i Tseylona: Materialy nauchniy konferencii*. Moscow: Nauka, 311-321.

Macphail, R. M. 1964. *An introduction to Santali*, Parts I & II. Benagaria: The Santali Literature Board, Santali Christian Council.

Maspero, Henri. 1952. Les langues mounda. Meillet A., Cohen M. (dir.), *Les langues du monde*, P.: CNRS.

McCawley, J. D. 1971. Tense and time reference in English. Ch. J. Fillmore & D. T. Langendoen (eds.), *Studies in linguistic semantics*, N. Y.: Holt, Rinehart & Winsron, 97-113.

Mellet, Sylvie. 1994. Les temps du passé: le plus-que parfait. In : S. Mellet, M. D. Joffre, G. Serbat. *Grammaire fondamentale du latin: le signifié du verbe*. Louvain : Peeters, 105-123.

Mithun, Marianne. 1995. On the relativity of irreality. Bybee J. L., Fleischman S. (eds.) *Modality in grammar and discourse*. Amsterdam: Benjamins, 367-388.

Neukom, Lukas. 2001. *Santali*. München: LINCOM Europa.

Pinnow, Heinz-Jürgen. 1966. A comparative study of the verb in the Munda languages. Zide, Norman H. (ed.) *Studies in comparative Austroasiatic linguistics*. London—The Hague—Paris: Mouton, 96-193.

Plungian, Vladimir A. 2001. Antirezul'tativ: do i posle rezul'tata (Anti-resultative: before and after result). Plungian, V. A. (ed.). *Issledovaniya po teorii grammatiki*. I: *Glagol'nye kategorii*. Moscow: Russkie slovari, 50-88.

Plungian, Vladimir A., van der Auwera, J. 2003. Towards a typology of discontinuous past marking. Ms.

SFT. 1923-1929. *Santali Folk Tales*: Ed. by Rev. P. O. Bodding. Oslo: Institutet for sammenlingenden kulturforskning, Publikationen. Vol. I–III.

Sitchinava, Dmitri V. 2001. Plyuskvamperfekt i retrospektivnyy sdvig v yazyke santali (Pluperfect and retrospective shift in Santali). Plungyan, V. A. (ed.). *Issledovaniya po teorii grammatiki*. I: *Glagol'nye kategorii*. Moscow: Russkie slovari, 89-114.

Sitchinava, Dmitri V. 2003. K tipologii glagol'nykh sistem s neskol'kimi formami plyuskvamperfekta: *casus latinus* (On typology of verbal systems with multiple pluperfect forms: *casus latinus*). *Voprosy yazykoznaniya* 2003-5: 40-52.

Skrefsrud, L. O. 1873. *The grammar of Santali language*. Benares: Medical Hall Press.

Stassen, Leon. 1997. *Intransitive predication*. Oxford: Clarendon Press.

Steele, S. 1975. Past and irrealis: just what does it all mean? *International Journal of American Linguistics*, 41.3, 200-217.

Urmanchieva, Anna J. 2003. Otritsatel'nye formy glagola v yazykakh Afriki: morfologiya i semantika (The negative verb forms in the languages of Africa: morphology and semantics). Vinogradov, V. A., Toporova, I. N. (ed.) *Osnovy afrikanskogo yazykoznaniya. Glagol.* Moscow: Vostochnaja Literatura, 460-487.

Vermeer, Hans J. 1969. *Untersuchungen zum Bau zentral-süd-asiatischer Sprachen (ein Beitrag zur Sprachbundfrage).* Heidelberg: J. Groos.

Zalizniak, Andrei A. 1995/2004. *Drevnenovgorodskiy dialekt* (The Old Novgorod Dialect). Moscow: Yazyki russkoy kultury (1st edition, 1995).

Zograf, G. A. 1960/1990. *Yazyki Yuzhnoy Azii* (Languages of Southern Asia). Moscow: Nauka (1st edition, 1960).

CASE DOUBLING IN KASHMIRI POSSESSIVE: ANOTHER LOOK

KASHI WALI AND
OMKAR N. KOUL

Abstract

Kashmiri possessive case marking has been described as an instance of case doubling by Payne (1995), while it has been analyzed as an agreement phenomenon by Wali, Koul and Koul (WKK) (2002). The object of our paper is to compare these two analyses and show that the latter is far superior to Payne's analysis. For example, the analysis proposed by WKK preserves the one case per nominal principle and explains the parametric variation across languages. Payne's analysis in contrast is purely descriptive and language specific.

Double case marking

Double case marking was first noted by Bopp (1848). He noted that in several languages, such as Old Georgian, Australian, Afro-Asiatic, and Indo-European the possessive case is suffixed with the case, and at times gender number features of the possessed head noun as in Old Georgian (OG) (1). Prima-facie it is an instance of double case marking on the possessor, that is, 'father' in (1)

(1) OG.	*sexel-man*	*mam-isa-man*
	name-ERG	father-GEN-ERG

'Father's name.'

This type of double case marking is in clear violation of the all-pervasive principle of one case per nominal. The principle is the backbone of most case theories, whether traditional, functional, or modern generative. There have been several attempts at describing the double case marking within a traditional morphological framework. The most accepted analyses amongst these are: the Adjective Theory; (ii) the Pronoun, or Appositive Theory; and (iii) the Phrase-Marking Theory. (See Moravcsik 1995.) We will not dwell on these theories. Here we will confine ourselves to the analyses proposed for the Kashmiri possessive. Towards this goal we first describe the composition of the Kashmiri possessive.

The Kashmiri Possessive

The Kashmiri possessive encodes an intricate network of the features of the possessor as well of the possessed noun as shown in (2).

Kashmiri Possessive complex:

(2) Possessor+(ABL/DAT+HUND+GNC of the possessed/ the head)

Possessor		Possessed/head noun
lADk-İ - sInd-	*is*	*doost- as*
boy-DAT-HUND-Msg-DAT		friend-Msg-DAT

'to the boy's friend…'

(i) Possessor is marked by a suffix -HUND
(ii) HUND assigns ablative or dative case to the possessor.
(iii) HUND declines according to the GNC-gender number and case of the possessed /head noun.
(iv) H/SUND has three allomorphs all cued to some feature of the possessor

(3) Three Allomorphs of HUND

Allomorph	Possessors
UN	Animate Proper Nouns
UK	Inanimate masculine singulars (mostly ending in consonants)
H/S-UND	All other nouns (all feminine forms, all plural forms, all animate masculine singulars) (HUND changes to SUND in certain contexts)

Following are the forms of allomorphs cued to the gender and number of the nominative head:

(3a) Allomorph Head noun in nominative case

	Masculine		Feminine	
	Singular	Plural	Singular	Plural
UN	-un	-In'	-In'	-Ini
UK	-uk	-Ik'	-Ic	-Ici
H/SUND	-h/sund	-h/sInd'	-h/sInz	-h/sInzI

(Note: These forms are further modified in the context of ergative, dative and other cases as noted in Wali and Koul 1997 p.164-165 and as is clear in examples in 5b and 5c.)

It is interesting to note that each allomorph of HUND refers to a unique class by itself. -UN, is used for animate proper nouns only thus distinguishing proper from common a grammatical distinction which is rather unusual. -UK is used only for masculine singular inanimate forms. -HUND is used for the rest of the classes such as all plural nouns, all feminine forms, and all animate common masculine nouns.

Another oddity of these suffixes is they mark the possessor with two different cases. The suffixes -UN and -UK, use the ablative case, while -H/SUND, uses the dative case. The case markers precede the suffixes and vary according to the gender and number of the possessor as in (4).

(4) Possessor

	Masculine		Feminine	
	Singular	Plural	Singular	Plural
Ablative (UN/UK)	-I/-i	av	-i	-av
Dative (H/SUND)	-as/-is	-an	-i	-an

Note that both -UN and UK employ only the ablative singular form –I/i. Secondly, the ablative form -av, never comes into play since -UN and -UK are never used with plurals. Third the ablative feminine -i is same as its dative counterpart. Clearly then ablative -I/i can be listed as a suppletive of the dative, as already suggested and adopted in Grierson 1911.

Features of the head noun affecting the suffixes

It is important to note here that all the three suffixes, -UN, -UK, and -H/SUND, decline according to the gender, number and case of the head noun. If the head noun is in the nominative the suffixes show only gender number variations. If the head noun is marked ergative/agentive or dative the suffixes are also marked with these cases. If the head noun takes a postposition (i.e., PP), the suffixes are not followed by the PP but they are marked by the suffix that is appropriate for that PP. (5a) shows the ergative case paradigm followed by examples of the possessive in all its declensions as in (5b, 5c).

(5a) Ergative case paradigm

Masculine		Feminine	
Singular	Plural	Singular	Plural
-an/C'	-av	-i/an	-av

(C' represents the exceptional masculine ergative singular forms of certain nouns. These employ their palatalized plural forms as ergative singulars as noted in Wali and Koul 1997, p. 151.)

(5b) Proper noun possessor with ergative and dative head nouns
Examples of ergative and dative possessive forms of –UN and –UK:

(Note that morphological forms of possessives and cases undergo certain sandhi rules and as such are not always very explicit as in the case of *mohn-In'* below.)

(i) *mohn-In'* *doost-an* *vod.*
Mohan-Msg-POSS-Msg-ERG friend-Msg-ERG cried

'Mohan's friend cried.'

(ii) *me* *dits* *mohn-In-is* *necvis-is* *kitaab.*
I-ERG gave Mohan-Msg-POSS-Msg-DAT son-DAT book

'I gave a book to Mohan's son.'

(5c) Masculine singular possessor with ergative and dative head noun
Examples of ergative and dative possessive forms of SUND:

(i) *lADk-I-sInd'* *doost-an* *pAr* *kitaab*
boy-Msg-DAT-POSS-Msg-ERG friend-Msg-ERG read book

'The friend of the boy read the book.'

(ii) *tse* *ditsIth* *lADk-I-sInd-is* *doost-as* *kitaab*
you-ERG gave boy-DAT-POSS-Msg-DAT friend-Msg-DAT book

'You gave a book to the friend of the boy.'

Note that In (5c(i)) -SUND has marked the possessor 'boy' with a Msg. form of dative and itself declined for Msg. ergative form of the head noun friend. In (5c ii) -SUND has declined for the Msg dative form of the head noun 'friend'.

Kashmiri possessive as Double case

Consider now Payne's (1995) analysis of the Kashmiri possessive as an instance of double case. He states that -UN, -UK, are genuine case markers representing CASE 1. He considers juxtaposed gender, number and case of the head noun as representing CASE II. (See 6)

(6) Double case in possessive suffix:

[possessive suffix (UN/ UK) + GNC of the head noun]
CASE I + CASE II

Payne adopts the morphological framework proposed in Zakharyin and Edel'man (1971), and Masica (1991). In this framework case markings in Indic languages, with split ergative morphology, are analyzed as representing three layers as in (7). Note that oblique case denotes the mark/suffix that precedes the overt cases as well as postpositions. The status of this oblique case/mark as a case is a dubious issue that will not be touched here.

(7)
Layer I: Direct/Nominative, Oblique
Layer II: Ergative/Agentive, Dative, (Ablative, Locative)
Layer III: Postpositional markings
Arrangement of Layers: [Nominal +Layer I+Layer II/III]

The Layer II cases – ergative/agentive, dative- mark the nominal with the oblique case, as is the case with postpositions. However, unlike postpositions, both ergative and dative appear with grammatical subjects and objects. They are thus assigned an intermediate status—Layer II.

Returning to Kashmiri, we note that the ergative, dative, and ablative, do not mark the nominal with an oblique case. These cases are essentially like Layer I cases. In Kashmiri the so-called oblique case comes into play only in the context of postpositions.

Arguments for -UN, -UK as Case markers

Payne argues that the possessive suffixes -UN, -UK and -SUND are a mixture of both inflectional and postpositional markings. He analyzes -H/SUND as a postposition and -UN and -UK as inflections. He argues that -UN and -UK are genuine Layer I case markers on par with the ergative, dative and the ablative. His arguments are based on his morphological reanalysis and the behavior of these markers in conjoined noun phrases. However, his arguments are problematic.

Consider the morphological reanalysis. Remember that both -UN and -UK are preceded by an ablative case marker. According to Payne, the ablative marker creates a complicated morphological sandhi problem. He suggests that -UN and -UK be posited as sole possessive markers on par with ergative, and dative. (Payne 1995, 291-292). However there is a problem. Both ergative and dative mark the adjectives (8 a, b) without being preceded by an oblique case/mark. The Possessive -UN, -UK markers never show up with the possessor without the ablative/dative case (9,10).

(Note: Adjectives in Kashmiri divide into two classes. Adjectives of class I inflect for number, gender and case with the nouns they qualify. Adjectives of class II do not show any inflection. See Wali and Koul 1997).

Adjective with ergative case nominal

(8a) *baj-i* *koori*
big-Fsg-ERG girl-ERG

Adjectives with dative case nominal

(8b) *bAD-is* *baag-as*
big-Msg-DAT garden-Msg-DAT

Possessive adjectives marked with dative case with –UN proper noun

(9a) *meen-is* *mohn-un* *makaanI.*
my-Msg-DAT Mohan-ABL-POSS-Msg house-Msg

'My Mohan's house.'

Possessive adjective without case

(9b)	**m'oon*	*mohn-un*	*makaanI.*
	my-POSS-Msg	Mohan-POSS-Msg	house-Msg

'My Mohan's house.'

Possessive adjective marked with ablative case with –UK masculine possessor

(10a)	*baD-i*	*kar'-uk*	*vazan*
	big-Msg-ABL	bangle-ABL-POSS-Msg	weight-Msg

'The big bangle's weight.'

Possessive adjectives without case

(10b)	**baD'-uk*	*kar'-uk*	*vazan*
	big-POSS-Msg	bangle-ABL_POSS-Msg	weight

'The big bangle's weight.'

Clearly the ablative/dative case marking is playing an important role in -UN and -UK possessors as emphasized in Grierson (1911), and cannot be that easily dispensed with as a mere sandhi problem as advocated by Payne. In fact the behavior of the ablative parallels the behavior of the dative which is controlled by the suffix -H/SUND. The -H/SUND marked NP requires the adjective to be marked dative (11,12).

Adjectives with -H/SUND

(11)	*bAD is*	*lADk-I-sind'*	*doost-an*	*vod.*
	big-Msg-DAT	boy-Msg-DAT -POSS-Msg-ERG	friend-Msg-ERG	cried

'The friend of the big boy cried.'

(12)	*baD'-an*	*kar'-an- hund*	*vazan.*
	big-DAT-pl	bangles-DAT-pl-POSS-Msg	weight-Msg

'The weight of the big bangles.'

The similarity of adjective marking shows the unity of -UN, -UK and -H/SUND. All the three have the same status as possessive markers, whatever that turns out to be–bound, inflectional or postpositional. They all mark the possessive with ablative/dative which some grammarians categorize as oblique since these cases have no syntactic function as such.

Consider now the conjoined noun phrases. According to Payne, suffixes -UN, -UK must be added to each NP (13a,b; 14a,b) in the conjunction. They are thus inflectional suffixes. In contrast, -H/SUND is a phrase final postposition since it need to be suffixed on the last NP only (15b).

(13a) *kul'-uk* *tI* *latshl'-uk* *rang*
tree-POSS-Msg and broom-POSS-Msg color-Msg

'The color of the tree and the broom.'

(13b) **kul'-* *tI latshl'-uk* *rang*

(14a) *mohn-un* *tI* *aslam-un* *makaanI*
Mohan-POSS-Msg and Aslam-POSS-Msg house-Msg

'Mohan and Aslam's house.'

(14b) **mohn tI aslamun makaanI*

(15a) *lADkI-sInd'* *tI* *koori hInd'* *doos* *chi* *jaan.*
boy-DAT-POSS-Msg and girl-POSS friends are nice

'The friends of the boy and the girl are nice.'

(15b *??lADkI tI* *koori hInd'* *doos chi* *jaan.*

Notice however, there are certain exceptions to both -UN, -UK and -H/SUND conjunctions. For example, when anything is represented as belonging to several persons and their names occur in a series with the conjunction -tI between the last two of them then the possessive occurs only with the noun before and after -tI. (Wade 1888: 123). This is exemplified below for -UN, classified as a bound suffix in Payne.

(16) *yi garI chu mohan laal, raam chand, javaahar laal-un tI bAAy laalun.*
this house be Mohanlal, Ramchndra, Javaharlal-un and Baylal-un.

'This house belongs to Mohanlal, Ramchandra, Javaharlal and Baylal.' (Wade 1888)

This sentence is acceptable to most native speakers, though some would prefer that the marker -UN be attached to every NP. In essence, the conjoined NP's are more acceptable when the suffixes are attached to every NP in the conjunction. Thus the rule about suffixation in conjoining provides only a weak argument for inflection vs. postpositional status of the possessives.

Payne's object here is to elevate the mere postpositional level of the possessive markers -UN, -UK to genuine genitive case. For him they represent the internal case (i.e.; CASE I in 6) of the possessive phrase. He further states that agreemental gender, number and case features of the possessed head noun represent external case (i.e., CASE II in 6). In sum, Payne has extended the case category to include the agreement features. He is equating the agreement features with a case category to prove the existence of Double Case in Kashmiri.

WKK analysis

We now consider the analysis proposed in Wali, Koul and Koul (2002) within the Minimalist framework. WKK argue that,

(a) -UN, -UK and -H/SUND are theta markers
(b) The juxtaposed case is concordial and is part of the agreement complex.
(c) The function of the agreement features including the case is to check the feature possessive.

The Generative framework

In the Minimalist theory, a possessive construction is a fall out of a nominal system. The noun phrase is analyzed as a DP, the maximal projection of the functional head-D, the determiner. According to Abney (1987), D node is similar to I, the so-called infl., in IP. D assigns Case to the possessor in the Specifier of DP

Similarity of IP and DP

(17a) IP structure : $[_{IP}$ DP (subject) $[_{I'}$ [I $[_{VP}$ V]]]

(17b) DP structure : $[_{DP}$ DP (possessor) $[_{D'}$ [D NP]]]

Consider now WKK's treatment of Kashmiri possessive.

(a) Status of -UN, -UK and -H/SUND

WKK argue that within a DP framework the suffixes -UN, -UK and -H/SUND belong to the D-node. The D-head encodes the referential content of its specifier. They argue that -UN. -UK, and -H/SUND are like the referential features of a nominal, since they are linked to a particular feature of the possessor such as a proper noun, a masculine singular inanimate, a feminine, or a plural. The proper nouns are highest on the referential scale. The inanimate masculine singulars have formed a class by themselves. They too legitimately belong to the D head. Since the suffix -H/SUND belongs to the same category as -UN and -UK as already argued, it too must belong to the D-node.

(b) Status of ablative and dative cases

WKK next consider the role of ablative and dative cases assigned by -UN, -UK and -H/SUND. These ablative and dative cases have no syntactic function as such. They appear like an oblique mark/case that is allotting a PP role to -UN, -UK and -H/SUND. However, unlike a PP, the possessive is expressing a relation between two nominals. More crucially, -UN, -UK, and -H/SUND bear the referential index of their possessor. They are like the carrier of a theta role. WKK emphasize that -UN, -UK, and -H/SUND are not possessive case markers as is assumed in Payne.

(c) Status of GNC elements

The head noun in Kashmiri is in an agreement relation with the possessor. WKK claim that the gender and number features project an agreement phrase, more precisely, an Agr. possessive phrase, as shown below in (18)

(18) $[_{DP}$ Spec. $[_{D'}$ D(-UN,-UK,-SUND) $[_{Agr'(poss\text{-}phrase)}$

$[$Spec(possessor)$[_{Agr'}$ $_{(GN,C)}$Agr NP]]]]]

The possessors in Kashmiri are always in the pre-nominal position. The possessive case is assigned/checked by the functional head -Agr- in a spec-head relation. (See Ura 2000 for technical details.) In (18) the possessor is not an internal argument of the noun. The possessor is not in a thematic relation with the noun. The theta role of the possessor is assigned by the D node as noted above. The possessor moves to the specifier of DP to receive its theta role. The Agr element moves to the D node where it combines with the possessive suffixes -UN, -UK or -H/SUND. WKK claim that the possessive in Kashmiri is very much a structural case. The possessor case and theta role resemble the case and theta tole assigned to an agent. The agent theta role is never assigned in a complement position of the verb. The agent must move to the specifier of IP as assumed under the Minimalist program. (See WKK 2002 for details.)

(d) Juxtaposed ergative and dative case

WKK next consider juxtaposed cases such as ergative and dative, which are copies of the head noun's case. Prima facie the juxtaposed case looks like an instance of second case marking on the possessive. WKK claim that the juxtaposed case is concordial and is part of the agreemental complex, namely, the phi features, i.e., gender and number, as discussed above. They argue that in a generative framework, a genuine case marker is either structural or lexical. The juxtaposed cases do not fit any of these categories. For example, both structural and lexical cases neutralize the agreement features on the verb as is well known from Hindi and Punjabi. The juxtaposed cases induce no such neutralization. They do not obliterate the agreement as evidenced in the examples in (5b, 5c).

Secondly, the structural case is assigned by a head to a specifier. The agreement features do not bear a specifier relation to the head noun. So the head noun cannot be assigning the juxtaposed case to the agreement node. It would be an odd combination. It cannot be argued that the juxtaposed case is an instance of a lexical case either. A lexical case is usually intimately connected with theta roles. The juxtaposed case does not bear any theta relation to the possessor. It is not a theta marker. As argued above the theta role is assigned to the possessors by the possessive marker itself. It is also clear that the juxtaposed case is not cued to any lexical features of the head noun. It is in essence a copy of the case on the head noun. It is purely agreemental. Its status here is the same as the basic inherent phi features. All these features of the head noun conspire to check the possessive relation. They are in essence performing the role of agreement. The possessive is realized when the agreement features move up to the possessive suffixes. They move in order to satisfy the possessive feature.

A crucial argument against the juxtaposed case having the status of a true case derives from the agreement features themselves. The agreement features are cued to the nominative case of the head noun as shown in (3a) above. The nominative is an unmarked/zero case. If the case, in the sense of CASE was the primary element being copied, then the possessive will be marked zero also and will not show any gender number variation at all. The variation of the possessive with the agreement features as shown in (3a) is a clear indication of the agreement element being in charge here. The agreement features justify the positing of the agreement phrase in (18). The juxtaposed cases-ergative, dative-are nothing but part of this agreement complex. In WKK analysis the case is clearly concordial contra Payne. In Payne's analysis the agreement is acquiring a case value. WKK analysis shows that case is acquiring agreemental value.

A bonus of WKK analysis is it makes a prediction. An agreement is a surface phenomenon and is always subject to cross language variation. Agreement in short may acquire a parametric value. The prediction is borne out. For example, in Turkish (T) the head noun itself is marked with the agreement features of the possessor:

Turkish: (Underhill: p. 92)

(19) T *Mehmed-in* *el-i*
Mehmet-gen hand-3sg

'Mehmet's hand.'

(20) T *ben-im* *el-im.*
my-gen hand-1sg

'My hand.'

Clearly, the differences in agreement marking across languages are instances of different parameters of POSS-MARKING. In some languages the Agr appears on the head noun - Turkish, Hungarian, and in some others it appears on the possessor – in Kashmiri, French, Old Georgian and some others. The two types follow from the same function. Both are used to establish a relation between the possessor and the possessum.

Payne vs WKK

We have compared Payne's morphological analysis with the modern DP analysis. Payne claims that the Kashmiri possessive is an inflectional postposition. The analysis classifies the possessive marking as a rare morphological strategy. It does not quite fit the double case marking as seen in other languages as noted in Plank (1995 b), and Moravcsik (1995). It also has no explanation for the difference between the three suffixes -UN, -UK, and -H/SUND and provides no explanation of their function. Crucially it classifies the possessive agreement as an instance of External CASE. It argues that possessive in Kashmiri is an instance of Double Case – CASE I+CASE II in violation of the universal principle of one case per nominal. The DP analysis, in contrast, shows the proper function of the three suffixes by generating them under the D-node. They are referential. Secondly, it shows quite convincingly that the possessive agreement complex is part of possessive case marking and the juxtaposed case is concordial. Being concordial, it is subject to parametric variation. It has no CASE value as such.

An objection against WKK analysis may stem from the current idea that agreement node is superfluous and case is [-interpretable]. According to Chomsky (1995), an agreement node should not be present in the clause structure. His hypothesis is based on the distinction made between [+interpretable] and [-interpretable] features. These features play a significant role at the LF level, which is interpretative. The nominative case feature, which is part of agreement, is [-interpretable] since its function is simply to express a morpho-syntactic relation. Currently, nominative case is checked by Tense and not by Agr.

The question now arises whether the same status should be allotted to the agreement features in the Kashmiri possessive noted above. In short, are the possessive features integral part of the D node. This is however a moot question and much research needs to be done. We leave it to future research.

Abbreviations

Abl: ablative; Agr: agreement; D: determiner; Dat: dative; Erg: ergative; Fsg: feminine singular, Fpl: feminine plural; GNC: gender, number, case; Msg: masculine singular, Mpl: masculine plural; PP: postposition; Poss: possessive

Special Note on the Transcription

In addition to the conventions common to the papers in this volume [see Note on Transcription at the beginning of the volume], the following conventions are used in transcribing special features of Kashmiri in this paper:

/A, AA/ = mid-central vowels, short and long respectively
/I/ = high-central vowel, short
/C'/, i.e. consonant + */'/* = palatalized consonant

References

Abney, Steven 1987. The English Noun Phrase in its Sentential Aspect. Doctoral dissertation, MIT, Cambridge.

Bopp, Franz. 1848. Über das Georgische in sprachverandtshftlicher Beziehung. *Abhandlungen der Königlichen Akademie der Wissenschaften zu Berlin:*

Philosophisch-historische Klasse, 1848, 259-339
Chomsky, N. 1995. *The Minimalist program*. Cambridge: MIT.
Grierson, G. A. 1911. *A standard manual of the Kashmiri language*. Oxford: Clarendon Press.
Masica, Colin. 1991. *The Indo-Aryan languages*. Cambridge: Cambridge University Press.
Moravcsik, Edith A. 1995. Summing up Suffixaufnahme. In Plank, Frans (ed.) 1995: 451-484.
Payne, John. 1995. Inflecting postpositions in Indic and Kashmiri. In Plank, Frans (ed.) 1995: 238-300.
Plank, Frans (ed.). 1995. *Double case: agreement by Suffixaufnahme*. Oxford University Press.
Roop Krishan Bhat. 1987. *A descriptive study of Kashmiri*. Delhi: Amar Prakashan.
Underhill, Robert. 1985. Turkish grammar. Cambridge: MIT Press.
Ura, Hiroyuki. 2000. *Checking theory and grammatical functions in Universal Grammar*. Oxford: Oxford University Press.
Vergnaud, J. R. and M. L. Zubizerrata. 1992. The definite determiner and the inalienable construction in French and English. *Linguistic inquiry* 23. 593-652.
Wade, T. R. 1888. *A grammar of the Kashmiri language as spoken in the Valley of Kashmir, North India*. London: Society for Promoting Christian Knowledge.
Wali, Kashi and Omkar N. Koul 1997. *Kashmiri: A cognitive-descriptive grammar*. London: Routledge.
Wali, Kashi, Omkar N. Koul, and Ashok Koul. 2002. Multiple case marking in Kashmiri possessivee traditional and modern perspective. In Koul, Omkar N. and Kashi Wali (eds.) *Topics in Kashmiri linguistics*. New Delhi: Creative Books.
Zakharyin, Boris A., and Dzhoy Edel'man. 1971. *Yazyk kashmiri*. Moscow: Nauka.

PaaNini's 'LOPA' AND ZEROING IN MODERN STANDARD HINDI

BORIS A. ZAKHARYIN

PaaNini's grammatical treatise on Sanskrit, the **Aṣṭaadhyaayii**[1], belongs, as is known, to the generative type of grammars. That is, relying as a starting point on meanings to be expressed, a grammarian, acting also as a language speaker and guided by his own skills and intuition, finally derivates - through operations with language signs - a desired unit: a word-form, a compound, a word-group or a sentence. According to PaaNini and his followers, there also exists the difference between the position of the grammarian and that of the speaker: the latter deals with wholes used in actual communication, while it is the former who analyses wholes into (virtual) meaningful parts.

PaaNini himself did not state explicitly what were his methodological procedures for abstracting parts from larger items and for determining which one of the varying units should be considered as basic. But there are evidences that he was well acquainted with the ancient tradition of presenting Vedic texts (specially of the Rgveda) in continuous (**saMhitaapaaTha-**) as well as in analyzed (**padapaaTha-**) forms - see, e.g., **suutra 1.1.16** of his grammar. Thus, we may agree with Cardona[2] that PaaNini might have adapted these Vedic procedures to his grammar. Only PaaNini's followers - Kaatyaayana and especially Patañjali - managed to formulate these linguistic procedures explicitly, and as they are quite compatible with PaaNini's own principles, we have the right to assume that PaaNini also would have accepted them fully.

As for Patañjali, he suggested two procedures for extracting meanings from the parts of wholes (that is, for determining individual meanings of words, stems, affixes, etc.): **anvaya** 'concurrent occurrence'

---

[1] The order and numeraion of rules (***suutraaNi***) are the same in any edition of the **Aṣṭaadhyaayii;** here and further on the edition and translation by Vasu (1962) is referred to.

[2] Cardona (1988): 499.

and **vyatireka** 'non-occurrence'. According to Patañjali[3], the main principle to be followed in case of these procedures is that the amalgamated meaning is referred to the common element of the utterance while the differentiated portions of meaning are connected with the [virtual] parts of the utterance. Thus, a differentiation is provided between the meaning of the whole utterance which is **sthitalakshaNa-** 'fixed in character', and the 'extracted' (**apoddhRta-**) meanings of virtual parts of the same utterance. The extraction is determined by differing analytical procedures undertaken by different grammarians, and due to this the final individual elements may also be different[4].

The **anvaya** and **vyatireka** analytic procedures may imply four logical possibilities. The first two of them (most important) are: (a) if a certain form occurs, the corresponding meaning is also there; (b) if a form does not occur, the meaning is absent. The additional variants are: (c) a form occurs, but the meaning cannot be extracted; (d) a form does not occur but the meaning is present[5]. It is evident that possibilities (a) and (b) roughly correspond to Greenberg's 'square principle' in morphological analysis[6]. As for the additional possibilities, (c) looks similar to the contemporary notion of 'empty morph', while (d) - to that of 'zero morph'.

It should be emphasized in passing that, in case we understand 'morpheme' as a class of semantically or functionally correlated allomorphs, the term 'zero' may be applied only to morph and never to morpheme, as the latter, being a class, must include, besides 'zero-morphs', also formally expressed morphs.

As the sphere of meanings is a starting point in PaaNini's derivational system, his position is that specific affixes and metalingual elements of different types must initially be overtly presented in utterances, and only at later phases of generation they may be replaced by zeroes. Thus, the emphasis is generally not on units, but on the processes creating these units, though, in the **Aṣṭaadhyaayii**, the same terms are used for processes as well as for the resulting elements.

Correspondingly, PaaNini in his rule **1.1.60** suggests the following definition for both zero replacements and zero elements: **adarśanaM lopaH** '[The term] **lopa**, 'elision', [signifies] 'invisibility/disappearance [of a language unit]'. The root lup- 'cause to disappear, elide' serves as a primary base for deriving nominal lop-a- 'loss, lack, disappearance;

---

[3] See his commentary on rule **1.2.45** of PaaNini and on the corresponding *vaarttikaa* No. 9 of Kaatyaayana in Kielhorn (1880): 219.
[4] Gune (1978): 1.
[5] Cardona (1988): 503.
[6] Greenberg (1960): 188-190.

failure'. These ordinary, non-terminological, meanings imply general usages of the noun lopa by PaaNini. Functioning as a term, **lopa** has the meaning 'elision (in general)'. It may be applied to any element - be it a language unit or a metalingual symbol - undergoing replacement by zero.

For example, in rules **1.3.2 - 8** of his grammar PaaNini explains the nature and functions of different metalinguistic symbols (the latter are termed **'IT'** by PaaNini and **'anubandha-'** by later grammarians). PaaNini and his followers note that **IT** may be used only in grammatical instruction (**upadeśe**). In rule **1.3.9**, implying that instruction given in rules **1.3.2 - 8** is over, he states: **tasya lopaH** 'The zero replacement of that (= of any of the metalingual markers mentioned earlier) (may take place)'.

Thus, in accordance with rule **1.3.9**, a complete and unconditioned elision of a technical symbol **IT** becomes possible. - E.g., pat- 'to fall; fly' + **ŚaP** + -ti = pat-a-ti '(he/she/it) falls', where **ŚaP** is a technical name for a set of affixes forming the so called 'present stems' from verbal roots of the 1st class, and symbols **Ś** and **–P**, belonging to **IT**, undergo a process of zero replacement on common grounds (following **1.3.9**).

The term **lopa** may also imply replacements of phonemes by zero. Thus, the phonemes /**v**/ and /**y**/ may be replaced by zero before any following consonant except /**y**/. The corresponding rule **6.1.66** says: **lopo vyor vaLi** 'replacement by zero [takes place in case of the phonemes] /**v,y**/ before [the phonemes denoted by abbreviation] **vaL** (= before all consonants excluding /**y**/)'. E.g., uuy- 'to weave' + -ta- (affix of perfect participles) implies **lopa** in between the root and the affix: uuy- + **lopa** + -ta- > uuta- 'woven' [compare with uuy- + -ya- (suffix of passive stem) + -te (affix of 3rd pers. sg. pres. Mid. voice) > uuy-ya-te 'is (being) woven', where, according to **6.1.66**, no zero replacement of /**y**/ in uuy- can occur].

Nominal or verbal inflections may also undergo the processes of zero replacement. For example, according to the Western tradition of presentation, the form of Voc. sg. of masc. stems in a- is equivalent to stem itself: deva 'o God!'. But PaaNini would explain it differently: first, the form of Nom.sg. devas 'God' (from deva- + **sU**) is produced, and then the inflection -s (together with **IT**-marker **'U'**) undergoes zero replacement; thus, deva- + **sU** + **lopa** > deva 'o God!'.

The terminological meaning of **lopa** in PaaNini's grammar is based on everyday usage of the common noun (see above). An additional support to this is the fact that **lopa** in a sense 'elision' is used in rules **1.1.4** and **1.1.58** that come earlier than **1.1.60** (in which the formal definition of the term is for the first time suggested). E.g., **1.1.4** is formulated thus: **na dhaatulopa aardhadhaatuke** 'no [**guNa** and **vRddhi** replacements may happen] before an affix of **aardhadhaatuka**-class [which determines] a zero replacement of a verbal base'. An abstract string of elements constituting a verbal noun from the root luu- 'to destroy' and having the meaning 'constant or intensive destruction' potentially would appear as lo-luu-ya-a, but, in accordance with **1.1.4**, (a) **lopa** (replacement by zero) of the third element takes place, and (b) no **guNa** of the second (root) element happens: loluu (reduplicated root) + **yaNG** + **lopa** + **aC** > loluu + **aC** > loluva 'constant or intensive destruction (of smb. or smth.)'.

Thus, we may draw two important conclusions from PaaNini's definition of the term **lopa** given in **1.1.60** and from the examples provided above: (1) a certain language unit before being elided must first be introduced overtly, and only afterwards it is reduced to 'invisibility' (**adarśanam**); (2) even after the elision has taken place, the functional trace of the deleted element remains determining other operations' applicability or non-applicability in the generation process.

How these principles operate, was well explained by G. Cardona, and here we 'll briefly repeat his argumentation (with some small changes in Cardona's examples)[7]. - Suppose, there are regular Sanskrit utterances: (1) atra tishThati payaH 'The milk is standing there'; (2) raamaH payaH pibati 'Ram drinks milk'; (3) odanam payasaa sińcati '(Someone) moistens rice with milk'. A non-Paninean modern linguist would simply extract affixes -H (variant of the set **sU**), -(a)m, -Ø from the constituents raamaH, odanam and payas and suggest for them the corresponding complexes of meanings: 'm. Nom. sg.', 'm/n. Acc. sg.' and 'n. Nom./Acc. sg.'.

PaaNini cannot act in this manner as the meaning Agent extractable for affix -H in raamaH of sample (2) cannot be also attributed to the modified stem payas in sample (1); as well as the meaning Patient, evident for -(a)m in odanam, cannot be referred to by the devoid of affix but phonetically modified stem payas in example (2).

The other complication is also a serious one: in accordance with rule **1.4.14 sUPtiNGantaM padam** 'A 'word' (is only that form) which ends in nominal (**sUP**) or verbal (**tiNG**) inflections', and, being a 'bare' stem, the noun payas does not seem to have any of the set of nominal inlections, and because of that it cannot be considered a 'word-form'.

The only way out for PaaNini then is, following neatly **anvaya - vyatireka** analytical methods and consistent with the general principles

---

[7] Cardona (1988): 503-504.

adopted (see above): first, to posit for utterances (1) and (2) the corresponding strings payas- + -**sU** and payas- +-am, structurally similar to (Nom. sg.) raama- + -**sU** and (Acc. sg.) odana- + -am, then to introduce zero replacements of inflections -**sU** and -am and at last to get the desired form payas in both utterances. - This latter form payas, having the 'invisible' traces of deleted affixes -**sU** and -am, may be now treated as a full-rights 'word' (**pada**) which undergoes the same type of '**saMdhi**' (payas > payaH before a surd consonant) as takes place, e.g., in raamas 'Ram' (...s > ...H after /**a**/ and before a surd /**p**/).

More specific grammatically, more determined by context and more important structurally are subdivisions of the notion 'elision in general' (**lopa**) as suggested by PaaNini in order to denote zero replacements of affixes alone. Characterized by abbreviation **lu-mat**-, literally 'having **lu**- (as a common element of the corresponding terms)', they are stated in rule **1.1.61** of the **Aṣṭaadhyaayii**: **pratyayasya luK Ślu luPaH** '(Markers) **luK, Ślu** and luP [signify replacement] of an affix by zero'.

Zeroing of affixes is conditioned in the **Aṣṭaadhyaayii:** by two important metarules - **1.1.62** and **1.1.63**. The former of them is: **pratyayalope pratyayalakshaNam** 'After an affix (as a whole happens to be replaced by) zero, the operation conditioned (by it still) takes place, (as if the affix has been manifested)'. This rule makes a naturally correlated pair with the statement of **1.1.60** (see above). - Reformulating PaaNini's statements in modern terms, we may say that according to him any affix, being a two-sided linguistic unit, must first be introduced in its full form, and only later, after **lopa** of its signifier, the unit becomes invisible (**adarśana-**), but, following **1.1.62**, the signified of the unit is nevertheless preserved intact.

Thus, by metarule **1.1.62** some general conditions for preservation of signified in the course of zeroing are formulated. The next rule, **1.1.63**, provides important restrictions for specific cases of zeroing, when zeroing of affixes is denoted by terms that have **-lu-** as a common element (**lumata-**) or, to put it differently, when zero-processes denoted by **luK, Ślu** and **luP** are to take place. Rule **1.1.63** is formulated by PaaNini like this: **na lumataaMgasya** '[In case zeroing of an affix is denoted by any term with the common element] **-lu-** [and the significant of this affix has correspondingly been deleted, an operation, normally applicable to] the preaffixal stem [in the presence of two-sided affix, now is] not [possible]'. E.g., a regular preaffixal stem from the noun garga- (name of a certain gotra) would be gaarg-ya- 'a descendant of the 'garga' gotra', generated (in accordance with PaaNini's rules **4.1.105, 6.4.48, 7.2.117**) from garga- + **yaÑ** (**Ñ** 'being an **anubandha**), where affix -ya- (= yaÑ) implies **vRddhi** - replacement of the first vowel of the base garga-. In case we intend to generate the form of Nom. pl. 'garga' descendants', a corresponding affix of Nom. pl. -as (=**Jas** in PaaNini's terms, with **anubandha 'J'**) is to be added; but addition of **Jas** implies replacement of **yaÑ** by zero-operation **luK** in accordance with PaaNini's rule **2.4.64**. The operation **luK** belongs to type **lumata-** described in **1.1.63**, and thus **luK** prevents any other operations on preaffixal stem (**aMga-**), namely, the operation of **vRddhi** of /**a**/ of the first syllable of the base garga-. Thus, garga- + **yaÑ** + **Jas** > garga- + **luK** + **Jas** > garga- + **Jas** > gargaas 'garga' descendants'.

Spheres of implementation of the three subtypes of affixes zeroing are not characterised unequivocally by PaaNini, as each of them is multifunctional in nature, determining usually not only an elision of a certain element but also some other related operations. For example, in accordance with PaaNini's rule **7.4.75**, **Ślu**, when introduced after reduplicated stems of some verbal roots, determines not only zero replacement of a final consonant of the first syllable of the stem but in addition implies replacement of vowel /**i**/ of the stem by its **guNa**-correlate, that is by /**e**/: nij-nij- (reduplicated stem from nij- 'to wash') + **Ślu** > ni-nij-> ne-nej- [and only from the latter stem (modified by applying some other rules) one may get, e.g., a correct word-form nenekti '(he/she) washes'- see below].

The linear order of **IT**-constituents preceding or following the common element **-lu-** in the names of specified zeroing operations on affixes is only of relative importance: the preposited **Ś-** may imply that the corresponding processes take place at the initial part of the substituendum, while postposited **-K** and **-P** often signify that the operations occur at the end of the substituendum, but there are also many violations of this. More important are functional differences between all the types (including **lopa-**, the general one,) determined by affixes affiliation with **kRt-** or **taddhita-** classes.

PaaNini does not give a proper definition of the **kRt**-class of affixes. His rule **3.1.93 kRd atiNG** means '[All affixes], excluding verbal inflections, [that are analysed in this section of rules - starting from **3.1.93** and lasting up to **3.1.150**, - constitute a class termed] **'kRt'**. Nor does he suggest anywhere a definition of the term 'verbal inflection' (**tiNG**), and only much later - in **3.4.78** - the list of these inflections, including 18 items, is provided. The same is also true for the notion '**taddhita-**': in paragraph **4.1.76** of his grammar PaaNini gives only a heading **'taddhitaaH'** implying that it extends up to the end of the fifth chapter and that all affixes mentioned in **4.1.77 - 5.4.160** belong to this set.

According to PaaNini, any affix (**pratyaya-**) is to be associated with either the **kRt-** or the **taddhita-** affixal classes, and the **kRt-**affixes serve to derive - from verbal or (rarer) nominal roots - more or less regular primary nominal bases (**praatipadika**), while **taddhita-**affixes form - generally with irregularity - secondary nominal bases.

The functional differences between the above analyzed zeroing-types may be stated like this: the use of **luP** is restricted to affixes of the **taddhita** class, while the zeroing processes denoted by **lopa, Ślu** and **luK** may occur with both the **taddhita** and the **kRt** classes of affixes. It should again be remembered that **lopa** implies operations not only on affixes but on language units in general (including phonemes or phonemic sequences) as well as on metalingual elements.

The difference between **luK**, on one side, and **Ślu** (and also **lopa**), on the other, has been demonstrated by Cardona[8]: i.e. an operation that is potentially allowed after a deletion of a certain affix, does not take effect if the zero replacing process is denoted by **luK**. E.g., when deriving the m. Nom. sg. form go-maan from the base go-mat- 'a person having many cows' we may replace the corresponding affix **-sU** (of m. Nom. sg.) by **lopa**, and in this case all subsequent operations, that are necessary for the derivation process, are allowed: gomat- + **lopa** (<-**sU**) > gomat- (in accordance with PaaNini's rule **6.1.68**); gomat- > gomaat (by rule **6.4.14**) > gomaant (by **7.1.70**) > gomaan (by **8.2.23**) 'a person having many cows'(m. Nom. sg.).

But if to the same affix **-sU** we apply the zero replacement operation **luK**, then the last three operations that might follow **luK** become prohibited, and we get only the stem gomat- (as a result of gomat- + **luK** (<-**sU**). This latter stem may be used when forming compounds - e.g., in gomat-priyaH 'one who likes a person having many cows'. Otherwise - if we were to apply general **lopa** instead of specific **luK** - we would get improperly formed compounds, like *gomaat-priyaH, gomaant-priyaH, etc.

As for **Ślu**, it is most often employed for zero replacement of the final constituent of the first syllable in a reduplicated stem, and zeroing is usually accompanied by vocalic and consonantal alternations inside the stem. E.g., when generating forms of Active Pres. III sg. from the verbal root hu- 'to offer oblation', that begins the main set of the 'reduplicated' class of verbs, we have first to combine the root hu- with the universal 'thematic' suffix -a- ('**ŚaP**' in PaaNini's terms, where '**Ś**' and '**P**' are **anubandhas**) and later to replace this **ŚaP** by **Ślu**. This latter, in accordance with PaaNini's **2.4.75** and other rules, besides 'zeroing' of **ŚaP**, also provides reduplication of the root with

[8] Cardona (1988): 53-54.

accompanying corresponding alternations of the root consonant and vowel: hu- + **ŚaP** > hu- + **Ślu** > ju-ho-; then to the reduplicated stem ju-ho- we are to apply the inflection -ti ('**tiP**' in PaaNini's terms) and, thus, to get the correct word-form juhoti '(he) offers oblation'. In case we are to generate the same grammatical form from the root nij- 'to wash, bathe' which begins some other verbal set of the 'reduplicated' class, we again replace **ŚaP** by **Ślu**, conditioning the necessary vowel and consonant alternations in the stem, and then combine the proper reduplicated stem with affix **tiP** - thus, nij- + **ŚaP** > nij- + **Ślu** > ne-nek- + **tiP** > nenekti '(he/she) washes, bathes".

It is remarkable that some contemporary linguists when dealing with zero allomorphs of different morphemes in New Indo-Aryan, intuitively follow a methodological pattern very similar to one suggested by PaaNini. E.g., V. Liperovskiy when characterizing the declination of masc. sg. nouns of the type kisaan- 'a peasant' in Hindi, introduces two different zero morphs for Nom. sg. and for Obl. sg. (-∅ ' and -∅ " correspondingly): kisaan-∅ ' 'a peasant' (Nom.) - kisaan-∅ " (+ ko) 'to the peasant' (Obl.), - on the basis of analogy with laRk-aa 'a boy' (Nom.) - laRk-e (+ ko) 'to the boy'. And it is not coincidental that Liperovsky also (implicitly) follows PaaNini in giving different notations for homonymous but functionally differing inflections - e.g., laRk-e' 'boys' (m. Nom. pl.), but laRk-e" (+ ko) 'to the boy' (m. Obl. sg.); PaaNini would have used different **anubandhas** in such cases[9].

But it is not just a problem of notation: PaaNini's refined system of zero replacements may be consistently used in grammars of New Indo-Aryan languages, i.e., it applies nicely to the Hindi data. E.g., in order to generate the word-forms of the agent noun 'boy' from the verbal root laR- 'to make war/ quarrel' we are first to combine the root with the derivational suffix -ak-, thus getting the primary stem (PaaNini's '**kRt**') laR-ak-, and then to add the necessary inflections: -aa (for m. Nom. sg.) or -e (for m.Nom. pl. or m. Obl. sg.). Before regular vocalic inflections in nominal paradigms /**a**/ in suffix -ak- is obligatorily zeroed, thus implying word-forms like laR-k-aa 'a boy', laR-k-e 'boys', etc. Then, by adding to the primary stem laR-ak- suffix -pan- of verbal abstract nouns, we get laR-ak-pan-, the secondary stem, (termed '**taddhita**' by PaaNini) which in its turn may be combined with -∅ inflection (of m. Nom. sg./ m. Obl. sg.), thus producing the word-form laR-ak-pan-∅ 'boyhood'. As is evident, /**a**/ of -ak- does not undergo zero replacement before suffix -pan- in this case, but there also exists the other variant of the same lexeme, that is, laR-k-e-pan-∅ 'boyhood', where /**a**/ of -ak- is replaced by zero.

[9] Liperovsky (1978): 23.

To describe these and other cases of derivation properly we have to turn to a zero replacement system very similar to the one offered by PaaNini. The deletion of /**a**/ in the '**kRt-**'type sufix of the first form might be denoted by the term **lopa**, and the latter implies that after zeroing of /**a**/ takes place, all other operations (e.g., adding of the inflections) are allowed. As for the second type of formation (of nomina actionis), we might first introduce the same vocalic inflections -aa, -e, etc. and then make their signifiers invisible (that is, to implement the null-variants for those inflections) through the **luP** zero replacement procedure, which also automatically prohibits the elision of the vowel in suffix -ak-.

The other variant of the form laRkepan- 'boyhood' might be described through the use of **Ślu** which triggers the zero replacement for vowel in -ak- and does not bar the subsequent operations: the addition of the inflections -e and -∅ and the insertion of the suffix -pan- between those two; as a result, the correct word-form laR-k-e-pan-∅, synonymous with laR-ak-pan-∅, will be obtained. Needless to say that in case we do not differentiate among the above described zeroing procedures (symbolized by **lopa**, **luP** and **Ślu**), the incorrect forms - like *laRakaa, *laRakepan, etc. - might be generated.

Taking into account PaaNini's concept of **luK**, a non-trivial description of the declension of Hindi nouns like ghar- 'a house' (masc.) may also be suggested. For this we might split the paradigm into two halves following the opposition 'plurality-non-plurality' and characterize the unmarked (nonplural) half independently from the marked one. The former would then imply, as the first step, combining of the stem with the above mentioned 'standard' inflections -aa (of m. Nom. sg.) and -e (of m. Obl. sg.) which, at the second step, would be deleted through **luK** zero replacement that prohibits any subsequent morphological operation. Thus, ghar- + -aa/-e > ghar- + **luK** > ghar (without any zero morpheme); e.g., ghar ban jaataa hai 'The house (Nom.) is being built' - ghar + me˜ 'in the house (Obl.)'.

Contrary to this pattern, the plural paradigm might then be described as implying **lopa** (and not **luK**) zero replacement: ghar-e (fictitious Nom. pl.) + **lopa** > ghar-∅ 'houses' (with zero morpheme -∅ denoting 'Nom. pl.') as opposed to, say, ghar-o˜ + me˜ 'in the houses (Obl. pl.)'. Such a description, based on the contrast **luK** - **lopa**, is, evidently, more economic and more consistant than the traditional one operating with three different zero morphemes (of Nom. sg., Nom. pl. and Obl. sg.).

The zeroing procedure similar to PaaNini's **lopa** may also be used for generating the forms of perfective participles in Hindi. The traditional approach is that the (dominating) participial stems in consonants do not imply basis-forming suffixes and simply add the necessary gender - number - case inflections straight to the stems, while their (much rarer) counterparts in vowels first combine with suffix -y- denoting the perfect aspect and only afterwards add the inflections: e.g., likh- 'to write' > likh-aa 'written (m. Nom. sg.)', but paa- 'to acquire' > paa-y-aa 'acquired (m. Nom. sg.)'. We might again first implement a 'standard' suffix -y- (overt only with vocalic stems) after stems of any type and later, before adding the inflections, in accordance with **lopa** principle replace this -y- with zero after stems in consonants: e.g., likh- + -y- + -aa > likh- + **lopa** + -aa > likh-∅ - aa 'written', but paa- + -y- + -aa > paa-y-aa 'acquired'.

This insertion of the universal suffix -y- (later deleted through **lopa** in a subset of forms) into bases of the perfective participles is consistent with the morphemic structure of the imperfective participles as in these latter the corresponding preinflectional suffix -t- (denoting imperfect aspect) is obligatory with all types of stems: e.g., likh-t-aa 'writing', paa-t-aa 'acquiring', etc. Thus, a morphemic symmetry may be provided for both subsets of participles. As for **lopa** of -y-, the conditions for applying this procedure must be stated more precisely: in perfective participles -y- is to be obligatorily replaced by zero after stems in consonants and before either the inflections of the masculine subparadigm (that is, before -aa of m. Nom. sg. and -e of m. Obl. sg./ m. Nom. pl.), or before the feminine base forming (second) suffix -ii. E.g., from paRh- 'to read' we may get paRh- + -y- + -aa > paRh- + **lopa** + -aa > paRh-aa 'read', paRh- + -y- + -ii > paRh- + **lopa** + -ii > paRh-ii 'read (fem.)'. With stems in vowels this base-forming and word-final -ii may imply optional **lopa** for the suffix -y-: e.g., from aa- 'to come' we get not only aa-y-aa 'come (m. Nom. sg.)' or aa-y-e 'come (m. Nom.pl.)', etc., but also aa -y-ii/ aa -∅ -ii 'come (f.)'.

For Hindi data it should also be taken into account that in all participial forms functioning as attributes, the feminine affix -ii is a word-final one (as participial attributes of feminine gender are inalterable). But it is not so if such participles (including the 'archaic' perfective participles that imply a past tense meaning) occupy the predicate slot - in this case the inflection -˜ (of fem. pl.) may follow suffix -ii-. Compare, e.g., aa-∅ /y-ii ciTThii-∅ 'a letter that has come' - aa-∅/ y- ii ciTThiy-aa˜ 'letters that have come', but ciTThii-∅ aa-∅/y-ii-∅ 'a letter came' - ciTThiy-aa˜ aa-∅/ y-ii-˜ 'letters came'; aa-t-ii aurat-∅/ aurat-e˜ 'coming woman/ women', but aurat-∅ aa-t-ii-∅ 'would woman come' - aurat-e˜ aa-t-ii-˜ 'would women come'. The solution then may be similar to one suggested by the Paninians: to have a list of verbal inflections into which to include -˜ (for f. pl. of the predicate) as well as its counterpart -∅ (for f. sg. of the predicate); the (optional) zeroing procedure **lopa** then would be reserved for the suffix -y- only.

A much more difficult case is presented by Hindi samples of the type bakraa 'he-goat' - bakre 'goats (m.)' - bakrii 'she-goat' - bakri(y)aa˜ 'goats (f.)'. Should we posit derivational zero in bakr-∅-aa, bakr-∅-e as there exist contrasting forms with evidently derivational -y-/ -iy- ? Should we treat the third form as bakr-ii-∅ because of the existence of bakr-i(y)-aa˜ ? - The answer to the second question must definitely be a positive one: -y- and -i(y)- are only allomorphs of one and the same derivational morpheme, while -∅ and -aa˜ are to be listed together with the other nominal inflections (see above); and -aa (of m. Nom. sg.) and -e (of m. Obl. sg. or Nom. pl.) should also be in this list.

If so, the answer in the affirmative to the first question is inevitable: we must posit derivational zero -∅ - for masculine forms, because only this decision would satisfy the demands of the internal logic of description. Otherwise we will be compelled to exclude zero -∅ - from the morphemic structure of bakraa-type wordforms and to treat final -aa in those forms as a portmanteau morpheme combining the derivational and the inflectional meanings. As other listed inflections of Hindi do not demonstrate the same amalgamation of meanings, this approach does not seem to be acceptable.

Still another solution might be based on Paninian theoretical postulates: to introduce the derivational zero -∅ - and to treat it as not denoting an independent meaning of its own (**vaacaka**), but as co-signifying (**dyotaka**) a covert meaning (of gender) belonging to the stem itself. The inflection -aa then would be treated as a nominal ending manifesting the denoted (**vaacya**) meanings of number and case. But the implementation of this model would demand a total restructuring of the descriptive pattern adopted, and because of this it is also unacceptable.

Thus, the adaptation of a model similar to the one suggested by PaaNini to the description of the zeroing processes in New Indo-Aryan (namely, in Hindi) has some irrefutable advantages over other possible approaches to the same problem.

References

Cardona, George. 1988. PaaNini: his work and its traditions. Delhi: Motilal Banarsidass.

Greenberg, Joseph H. 1960. A quantitative approach to the morphological typology of language. International Journal of American Linguistics, vol. XXVI, No. 3: 178 - 194.

Gune, Jayashree A. 1978. The meaning of tenses and moods. Pune: Deccan College Postgraduate and Research Institute.

Kielhorn, L. F. (Ed.). 1880-85. The Vyā:karaṇa-mahābhāṣya of Patañjali, 3 volumes [= Bombey Sanskrit and Prakrit Series 18-22, 28-30]. Bombay: Government Central Press. Vol. 1: 1880, vol. 2: 1883, vol. 3: 1885.

Liperovskiy, V. P. 1978. Imennye chasti rechi iazyka hindi (= The nominal parts of speech of the Hindi language). Moskvaa 'Nauka'. Glavnaia redaktsiia vostochnoi literatury.

Vasu, Srisa Chandra (Ed., tr.). 1962. The Aṣṭaadhyaayii: of PaaNini, edited and translated into English, 2 volumes. Reprint: Delhi, Motilal Banarsidass [= 1891. Allahabad: The PaaNini Office].

INDEX

Authors are listed in this index only when reference is made to their work or arguments, or when directly quoted, and not as more sources of examples, for which bibliographies are given at the end of each chapter. Boldface numbers indicate material on tables and maps.